T H E
DOOR
INTERVIEWS

EDITED BY
MIKE YACONELLI

Zondervan Publishing House
Grand Rapids, Michigan

THE DOOR INTERVIEWS
Copyright © 1989 by Youth Specialties, Inc.

Library of Congress Cataloging-in-Publication Data

The door interviews / edited by Mike Yaconelli.
    p. cm.
    "The best of Wittenburg door."
    ISBN 0-310-29591-2
    1. Christianity—20th century. 2. United States—Church
history—20th century. 3. Christians—United States—Interviews.
I. Wittenburg door.
BR481.D66 1989   89-31860
                                                              CIP

Unless otherwise indicated, the Scripture text used is the *Revised Standard Version,* copyright © 1946, 1952, 1971 by the Division of Christian Education of the National Council of the Churches of Christ in the United States of America.

Edited by Bob Hudson, David Lambert, and Lori Walburg

Printed in the United States of America

89 90 91 92 93 / DH / 10 9 8 7 6 5 4 3 2 1

Contents

Introduction

THE DOOR INTERVIEWS:

Will Campbell   *11*

Charlie and Martha Shedd   *21*

Wesley Pippert   *33*

Dr. W. Stanley Mooneyham   *43*

Donn Moomaw   *54*

Martin E. Marty   *62*

Dr. James Daane   *76*

Andrew Greeley   *84*

Mark Hatfield   *90*

Martin E. Marty   *95*

Mr. Fred Rogers   *101*

Howard A. Snyder   *110*

John Claypool   *120*

Sheldon Vanauken   *135*

Lewis Smedes   *144*

Ron Sider   *151*

Frederick Buechner   *159*

Harold Lindsell   *165*

Jack Rogers   *171*

Tim LaHaye   *177*

Juan Carlos Ortiz   *183*

J. Rodman Williams   *191*

Reinhold Niebuhr   *198*

Richard Ostling   *204*

Robert Webber   *208*

Tom Sine   *214*

Ed Dobson   *221*

Robert Capon   *227*

Roberta Hestenes   *235*

Os Guinness   *241*

M. Scott Peck   *247*

R. C. Sproul   *256*

T-Bone Burnett   *262*

Richard John Neuhaus   *266*

Calvin Miller   *272*

Henri Nouwen   *278*

Walter Wangerin   *285*

Ben Patterson   *292*

Madeleine L'Engle   *298*

Introduction

The Wittenburg Door was first published in June of 1971. We spelled "Wittenberg" incorrectly. We didn't mean to spell it wrong; it was obviously an omen of things to come. *The Door* became known for its mistakes. It was to be a tongue-in-cheek, humorous, smart-aleck magazine for professional youth workers. But it only took a few issues to recognize that *The Door* (at first a nickname, now the real name of the magazine) and the word "professional" just didn't go together. *The Door* quickly evolved into a satirical evangelical magazine that refused to take anyone or anything in the church seriously.

The Door, often called a religious *Mad Magazine,* lampooned the sacred cows of the church. Within a few short years the Green Weenie, the Theologian of the Year Award, and Truth Is Stranger Than Fiction struck terror into the hearts of the leaders of the Church. (Terror? Terror? Uh ... how about a mild case of indigestion? To one leader once—who, incidentally, had just finished a chili dog before reading *The Door.*) Those were the features that everyone talked about. (Everyone? Everyone? Uh ... a couple of people mentioned it once at a *Door* staff meeting.)

Gradually, it became obvious that *The Door* was not just a humor magazine published to give a few people some chuckles. *The Door,* as it turns out, *was* serious about something— the direction the evangelical church was going. People began to realize: "Hey, the interviews in the *Door* are pretty interesting. Who did them, *Christianity Today?*"

The interviews were different. They were with people who really had something to say, and the questions were not from the press-release package. The questions were honest, and so, for the most part, were the answers. *The Door* interviews actually contained insights into the church and the world that were very helpful for the rest of us.

The three subscribers who recognized how good our interviews are have continued to harass us with a phone call asking us to compile all of the *Door* interviews into one gigantic ... er ... large ... uh ... regular book. We thought that was a great idea, but then the caller had to add, "Let someone else publish it, or we'll never see it." *The Door* is known for not being published on time once or twice.

Okay. Okay. So we conned ... er ... asked Zondervan to publish the book and they actually agreed. (That's because they've had so many owners in the last few years, we kept telling the new owners that the previous owners had promised.) So here it is at last, *The Door Interviews*, all in one place, except for the ones that aren't in this place. (Hey, not every interview was a winner, and for some reason, some people didn't *want* their interview in this book—or any book.) We think you will find, as millions (uh . . . you know what we mean) of others have, "You know, those people at *The Door did* have some socially redeeming value." What a surprise!

We think you will find the interviews to be a pleasant surprise.

Mike Yaconelli
Senior Editor, *The Door*

The Door Interviews

WILL CAMPBELL

Will Campbell won't fit in a box. He's been "Country Boy" (Amite County, Mississippi); he's been "Ivy League" (Yale Divinity School). He's been "conservative" (Southern Baptist); He's been "liberal" (National Council of Churches). He's ministered to poor blacks; he's ministered to members of the Ku Klux Klan.

Mostly though, he's "down home" and Christian. Several years ago a professor of theology at a campus where Will spoke years ago kept demanding of Campbell, "But what's your actual *business*, Rev. Campbell? I mean, what do you believe in?" Will snapped back, "Look, I been trying to tell you, I believe in Jesus, goddammit. *Jesus!*"

Life magazine described Campbell as being "engaged in a quiet assiduous guerrilla ministry" to a congregation of the "desperate and dispossessed." Most of his witness is made up of haphazard occasions as he attempts to respond to the people God has placed in his path. He makes his home now on the outskirts of Nashville, Tennessee.

Will Campbell grew up in Mississippi, was baptized at age seven in a creek behind the East Fork Baptist Church, was ordained at age seventeen, later graduated from divinity school, and subsequently joined the civil rights movement in the South. He dropped out of that when he became disenchanted with the political approach to solving the world's problems. Today, under the auspices of the Committee: Witnesses to Reconciliation (formerly Committee of Southern Churchmen), Will does, in his words, "whatever a country bootleg preacher does—givin' speeches, writin', marryin', buryin', baptizin'." His recent books include *Forty Acres and a Goat*, the children's parable *Chester and Chun Ling*, and a parable for grown-ups, *The Convention: A Parable*. Even in 1973, the time of this interview, he spoke from a rich background of experiences and ideas.

DOOR: Many of our readers aren't familiar with the Committee of Southern Churchmen. Could you tell us what it is and what it does?

CAMPBELL: You're looking at most of it. It's a small group of primarily steeple dropouts (that's the term we use) in the South representing every denominational background from Church of God to Roman Catholic (depending on which way you move up and down the scale), and every occupational group who have for the most part dropped out from under the institutional, structured, steepled canopy, but who still believe very firmly some things about the Christian faith. I think we've seen, particularly in the South and I assume everywhere else, an awful lot of people who've become disillusioned with the institutional church. They drop out of that, and they drop out of the Christian faith . . . which is indicative of the fact that they had an idol in the first place. They assumed that the institution had something to do with the Christian gospel, and it doesn't.

DOOR: You make quite a distinction then between the steepled institution and the Body of Christ.

CAMPBELL: Absolutely.

DOOR: I read where you said that "the steepled institution is one of the greatest barriers to the proclamation of the radical gospel." Could you get into that a little more and tell us what you mean by the "radical gospel?"

CAMPBELL: It's difficult to summarize. I believe that the Bible ought to be read like any other book—at one sitting like a novel or a physics book—and then you can tell what it's about. But you can't do what all of us have been taught to do because some guy back there very conveniently divided it up into verses and chapters. That wasn't the way it was written at all, of course. And we pick out one and say, "But it says here!" Well, that's like trying to exegete a chapter from a William Faulkner novel. You've got to read Faulkner's entire novel, and then

you can say this book is about such and such. The Bible is a book not about love, or about justice. It is not a book about mercy, not a book about judgments, but a book about who God is, and who man is, and then who God is in relationship to what man does and tries to become. I think the radicalism could probably be summarized by Paul when he talks about the fact that we no longer judge any man by human standard or human categories. And that is radical because it wipes out all the things that man has done—like national boundaries, race, flags, education, who's smart and who's stupid, and all the things that we have used to describe one another and divide one another.

DOOR: Is that one of the main distinguishing marks you see in the institutional church—they keep building boundaries?

CAMPBELL: Well, the church is an institution. This is one of the things we've been talking about this weekend—the inherent evil of all institutions. At least that's what I've come to talk about. All institutions are inherently evil if by definition (I hope I can remember—it's been a long time since I've studied sociology) an institution is an organization set up to meet the continuing needs of the group. Then you make one other assumption which has to do with anthropology, the basic nature of man, what man is really like. Whether you put it in theological terms, or sociological terms, or psychological terms, it comes out to the same thing: namely, that man is basically less than all right. He's basically self-loving, self-serving, and self-seeking. Theologians used to call it original sin. Folks got the notion that original sin had something to do with a snake crawling around and an apple, and genes, and zygotes. All original sin means is that if you and I are standing on the side of a mountain on a ledge the size of this, we might be able to work it out where we both could stay there. We might. But we haven't been able to do it on a world scale, because there's plenty of room to stand now, but we keep pushing each other off. We go all the way around the world to drop bombs to kill one another. But you and I might be congenial enough or even smart enough to say, "There's room for both of us here, and let's stay." But if the ledge begins to crumble and pretty soon it's about the size of this tape recorder, then if I had anything to do with it, I'm pretty sure which one of us would go off plummeting down the side of the mountain. If you had anything to do with it, I know who's gonna go. That's original sin; that's all we're talking about.

Now you assume that pretty soon in the life of that organization, it's going to come to exist to meet the needs of itself, no matter what it's set up to do, whether grandiose or idealistic or anything else. Very soon it's going to be existing to meet its own needs, and the classical example of that is the Christian church. It's not the only one certainly. But institutions are not run by pastors, or boards of deacons, or trustees, or committees. Pastors, or presidents or chancellors or boards of trustees or deacons are run by the institution. They just think they run it, but they don't have anything to do with it. So the pastor very early learns to fit in, and we put it in all kinds of terms: "We have to get our people to love us before we can preach to them," or "We're gonna behave like a rubber band—we know just how far we can

go." But we all learn to behave. A good chancellor or a good college president doesn't have anything in the world to do with education. He has to do with meeting the needs of that institution. What are the needs of an educational institution? Building, libraries, more Ph.D.s on the faculty who may or may not be teachers, or even scholars for that matter? The good chancellor doesn't exist for any reason that has to do with education. The good chancellor is one who does well by that institution. The good president of the United States is one who does well by the United States, and this is what the Christian has never understood in the Vietnam War. I have been against this war, but I have never taken the position that what we did over there was not good for the United States. I think in all probability it was. You can make a rational argument either way on that one.

But I don't serve the United States. I'm not called to serve it. I don't think God created the United States. But the good president and the good Senate and the good House of Representatives are those who are meeting that needs or doing what is best for the United States without any regard for moral judgment or Christian views of vocation or anything like this. And I think you can apply that, I believe, to any institution in existence.

DOOR: How do you see your group overcoming some of these problems and not becoming an ongoing thing, or not being run itself?

CAMPBELL: When I talk in those terms, I never mean to imply that I'm some kind of an exception. I was meeting with a group in Toccoa, Georgia, and I made the statement that I thought the demise of the Christian faith began when some P. R. man dreamed up the gimmick of full-time Christian service and we started paying one another to be Christians. One of the brethren jumped up, red-faced, and said, "Well, you get paid!" I didn't mean to imply in any way at all that I'm an exception to what I'm talking about. Sure I'm trapped by institutions, and the Committee of Southern Churchmen is, in a sense, an institution. And the fact that we bend over backward trying not to be an institution is probably the very thing that is institutionalizing us. You can't escape those things.

I'm reporting and trying to interpret what I think is happening in the world today: mainly that the nature of institutions is involved in what that crazy Frenchman, Jacques Ellul, talks about in his book, *The Technological Society*—the process of technique. He applies it in particular to politics. There is a way, a technique, to running government. And this is why it seems ridiculous to me when someone becomes disillusioned with the Stars and Stripes and goes and unfurls the banner of Hanoi or Peking or Havana, as if there's anything different happening there. There's not anything different happening there. This technique, this sort of automatic pilot we seem to be on, the technique for running government, is just as true in Hanoi as it is in Washington. That's the way it's done.

That's why I don't vote anymore. It just doesn't make any difference. It's not that I think that politics has become that corrupt; it probably isn't as corrupt as it has been in many other periods in American history or world history. It's not that I despair of the kind of people that run for political office. You know some of them are

"good people." The only reason I'm tempted to go back and register and do all the stuff you got to do to vote, which isn't much, is just a matter of casting. I get tired of getting up every morning and seeing and hearing the latest utterances on the "Today Show" when I'd rather see somebody else. But it's in the same sense that I'd rather see Liza Minnelli than see John Wayne. It's a matter of casting. Neither one has anything to do with what's happening in the script. But other than that it doesn't make any difference who the president of the United States is. That's not the way power operates. That's not where it's at. It seems to me that there's been ample precedent in American politics that we could learn that by now. When Lester Maddox was elected governor of Georgia, a friend of mine who's in the House of Representatives refused to run in the general election even though he'd won the primary. He said, "I'm not going to leave my name on the ballot because two years from now there won't be any constituency in the fifth district. I won't have any constituency. This man is crazy, and the state of Georgia is going to collapse because a crazy man can't run something as big as a state government." Well, he not only ran it, but some of the New Left writers are hailing Maddox as a sort of new Populist—Lester Maddox whose only claim to anything was the sale and distribution of axe handles to people to keep black folks from eating his fried chicken. He might have been crazy, but he's not the first crazy governor in the United States, and he won't be the last. He's about as much a Populist as William Buckley. There's not a Populist bone in his body. But the point is that Georgia as a government entity, as a state, went merrily on its way and nothing happened.

DOOR: So you don't see not voting as a cop-out? You think things are going to keep going regardless of whether you vote or not?

CAMPBELL: No, it's not a cop-out. Who cops out? The one who exhausts whatever energy, time, effort, and muscle he has somewhere else, or the guy who keeps on waving one banner or another and saying that things are going to be different?

And if you or anybody else disagrees with the process of technique, then I challenge you to show me one secretary of Agriculture since old man Hyde who has done anything but make the situation worse. Now there have been some people that we would call good people. I thought Henry Wallace was a good man, but the policies of Henry Wallace have been the things that have driven the people off the land and into the cities. TVA (Tennessee Valley Authority) is an example. I was glad to see it. I thought that it was progress and good for my people and for me, and yet today TVA is the biggest buyer of strip-mine coal. It has taken more people off the land than any other agency of government.

I went up to Kentucky not long ago and had a funeral for a whole town which the TVA had decided they wanted. They had built Barclay Lake and Kentucky Lake (or vice versa), and here was this land left in between. So again some technician, somebody in TVA who is ruled by this process and who is ranked by the programs he designs and carries through, says, "Let's have the land between the lakes. We'll name it Land Between the Lakes, a very romantic, pretty sounding name." It just happens there are a lot of human beings in there, some of them being thrown off the land for the third time. So they had a funeral for the whole town of Golden Pod, and the folks came by with little artifacts, threw them in a casket, and we buried it. Now the Land Between the Lakes is gonna be for folks who make $25,000 and up. They come in with their camping equipment and all the rest, big boats and yachts, and get close to the lakes. There's even going to be a Camp-a-port there. A Camp-a-port is where folks fly their plane in and camp alongside the runway. And not many people on food stamps have jet airplanes.

Now these aren't bad people. Frank Smith, who's a former congressman from Mississippi and was defeated because he refused to run a racist campaign, is one of the world's foremost ecologists who's written books on the subject. Frank Smith is not a bad man, and yet it's the Frank Smiths of the Tennessee Valley Authority that persist in these policies—buy the strip-mine coal because it's the cheapest. And the same thing for all the Department of Agriculture, the same thing for the military. It exists not even for national defense any longer, which would be bad enough, but to serve the needs of the institution called the Pentagon. And all what we call liberal progressive Programs somehow turn out to make worse the things that they were designed to correct. So after a while it's not a matter of despairing; it's just a matter of two and two do sometime, sooner or later, make four.

DOOR: What would you tell Christians then? If you can't change the church and you become part of an institution yourself, what creative things can you do as alternatives?

CAMPBELL: I can't deal with that question. The answer is all about you. It's everywhere. All I could do is give acts of this apostle, but arrogance, humility, or modesty circumscribe that. But there is plenty to do. I can tell you what I'd do, but that's kind of an exercise in vanity or something. All I can say is I'm never idle and I'm never bored.

DOOR: So you see a person as responding to a situation and doing whatever comes up? That's the basic way he should handle it?

CAMPBELL: I can see him responding in the spirit of the Christian faith. Sure that involves some risk, and he even may do the wrong thing and he too may make it worse. I know that. What I see him not doing is trying to devise an institution that's going to be any different than any other institution. I do a lot of cussing about the public schools, but if somebody asked me to build a better public school system—I can't do that. Some folks say, "If you're so critical of the United States why don't you go somewhere else?" Well, my answer to that is why don't *you* go somewhere else. I don't want to go anywhere else. They say, "Can you think up a better Constitution, say, or a better government system?" No, I can't, and that's not my job; I'm not going to try to. Because to try to do that would be a denial of everything I believe in. If all institutions are inherently evil, then the one I build would be inherently evil. Much as I'd like to, I haven't been exempt from original sin.

DOOR: Then what's the purpose of being critical since you know people are going to respond with, "What's your alternative?" Do you see your role as a prophet?

CAMPBELL: I'm a reporter. I'm not being critical. I'm saying that in my judgment this is the way things are. Now there may be preaching involved in that. It seems to me that the role of the preacher has always been to sound the alarm and point out where the idols are. I think what we're talking about is a lot of idols that we fall down and worship. We worship the church as an idol. We worship education as an idol, and it has been absolutely nothing but an idol. Education hasn't helped us solve any of our problems. And we worship politics as the Messiah. And in the Christian tradition, I think, this is the role of the preacher too. Point out where the idols are. You stumble and bust your ass, but you persist in going down that road. Other than that I don't see myself as being critical. I see myself as a preacher, as a reporter. The only efforts are not man's efforts. There's something else going on.

DOOR: In specifics, how do you see the institutional church today in the United States? How does it differ, say, from the scriptural norm?

CAMPBELL: In the church described in the New Testament, as I understand it, there is first of all absolutely nothing to suggest that it ought to have a building. Certainly there might be a building, but then we all go on to behave as if the building was the church.

In apostolic days, I think, a theological seminary would not have been thought of. The bishops rose out of the congregation. If you needed somebody to do a specific job, you ordained them. The original ordination was just for somebody to do the shit work, waiting on tables so the apostles could be free to do some preaching. I don't have any quarrel about giving people specific jobs, but there's just nothing so complicated about the Christian faith that it's going to take you three to seven years to learn what it's about. There's no reason in the world for that except institutional reasons. Today the major institutional reason for divinity schools, and seminaries to a lesser extent, is because we too have fallen down and worshiped at the shrine of academe. Our learned doctors are just as learned doctors as any other scholar of any academic discipline. And if we run out of things to be academic about, we write papers and footnote them in German. We just reach out and create something. "God is dead"—now what the hell is that supposed to mean? And yet the learned papers and journals were filled with this for four or five years. Of course right now we're in kind of a dry, dry spell . . . there's no telling what some learned doctor is going to create to write papers in theological journals about. That's a difference from the apostolic church.

There's also the whole fashion in which we have identified with the culture. I referred to it last night as equating the Christian faith with sixth-grade civics. The good Christians are the ones who behave the way a good boy and girl behaves or learns to behave in a sixth-grade civics class. This is what we preach and this is, for the most part, the way we live.

So naturally we look at the court prophets as the highest, most influential religious leaders today. Elton Trueblood, Billy Graham, Norman Vincent Peale. These are the people who speak to the alleged leaders, the presidents—they are the court prophets. This is really to be expected as long as we go racing to Caesar, trying to make a pope out of him on

every moral issue in the world. Right now it's the one on abortion. So Caesar's with the Catholic church. We want to get a constitutional amendment passed. We simply don't have the moral leadership to state that abortion is murder, which I happen to believe it is. We don't need to ask the state if this is morally right. What we do, you see, is base everything on the law. If it's not against the law any longer, that makes it morally acceptable within the community of believers. That's not rendering to Caesar the things that are Caesar's; that's rendering to Caesar the things that are God's.

We saw that in the civil rights crisis that boomeranged so badly on us. In the activist days of the liberal wing of the church we said very little about the morality of race. We said, "Let's be good boys and girls and obey the Supreme Court. It is now the law of the land," as if that had anything in the world to do with it. Then we put it into terms of law and order. We were really the ones who dreamed up that term, law and order, so that in a span of three short years we saw that term appropriated by the bigots, and we saw a presidential campaign waged on law and order. Dick Gregory said that law and order became the new word for "nigger." So when do we learn? I'm not being critical or negative. I'm just trying to report what I see.

DOOR: Do you feel that this is something peculiar to today's culture or that it's something that's always been?

CAMPBELL: I think it has always been, but the difference is that before it has always been possible for the rebels to bitch up the system. In the technological era I really think that's not possible any more. It's just virtually impossible to bitch up the system. Again, in the name of progress, in the name of liberal politics, we have programs. I was riding down south of the city of Chicago a couple of summers ago, and my host, who was an outstanding liberal Christian layman, showed me all these miles and miles and miles of high-rise apartment houses built for low-income people. That meant black people. He said, "There are schools there, churches, supermarkets, gymnasiums, swimming pools, department stores, everything. These people never have to go outside." I thought, you know, that's cool. The only problem is, if necessary, they may *not go* outside. So you don't have to gun people down or gas them or build barbed-wire entanglements—that would be too easy. The radicals could bitch that up by throwing their bodies on the wire and chanting "freedom" and making a witness. But how are you going to throw your body at high-rise apartment buildings, which in the first place were put there for the people you claim to have in your best interest. Are you going to say, "Well, we don't want adequate housing for these folks!"? But we build the concentration camps. They're technological in nature and they're ours done in the finest democratic tradition, so anybody would be a fool who's opposed to it. It's not like Nazi Germany, as yet. But the real paradigm for concentration camps in the technological society is the things we're doing in the name of progress. Am I saying let's not have progress? I'm just saying we don't apparently know what progress is. I think it results in the fact that we have somehow forgotten what education or anything else has to do with the quality of life.

DOOR: Is there such a thing as progress? Maybe it's a value we don't understand and shouldn't strive for?

CAMPBELL: I don't know. If it is, we don't seem to be making it. I can speculate in theological terms that all these towers that we build in the name of man are Babel. They're towers of Babel because the Lord is not in them.

DOOR: Many of our readers are youth leaders in the church. They have a lot of questions and are doing a lot of struggling, but they're still there. Would you have a word for them? Would you tell them that they are perhaps wasting their time in an institution and they should begin to move in creative ways outside the steepled church?

CAMPBELL: No, because right away they're going to want to know, "like what?" And I can't tell them like what. All I can tell them is: If God be God, he can work anywhere he wants to, including the mahogany pews, the red carpets, the stained glass, and all the rest. I'm not trying to limit God; all I know is he's not calling me under the steeple. I can't say that for anybody else.

DOOR: The word "renewal" has been big lately. Do you feel that as long as renewal remains under a steeple, it's a waste of time? Or do you think that real change can take place in the church that's going to change from being a self-serving institution to becoming more God serving?

CAMPBELL: I don't believe that it's possible to reform an institution from within. There are people trying, and I respect them and love them. They say we are going to stay and fight this thing out. But the minute you really get close, something goes wrong: you're sleeping with the organist, or your hair's too long, or you drink whiskey, or something. So you're not going to be there any longer. And if you really start getting close, if you really start saying, "We don't need a building, let's sell this thing and give it to the poor," they'll have you committed for that one. You have to remember the nature of an institution.

DOOR: Do you feel there are some strides being made toward what you feel would be an acceptable form of the church?

CAMPBELL: Well, you see, I can't talk in terms of what would be an acceptable form for the church.

DOOR: Do you think it should have a form?

CAMPBELL: I think it's inevitable that it will. I know that, but again, I don't find in the New Testament that it is, in fact, anything but a relationship.

DOOR: How about church leadership? I think the people here are going to be influenced by what you've said, and I think the people you work with in the South are influenced. Whether or not you want to be a leader, you are. Do you see this as legitimate?

CAMPBELL: Well, I'm not a leader. You're wrong about that. I'm not a leader, and I don't want to be a leader. I don't want any disciples and I'll never have any. If I looked back at a bunch of folks following me, I'd fall apart. I'm trying to *be* a disciple, and I think that's all it's about. I'm trying to be a follower; I'm not trying to be a leader. I'm not any smarter than anybody else; I don't know more than what other folks know. I think an awful lot of people see what I see because it's so obvious that they can't miss it.

DOOR: I'm not trying to drive this point into the ground, but it seems to me that in the New Testament they

had some leaders that provided them with direction. . . .

CAMPBELL: Who rose out of the ranks. . . .

DOOR: Yeah. Do you see this happening? Should it happen with the community of people that you might have?

CAMPBELL: Well, not if you structure it. Because once you do then you've got to set up guidelines and standards—"We don't want a minister unless he's got a B.D." Again, I can't improve on the structures we already have. If we're talking about structures, let's just keep what we've got. Keep showing them up. We'll have a "Key '73," and if that doesn't work we'll have "A Million More in '74" and whatever rhymes with '75 and '76 and all the rest. Which seems to me is going down a bit in history. I'm not saying we're not going to have institutions; I know we are and I know I'm involved in a lot of them. All I'm saying is you don't ever take them seriously. And that you see them as the enemy. You know that they're after your soul—every last one of them is after your allegiance.

DOOR: Would you amplify that?

CAMPBELL: Well, I know, for example, that Caesar can make me bow down to him. It happens all the time, and it's going to happen next week when I make out my income tax. He'll force me to do it, and if I don't send it to him, he'll come get it with a little extra to pay him for coming to get it. It's again a part of that technological society where every penny I make and everything goes into this computer and it's impossible to bitch up the system. It's so built in: if you don't do what you're supposed to do the machine kicks your card out and they come and take it away from you. And all these institutions make me bow down and worship them, and the only thing I can do is try to hang on to a little tiny shred of humanity and be able to chuckle or snicker when I bow down and put a pinch of incense on their altar. I used to say that "I'm free and I'm not going to do that," and so on. All I know to do is to go on shaking my head negatively to Caesar and to all institutions as much as my gut and my nervous system will let me do.

CHARLIE AND MARTHA SHEDD

Charlie and Martha Shedd made a lot of people jealous. They were too darn successful. In the pastorate, C & M took a church in Houston that grew from less than fifty members to over 3000. In the process, warm human relationships were developed. And the church gave one dollar to missions for every dollar spent on themselves.

In physical fitness, Charlie battled the bulge and won. Despairing of obesity, Charlie shed over 100 pounds and kept it off. Then he wrote a book about it.

In publishing, the Shedds have written over a dozen books (most recently, *Bible Study Together: Making Marriage Last* and *Praying Together: Making Marriage Last*) that have sold thousands of copies. The books have made money. And C & M have given over half of their book royalties to missions.

In media, they succeeded with Charlie's syndicated radio program, "Parent-Talk."

In addition to writing and speaking, Charlie and Martha pastored a little Presbyterian Church in Jekyll Island, Georgia. A few years after Martha's death, Charlie has now remarried (inheriting two teenage boys in the process), serves as interim pastor here and there, and still writes.

DOOR: Where do you think marriage is in the Christian church today? Especially among clergy.

CHARLIE: I think that marriage is awfully good in the ministry and awfully bad. Some of the strongest marriages that I see are in the parsonage or the manse or the pastorium, or whatever it's called. But some of the sorriest are also there. By and large, our research on the whole thing doesn't mark marriage in the ministry a whole lot different than other marriages. And I was sorry to report that we don't think that more than about ten percent of marriages in America are anywhere near maximum. It's maybe closer to five percent.

DOOR: Why is that?

CHARLIE: Mostly because people aren't honest with each other. They're afraid. They've never learned to live in the grace of God. They've never extended to each other the mercy of the Lord. As such, they have to live behind masks and move behind a facade in everything they do. And as a consequence, they go through life looking for some place to relate. And some of them find it, including ministers.

MARTHA: I think that's basically it— a matter of communication, being honest in communication. But people don't take time for in-depth communication so that they can be friends and have a good time.

CHARLIE: We have a real thing about this time deal in the ministry. The easy excuse for the minister is "we just don't have time." The minister's wife has been programmed to read back— "I don't have time, darling." And she goes around saying, "My husband doesn't have time." That is just as phony as it can be. Everybody today is busy. I don't know anybody who is doing anything worthwhile that isn't right up to here with activity. It seems to us that one of the basic problems is that couples in the ministry and elsewhere just don't put priorities where they ought to be: mainly for relationship. We have a real thing about this. Almost a holy zeal about the fact that in order to relate well to other people—to the masses, to a congregation, to youth, to other couples—we have to relate well to each other. For us this is theological. You can't be charismatic to a whole crowd, in our judgment, unless you have been honest with one other person. You can be charismatic in appearance, but to really have the charisma that turns people on to the Lord, you've got to discover it with a relationship one on one.

DOOR: How do you begin to pull a marriage back together after five, maybe ten years, of mediocrity?

MARTHA: Set up some goals together. Everybody has twenty-four hours a day, and you can decide what to do with it. Charlie and I decided long ago that we would go out once a week alone on a date and we'd communicate. And we've stuck with that, and it's meant everything to our marriage. And it means a lot to the kids. They love it. They send us out if we haven't been out through the week.

DOOR: Did you do this right from the start of your marriage?

MARTHA: No, but pretty early.

CHARLIE: We didn't begin it immediately. But we were pretty estranged from each other too. One of the amazing things that happened in our marriage was that we'd gone together a long time, and we felt we knew each other just as well as two people can know each other. We got married, and suddenly we began to withdraw from each other. Martha had been raised in a home where she had picked up a very definite shyness and inferiority complex. A withdrawal, a barrier type of life. I was a very much outgoing, flam-bang, move-right-in-on-them kind of guy. A phony. I was moving out so I wouldn't have to go in. We decided then since we were becoming estranged from each other and didn't want this estrangement, that we would (a) give it the time and (b) try to be honest with each other. It took a long period with us. But the thing that we're really hepped on for marriage is if we can get a couple praying. If a couple will agree to pray and study prayer together, and really commit themselves to a duet of prayer, it doesn't matter whether they've been estranged from each other for thirty years—they can build a good marriage. Because this is where it's at in our experience. Once you begin to relate to the Lord through each other then your own relationship grows in depth and you become able to relate to other people.

DOOR: What if the two of you can't seem to pray together out loud?

CHARLIE: We began our prayers in silence. Why don't you tell them about that, Martha?

MARTHA: We have a favorite place where we sit down—a rocking love seat in our living room. We hold hands and talk about the things we want to pray about—anything that is troubling us or that we're grateful for or whatever. Then we pray silently. We started this way, and we still do it. And anybody can do that. Then say amen or the Lord's Prayer or some closing when you think you've gotten through.

CHARLIE: We find that even in the ministry, a couple that should be schooled in prayer, clam up completely when they begin to pray with each other. Or if they don't clam up, then they are simply parroting words. They're not effectively sharing the deep places of their lives together.

Another part of our prayer life together would definitely have to be our study. We have four goals at our house for a praying home.

DOOR: What are they?

MARTHA: One goal is that each one of us has our own quiet time every day. Charlie and I get up early—he gets up real early, and I'm ahead of the rest of the gang—and we have our own quiet time . . . reading the Bible or an inspirational book. It's a time of meditation. Another goal in our family is that everybody prays for everybody else

every day. There are thirteen in our family now including in-laws and grandchildren. Then we pray together—husband and wife. And the final goal is family devotions. We try to gather whoever is at home together.

DOOR: Do you try to do that every day?

MARTHA: We try to, and we make it over half the time. It's a fun time. We have a real celebration at it. We hang loose.

CHARLIE: Our study is a big part of our prayer life, and we are constantly in our quiet times studying materials that we're sharing with each other. Now we don't share these study times together. Once in a while we read a book together. She reads to me or I read to her. We do this sometimes when we're in the car. In our quiet time, we're reading the Bible. In the living Word are the dates of the different times when we read, Martha's marked in green and mine in red. And they're dated when we read them. Then we will discuss later what we read that we want to share with each other. "I came on this verse, honey, and it said this to me, what do you think?" And she gives me feedback. We're also reading something on self-help psychology. We started out with some pretty surface material, but we've gotten now where we read straight psychiatry and psychology. Depth stuff. Some of the heavies. We will read material of this kind together and then we will mark. We have four marks we use. This is an old Swedish system. We have an arrow if it convicts us, a candle if it's new light, a star if it's something that's quite important, and then we underline. And then when I find some crazy part of me coming to the surface, I write "Me" in the column and discuss this with Martha. She writes "Me" in her column. And then we talk about that. And one thing we do is never to demean each other's dignity. I never write "Martha" in the column and she never writes "Charlie." So this is part of our prayer life too. We're researching each other all the time. I guess you could say we're being each other's psychiatrists. This could be very dangerous for a couple that isn't in tune, or isn't honest, or isn't praying. I think it could be pretty savage. But doctors have told me there's no way that could be harmful to you unless you are really psychotic. If you're just neurotic like we are and like a few other people are, it could be extremely helpful. And we spend about fifteen minutes a day on this in addition to our prayer life together.

DOOR: Some forms of public prayer seem to inhibit communication like a façade or mask. We make speeches to each other. Don't you think that kind of prayer would only add to the problems of communication in marriage as opposed to the right kind of prayer, which is precisely the opposite: taking the mask off, becoming naked before God, and letting it all hang out?

CHARLIE: Oh, you're right on.

DOOR: How do you handle that?

CHARLIE: I am so much in tune with what you say that we have scrubbed the pastoral prayer in our church services. We just don't have it. Instead we have a period of silence, which blows our people's minds. There is something about corporate silence that is a tremendously dynamic thing, and this is how Martha and I feel about our own silent prayers. The vocal prayer that we can share together now first had to be learned in silence. Part of the reason why prayers out loud are

phony is because we are invariably telling God how we want it. Real prayer is just the opposite: God telling us how he wants it. So instead of us putting God into a manipulative position, prayer is for us to put ourselves where God can manipulate us. This is great prayer. So I think you're just so right on about the whole business of praying out loud. Praying out loud can be an enemy to an effective prayer life between husband and wife unless it's properly managed.

DOOR: Do you feel that in the type of fast-paced, go-go-go culture we're involved in that a couple must be disciplined to survive in communication?

CHARLIE: Exactly. I would say that we do not know any couple that has a vital prayer life that is undisciplined. Now that's amazing, isn't it?

MARTHA: But ours isn't rigid at all. It really is a relaxed discipline. And it's something we have a good time at— like our family devotions. It doesn't seem like a rigid schedule at all.

CHARLIE: It isn't. We've had people tell us, "I don't believe in scheduling my love." The only answer to that is, "Great, do it your way. Only do it." Only we don't know anybody that does it if they don't schedule it. Just to float into this kind of a life because you're so in tune with each other and the Lord . . . there may be people like this, but we don't know them.

DOOR: You mentioned once that great sex comes from great prayer.

CHARLIE: Yes. I can say without question that our prayer life led to a vibrant sex life like we never thought possible. We had always had a good sex life, but it was after we began praying together that our sex life really took off. And we don't know of another couple that has as potent a sex life as

Charlie and Martha Shedd. Now we don't know another couple that has a better prayer life either. Do they go together? We think they do. I also think it's very dangerous for couples, seminary students and so on, if they're engaged and a couple of years away from marriage, to begin praying together. Because it's going to lead to sex. It's a fact time and time again: a spiritual approach to union will lead to physical union. Now we're fifty-eight years old and there's nobody that we ever talk to that has a sex life any better or as good as ours. And we don't think that this is physical. We think that this is a turn on direct from the Lord which says, in essence, that sex is a gift of God, and that the closer you draw to God the more you get turned on all over. I get around with young people, of course, just like you guys do all the time. I get pretty weary of these poor kids who have been brought up in that ultra-severe background where they have been taught if you just believe in Jesus enough, you won't have any sex feelings. And I tell them, "Kids, this is absolutely the reverse of reality. The more the Holy Spirit turns you on, the more he's going to turn you on all over. Unless, of course, the vagina and the penis are bad organs. If everything about man is good except the vagina and the penis, then you are perfectly within your right to believe that when you get turned on by the Holy Spirit, you're going to get turned on all over except there. But if you look at the first chapter of Genesis where God says everything that he had made and, behold, it was very good— no exceptions—then you've got to believe that if the Holy Spirit is really living in your heart, he's going to turn

on everything." And that is our witness. That is our experience.

DOOR: That explains why Assembly of God girls were so sexy in high school.

CHARLIE: Do you have anything to add to that, honey?

MARTHA: No, I agree.

DOOR: What kind of advice would you give couples that are having problems relating to each other sexually? Where could they go to get help? Or is it simply a matter of building up their prayer life?

CHARLIE: At the risk of sounding like a one-song singer . . . and I mustn't apologize for that because I am a one-song singer about sex and prayer. I think that any couple that is having sexual problems ought to begin at the point of prayer because this may do a whole lot to work their problems through. Now I think there are a few cases where it's physical. And sadly enough, where that is true, it's usually on the male side. There are a number of situations in every group that we get into where the male has just lost his ability or his interest and there's a very frustrated female in the relationship. Now that guy needs help. But without that problem and given everything else, a couple doesn't need to sit still for a weak sex life. Not with all the wonderful counseling there is available. I think if a couple can't pray together, they ought to get a psychologist, psychiatrist, counselor, or someone else who can help them develop a oneness that will lead to some sort of physical union. As far as technique is concerned, I just don't think I'd have anything unique to offer except perhaps to say the average man is an idiot when it comes to turning on a woman. Really. Most ministers particularly.

That's not fair. *Most* men are really dumdums sexually. They don't know what a woman's like. And a guy who knows what he's doing, if he's got any relationship with his woman at all, can sit across the room and never lay a hand on her and get her so excited that something's going to explode. But this takes a fella who's got a lot of imagination, a lot of ability, and a lot of understanding of what the female is. Most of the sex problems that I see are the man's fault, probably because he doesn't understand that sex with a woman is an all-day-long quality. For him, it's just quantity. "How much am I going to get?" And she wants to know, "How am I going to get it?" We think that more women would cooperate in a good sex life if more men would.

DOOR: How could a man find out more about what turns a woman on?

CHARLIE: Martha, I've never been a woman. What do you think about that?

MARTHA: I think it's back to what we've already said. It takes time and work and communication and honesty—if they'll talk and visit. And if even during the sex act they talk they can learn what turns each other on.

DOOR: So it's a matter of learning from your spouse—communicating and finding out what turns her on.

CHARLIE: Plus learning from people who know what they're doing. One of my favorite books on this particular question is a book called *Letters to Phillip*. I happened to write it. It's a superb book. But I don't see how any man could read *Letters to Phillip* (thank God many men have ... and you wouldn't believe the letters I get from fellas who have read it) without understanding that sex to a woman is not an act, not a happening; it's a creation. It's a twenty-year warm up.

And if he comes at it from this point of view, he's more likely to get the job done. Since the twenty years are going to pass anyway, he might as well put them to good use.

DOOR: Why is it that so many people consider men and women in the ministry to have less sexuality than the average person? If a pastor looks at a girl in a bikini and smiles, people question his spirituality.

MARTHA: I think it's like Charlie said, pastors are probably more turned on than anybody because the Lord turns you on all over. I feel if Charlie doesn't keep on responding to girls in bikinis, he's not going to be much good for me. We encourage it.

CHARLIE: Martha is superb at getting me to evaluate the various arrangement of molecules in her presence. We live on a beach and watch these girls go by in bikinis, and she very often will say to me, "What do you think about this one?" or "Which of those three do you like?" But to answer your question, I think the church has sort of put a shamey-shamey on sex; therefore, the churchman is supposed to be above sexual feelings. Whereas, what the church really needs to say to its people is: Sex is beautiful and from the Lord. And when it's right, there's nothing that could be wrong with it. Now whenever we begin to look at other women in lust, when we begin to plan and connive, and our mind gets carried away, that's something entirely different. But I believe the church has tried in the past to get people to be subhuman, or to be more saintly than they really are. So I think that this is part of the reason that people look at the preacher and say, "Oh, bad boy." Well, he isn't any worse of a boy than the guy selling computers, is he? They've both got the same kind of response. I think that the church has grievously put down sex through the years. It's tragic.

DOOR: Martha, wasn't it difficult at first to have him look at other people and help him in his evaluation? How did you get secure enough to do that? A lot of wives just couldn't handle that.

MARTHA: It was difficult, and we had a struggle with it for a while. The jealousy problem was an awful one. I think this was answered through prayers. I know when I finally got the feeling that I was important to the Lord, that he loved me, this was the biggest step.

CHARLIE: One of the most beautiful things that ever happened in our relationship was right there at that point when Martha, out of her prayer life, came to me and said, "I'm never again going to be jealous. I've turned it over to the Lord. And the answer I got was that you are free to be you. I was afraid that I wasn't good enough to hold you, but I believe that the Lord made me and accepts me, and I accept that. So I'm just saying to you, it's yours to do with as you wish. And if you do ever have intercourse with another woman—which I have been jealous for and afraid of—if you want to come home and tell me about it, then we'll talk about it, and we'll pray about it, and I'm just going to love you." And then she said something further (can you imagine a woman saying this to her husband), "While you are having intercourse with this other woman, will you remember that I am there loving you?"

DOOR: That did it right there, huh?

CHARLIE: What have you got left? That's a beautiful way to ruin a man's

fun. And through the years, for thirty-five years, I have never once been unfaithful to Martha. Not because I'm good, but because she is. And she would say not because she is, but because she was in the grace of God when she said this to me. She's standing there right in the middle of the free, unmerited favor of God and saying, "I'm going to love you no matter what." This is what you call holding a man by loving him. I wouldn't say every marriage is ready for that. I wouldn't recommend it for everybody, but it's a true story of what happened in the life of one couple.

DOOR: Sometimes a couple can have a fairly good sex life, but they've been brought up in a church where they feel that a lot of things are taboo for a Christian married couple. Is there anything a Christian married couple can not do—oral sex, etc.?

MARTHA: We don't think there's anything a Christian couple can do that would be wrong if they both want to and it isn't harmful to either one physically, emotionally, or mentally. The more uninhibited you are the better.

CHARLIE: The more uninhibited you are the more likely you are to really reach the potential that God wants you to reach. Now, here again, I think the idea that sex organs are bad and everything else is good is one of the reasons that many people shy away from such things as oral intercourse. But our thing with each other is, if you enjoy it and if it isn't harmful to each other physically and mentally, then enjoy it. We feel like the full expression, the free expression of your love ought to be a part of a vital Christian marriage, so long as you both are enjoying it and not hurting each other physically or emotionally. We go very big for variety. We think that one of the tragedies of sex in couples that we've worked with is that many people have no imagination. We were in Cincinnati a while back. We went into a bookstore and bought a book on 147 different positions for intercourse. That is more than twice as many as the Japanese say there are. Of course, there are only maybe a dozen basic positions and variations from them. We were so excited because when we got home and read this book, we discovered that our favorite position wasn't in there. We thought that was pretty good. I'm real proud of that.

MARTHA: People get in a rut too on the time and place for intercourse. We had a couple visiting not long ago who only had intercourse every Saturday night or something. Anyway, it was once a week.

DOOR: Like a Saturday night bath.

MARTHA: And that's too bad.

CHARLIE: Yeah, sex is good anytime, we think. And variety and frequency are a big part of it.

DOOR: We recently ran across a fellow who thought it was wrong to have sex on Saturday night. He was a minister, and he was afraid that would cause problems for his ministry on Sunday.

CHARLIE: We like it on Sunday morning too. Not immediately before the sermon. . . . Anyway, we think it's a very nice part of programming Sunday mornings.

MARTHA: I remember the doctor I went to just before we were married— a lady M.D. who was also a psychiatrist—and she said a minister really needs it *after* his sermon on Sunday.

CHARLIE: There you go. Thank you, darling. I hadn't realized it, but that is a great healer. You can bomb out on the sermon, but there's one place you're going to do it right.

DOOR: Do you have anything to say about the whole area of climax?

CHARLIE: We have had a very interesting development on that in our own marriage. I was brought up like I think most boys are on the assumption that unless a man can put his wife into orbit every time they have intercourse, he just really is a failure. I think one of the big steps forward in our sex life was when Martha convinced me that she loved me and loved my loving her and that's all she needed sometimes. There are some couples who climax every time. But rarely do you find a couple that climaxes together every time. But what's the difference? The psychologist say it doesn't matter as long as you both get what you need. I think it was a big beautiful moment in our marriage when I finally got it out of my thick skull that I had to make Martha be what Charlie wanted. And I finally could surrender my coercion of my wife and accept her as she was and be joyful. And when a woman can say to her man and convince him it's true, "I just want to be a missionary to your needs tonight," this is a big leap up. But here again we're back to prayer. I don't think that you're going to have that kind of relationship until you finally through prayer come to the realization that though you are one, you are still the combination of two unique creatures before God and the priesthood of believers. The right of the individual to be himself before God is a big part of a great sex life.

DOOR: So you think there are problems peculiar to a minister's marriage relationship that laymen do not have?

CHARLIE: I don't think I see any. I'm hesitating on this because I could be wrong. (Amazing thought.) I can't see marriage problems peculiar to the ministry that aren't peculiar to every other marriage. Honey, do you have any thoughts on that?

MARTHA: I'm not sure. It seems to me that ministers' wives and doctors' wives are among the loneliest of wives, because men in these professions often seem to put the profession ahead of other things. There are so many ministers that run around and escape from home it seems to me—meetings, calling on people. They're gone a good deal more than they need to be. I don't know whether that's true or not.

DOOR: So you see it as a time problem.

MARTHA: But that could be any profession.

DOOR: However, it seems to me that because it's a spiritual calling, we can somewhat put the blame on God: "God has called me into this. If you were really fulfilling your spiritual obligations, you'd stand behind me and you'd be hanging right in there." That's different from someone who's a doctor.

CHARLIE: In that light, I think you are probably right on. There is more temptation, I think, for the minister to justify some of the bizarre in his life and to turn it over to the responsibility of God and project it onto the people around him rather than face up to it as his problem. There might be more temptation to do this. There's nothing neater than being God's man. I think in the ministry there is a tendency to believe that we brought down the Ten Commandments from Mt. Sinai; therefore, whatever we do has a holy aura. But other than that I just can't see much difference between ministers' marriages and laymen's marriages.

DOOR: Obviously, your priority structure is God first, family second, and then church. How did you set that up in the ministry? You were in a big church in Houston, weren't you?

MARTHA: A big, fast-growing one, and we just set our priorities. Anybody can. This church had fifty-five members when we went there and over 3,000 when we left. So it was fast-growing, and Charlie also wrote eight books in that time. It was a dollar-for-dollar benevolence church, so there wasn't any staff. We sent a dollar to missions for every dollar we kept, which meant sometimes we hardly had pencils, or office paper, or anything. And during this time, we decided that God was first, then our marriage and our children. And that's when we decided on one night out a week and fifteen minutes a day to sit down and visit. We also had one night for family night with the children, and this was the best witness Charlie gave in that church. I know of marriages that were saved and homes that were happier because they knew their preacher wasn't coming out to a committee meeting or a social meeting on the nights that were set aside for his wife and children.

DOOR: You had two nights a week— one when you and Martha got together and one for your family. So the maximum the church could expect from you would be five nights a week and maybe less?

MARTHA: That's right.

CHARLIE: Plus another night once a month. We have five children, and I took one of the children out to dinner alone—just Daddy and child. That was sacred. That was holy ground from the time they were two years old. It was absolutely beautiful.

MARTHA: One other thing I think about ministers is that Charlie also organized the church. He was able to because it was a new one. But he organized it so there weren't committee meetings. He assigned one-man-responsibility areas within the officers. And they took care of it instead of having committee meetings every night of the week. And instead of having clubs and social organizations, we recommended to the people that they stay home with their family. So the whole church was set up to emphasize family instead of running to meetings.

CHARLIE: One of the interesting things that happened along this line was people saying you're a bad guy for taking time off. I had a fascinating experience with a man in a church in Oklahoma where I was pastor who really gave us fits. This guy was a needle though. And he resented terribly all my time for the family. I discovered after the big resentment that he was resenting me (a) out of jealousy (b) out of the fact that he didn't want anybody around there showing that kind of example because he didn't want his family to see it and certainly not his wife. And the way I found this out was that this dear man later became a close friend of mine and confessed it to me. Now isn't that interesting? It was to me. So I wonder if people who point the finger at ministers and say, "Shamey, shamey on you . . . you're taking the day at the beach," aren't saying, "Boy, I wish I could take a day at the beach" but "I ought to, so I don't want you to because I can't or I won't." I think that the minister and the churchman as he works with people needs to go behind the criticism often to the deeper motives of the criticism.

DOOR: Do you think that a church should expect a minister's wife to share in his ministry? Should the minister himself expect when he marries this girl that she should share his vow of poverty and some of the trials he'll go through as a pastor?

CHARLIE: Do you know that we have in the Southern Presbyterian church right now a very interesting situation at Columbia Seminary in Decatur, Georgia. One of the senior student's wives is teaching belly dancing in a night school. Isn't that something. I just think that's super. She says, "Why shouldn't I? Belly dancing is a very healthy activity." He wasn't in the ministry, and apparently they have a very fine relationship where she can say that. I think it probably requires a stance on the part of the minister about his wife to the church. I want her to be what she feels the Lord wants her to be. Martha has always said loud and clear to the women of the church, "I'm going to be a wife first, a mother second, and if there's anything left, you can have it." I think that's pretty good.

MARTHA: I know that lots of women who are minister's wives work now and earn money to help with this sort of thing.

CHARLIE: This is one of the things we see, and there are many places where a home is better off if the wife is working. If she's doing it out of necessity, really grinding, I think there ought to be a limitation, "Well, we're going to go on like this so far and no farther." Then they have an understanding. I don't believe that we have any good advice on that particular thing. Martha taught school a year or two . . . longer than that after we were married. It was very healthy for her and our marriage and our pocketbook. I feel that the problem is maybe aggravated by the man not realizing that what he has married here isn't his woman, but a wonderful daughter of the Lord who has rights of her own and a uniqueness to live out in their togetherness. Gibran's "Let there be spaces in your togetherness" is a very precious phrase in our marriage. And the dignity of me saying to her, and her saying to me, "Honey, there is one thing more important than pleasing me and this is pleasing the Lord." This frees up a whole lot of problem areas.

DOOR: When a woman is tired of living the lifestyle she's been forced into, I think sometimes a bitterness comes.

CHARLIE: Exactly, and I don't blame her.

DOOR: I guess it would be sensitivity on the husband's part to say, "I've poured ten years of our life into this and given it my best shot, and maybe to be fair to my family, it's time to move into a different form of ministry."

MARTHA: For sure you don't have to be in the ministry to be God's man.

DOOR: With the pressures of a church ministry and the time devoted to the family, how do you develop relationships with other couples?

MARTHA: I think the only time we've been frustrated by it was in a big church. We didn't have much time and we had five children and there were so many nice people that we never had time to spend with socially.

CHARLIE: I think there's a danger of developing exclusivity in friendships in your own relationship and in your own home to the extent that you don't take in other people. That is a viable threat, I think. We try to watch it. We've never lacked for friends and never had any dearth of relationships like this, so I'm not sure we could give good advice. One thing we have found to be very helpful is to develop friends of an entirely different lifestyle.

DOOR: How do you view Paul's view of woman, the view he had of the ministry, and the view he had of celibacy? How do you handle the apostle Paul?

CHARLIE: As an amateur theologian . . . my standing as an amateur has never been questioned . . . this isn't my thing. I'm more of a practical day-by-day religionist, I think. I have a great deal of respect for the apostle Paul. So I always tip my hat in that direction. I think there were also areas where the apostle Paul was very, very off center in his attitudes toward people. Most of which, I think, are hang-ups out of his past. We know that he had a pretty traumatic childhood and history. And I don't think he ever got completely over it. I preach from Paul and I love some of the things he's written and I believe in his thirteenth chapter of Corinthians, if he wrote it, which of course is open to question. It's the great symphony, word-wise, of love. But I don't think he has all the truth, and I certainly don't think he has all the truth about man and woman and womankind. I have to remember all the time that he very likely wasn't married. That may be a put-down of the apostle Paul. I don't mean it to be, but he was human. He wasn't divine any more than you and I are divine. So theologically, I just simply don't buy his whole bag about women.

MARTHA: I don't like him.

CHARLIE: But I don't think we have to get hostile toward Paul because we can look at a guy and understand his background and say, "Well, he's got a problem." And he obviously had a problem. One of the most wonderful things that the apostle Paul teaches us is that God can use people with problems.

MARTHA: If you read the books in the order that he wrote them, he seemed to improve through the years.

DOOR: How do you see the inspiration of God coming through a guy who's got a hang-up?

CHARLIE: Well, I see it first as a witness to the glory of God, that God can take an imperfect being like Charlie Shedd and use what he has to say to bless somebody's life. That's the first thing we can say about somebody like Paul. The second thing is "praise God we can think as straight as an arrow in some areas whereas we may be really flaked out in other areas."

The Lord can use the part that is going straight to the mark if we understand this and can discern it. Theologically, I have never felt that a person had to be perfect to be used by the Lord. It's amazing how the Lord can use people so much different than we are and use that person to his glory, isn't it? A humbling experience, but still beautiful. I think this is also true in the whole religious area—the whole realm of fundamentalists, modernists, liberals, conservatives. It's just so great to realize that we don't have to agree about everything to get good vibes from each other and to do our thing together. I get invited to circles where theologically I am just completely at the other end. But we get along fine. There's only one thing that counts and that is the lordship of Jesus Christ. And as long as we both agree that the lordship of Jesus Christ is the crucial point, we can harmonize.

WESLEY PIPPERT

Wesley Pippert, fifty-four years old, was a principal UPI Washington correspondent during the Watergate years before a stint as bureau chief in Jerusalem and Middle East correspondent. Pippert now directs the University School of Journalism's Washington Graduate Program in Washington, D. C.

Pippert, a former Iowa farm boy who attended a one-room schoolhouse with ten other children, graduated Phi Beta Kappa from the University of Iowa. He also picked up a master's degree in biblical literature from Wheaton while working with UPI in Chicago.

His political background is no less varied than his journalistic one. He covered the state-capitol scene in both North and South Dakota, was press aide to Senator Charles Percy, recently spent some time as special assistant to Representative Paul Henry, and voted a straight Democratic ticket in the '72 election. He left UPI in 1986 for a sabbatical at Harvard, where he held two consecutive fellowships in the fields of politics, public policy, and the press. He is married (to Becky Pippert) with two children.

While a political reporter in the Dakotas, he served as lay pastor of two small country churches.

His latest books are *Land of Promise, Land of Strife: Israel at Forty* and *An Ethics of News: A Reporter's Search for Truth*. The *Door* flew Pippert out to San Diego in 1974 for an interview shortly after Gerald Ford's pardon of Richard Nixon.

DOOR: What are your immediate views on Ford's pardon of Nixon?

PIPPERT: I personally think it was a great tragedy. It really prohibits us. There's nothing like a trial to bring out all the facts and permit cross-examination. What Ford has done is simply shut the door on us ever finding out the total, full story of what Nixon was up to during his first term. I don't know what the American people are going to think about it. I don't know that the telephone calls and the letters are a reliable gauge, but it would seem to me, maybe I'm projecting my own wishes, that the people would really be outraged by this. It might well give the Democrats a fresh issue for November. When it looked like Ford had absolutely preempted the whole ball game as far as November elections are concerned ... it may mean that the Democrats have new life. Maybe that's the redemptive part of what's happened.

DOOR: How long have you covered Watergate?

PIPPERT: Since March of 1973.

DOOR: With Ford's action, does it seem like all the trials and special committees were kind of a waste?

PIPPERT: Absolutely not. I think that Watergate was a sad and sordid story. But if there had not been this full and complete coverage of Watergate with all the revelations, the American people would never have known how seriously our system of government was threatened by such things as the Ellsberg break-in, the domestic intelligence gathering, and the impact big money had. Watergate laid this open for all the people to see and to observe and hopefully to set a different standard for what follows in the next few years.

DOOR: Do you see any positive results coming out of this thing? It seems like the campaign reform laws have been very slow in coming.

PIPPERT: I don't think the most positive thing will be in the area of legislation, although obviously some legislative changes are necessary, such as in the area of campaign financing. But it really points out once again that our government is no better than the men who run it. And our system of government is no stronger than the conscience and the concern that each one of us citizens has for it. The strongest fruit that can come out of

this all will be a quickened concern on the part of all of us. And a quickened conscience on the part of those who hold office and seek office.

DOOR: In *Memo for '76*, you mentioned a lot of things that Christians could do in politics. Would you comment on some of these, especially after Watergate?

PIPPERT: I think it's pretty obvious that all of us are not called to be active in politics. I don't think that God ever intended that this be the case. That isn't the way he has apportioned his gifts among us believers. But the minimum we can do as Christians is certainly to be concerned and be aware of what's happening around us in the political sphere. If we're concerned and we're aware, hopefully we can pray more intelligently. And if we can pray more intelligently, perhaps those of us who do have particular and specific gifts will be more sensitive to being led into the political area if God intends that for us.

In *Memo*, I talked about the various degrees of involvement and the different types of involvement. I didn't talk so much about philosophy. I talked about the Christians who are so disenchanted with the system that they've dropped out entirely. On the one hand you have the Jesus People who have completely dropped out of any involvement with the system or the establishment at all. Then you have the Berrigans and the Bonhoeffers and the Reies Lopez Tijerinas who feel strongly that the system is so rotten and so decayed that it has to be assaulted and torn down and built over again as Jeremiah talked about. That is a legitimate, biblical possibility for Christians who feel that strongly and are led by God in that direction.

On the other hand, there are many people who don't feel comfortable being a revolutionary. They choose to do something else—work within the system. As you work within the system there are several paths you can go too. There is Carl McIntyre, for instance, whom I mentioned in the book, and Martin Luther King who worked within the system . . . within the established laws. They organized political action groups in the name of the Christian faith. Now it might seem absurd to compare Carl McIntyre and Martin Luther King, but really their technique was the same even though philosophically they were poles apart. Carl McIntyre acknowledges that he is a firm social activist. And he is. He uses demonstrations as Martin Luther King used demonstrations. That is another legitimate option for a Christian group who feels led in that direction.

On the other hand, there are those who don't want to follow that particular path. They want to be involved, but they want to be involved within the system . . . within the established groups of doing things. We come to the John Andersons and Vinegar Ben Mizells and the Mark Hatfields. They have chosen to infiltrate the system and to position themselves in decisionmaking places and in that way try to affect change within the system. Now I'm still confused personally as to what the Bible has to say to us. How can we have a Vinegar Ben Mizell who has a 100 percent conservative voting record and a Mark Hatfield, on the other hand, who has a nearly 100 percent liberal voting record? Both are professing Christians and both are firmly in the evangelical mold, but they are poles apart philosophically. And I don't know the answer to that. It might be

that God uses our particular points of view, our abilities, and our skills and allows us to have differences of opinion. But we've all got to be responsive to the biblical mandates of justice and mercy and compassion.

DOOR: Some of those people like McIntyre don't seem to fit the mold of compassion. But you see all of these as part of God's balance? They're all okay?

PIPPERT: I don't think so. I said in *Memo for '76* that we could fault both McIntyre and King. King failed because he did not preach the complete gospel. He preached a socially activist gospel of which I'm totally sympathetic. But he failed to preach the complete gospel in that he failed to preach a personal gospel as well. Now Carl McIntyre also preaches a distorted gospel in that he completely links his version of what the Christian message is with what the American flag represents—capitalism and essentially a Waspish lifestyle and way of living. In that sense, he's preaching a distorted gospel too. I'm not saying that all these men are always okay. I'm saying they are following valid options. But they must continue to be open to what the Bible is saying about these bedrock, unchanging positions of justice and mercy.

DOOR: What would you say is the spiritual climate in Washington now? Would you agree with some recent magazine articles about a "revival in Washington"?

PIPPERT: I can't believe it. I know it's not true. Just because Gerald Ford is now president and Charles Colson is a professing Christian doesn't mean that somehow revival is sweeping Washington. I see very few evidences of that. I see signs of God at work in Washington, but I see no signs that revival is sweeping Washington.

I think it was very significant that one of the key things that happened in the Watergate unraveling was that Charles Colson pleaded guilty and thereby offered his testimony to the House Judiciary Committee and the various criminal trials that were coming up. He didn't do so merely because he had become a Christian, because you remember two weeks previous to his pleading, he told Mike Wallace on CBS, "I don't see how I can go back and make things straight. You can't expect anybody to do that." But in a two-week period after that interview, something happened to change his mind. I think what happened was this group of men he prayed with somehow . . . not by consciously prodding him but just through their continued prayers for support and the growth of the entire group . . . pointed him in the direction that he could do something about his past. And that led to his plea of guilty. Well, look at that group: Harold Hughes, a liberal Democrat; Al Quie, a moderate Republican; Graham Purcell from Texas, a southern Democrat; and Doug Coe who's apolitical. They certainly didn't have in common a political bind. Chuck Colson, on the other hand, was the epitome of political pragmatism, probably a philosophic neuter (and what Jeb Magruder called "an evil genius"). These men didn't reach the point where Charles Colson could step before the judge and plead guilty by virtue of their political bond. It was their bond in Christ which resulted in a quickened conscience on Colson's part. So really one of the most significant things that happened in the Watergate unraveling occurred because of a quickened conscience that

evolved out of an evangelical circle that was a political mixed bag.

DOOR: So you think the spiritual climate has been overrated in terms of being very significant.

PIPPERT: I went back to Wheaton in 1968 after the election. In that campaign I had worked for Percy, and in Percy's attempt to reconcile with the Nixon end of the party, I had been farmed out to the Republican National Committee to work on a project half-time during the fall campaign. The project was headed by Kleindeinst. I think I talk about it in *Memo*. And I was so disillusioned I voted straight Democratic that fall. I went back to Wheaton after the election with my family, and you know the people around Wheaton almost interpreted the election of Nixon as being the Second Coming. I don't know why they did it. I think it was partly Nixon's identification with Billy Graham and their trust in Graham. Anybody who was a friend of Graham was a friend of theirs.

But I think that's too superficial. More likely is the fact that most evangelicals have in common (except for you guys) a conservative thread in them. And that makes me very uneasy, because if you're a conservative in all areas of life and your lifestyle, and if that's the reason you're theologically and doctrinally conservative, that's not a very good reason. It doesn't mean that you're a conservative theologically by conviction; it just means you're conservative theologically because you're conservative every other way. So what happens? We bought Nixon hook, line, and sinker—and look what happened. Look at the disillusionment. And now we see Chuck Colson coming to Christ and we rejoice in that. So here again it looks as if we evangelicals have a compulsion to reach out and grab the most recent conversion or the slightest little example and then convert it into a revival. I think Hatfield said it: "Let's not try to make an evangelical out of Ford, which he is not, and then set ourselves up for another disillusionment."

DOOR: What do you think is the reason for evangelicals acting this way? Why do we have to go out and grab somebody who's hot, abuse him until he is used up, cast him aside, and get the next hero?

PIPPERT: I don't know, but it makes me very uncomfortable. When I grew up, my dad was a tenant farmer. I went to a country school, and when I finally got around to going to high school, I felt very peripheral because I wasn't a city kid. I went to a little, brick tabernacle church down the street, and not very much of what I did either socially or where I came from was very acceptable or very middle class. And I think that is probably true of many evangelicals. Evangelicals were essentially lower middle class economically; they were certainly not in the mainstream of the social life of any community. And all of a sudden we arrived. (This isn't my idea, it's been talked about before.) One of our men got elected president. A lot of evangelicals have good jobs and are making good money. Now we evangelicals drink, we go to movies, and we're very accepted. We're in there. We enjoy being accepted and being part of the mainstream. We want to continue that. One of our men was president. But he fell. So we grab the next guy, Ford.

We were doing better when we were struggling. We were doing better when we were a country-school kid whose father was a tenant farmer.

DOOR: Do you think that the evangelical church is contributing much to our society?

PIPPERT: I'm very critical of the institutional church, but having said that, I have not abandoned the institutional church. I am a part of it. I work in my own church. It seems to me that what the evangelical church is doing now is of infinite value. It is reminding us once again that there are absolutes. In a day of moral relativism and situational ethics which created the atmosphere in which Watergate could take place very easily and comfortably, the evangelical church is reminding us once again that the Bible does say some things that are absolute. Truth is absolute. The reality of sin is absolute.

DOOR: Is that all we're doing—just talking?

PIPPERT: I wouldn't go that far. I'm sure my parents are segregationists. And I'm certain you could extend that into other areas. But in my home my parents had feelings of love and kindness and mercy, I think toward everybody. I don't know that you can draw that distinction, but even though they might believe in segregation, it was not accompanied by hatred. I never met a person who has had a genuine Christian experience who has feelings of hatred, or bigoted or extremely prejudiced feelings. Now you may have, but I haven't.

All these years the evangelicals have preached about the reality of sin. And the evangelicals are now saying, "That's what we've been telling you for a long time." Now we're awakening to that fact. But the evangelicals also hold out the possibility of redemption, and that's one of the things we get out of Watergate.

DOOR: It seems to me that you've pointed up one of the major problems in the evangelical church. They point to what has happened in society— social sin. But then do they talk about personal sin? If the gospel has broader implications, we can't isolate personal sin from social sin. The church is trying to separate the two and basically say, "The problem is sin, and we're going to stay nonpolitical and not get involved in it."

PIPPERT: I'm not saying that they're totally right. I'm saying that their bedrock position was accurate. But in the living out of their beliefs there were some grievous distortions.

I know what you're saying and I agree with it. And in that sense, the evangelicals have been sitting on their behinds. That's why I can't understand why the Declaration of Evangelical Social Concern that came out of the Chicago workshop last year was so widely applauded. It was weak and it was spineless. It said nothing that should not have been said fifteen years ago. I don't know what everybody was shouting hallelujah about.

I'm just saying that the one crucial thing that the evangelicals have been saying all along is something that really needs to be said right now. The evangelical emphasis on sin and redemption really is the one central message that we need right now.

DOOR: How do you feel about the church's tax-exempt status?

PIPPERT: I don't know much about this. But churches, evangelical churches included, have become so institutionalized, and therefore suffer all the ailments of institutionalization: top-heavy in structure, too much bu-

reaucracy. There's as much politicking in evangelical denominations and institutions as there is in Washington. I think all denominations ought to be treated just like any other corporation. They should be taxed. They should pay taxes on their income, and they should pay real taxes on their property without exception.

DOOR: You don't think the church should be treated differently?

PIPPERT: There's a smugness that sets in an organization that becomes sound and entrenched. I don't know why a church should receive special treatment. I don't see why we in the church shouldn't be treated just like everybody else.

DOOR: Is part of your motive on taxation due to the feeling that it might force the church to move into the homes and go back to the style of years ago?

PIPPERT: That might be a good idea.

DOOR: What are some of your views on the press? Are they power hungry? Prejudiced?

PIPPERT: The press certainly played a key role in unraveling Watergate. But I don't think this gives us any particular reason to be proud. I think it pointed out the poverty and the lethargy of the press until now. Think back on the Agnew case. Agnew was elected county executive in 1962, governor in '66 and vice president in '68. All this time he was on the take. George Beal, the U.S. attorney, told me Agnew took about $150,000 in kickbacks. Now what was the press doing all this time? If the press had done the right kind of investigative digging when Agnew was county executive and governor, he never would have been vice-president. He wouldn't have been there to add further embarrassment to Nixon. The press was lazy.

The seeds that bore the bitter fruit of Watergate in '72 and '73 actually were sown in 1970 when the plan for domestic intelligence gathering was conceived and put into effect. It provided for mail interception, for surreptitious entry, for expanded infiltration of campuses. The White House plumbers are another example. They were established in 1971. What was the press doing then? The White House correspondents were sitting there in the lounge listening to Ron Ziegler's twice-a-day briefings. That was the extent of it. Only the *Washington Post* and CBS to a lesser degree did anything about the Watergate break-in for nine months afterward. Until March—then everybody seemed to awaken to the story almost simultaneously. It was nine months after the break-in and four months after the election before the American press as a whole finally got around to covering Watergate. So what do we have to be proud of? If we had been doing our job when we should have been doing it in 1970 and '71 and '72, we might have headed off a lot of these things. We have nothing to be proud of. We just did in '73 and '74 what we should have been doing all along.

DOOR: The press has been criticized for being prejudiced in their handling of Nixon. What's your feeling?

PIPPERT: I just got back from Iowa and South Dakota, and many people still feel that the press ran Nixon out of office. It's nonsense. I covered the '72 campaign from the McGovern side and I would imagine that every reporter who covered McGovern voted for him, almost without exception. But you tell me who had a favorable press

in the '72 campaign. It was not George McGovern. Richard Nixon sat in the White House and made very few trips. And the press did nothing about it. He had a good press through the entire campaign. George McGovern, on the other hand, had some problems. And those problems the press exploited to the fullest, as they should have. The Eagleton affair ... the $1,000 a year bonus plan ... whenever a minor staff problem came up, it was all over. The press hit it hard. It was George McGovern and not Richard Nixon who had the bad press, if there was a bad press in '72. So I don't think the press has been hounding Richard Nixon. I think that's an excuse so that the Nixon supporters can get the spite vote out.

DOOR: Do you see a place for investigative reporting in the church?

PIPPERT: Sure, why not? As I said earlier, a smugness sets in entrenched institutions. And the smugness has all kinds of ramifications. You think you're above questioning, like your good friend Gothard. And you think that somehow you're exempt from being answerable to anybody. And pretty soon, not only are you exempt from being questioned by anybody, but you think that your word is tantamount to Holy Writ. That's simply not true. Someone needs to go to it.

DOOR: However, a lot of true things you find out about people, even if they're not dishonest or shady, could tend to be embarrassing or damage a person's reputation and would not serve any useful purpose. Do you see that kind of thing happening very often?

PIPPERT: I have mixed feelings about this kind of intense recording of every detail of a politician's life. On the one hand, it may seem that one bit of information is meaningless and has no significance at all. On the other hand, it adds to what eventually becomes a mosaic of the person's life. So it takes a lot of different stories about a lot of different things about an individual to create the whole panorama of who he is and what he's all about. Or who she is and what's she's all about. Like the four Gospels—the four views of Christ—you need the same thing. You need a lot of people covering and writing and approaching the presidency or the politician who's running for office to build that kind of a multi-faceted panoramic and multi-dimensional picture of the person. On the other hand, I can't for the world imagine what it adds to our body of knowledge that Gerald Ford when he gets up, before he puts on his necktie, toasts himself an English muffin. There's a tension there. There's a tension between prying into a person's affairs that don't contribute much to what we really need to know about what kind of officeholder that person will be. On the other hand, we need to fill in the mosaic.

DOOR: Say an evangelist has been having an affair during his crusade. Should we print that or should we go to the evangelist and say, "Look, man, you need to repent and get this thing out of your life." Do we tell the rest of the Body of Christ about it . . . or are we on a different set of rules?

PIPPERT: Is there a difference between the way one approaches Christian journalism and the way one approaches secular journalism? I'm not sure that there is. Obviously in the secular press, if we come across a story and it involves sexual indiscretion, we treat it with delicacy. It's only the tabloid who would take that and

blast it all over the front page. So I think whether you're a Christian journalist or you're a secular journalist, what you say you say with delicacy and sensitivity and with some restraint. The rule that we have in covering a story or in covering a charge or an allegation that comes up involving a person is to get that person's response to the charge, and to include that response in the same story, if possible. We're admonished again and again to do that. And I think that what you suggested might be a good idea. You could go to the evangelist, just as we would as a secular journalist, and say, "Here's what we've uncovered, what about it?" It's a tough judgment, and I certainly couldn't call it. There are probably a lot of factors to consider.

Let's be specific in talking about investigative reporting. What about Kennedy and Chappaquiddick. I don't know whether you saw it, but the *New York Times* magazine had a piece about six months ago by Robert Sherrill, who is a liberal writer. I think he's editor of the *Nation*. And one of the women's magazines had an article about the same time . . . they were devastating. Teddy's counsel, who's a friend of mine, told me that that finished Ted. The two articles raised extremely probing questions about that whole affair. They traced events of that entire episode from the time it happened that night through the grand jury proceedings which apparently were locked up, and the discrepancies in the various stories of the persons who witnessed it. That is legitimate journalism whether it's Ted Kennedy or Richard Nixon.

DOOR: There's an example where the press really didn't pursue that story when it was pursuable.

PIPPERT: It really didn't matter then. It did in a sense, but Ted Kennedy was a senator from Massachusetts. I think the revelation of that story at the time kept him from running in '72, if he had any notions. And now at the right time, as '76 approaches, the reporters of those two articles have gone into it. So the timing is once again right. That also helps explode the myth that the press is exclusively anti-Nixon. They put McGovern's campaign under an Xray in 1972, and now they're doing the same thing, as they ought to, on Kennedy as '76 approaches.

DOOR: Who have the Democrats got for '76?

PIPPERT: Zilch.

DOOR: How do you see Christians becoming more aware politically? Do you have any concrete suggestions?

PIPPERT: Well, for a starter, you can start reading the paper. Just read the front page and catch a couple of newscasts and pretty soon it becomes like a comic strip. You find yourself becoming more and more interested. I suppose that's too simple, but that's the best way I know of to get started.

DOOR: Do you think you can be a Christian and a politician?

PIPPERT: Can you be Christians and editors of the *Wittenburg Door*?

DOOR: Yeah, because we're not totally dependent on a constituency to keep us going.

PIPPERT: Well, I think successful politicians have different sets of skills than the rest of us. I think one of those skills is the ability that Johnson had in such abundance—to compromise and to find a common bond. That really is one of the most effective skills that particularly a legislator can have. Hopefully, a politician can have that ability and yield on certain points without compromising his basic beliefs. I think a lot of politicians do that. They're able to yield occasionally ... particularly the ones who are effective. But the zealots play more of a prophetic role and get out and hammer away with little expectation that what they're talking about is going to be achieved.

DOOR: It sounds like you're saying that you think it's possible.

PIPPERT: In a word, yes.

DOOR: It just seems that if a politician has a decision to make regarding anything—whether it's the content of a speech, which way to vote on a bill— the question becomes, "What is best for me politically?" You don't vote the way you really feel; you vote politically.

PIPPERT: It's obvious that the Nixon White House looked at it in precisely that way. They gauged everything in terms of what the reaction to it would be. They looked at everything in a PR way rather than looking at the essence of it. I don't know if that was even shrewd politics. Every politician who gets elected to office probably has a hard core of support—people who are with him or her, people who have voted for that politician because they are in agreement with his basic positions on things. Now he can go ahead and vote his convictions, which most times will pretty much follow what the hard-core supporters expect him to do. They're the ones who got him into office, and if he's thinking continually about those others out there who had nothing to do with his being elected anyway, he's going to be continually interpreting things in that Nixon kind of way. The safest thing that any politician can do is to go ahead and vote his convictions, which probably will be found satisfactory to the hard-core group of supporters who put him in office in the first place.

DOOR: You're assuming that this politician is in office and he's got supporters. But how do you get supporters unless you become politically minded and not tell too many the fact that you're a committed Christian? You've got to kiss the backsides of people who are influential in order to get the support in the first place.

PIPPERT: Politics is, after all, the art of compromise. And you can have your bedrock position beyond which you will not compromise and you shouldn't. The point I've been trying to make is that it's not even good politics to chip away at your bedrock position to compromise those views, because you alienate your own people. On the other hand, there are a vast amount of things in that gray area that you can give a little on that you may not feel totally satisfactory about, but you don't really compromise your basic beliefs about. Now if you want to be a Bella Absug or a Jerome Waldie, you don't care. You're going to adhere to that line and you're not going to budge an inch. That's fine. You're filling a role and speaking out and maybe attracting an audience, but you're not going to accomplish very much immediately. The master of the art of compromise was Johnson. And I don't think he yielded a lot on his basic principles. By adhering to his bedrock position, and being willing to give a little bit on the others, he could get things done. And

that's what politics is all about. That's healthy. And I think that's a role that a Christian can play very well.

DOOR: But how do you attract initial support?

PIPPERT: What attracts people to a politician? Is it his or her stand on the issues? I think there are other elements that attract people to a person. I don't know what the mix is—whether it's 60–40 or 50–50 or 80–20; I don't know. But Iowa was not attracted to Harold Hughes because of his stand on the issues. Nor was South Dakota attracted to George McGovern because of his stand on the issues. In the case of George McGovern, whom I know better, he really communicated a sense of presence, gentleness, compassion, and concern. And the way he spoke was clear and simple. He just drew people to him. He was elected despite the fact that he had been accused of teaching Communism at Dakota Wesleyan, and despite the fact he advocated recognizing Red China. In '72 he made a speech out there and he said, "Well, people said that if I got elected, I'd go to Peking. But somebody else got there first." What drew South Dakota to McGovern was not his position on the issues. They were drawn to him; they were willing to listen to what he had to say about these things. And it might well be that he changed some minds, that he helped mold his constituency. But it's a mix. You're drawn to a politician partly because of his issues, but partly because of who he is and the kind of rapport that he establishes with you.

DR. W. STANLEY MOONEYHAM

Dr. W. Stanley Mooneyham was president of World Vision International from 1969 to 1982, during which time he administrated an annual budget of fifteen million dollars for programs of child care, social welfare, Christian-leadership training, evangelism, and emergency relief. He now lives near Palm Springs, California, where he heads an international consulting firm for non-profit organizations. His recent books include *Dancing on the Straight and Narrow, Is There Life Before Death?* and *Traveling Hopefully.*

The *Door* Keepers interviewed Stan late in 1974 just after he had returned from an eight-week tour of the hunger belt.

DOOR: Would you give us an overview of the world hunger situation?

MOONEYHAM: I've just come back from eight weeks around the hunger belt. I get into the Third World about four times a year, but I went this time with a different set of eyes because I was doing a book. I wanted to see hunger. I wanted to see from a non-organizational perspective the problems as well as what was being done.

Let me briefly take it continent by continent. Africa, of course, is still in very deep trouble, although they did have some rains this year in the Sahel. They just didn't have enough rain. One rain doesn't break a seven-year drought, because the water table is very low. The whole lifestyle of the people has already been changed. Africa is still in trouble even though I would have to say that the crisis edge for at least some of the drought area is off as of this moment. They will get a small crop. Ethiopia would be the exception to that. Ethiopia is still in very deep trouble because their rains were too little too late.

I would say that the two areas of the world that are really crisis areas now would be India and Bangladesh. Almost half of India has had one of the worst droughts since the turn of the century. I went into one of those drought areas in Gujarat State, and I can confirm that the area is literally devastated. Besides that, India just can't feed its population anyhow. They are always short and have to import. That coupled with even one year's drought creates a disaster which pushes India over the brink.

Bangladesh is in the same situation. Publicly, the government was saying they had about twenty-three days' food supply. Privately, they were saying there was more like ten days' worth.

Southeast Asia and the Philippines are kind of a different world because here you are dealing with chronic malnutrition. In Vietnam and Cambodia it is a result of the displacement of persons caused by the war. In the Philippines it is a result of a combination of economic factors as well as the need for the conservation and proper use of water. But you have endemic malnutrition. It's not the crisis situation you have in Sahel, India, and Bangladesh. But in some respects I think it may be no less deadly, although its effects will take longer to be felt.

Latin America is a bit like Southeast Asia except you don't have the problem exaggerated by war. You have terrible economic inequity within the country. Again you have endemic malnutrition due in large part to the inability of the people to buy food. They just simply don't have money. They don't have jobs and they don't have money.

DOOR: The food is there, but people just can't afford to buy it?

MOONEYHAM: The food is there with some qualification. There isn't an adequate supply in every place. But generally speaking, there is food available. The people just can't buy it.

That's kind of an overview of the world hunger situation. Acute in some places, endemic and chronic in other places. The total problem represents about 40 percent of the world's population. Just slightly under two billion people are affected with acute hunger or endemic malnutrition.

DOOR: A state is considered a crisis when people don't have anything to eat, but when they're malnourished that's not considered quite a crisis?

MOONEYHAM: It isn't considered a crisis except for the children because many of the deaths that result are among the children. They actually don't starve to death, but their bodies are so weakened and their resistance is so low they contract diseases which they cannot resist and from which they can't recover. Also, a malnourished child cannot produce a healthy brain. This, I think, has been the most devastating tragedy I have seen. When I see people who are just skin and bone, and talk to families who fully expect to be dead from starvation within three to six months, that's devastating to me. That just tears me up inside. But then I look into the face of a little six-year-old girl who looks bright, alert, and normal in every way, but because she was malnourished as an infant and that malnourished body produced a small brain, she is incapable of learning. When I realize that child is doomed to a cruel twilight world of being a mental cripple, I must confess that it just tears me up inside too. Not all the food, not all the good wishes, not all the congressional appropriations, not all the prayers, *nothing* is ever going to change that irreversible damage in the life of that child.

DOOR: You mentioned weather, but what are the other major factors involved in this famine?

MOONEYHAM: One is overpopulation. There is no question about that. Another is changing weather patterns, which I think if not permanent are at least cyclical. The third factor is economic. And the fourth factor is political.

DOOR: Should an organization like World Vision spend time and money attempting to change political structures?

MOONEYHAM: I'm not sure that simply changing the political system within a country is going to make more food available. In some countries in Latin America, for instance, a change in the political system just means a few new names at the top. The rest of the structure remains. Your educated elite are the only ones capable of governing the country, and for the most part they really don't care about the people. Now again, there are exceptions to that. But generally, it doesn't matter whether there is a coup, whether this general is in charge or that general is in charge, the people aren't going to be fed. In Bangladesh the problems are so horrendous that I don't think anything short of a complete restructure of the society and the governmental infrastructures can save Bangladesh. When I talk about saving it, I mean in a sense where people can live with a reasonable degree of dignity. I'm not saying that some governments don't need to be changed, but I don't really see this as being an answer.

DOOR: If these structures remain and you pour food, supplies, and knowledge into a country, isn't it just like applying a Band-Aid to the situation?

MOONEYHAM: World Vision of Canada has just flown a planeload of food, powdered milk, and baby food (I think $85,000 worth or something) to Bangladesh in a special airlift. But we would not turn this food over to the government, because we have our own distribution infrastructures which we set up in these countries. Within twenty-four hours of the plane's landing, we had food out to the people who needed it. They were being fed. Now that may be a Band-Aid. I'm not going to argue. I couldn't even argue to myself, because I have mixed feelings about this. All I know is that it's following the example of Jesus. When there are people in front of you who are hungry and you have some resources to meet that need, the emotional reaction is to do what you can. And frankly, that's the way we react in those emergency situations, although about 80 percent of our resources now go into medium-range developmental projects.

DOOR: Could you comment on those projects?

MOONEYHAM: We're a relatively small, private organization. We don't have anything like the resources available to governments today and to multinational organizations like the U.N. If the job were left to us, there is no way we could feed a whole country. So we carve out for ourselves what we believe is a manageable situation so that we can, by investing the dollars that we have available, produce the maximum results to make people self-supporting in one year, two years, or three years. Those are the developmental programs. That says something that I don't like to have to say. "Okay, for twelve months you're willing to sacrifice the lives of some people so that you can save the lives of others later on." And I suppose when you reduce it to that kind of bald statement, that's really the reality with which we have to live. I know that the answer for us is to try to make people self-supporting—as many in a country as is possible for us to do with our limited resources. So we will take one village or one area and we will invest our money there through a local infrastructure. In the case of Bangladesh, we're working in an area about 25 miles wide and 125 miles long. That's manageable for us. We can deal with that.

DOOR: What do you do to help people become self-supporting?

MOONEYHAM: We provide seed for the first crop, and in some cases we provide animal traction where farmers have lost their animals and don't have mechanical traction. This is particularly true in Ethiopia, where we have bought scores of ox pairs, seed, tools, hand tools, plows, and animal traction so they can farm. Many of them do have land.

If they don't have land then all we can do is give them task relief work—where they will work to earn money to buy food that is available in the market. In Bangladesh that takes many forms, but one of them is building roads. For five months in a year the little isolated villages in Bangladesh find themselves completely cut off from the outside world because of floods. Bangladesh is one vast delta. So we pay the people to go in and do hand labor to pile up dirt which may be six feet high and connect their village to what we would consider an all-weather, farm-to-market road. Then

during the wet season they have access outside. We pay them to do this work. In India we invested about a quarter of a million dollars in well deepening and well digging. We paid the villagers to dig or deepen their own wells. This is what we call "labor-intensive" programs, which is what I think the developing world needs today. They do not need "capital-intensive" programs because we've already seen that the so-called trickle-down theory doesn't work. When you invest huge amounts of capital in a country it doesn't trickle down. The guy down there at the bottom doesn't get it. It stays with the elite strata at the top. Instead of bringing well-drilling rigs, for instance, and employing three people, we'll employ scores of people in the village to deepen that well maybe sixty feet simply by hand labor.

DOOR: Do you make any attempts at improving the political structure of our own country? Do you make any effort to change the minds of our government or to influence the way we react toward other countries?

MOONEYHAM: Yes. We don't lobby because we aren't a lobbying organization. But I use my personal influence in talking with governmental leaders. And our board members, like Senator Hatfield, use their influence. As you know, he has a very deep conviction about these matters. We had a press conference recently in Washington where we had a non-luncheon and invited some members of the Senate and some ambassadors to come. And they did. We also had about seventy-five media representatives there, and we served a sixty-seven calorie meal which cost 8 cents—the same meal that I saw people eating and trying to exist on in my recent trip through India. This was one of the ways that we were trying to help people see that when you talk about hunger, it's not a euphemism, it's not a metaphor—it's for real.

DOOR: How about in a place like Bangladesh? Are you able to have any influence there with governmental leaders?

MOONEYHAM: Influence would be a relative word. We are friendly. We speak to them about problems. But it's awfully hard to effect real, lasting changes on a culture that stretches back over centuries. So from that standpoint, I don't see that we're having any real influence in changing the way the government operates.

DOOR: You talked about setting up infrastructures to distribute food and supplies. How do you go about that? Does it bother the politicians of that country?

MOONEYHAM: I don't know whether it bothers them or not. But we have not yet been turned down when we have gone in with a program.

Number one, we never hide the fact that we're a Christian organization. We tell them we are motivated by our Christian faith, but we are there to help people regardless of their faith. We say that our relief work is not at all geared to proselytizing. We are not out to make "rice Christians." We give the assistance that we have available without any strings attached whatsoever, but we want the privilege of setting up our own infrastructure in that country through other private agencies. We do not work through governments. We will coordinate through governments because we don't want to go off on our own without the government being aware of what we're doing. But they

don't seem to resist us. In setting up that infrastructure, it's been our experience that if we can find mission agencies or Christian churches that either are already involved or can be motivated to be involved, then we have a responsible agency through which we can work.

DOOR: What specific things must the U.S. government do to help alleviate the hunger problem?

MOONEYHAM: One of the big problems that I talked with Senator Hatfield about is what we call the futures commodity market. It's a very mercurial way of gambling where people buy paper against food production, against crop production two or three years from now. And they are gambling that either prices are going up or prices are going down. By speculating and gambling on food production in the future, we are creating an artificial rice level in years of surplus because it's not pegged upon what was produced that year. It's pegged on what was the anticipated production two years ago or a year before that. And I really think that there needs to be some regulation of the commodities futures market in order to help stabilize the price of grain and the price of other food items.

DOOR: It seems to me that you can't take food relief or anything else and separate it from the whole. "All I'm interested in is the fact that these people need to eat," sounds good if you write it on a piece of paper or talk about it in a vacuum. But we have to talk about the whole complexity of matters. And it seems to me that in this country, if people eat less, then business will try to figure out ways to convince people to eat more. So it seems you have even more encumbered upon you to do something politically and structurally in this country.

MOONEYHAM: But at this moment, you see, there is no surplus of food. I'm not saying that what you're saying doesn't have any relevance at all. But the problem today is a food shortage. We have people begging at the doors of the Export Commodities Corporation and other places to buy grain. So it seems to me that right now, at least, the immediate problem is to make more food available for the rest of the world. That's the immediate need. Now to say that there's no validity to changing the structures wouldn't be true because there is validity in both the need to change the commercial structures and to change or at least sensitize the governmental structures. We are doing some things and we will be doing other things. But we want to do the right things and not just do something in order to create a lot of activity. For instance, I just read the other day where some religious leaders had issued a statement stating that government must make X amount more tons of food available to the rest of the world. Well, that sounds real good. But I would ask these church leaders, "What are you doing to restructure your own ecclesiastical systems in order to make more resources available to the rest of the world? What are your priorities?" It is one thing to speak to the government prophetically, as it were. It is quite another thing to reassess and reevaluate what you spend on perpetuating your own ecclesiastical system. The answer is in a philosophical change of the mind-set of people—in sensitizing the conscience of people so that they will voluntarily make these changes. That's true for ecclesiastics as well as politicians.

DOOR: What would you tell the little man to do? What can he do to fight the hunger problem?

MOONEYHAM: I'm living with this emotionally as well as organizationally and pragmatically. And in a sense what I would say is what I'm trying to do for myself because I've had to make this very personal, as has our whole staff. Number one, don't make it just an intellectual exercise and say, "Okay, I'll skip this meal or fast this day," or whatever. Instead, begin to reevaluate your lifestyle in the light of Scripture, your needs, and the needs of the rest of the world. Those three elements ought to be brought to play in a reevaluation of one's lifestyle. Then this begins to become an emotional and philosophical experience as well as a pragmatic experience. This process may take a little while. Second, decide on specific things that you can do that would help demonstrate your own personal concern and involvement and would be meaningful to somebody else in the rest of the world. You notice that I've avoided saying, "Skip this meal," or "Set aside this amount of your income" because I think the tangible response, if it's going to be meaningful, will have to arise out of each individual's own understanding of his situation and what God is saying to him. I think out of that can arise hundreds of ways for personal involvement. We have some people in our own organization who decided some time ago as a voluntary action that they would forgo any salary increases, including cost of living increases. They instead would contribute any salary increases which they were to receive to programs designed to help the hungry. Not just relief programs, but development programs. Other people can't do that. So you see, it would be a mistake to say that everybody ought to do this. I'd be very reluctant to say to anybody, "Here are the specific things that you ought to do." But I would say to everybody to go through the same exercise that many of us are presently going through. Evaluate your own lifestyle in light of the Word of God, your own personal needs, and the needs of the rest of the world.

DOOR: Well, isn't that so vague that it lacks any real punch? Where do you draw the line? How much is too much? We could all get by on less, we know that. We could get by on a lot less. It seems to me that you folks who are in a position to know ought to be able to provide some helpful guidelines.

MOONEYHAM: The book I'm writing will include a chapter on things that you can do. But you see that list could be five things, or it could be twenty things, or it could be five hundred things. I personally believe that if a person gets very serious about world needs and his personal response and begins to reevaluate, then the Holy Spirit will lead that person in the specific things to do. So I really can't feel that it's a cop out not to tell them, "Do this." I do know that Americans particularly, being very pragmatic, like to have things spelled out pretty well. But at this point, I am reluctant to start listing things for people to do except for the very elemental things. Don't waste food. That would be the first place to start. Secondly, reduce your food consumption. I find as a result of my own experiences in seeing the hungry that my appetite is diminished. That's a very strange thing that I

cannot understand, but it is definitely true. It does not take as much to satisfy me as it once did. Then thirdly—and these are all so elemental that I almost feel that they go without saying, but maybe they ought to be said—contribute or see that your church contributes to programs designed to meet human needs. Not just to missions generally, but to programs designed to meet human need through some responsible agency. Fourthly, use your influence in writing letters to your congressman and the newspaper to help sensitize the conscience of other people to these same things. If I went beyond that list I would only be suggesting things that might fit some people and wouldn't fit other people. But these are things that can fit all of us.

DOOR: On a personal level, I think it's easy to feel guilty as heck in this country. Somehow in the last year or so I've discovered that I'm a materialist through and through. From looking at pictures in *Time* magazine, reading the paper, etc., I've found that I am what I haven't wanted to be. I haven't tried to be greedy. And suddenly, I'm starving all of these people all around the world. Am I a victim of the culture? Am I greedy? Where does guilt stop and compassion begin? What do we do in this country to relieve the guilt that all of us feel?

MOONEYHAM: Well, I hope this won't make you feel any better—and it won't. But let me just say that I feel exactly the same way you feel. I feel guilty. It bothers me so deeply that I can tell you right now that my emotions are raw. I feel guilty, and yet I can't change the place I was born. I can't help personally the lifestyle which was handed to me. And that lifestyle has been developed over forty-eight years because that's how old I am. And I cannot suddenly tomorrow say, "Okay, that lifestyle gets cut by 50 percent or 40 percent or whatever." I don't think any of the rest of us can do that. What I think we can do is agree that over a period of time in deliberate actions we can reduce that lifestyle so that we do free up more of the earth's resources. In the U.S.A. we represent about 6 percent of the world's people and we consume about 40 percent of the world's resources. By reducing our lifestyle, by driving the car one year longer, by not encouraging the commercial enterprises in our country to be built on planned obsolescence so that we just gorge our furnaces with the world's resources. I think by doing that, we can have an effect on the world and on the amount of resources available.

DOOR: But can't we change our lifestyle by 50 percent? We know people who've done it.

MOONEYHAM: Radically.

DOOR: Yeah, radically. We've seen it. Maybe we don't want it, but it is possible. We all could do it if we really felt committed to it.

MOONEYHAM: I think about myself; I have kids in college. I've got myself committed to that expense right now. Of course, I could do it, any of us could do it, but it would mean such drastic alterations that I'm not sure at this point that I could do it without damage or effect to my family or to the situation where I find myself. I think over a period of time we could certainly do it. But I'm sure you're right. If I lost my job and couldn't find another one, I'd undoubtedly do it.

DOOR: There are a lot of other things involved here. If you don't buy the cars on a regular basis, then that's going to kill the auto industry which is going to kill a few other industries which is going to put a lot of guys out of work which is going to limit the amount of money America has to give to the hungry. You've got to look at the whole picture. I'm not saying that's the answer, but I'm saying if everybody cut back, there'd be a tremendous upheaval. Now it's true that not as much stuff would be used, but it's also true that we would not have the financial resources to help very many other people because we would be taking care of our own welfare rolls.

MOONEYHAM: I don't have any answer to that. I wish I did. If I had an answer I wouldn't have to live with my own guilt. I think maybe the answer is to learn to live with the tension. With guilt and with thankfulness. I don't think we should entirely stop feeling guilty because I think guilt is a motivator. But on the other hand, it would be bad for us psychologically to feel nothing but guilt. It would be equally bad to run along in glib thankfulness and keep wasting what we have. So I think the answer is to learn to live with that healthy, creative tension between guilt and thankfulness.

DOOR: What percentage of the money that is given to an organization like World Vision really goes to relief?

MOONEYHAM: Of our income, 20.6 percent goes into overhead, administration, and fund-raising. Some organizations don't break their income down like that. They say so much for overhead and administration, but they don't mention fund-raising. But we put all three together.

DOOR: What was your percentage for fund-raising?

MOONEYHAM: Our percentage for fund raising, everything included, was 7 percent.

DOOR: What is the overall gross budget?

MOONEYHAM: We have a U.S.A. operation and an international operation—World Vision Canada, World Vision Australia, World Vision New Zealand. The budget for the U.S.A. operation is over eleven million. International is close to fourteen or fifteen million, counting the other countries.

DOOR: What's your philosophy in using an outside advertising agency to handle promotion?

MOONEYHAM: We would have to use somebody. In other words, you either have to use your own staff or you have to buy brains to do it. We feel it is cheaper for us to use an outside source than it would be to create an in-house public relations department.

DOOR: How much do they influence what you write? Does the agency say here's an angle that we could use?

MOONEYHAM: No way. We consider the Reid agency a kind of arm of World Vision. They know a great deal about our philosophy and about our programs. We interact with each other, but we would never pitch an angle simply because it seems a good angle to pitch.

DOOR: We were wondering about the philosophy of appeal letters. It seems that if you're on any mailing lists at all, you get tons of letters asking for the same thing. And it seems like the letters are very, very similar. They try to grab your nerve endings. What's the philosophy behind your letters? What are you trying to do? How are you trying to grab a person?

MOONEYHAM: The object of a letter is to raise money. To get money for a project. So first of all, get the person's attention.

DOOR: Do you try to motivate a person with shock treatment? Guilt? Or do you just present the need?

MOONEYHAM: We don't use shock treatment. Now and then I'll get a letter from somebody complaining about the pictures in our magazine because they don't believe that we are presenting the realities. They think we are picking up the exceptions, the exaggerations. We aren't. In fact, if we were to print the worst pictures, they would just simply be so revolting that people wouldn't look at them. So we try not to use shock treatment. We never manipulate. That's a matter of conscience with me—to never use something because it's manipulative. On the other hand, we try to write it the way it really is and tell it the way it really is. I think to do any less than that, in other words to do it more academically or without the adjectives, would be less than honest. For instance, this weekend I labored over an article which will be the lead article in our magazine. It's called "Famine in One Man's Family." I went into the village of Singhali in India, and after talking to the village chief and talking to a lot of people, I went in and talked to one Christian family. I tried to probe in-depth how they are starving to death. This is a family who expects to be dead six months from now. The monsoons failed and they don't have a crop. He doesn't have a job and they have been just subsisting. So I asked hard questions, questions that to me seemed a little brutal, like, "Do the children cry?" I wanted to know so that I would be able to interpret this for people who have never experienced hunger. Well, this mother began to weep because I was opening a very deep wound with her. The only justification I have for that is that I wept with her. She told me that the children sleep anyhow, but she said, "My husband and I stay awake a great deal because we worry so much about the children." And she said, "Yes, we cry, and the children cry a great deal when they're hungry." Okay, that's very emotional, but for me not to tell that would be less than honest in telling the story of this woman and this family. I can only say that in the appeal letters or in the article, I try to write as an act of conscience on my part. My philosophy is to use nothing that is simply manipulative and yet to tell the story as honestly and truly as I know how. In the appeal letters I do know what I'm writing because it's coming out of my own experiences.

DOOR: What does starvation do to a person's theology? A person reads PSALM 23, "The Lord is my shepherd, I shall not want," and their children are starving. They don't have a job. What does this do to their belief in Christ and God and Psalms?

MOONEYHAM: You're talking about the people now who are suffering?

DOOR: Yes.

MOONEYHAM: I really wrestle with this theologically. I asked this family, "How can you believe that God loves you and yet lets you starve to death?" That's one of the questions that I said was almost brutal. She said (and let me read this interview), "It's difficult to keep the belief, and also the children cry all the time because they don't have enough to eat and they're hungry." And then the father said, "For the next crop we have to wait until October. So there's one more year. So if God keeps us alive, we will remain alive. Otherwise we will go back to God, and that is what we expect." And

I said, "Do you feel jealous about your neighbors who have food when you don't have enough to eat?" And the mother answered, "We don't envy any of the others although they have food. For whatever God wants today he'll give us. And we still depend upon him. We're not envious of anyone who has bread or enough to spare."

The kind of serene confidence that these people have is just incredible. Let me put in a quick postscript. Fortunately, the family I talked to is not going to starve to death. I left some money, and this January an appeal will be for that village, not only for the Christians in it, but for the Moslems as well.

I saw NBC's White Paper on hunger about a week or two ago on Sunday night, "Who Shall Feed This World." I was intensely interested, but I disagreed with one thing they said—that there is going to be a revolution in the world by the hungry. In other words, in order to protect our own life and our own livelihood, we'd better do something about the rest of the world. The people with whom I talked and interviewed agreed that it is not the hungry and the starving who are going to revolt. They have a kind of serenity and a kind of trust that is incomprehensible to me, whatever the religious faith, whether it's Buddhism, Islam, or Christianity. There are two reasons why they will not spark the revolution. One is this serene faith. For the Moslems, it's "If Allah wills it I will die and if Allah wills it I will live, whatever Allah wills." The Christian somehow just believes that God is going to provide to the last breath.

Religious faith is the first reason. The second reason is that they are so weak. They have lost the ability to resist or protect, much less mount a revolution. All they can do is die. They can't revolt. If the revolution comes in some of these countries, and it well may, it's going to come from those who are not starving, but who are economically deprived—people who find themselves somewhere above the bottom rung of the ladder.

I read and I talk to these families and see them starving to death. But I admit I do not know how to reconcile starvation theologically. I find my simplistic theology challenged by the world's realities.

DOOR: Some people say that the most Christian thing we can do is not to send food, which is just a drop in the bucket. We need to send birth control pills. Would you comment on that?

MOONEYHAM: There's no question that we've got to have some control on the world's population, because we cannot continue to people the earth and expect to feed it. Even though we might have the technology to feed the world, there is not the governmental will to say pragmatically, "We have to do something about the world's population." On the other hand, there are some countries in the Third World who feel that the West should not try to make its priorities their priorities. A leader told me, "In our country we are underpopulated. We feel threatened by our neighbors around us, and so we need to increase our population." Okay, that may be the shortsighted view, but, nonetheless, that's where they are and we have to take them where they are—not where we wish they were or where we think they should be. To simply export means of birth control to a country like that would be of no value at all because the government does not accept this as one of its priorities. On the other hand, we have India, which has placed high priority on planned parenthood and birth control. But it's had almost no effect throughout the countryside for several reasons. Lack of communication in the structure. Lack of medical facilities available at the village level for dispensing contraceptives and birth control methods. And a culture that makes it necessary for a family to have enough children to till the soil that has been handed them by their ancestors. This is the only way a father views the situation. He has a few acres and he knows that it takes maybe five children or six children to make that land productive. If he can irrigate, he has to do this by hand. So he knows from generations of experience that it's going to take six children (or five or seven or whatever number) to make that land productive. When you tell him to cut his family to two, he says, "What are you trying to do to me? I can't possibly exist with two children. I have to have five." And in order to have five reasonably healthy children live, he will probably have to have eight or ten. Because half of them may die. But some may not die and he may wind up with eight when all he wanted was five. You have enormous complexities, and it is the height of simplistic answer to say, "Give them birth control pills, intrauterine devices, or involuntary sterilization." And yet, having said all that, having presented the complexities, I have to say that we have to deal with the world population as a major factor in dealing with hunger. But it's going to have to be done sensitively and not with the heavy hand that we in the West so frequently want to use.

DONN MOOMAW

In 1952, Donn Moomaw was everybody's all-American. The big, fast, tough linebacker was voted "Lineman of the Year" by both Associated Press and United Press. He was named the Most Valuable Player in the North-South game. He was drafted Number 1 by the Los Angeles Rams.

That was nearly forty years ago. And for years afterwards he was still recognized as a jock.

The transition from Christian athlete to a Christian who used to play football was a real pilgrimage for Donn. He describes it in this interview with the *Door*. The Keepers interviewed him in 1975 at Bel Air Presbyterian Church (just a long punt from UCLA), where he is still senior pastor.

DOOR: As a college athlete, did you feel exploited by Christians?

MOOMAW: Yes. But I didn't feel exploited until I looked back in retrospect. While I was going through it, I didn't feel exploited or abused. But I really was. I was used to build an organization. I don't want to overly criticize those who "used" me because I know they were trying to make inroads and I was the big man on campus. And I really think that God used my conversion to help an organization get off the ground and go.

I don't think the organizational

leaders felt, "Let's use Moomaw." But I think the nature of their position at the time and my vulnerability to be liked by Christians led me to fall right into exploitation. The wounds didn't come until years later as I began to look in retrospect at how I was not really appreciated for being me.

DOOR: What were some of the results of the wounds surfacing? Did you go to extremes? Did you deny your athletic background?

MOOMAW: Both. In the very beginning I came into a community of very zealous Christians, both in Campus Crusade and in Hollywood Presbyterian Church. One who is driven to be an all-American on the football field is often driven to be the all-American Christian of the group that he's brought into. So I tried to be A-1 Christian. If people were praying an hour a day, I'd pray longer. If they memorized Scriptures, I would memorize more. Because I felt that my worth always was on the basis of my production, my being better than other people. This wasn't necessarily bad when it came to football because I wanted to be the best there was. That was a goal. But in the Christian faith when my worth was directly tied up with my achievement, that began to get me in trouble.

I was drafted by the Los Angeles Rams—their first draft choice—in 1953. What better way to dramatize the fact that you're a good Christian than by turning down the draft. So the day I was to tell the *Los Angeles Times* that I was turning down their draft and going into the ministry, Bill Bright suggested that I have the press conference in his home. I didn't know what was coming off. I didn't foresee at that time that I was being used. I was getting a lot of pious advice. But I wasn't getting a whole lot of earthly, loving support.

I decided to go to seminary. But before I went to seminary, I went to Canada. I probably felt the best I've ever felt about myself up there. There I was only a professional football player. I had no expectations from either myself or other people other than being a good football player. I didn't have to "live a lie." I didn't know anyone. Very few people knew me. I went to church. I didn't have to speak at church—I went to church. And surprising as it sounds, some people at the People's Church up there really loved me. There were a bunch of fundies who said, "Hey, come on in." And I was blessed.

DOOR: Was that in Toronto?

MOOMAW: Yes, in Toronto. I played seven games of a fourteen-game schedule. I was all-pro. But I was a recluse. I lived in a crummy hotel. But I really felt human.

DOOR: Then you went to seminary?

MOOMAW: Then I went to seminary. Okay, you go to seminary. You're an all-American big shot and you're unconsciously trying to climb the ladder, trying to gain something that you already have by grace—unconditional love. I didn't have it for myself. I had it for everyone else. I was trying to love everyone else, but I couldn't love myself unconditionally.

I never had the freedom to fail. Coaches never permitted failure. And I would never permit myself to fail. You missed a block, that was bad. If you made a block, that was good. Well, you interpret that, "If you miss a block, *you're* bad. If you make a tackle, *you're* good." You don't have any unconditional love or unconditional feelings of worth. Worth is all tied up with success or failure. I don't want to blame athletics necessarily, but that's the way it worked out for me.

So what do I do? I go to seminary to prepare for the ministry. But a lot of people do that. I want to be tougher. I want to go into the foreign field. So all the way through seminary, I either wanted to go to China which was closed or to Saudi Arabia which was rough. My hero through seminary was Bill Borden of Yale who died of spinal meningitis in Cairo, Egypt, eighteen months after he graduated from seminary. He was a great football player. He was my idol. He had climbed to the top of the spiritual ladder in my eyes.

I was always trying to win the approval of someone. I guess what I'm saying to you is that I was very ripe for exploitation because of my own needs. I guess I never felt real good about myself unless I was achieving. It's no one's fault so much as the circumstances of the time which made me open and vulnerable to those kinds of people who would take advantage of me.

DOOR: You once remarked that when you began your ministry, you didn't use an athletic illustration for several years as a reaction to what you'd been through.

MOOMAW: That was primarily when I came to Bel Air. In my first eight years I served in the Berkeley church where I was the assistant pastor. I could swing any way I wanted. I could be the athlete or I could be the minister or the Bible teacher. It wasn't so acute. But when I came back here, a lot of people had preconceived ideas of who I was and what I was. They identified me solely with the past. So I completely stayed away from anything football. As a matter of fact, I barely acknowledged the USC/UCLA game. I assume it's like some women in women's liberation who have a difficult time even admitting they're women until the pendulum swings back and they can say, "Aha, I can celebrate I'm a woman." Like, "Aha, I was Donn Moomaw, the all-American. That's great. You're right. That's who I was. That's what I used to be. I'm a fair athlete now. Okay, but I'm also something else."

But in order for that to swing, I had to get completely away from the image of being an athlete. For a lot of reasons. It's always been in my psyche that an athlete is dumb. Especially a linebacker—he has to be dumb to play the position. Now that's not true. It's not proven out. But we still have that in the background. So I wanted people to know when I came here that if I was

an all-American it was because I was a super biblical theologian. I had a lot of head trips. I was still trying to be above everyone else. And it wasn't until the death of Martin Luther King that I turned the corner. When Martin Luther King died, I was in a meeting with Wilson Riles, the black state superintendent of schools. We cried together. It was the first time I ever cried with a black man.

On the Saturday after King's death, three people called me and said, "Don't mention King's death from the pulpit on Sunday; you'll split the church."

I didn't want to split the church. Some radicals get really cocky and say, "Well, I lost twenty members this year. Praise God, I'm really preaching the gospel." I say baloney. They're probably rejecting you more than your ideas. I didn't want to do that, but I wanted to be a man of integrity too. Before I had always played it safe . . . wanting to be liked and not criticized. But more and more I was wanting to be a man of integrity and wanting to risk some things. If I was rejected, I would have to deal with that.

So that Sunday morning, I talked about forgiveness. I said I needed God's forgiveness mainly for my blindness to what was going on in the world around me that I hadn't wanted to look at. I didn't eulogize King, but I said some things about how God had used him. After I preached I went back to my little closet behind the pulpit and cried harder than I've ever cried in my life. It was kind of a laughter cry, the emancipation cry of becoming. And since that time it's just been magnificent. Since that time I feel I've been growing, becoming more vulnerable, personal, and human. There is no ladder of authority at the church anymore even though by my size, by my position, by my voice, by everything, I still come over heavy. We've got a great kind of equality. How that relates to athletics, I don't have the foggiest dream. But I'm sure a psychiatrist could really weave some things through there.

DOOR: I think it's interesting to see how an athlete struggles with who he is and works through it. A former jock has a lot of stuff to carry with him.

MOOMAW: I think most athletes to be good athletes have to have a lot of ego needs or ego strength, because it's rather foolish to do all they have to do to play a game when they could play a game without all the rigmarole. If you wanted to play football, the four of us could get up a game and go down to the high school right now. And we could even get some pads, if you wanted to be sophisticated, and we could wallow around out there and have some fun. But what is it about professional or collegiate ball? In the pros, you're being paid for doing it. In collegiate athletics, you get your strokes from the audience. Why else do you go out for the first two weeks of September two times a day and then every afternoon of the fall for three hours and go through a lot of physical drill and a lot of combat to play for two hours on Saturday? There is something within us that is not altogether bad—don't get me wrong—it's a discipline for a determined objective. But if we didn't have the ego needs, I'm sure we would settle for intramural sports every time. But the question is how can we as Christians harness some of that and yet let a Christian guy feel that he is very much first-string in the kingdom whether he gets up and gives

his testimony at a father-and-son banquet or not.

DOOR: There's a lot said today about the violence of sports—the dehumanization of pro sports where men are made into things. How do you feel about this competition and dehumanization?

MOOMAW: Well, I'm not very radical at this point because I see the athlete having a choice. I see the athlete as very well paid. Not just your professional, but your collegian. He's paid in ways other than financial.

I can agree with the dehumanization, but here again it's choice. If I find my worth based on success, then I'm going to dehumanize myself. Because when I finish playing, I have no worth if my worth came through my playing. A guy can get hurt at the peak in his career, especially in professional football, and within hours he's a forgotten man. And the tragedy is what happens to himself, not what happens to the crowd. The crowd remains fickle. You can't change the crowd. But if we as Christians get to that guy and explain to him who he really is before God, then I don't think he'll be used. He won't permit himself to be used. He may have to take the radical step of getting out of athletics. Hopefully not. But if he feels he's been used as a gladiator for someone else's financial benefit, and he feels he cannot maintain his own integrity in the midst of it, then I say he has to go. But that isn't the only alternative. I would also have to be defensive a little and say that as I look around town, most of the guys that played with me are in very significant leadership positions.

DOOR: But might that not be due primarily to their popularity?

MOOMAW: I think it has a lot to do with it. Guys make capital of it and cash in on it. But I don't think they would stay there long if they didn't have what it takes to produce. I think lots of times their names are used. But they permit themselves to be used that way.

DOOR: We were talking to a guy who did a chapel for the Bears at the Jets' game. I don't think he has a lot of experience with pro teams. But he was amazed at how immature the ball players were. They seemed like huge adolescents to him. He tried to present an honest, realistic picture of the gospel—that Christianity doesn't always make you more "successful" in athletics—and the players came up to him afterward and said, "Hey, we haven't heard that before."

You're tied into FCA, Donn; is there anything you or FCA can do to help these athletes prepare for the future when they do get broken down and can't be a star anymore?

MOOMAW: Yeah, I think there is. I don't think we prepare them well enough. I don't think we get down to the specific dynamics of what happens when you're no longer Saturday's hero. Guys do have a cultural shock when they're no longer Saturday's star. And they need to be taken care of because they were taken care of by the team. They were never responsible for their uniforms. They weren't responsible for their meals. They weren't even responsible for the money. And they were trained in a very limited sphere of life: physical combat. I also don't think we prepare a Christian college star for life in the pro ranks. It means a shift in his whole emotional and domestic lifestyle. You get a guy who was such a good straight Christian college guy,

and he gets into that rough professional world. He's away from home so much with guys who don't march to his spiritual drummer, guys that are unfaithful, guys who have a different approach to life than he does. And it is rugged. Especially when you get into the basketball and baseball world. Basketball and baseball are harder than football because the players are gone much more and they go to the same cities time and time again. They begin to build up "their friends," and a lot of guys who complain about road trips really like road trips because when the going gets tense at home or tense in business, they can let their friends and the management take care of them. They can close themselves off from the wife and children at home and their involvements in the secular world and go off and be the star.

DOOR: Do you feel that certain things you learned in athletics have been helpful to you in the ministry?

MOOMAW: Yes. It sounds like a cliche, but very definitely I have. I learned to continue to go on when I felt that I didn't want to go. You're in the midst of combat, and you go whether every bone in your body and every muscle says slow down or not. You're working with a team and you go beyond the point of endurance.

I learned discipline. When I have an assignment to preach every Sunday morning, I take all day Thursday for study. I don't go out on Saturday. I'm not sure whether I would be as disciplined today if I hadn't played football.

I was taught coordination with a team. I'm on a team now. We have twenty-seven people on our staff here. I learned a lot about what it means to work within the team structure through athletics. I also learned a lot about doing a job the very best I can do it. I was a single-wing center for Red Sanders. He wanted the ball in a particular spot every play. So when he wanted it on the ear, he wanted it on the ear and not the chest. I centered 150 times one night after practice because he wanted it on the ear and not the chest. Well, what is this saying to me, to my psyche? "Get it down so you can do it right. Work to do it right." I don't know if there's anything else in society that demands that kind of exactness and pressure.

I'm grateful also for the physical activity, just plain old physical activity. I learned what it was to feel my body, and so I want to continue to. I believe there is something very sacred about the body being kept well.

DOOR: The thing that gets me is the whole concept of winning and success. How do you judge success? Our culture worships winners—guys who make it to the top. Does Christianity cut across that?

MOOMAW: Only if we can get across some principles of unconditional love. The crowd is going to do what it wants to do. You're not going to change the crowd. It's been true from time immemorial. The hero is going to be eulogized by the people. The place where we need to work is on the athlete himself—not getting sucked into that kind of philosophy which says, "I'm a winner if I win—I'm a loser if I lose." I really can't change the bib-overall guy who goes to the game on Sunday afternoon and screams his head off and gets mad at the referees if a call goes against him. Right now I'm focusing in on what the athlete does within himself to feel that God created him and loves him. It has nothing to do with win or lose.

DOOR: Are you personally going through the same thing with movie stars that non-athletes go through with you? Do you think, "Gee, I had Robert Goulet sing, or I met this guy today...."

MOOMAW: I hope not. No, with movie stars I treat them the same way I treat athletes. No different. I really don't want people to feel when they come here that they're going to be used. When you get them up front and advertise that they're going to be there—they can only talk success. They're there to give an endorsement on God. I want people to be real, and I'm just afraid that when you put a mike in front of them, you're eliminating the possibility for them to be real. The Christian church must begin to let people be real, to let them give a witness no matter where they are and not feel that we always have to defend the dignity of God by using the right words.

I was crying some nights when I went out and spoke about joy, peace, and happiness. I felt I had to phony up a crummy life. And I wasn't nearly so crummy as I told people, but it made a nice black-and-white distinction. But that's not because of athletics. That was my own hang up.

I remember one time, however, when I really felt used. A man who's a very responsible Baptist minister called me in the midst of my senior year after I'd gone out four nights a week for the past three weeks. He called and said, "Would you come to our father-and-son banquet?" I said, "I'm sorry, sir, I would love to, but I just can't. I've been gone all this time and I'm really going to stick to my guns and not schedule any more meetings until...."

And he said, "What are you, too big for us?"

I was a thin-skinned guy. You talk about scars. I lived with that a long time.

DOOR: Does it bother you now to be introduced as Donn Moomaw, former all-American, when it's been over twenty years?

MOOMAW: It really doesn't bother me because it's really true. I was a former athlete. It would bother me if I didn't have a present.

DOOR: Would it bother you now if you were introduced before a large audience who didn't know you only as "Donn Moomaw, pastor of Bel Air Presbyterian Church."

MOOMAW: All right, that's the other side of it. To some groups I would like you to say I am a former athlete.

DOOR: If there is a structure that takes a person and manipulates him, uses him, destroys him, whether he's a Christian or not, do I have a responsibility to say something? In terms of athletics, if pro sports are so structured to win that a man loses his humanness, shouldn't I speak out?

MOOMAW: That's your bag. I'm not sure if a lot of guys who are playing professional athletics would agree with your presuppositions that they are exploited.

DOOR: Wasn't the football strike saying some of those things? Weren't the players saying that they were treated by management like cattle, just traded around without much to say?

MOOMAW: I think a lot of that was because of a desire to get what they wanted in their contracts. Maybe I'm overly naive at this point. Maybe I'm just a country bumpkin who doesn't think very deeply in these areas, be-

cause I really enjoyed it. I really loved playing ball.

DOOR: But you were a star. Don't you think there's a difference between a star and a third stringer?

MOOMAW: If I were playing third string and my whole worth was dependent upon success, I would feel a failure all the way through college. But I didn't; I felt that I was king.

DOOR: How about the church? What can we say to church leaders about how to take care of an athlete?

MOOMAW: I've never had an athlete in the pulpit. I have scars all over from people inviting me saying, "We want you to come because we know you can get a crowd." And they'll be frank about it. They don't say, "We want you to come because you really have something to say." I'll get people who call me and say, "Hey, do you know an athlete who can come and speak at our banquet?"

I say to them very frankly, "Do you want an athlete who may not be able to say very much, but who may be a star athlete? Or do you want one who can say something, but who may not be a star?" Very often they can't answer that.

DOOR: So you answered the question in your church by not putting an athlete in the pulpit.

MOOMAW: I don't invite an athlete to preach, but we have athletes stand up and witness when we have free-wheeling witness times. Sure, bless God. And we had Robert Goulet sing in our service. He worships here. We never advertised it. No one knew that Goulet was going to sing until they came that night.

DOOR: Because it gives you a better entree with the group?

MOOMAW: Yeah, and I think we need to be honest about that. There was a time when I reacted very much against that because I wanted to be known for something else, but I don't do that anymore. I want to say athletics has opened an awful lot of doors for me. In the secular world in particular.

MARTIN E. MARTY

Martin E. Marty, Ph.D., is a balding free spirit. A Nebraska small-town boy, Marty grew up with the idea of either being a pastor or an artist. He left Nebraska and headed for Milwaukee to attend a Lutheran preparatory school "where we had a rather seedy environment, but we did manage somehow or other to get a good classical education."

Martin worked his way through school as an artist, but he had an inner feeling that he never would be really good at it. ("You sense your own level of mediocrity.") And with this feeling, he journeyed more and more into art history. "I got interested in the German art of the fifteenth and sixteenth centuries ... and in the process got more and more locked into history and combined the ministerial interest with the historical interest."

After becoming ordained in the Missouri Synod Lutheran Church, Marty did not plan to attend graduate school. But he ended up there as punishment for being too satirical. "We invented a fake theologian as a satire on the system, and I carried it a little far. The faculty didn't like it. I had been destined to be a minister in England to the Baltic DP's, but when they heard of Franz Bibfeldt (Marty's theologian), the faculty decided I was too irresponsible and immature to represent Lutheranism in England. For punishment, they made me an assistant pastor. And the church where I was an assistant pastor said you had to work on your doctorate while there. A very fine head pastor pushed nine of us in a row into a Ph.D. through that program."

Marty served ten years in the pastorate before joining the faculty of the Chicago Divinity School in 1963, where he is now the Fairfax M. Cone Distinguished Service Professor of the History of Christianity. He is also senior editor of *Christian Century*, coeditor of *Church History*, and editor of his biweekly newsletter *Context.*

The Keepers interviewed Dr. Marty in 1976 between plays of the Ohio State-Michigan game in his hotel room in Scottsdale, Arizona, where he and his wife, Elsa, were participating in the Laymen's Leadership Institute.

DOOR: How do you feel about the Bicentennial?

MARTY: The commercialization I simply assumed and, therefore, wasn't surprised, horrified, or shocked by it. We don't seem to do anything without the Franklin mint going into action with sterling silver duplicates of Paul Revere's bridle bit and so on. I promised myself before the year started that I wouldn't put a lot of energy into that side of it because it's going to happen whether you put energy into it or not. The second thing that I noticed and I suppose am more cheered by is that I don't think the Bicentennial has resulted in the uncritical civil religiosity that everyone was worried about. There are more editorials saying, "Let's not let the year develop into civil religion," than there are evidences there is civil religiosity. It's very obvious to me that the nation is morose and directionless and, at worst, not rising to anything in the name of Bicentennial. At best, I find some self-criticism and some attempt to get direction going. But you can't say that the American Legion, VFW, John Birch, DAR, or anyone else like that is having an ominously good year. I would hate to have had the Bicentennial in 1956, let's say, when it would have been part of the crusade. And I'm not sure I would have liked it around 1966 or whenever we were so hopelessly polarized. So it's not as dangerous a year as some earlier years to have it.

DOOR: Do you consider America a Christian nation?

MARTY: No. It isn't by legal definition very clearly. The founding fathers not only didn't casually overlook that theme, but debated how to define a nation and decided it shouldn't be defined in metaphysical terms. There is no kind of metaphysical theology formally applied to the Constitution—which is the only base we have. "Wholesome neutrality," the Supreme Court called it. So on legal terms, it isn't.

On ideological terms, I see half-and-half historic input. On one side, you have the historians who've traced the Puritan, Quaker, and Anglican impulse. For a century and a half, they saw to it that we were genetically programmed to be reflexively biblical about many things. That is, the United States is "a nation under God." America has some sort of "mission" or "destiny." Our ideas got planted by people who believed those things. And that always provides a later base for people who want to rework the symbols or myths of American life. To that extent we have a Christian reminiscence. The way a society first packages itself has a lot to do with what its nominal teaching or thought will be for a long time to come. You can change the content of the symbols. You can neglect them. You can refurbish them. You can turn them inside out. You can turn them against themselves. Yet they remain. Thus mission, which can be a good concept for some purposes, is also what gets us into Vietnam. But in both cases it is mission.

The other half of the historians are legally probably more correct with their idea that we are a nation based on enlightenment philosophy, which isn't Christian. It wasn't casually not Christian; it was formally not Christian. These were people who were vestrymen in the Episcopal churches, but who took great pains not to let anything particularly Christian get into the genetic programming. Their attitude was: it makes no difference to me if you have one God or twenty gods, or whether you're Episcopalian, as long as you don't violate the law.

But I don't know what a Christian nation would look like. I guess I don't expect a nation to be Christian. My own distinction between how the law of God operates in creation is such that the adjective "Christian" would apply for me more to the gospel. And I don't think any state lives by the gospel. So no, we're not a Christian nation.

DOOR: The case often made is "Look how God has blessed us. Obviously, God must be on our side." Do you have a reaction to that kind of thinking?

MARTY: Yes, I have a biblical reflection on it, picked up by our mentor Martin Luther who says God lets his rain fall on the evil and the good, on the just and the unjust. I don't think you can go through history and say that God grasped by Christian faith has endowed things a certain way because the people who live there are Christians. These hills would have had minerals and oil whether or not they were settled by Christians. Suppose we had been settled by Japan instead of Europe. They would have found the same resources and probably would have been as skilled at developing them.

I do think as Christians we can say that in some overall way God acts in history. I think that you can say that your life is hidden with Christ in God. All things are yours, but you are Christ's and Christ is God's. But I think it's pretty tricky when you then apply it to each detail. We won that battle; therefore, God was on our side. Maybe we won our best battles at our religiously worst moments and there may

have been times when we have been very faithful when we suffer most. So I would be very uneasy in that kind of a conclusion. That doesn't mean you can't have a Eucharist or a Thanksgiving service in which you acknowledge him as the giver of all good things, including all things that happen here. But I wouldn't put it on a system of brownie points or merit badges, or a score card.

DOOR: Why do you think that many Christians want to create a concept of a Christian nation? Why do they make Washington and Jefferson and the other founding fathers look like great pillars of the church?

MARTY: I think because they lack a theology of common grace or civil righteousness. That is, in the mainline Christian tradition, Augustine, Calvin, and Luther believed that God is active in the world even apart from the way in which he is active in the plot of human salvation. For Augustine there is something he calls nature, which is potentially usable either for good or for evil. The good use of nature doesn't make you a part of the city of God or the people of God. It doesn't "save your soul." But it affects the purposes of God for the city. So Augustine could look at Rome and see the hand of God active in people who didn't believe in God. That's very deep in the Christian tradition. And I think nineteenth century American piety or Protestantism forgot that. Catholicism has kept it through its natural law theory. Some reflective conservative Protestantism kept it. And some liberal Protestants kept it. But the Protestantism that focuses mainly on personal piety, what Stendahl called Western egotistic, anthropomorphic soteriologism—"Are you saved? I'm saved. The preceding sentence is incomplete. Is Jesus Christ your personal Savior?" Letting that individual question exhaust everything that the message of God is about means that you don't quite know what anybody else is in the world for except as an agent in the conversion process. I always like to quote a parody of a sermon that W. H. Auden said: "We are all in the world to save all the other people. What all the other people are in the world for, I haven't the faintest idea." In other words, if you put it all in that one theme, then you don't really know how to account for anything good happening beyond it. Therefore, since good things are happening, or since you want to be sure that you can call on God to make good things happen, you have to restrict it to that one mold. Therefore, it's important to elect a politician who is godly in your way. He can be an inadequate politician, but if he's pious, he gets extra points. That's not in the Christian tradition. Certainly Christians have enjoyed pious and godly rulers. But there is a theology that makes plenty of room for their absence.

I remember even when U Thant was elected General Secretary of the United Nations, the *Christian Century* ran an editorial saying it's too bad a Buddhist is running the U.N. because if he were a Christian we would have more confidence and he would be more responsive to the call of God. Now I don't think there's a reason for the Christian to say better or worse on those grounds. I do think that the Christian has special reasons for being responsive to the law of God in the affairs of humans. I see the law of God, the power of God, not unto salvation, to use a biblical term, but for the care of the neighbor. The church is the place where one should be especially responsive to the call of the care of the neighbor. But I don't think that you can empirically as a social scientist measure that those civilizations in which the church is present has assured that much better social justice.

DOOR: What do you see good about America?

MARTY: The good I would say is on two levels. One level is what Walter Lippman called the public philosophy, which is a blend of the two things I talked about earlier: a potential responsiveness to the prophetic note in biblical religion and the potential responsiveness to the working hypothesis for the good society that is asserted in the Declaration of Independence. I stress the word *potential*. If that's all it were, that wouldn't be the good thing about America. But I would say there have been moments. I am not embarrassed to go in front of the Court of the Nations with the American record in contrast to other nations, but not in contrast to an ideal. I'm not embarrassed to show the record of the humanitarian impulse, for instance. I think the record of the nineteenth century errand of mercy grew up on evangelical soil. Or the Catholic concern for the immigrant peoples of the cities. You can take that record and say there's a remarkable stirring here of the impulse born of the conversion experience; born of a sense of belonging to the church; born of a vision of people as victims of society. That would be one illustration of how these two things have worked out. And the other one would be that at moments in our history we have inconvenienced ourselves in the light of what's imparted there. An illustration in the early sixties is Martin Luther King at his peak. If you'll notice, his appeal was not pragmatic—do it because it's the best thing for society or do it because in the long run you'll save civil peace. It was first "let justice roll down like streams" to a society in which 100 million people were still reading that language. He talked the language of unalienable rights, which is an unqualified term. And again, there were just enough people around who made room and just enough people who were in Congress for just enough weeks in the spring of '65 to enact a few things. I use that as a moment. There have been other such moments. That's the good side. And it's the combination between what I was calling the public philosophy and what I would call a kind of inherited, intuitive goodwill on the part of a lot of people who would like to make the society work. You can't tell the story without recognizing that there's been that.

DOOR: What's bad about America?

MARTY: The bad side, I suppose, is really the negative side of the virtues. I think pride of nation is a very big theme here. I didn't agree a few years ago when Harvey Cox was saying that pride wasn't the great sin. A nation with the potencies of our own in human and natural resources and some good luck has always been tempted to find ways to throw its weight around in the world or to justify its neglect of its own victims. We try to remake the world in our image and don't comprehend why we aren't liked, understood, or followed. That's what has given us our worst moments. The worst moments are the Mexican war, the Spanish-American War, and the war in Vietnam, where none of the public philosophy or the inherited intuitive wisdom of the

people shone through for the moral purposes I described. Or it shows up in the subtler forms of economic imperialism that we've shown.

On political/military imperialism, America has a pretty good record. If you look at the number of people and the number of square miles that were seized in the imperial era, we're way below England and Russia. Russia was far more imperialistic than the U.S. We picked up a few islands, but we didn't need them. In our case, it was an economic imperialism. In order to sell our goods and have our markets, we found ways of letting other governments remain. We didn't have to topple the government as long as we could control the entire internal life. And that's been our problem in the last ten or fifteen years with the multinational corporations and our determining who to assassinate in which country. I am not naive about the self-interest of nations. But when it is self-interest, then we should call it that instead of disguising it. So I guess pride of nation, pretense, confusing our mission with God's has been the overall central problem of our history.

DOOR: Do you think that as America becomes less powerful we'll lose this sense of pride and be a better nation for it?

MARTY: I have an imaginary pride-humility scale. If we as Americans have a feeling of self-worth on a scale of 51 out of 100, we're in good shape. If we have the humility based on a scale of 49 out of 100, we're on the end of the scale, we're in trouble. And if we go below 49 on the other, we're in trouble. There is no question about it; we're going to get a little more honest about some things because we can't do everything. We've really learned over ten years that we can't nail the coonskin to the wall and run even a little nation like North Vietnam off the map. There are things that cannot be done, and we now know that. The masks are off in the eyes of the world, and we know that they know that. Some of the better moves in our foreign policy in recent years have recognized this. By better, I don't mean perfect. I think detente is necessary and good, but there are a lot of things about the Soviets I don't enjoy detenting with. But it's better than if we weren't. The recognition of the existence of China with their 700 million people helps us join the human race. And some of our Middle East attempts at accord are good. So I'd say there have been some good things growing out of that. But if we get below my partly arbitrary 50–49 scale, we're in trouble. I would not trust a nation that is too full of self-pity. I think anytime a people comes on like a crippled giant, a Wallace in a wheelchair, it's dangerous. If we just keep looking back on the days when we could really flex muscle and now we can't, we're in trouble. It's far more important to find what new things we can do. And I don't ever for a moment think we lack such things. If we began to begin to put our imaginations together as a nation, I would think the last part of this century would be a most exciting time, because of the delicate interplay between ecology and environment, the question of world population and hunger, the possibility of changing human nature in the test tube in the laboratory. We know the game's over if not played right in the next twenty-five years. You don't have to have all the military might to work on the problems. You don't have to throw your weight around. You might

have to apply little bits of economic pressure. You apply certain moral pressures. You use imaginative arts. And try to quicken your own population to it.

DOOR: What do you see good about the church?

MARTY: I guess my pro would go back to the word *experiment*. I'm always astonished at the resilience and the vitality and the ability so many Christians have to find new outlets for, in this case, Christian energies when one outlet gets dammed or aborted or perverted. I don't necessarily always enjoy each new direction the energies take, but I try to teach myself to be a little tolerant of them until a new channel is found. Overall, I am impressed that after the expenditure of a certain kind of spiritual capital in the sixties, suddenly across the board, there seems to have been some attempt at least to see a renewal of faith and life in the church on experiential grounds, on the grounds of immediacy, locality, or whatever. There's just a kind of instinct by which people who want to be religious today are trying to be that on a different set of terms. That's a marvelous experiment of character. And it shows up in their immediate claim to the local.

DOOR: What's bad about the church?

MARTY: When I say what's bad about the church, it's not going to be my big bad, it's going to be my little bad. I said experientiality is good, but we tend to freeze there. In any fulfilling religion, or certainly biblical and Christian faith, the impulse has always been to move from the experience into either or both interpretation and action. You have an incandescent experience and then you go back to the world of malignant tumors and hunger and scientific questions and you try to make a connection, a theoretical address to it. Because life is *not only* interpretation. If you cop out on those lines, you simply turn interpretation over to something else. I haven't yet seen a great deal of use of this experiencing God. I see traces of it. But I don't see much action.

I mentioned that the second good about the church was the creative revolt against the impersonal and remote which takes the form of the affirmation of the local. And the little bad about that is that we are not only local. We live in a world of interconnections. We're almost idolatrous about the local because we can control the local. We can pick our minister, we can set our budget, and we can stop being members one of another with people overseas or wherever. And that's what the rest of the century is going to be about. Those are the little bads.

DOOR: What's your big bad?

MARTY: My big bad might be a strange choice. My big bad is that in America, religion for some good historic reasons, I suppose, is made up so much of people who steadfastly, self-consciously, and joyfully embrace and endorse mediocrity on all dimensions. By that I mean any kind of rhetoric passes for a sermon and the public is trained to say, "Well, that was a good sermon because at least it wasn't intellectual. It didn't push my thoughts at all." Anything goes in the name of church art. There's been some great church art. There's been some wonderful architecture since World War II. And we're better off in some ways than we were. There have been a few people who have really set an example. But overall, I still don't find the New

York gallery having to reckon very seriously with any of the art that the Christians are producing. The music world is about the same. There have been a couple of nice little improvements, but it's about the same. If you notice the obsession Christians have with, say, C. S. Lewis, or W. H. Auden, or T. S. Eliot, or Dorothy Sayers, and so on, it's because that's about all we've had. We'd be just as happy with others, but that's the number of people who could put sentences together out in the world that is honestly dedicated to Christian believers. Now you can't produce genius. But you could produce the audience out of which genius arises. But almost any time anyone begins to get a little expressive about these things, they have to move out of the context of the faith in order to get their hearing. And to the degree that they get a hearing, the further they get out of that original context. That would be the arts. But it's also true of professionalism. I don't want to put a good word in for the content of prime-time television, but now and then I come into contact with the people who put something on television. And I cannot get over how someone will have a 103 degree fever and he'll retch between camera takes. But when he's on camera, you don't see any self-pity, not a glimmer of a lapse from the best. But I get into a church and the minister will get up and clear his throat and mumble and shuffle and say, "Tuesday I had to make an extra hospital call and I never quite got the week back together." It's kind of an apology for the chaos that's going to follow in administrative or organizational form. This is choice of mediocrity. It's sort of a conspiracy we have with each other to dare anybody to offer their best gifts to God. If you offer a good gift in a safe context, that's all right. But really let it erupt into the margins and you're in trouble. **DOOR:** In your book you discuss community and loneliness in the church. The form of the church is part of the message of the church. And when it is basically in our culture a large business enterprise organized to the hilt, doesn't that in itself preclude people from being a community?

MARTY: I think that on this level, what is often called the small group movement—for which you don't need a movement—has been at least a partial corrective. The church you are describing is the one on which our society places a premium for to me incomprehensible reasons. They strive for the one big show that's better than the other big show. The big problem there is you have something that looks like sociability and sociality, but it's on the terms of, "We really need you because we've got a program. You're really great; we have a stewardship campaign coming. You're really great; we've got a supper and we want a big crowd." You are affirmed to the degree that you are a reasonably healthy, able-bodied, good career potential person. Watch any such church or listen to its minister and notice the higher premium placed on the young executive and his two children and beautiful wife who just moved in and who can exert a great influence in the world as opposed to a woman in an old peoples' home or an unemployed person.

All you can say is, "Will you love me forty years from now?" Because forty years from now that executive will be creeping around in a wheelchair. We don't really see that soon enough because in our social-organization

congregations, all the people who are in that stage are living in a congregation at a certain time with a certain kind of church that has gone ahead with career-oriented, healthy, happy, potent people. You can have all the theologies geared up for them. And then when the people are on a decline—and we're all destined for a decline—they're going to move to places where they aren't going to be noticed anymore, and it often works to new loneliness. The compulsive friendliness breaks down when tested.

I think of little white ghetto churches, like a little Baptist church near Mayor Daly's place in Chicago that can't get more than a few people to church. And every week its minister has to look out and see the buses from First Baptist Church in Hammond, Indiana, invading the neighborhood from forty miles away. But I wouldn't worry about the overcoming of loneliness among the people at that church. They need each other. Their danger is the siege mentality—the whole world's against us. They need each other and they'll find each other. The only visit they'll get all year, if they don't visit each other, is when the precinct captain comes by.

But I'll tell you how loneliness shows up. This Thursday is Thanksgiving Day, and you could go into almost any church in the U.S. and hear the minister say, "Now later today as you gather at your groaning boards with all your family and relatives gathered for that hearty turkey dinner . . . the candles will glow," and so on. And a third of the people there are going to go to a little place and have a TV dinner and watch the football game and be absolutely alone. How many churches are having a Thanksgiving dinner on the premises for the people who are in that circumstance?

DOOR: How about the system that contributes to loneliness? You mentioned mobility extensively in your book. Should we fight that system or should we accept it and try to work with it? What about the destruction of friendships, the loss of the extended family, and other factors caused by too much mobility?

MARTY: I think we should fight it as part of the bigger fight. And I think there can be some gains. I'm not saying it's immoral every time someone moves. But I think we should put a premium on the times when people might refuse to move even at a little bit of status loss. I'm saying that against the background of a *Times* cover story I read about two weeks ago. It personalized it by telling of a man who had been forced by his company to move eleven times in eighteen years and this time he said no. He said, "You can fire me or you can side channel me or you can demote me, but I'm just sick and tired of moving. I never have roots. I never have contacts." The article went on to say that this is getting to be a more widespread revolt. All right, if enough people started protesting, I know the large firms would have to begin to reappraise their policies. They've been able to work the last quarter of a century on the premise that all of us want to move upward as fast as possible and the way to do that is to be moved to a new place where there is a slot for our talent. And if we start saying, "I'll really give you my best here where I am, but I don't care if you pass me up for somebody else," and if enough other people protest the move, they're going to find enough talent in

the other branch office. I'm not naively or optimistically romantic about this kind of thing. I'm saying it's one little part of a big mosaic of altering premium scales. I know that was our case when I moved to the University of Chicago thirteen years ago. I've been in the Chicago area my whole career. And I intend to spend my life there if I can. When I moved to the university, we moved into a big old house. We had foster children and by Illinois law, they can't be taken geographically away from their parents. And therefore, from then till now, anytime I get an offer from anywhere, I just write a little letter saying I can't even entertain it because if I did it would break up our family. That's been a tremendous luxury for me because it makes people say, "Sorry I asked." It's kind of a sacred bond I wouldn't violate. And it's prevented me from having to get involved in the seductions of whether I'd be happier in Europe or whether I'd be happier somewhere else. Now I know good and well that if I felt a call to go someplace else, I could pull rank on myself. But it's been kind of a natural, nice device. The beautiful thing about that is in the crucial years of our own children's development, it has given my wife and me what Santayana called a *locus standi*—a place to stand to view the world.

We've been privileged. We're upper-middle class and we can name our ticket a little better than some. But I think a lot of upper-middle class and middle-middle class people through these years have been the disease instead of the beginning of a cure. And these are the classes that make the decisions about mobility. Mobility by itself is not a vice. And the Christian faith happens to be a mobile faith. It's not a tribal faith tied only to a local deity. So we're better off than some for that. But I think we've been psychologically harsh on the coming generation by this approach.

DOOR: How can the church help people with decisions like the mobility question?

MARTY: I'm not making a categorical imperative out of this, but we're talking now about the subtle, little things that we can do to humanize the order. I work on the assumption that our future is somehow technological. That is, I don't think we can dream ourselves into the future in which pure innocence returns. If we want cancer research, if we want high-speed drills, if we want anything like that, we have to have the logic of technology. The issue then is, how do you make it a humane order? I don't think we've begun to explore the resources that the Christian tradition with Jesus Christ, with the biblical view of nature, has for us. How many of us would have to say, "I've been in the church all my life and I've never been in a place where anybody discussed technology theologically or morally"? It doesn't come up. But I think the fortunate side of this is that you could right now take up most of the best issues and they wouldn't yet be directly seen as "meddling in politics." That is, these are not yet polarized by parties. Some of the populistic features implied in what we've been talking about here today are advocated by a Jerry Brown who people thought was liberal and the New Hampshire governor whom people thought a conservative. Both of them have said, "I don't have to have a style of living that only flaunts affluence." I'm not here to endorse either one, and I know a lot of flaws

about both, but there is some symbolic weight to someone saying, "I don't need the limo, I don't need the big mansion. I don't need conspicuous consumption. I don't need endless proliferation of staff, etc." It doesn't solve all our problems, but it lets a little signal out. And while our people can sense this on both sides of politics, I know it will all get political in the end. As far as changing minds is concerned, at this stage, we have a lot of areas in which the church could be busy. And by the church I mean not only the pulpit, but *the* church which has twenty outlets to one over the pulpit in education and other areas.

DOOR: In your book, you suggest that without an understanding of history, we lose our identity.

MARTY: I guess I'd say coming from a liturgical background it hit me harder these two days than it has for years. And it's helpful for me as a chronicler of American religion. If you're Catholic, Lutheran, or Episcopalian, you are liturgical. By liturgical, I mean you sort of cohere to an ongoing life of the church and you have your ups and downs and you grow in grace or you see spiritual decline. And you might even witness, but your witness is more just to the power of God or the love of Christ. But not so much this, "I was driving along and God spoke to me." Maybe one in five hundred in the liturgical church has his or her story to tell.

In that sense, I would say the liturgical churches do have it easier to think historically because the only identity I would have as a Christian is in that group of people who brought me as an infant to be baptized. I'm not saying that the typical Catholic, Lutheran, Episcopalian, or whatever is better informed historically. I'm not saying that at all. A lot of them know very little of their history. But their history is pre-packaged for them. So in a sense, whether the big deal happens to them, God's process goes on anyhow. But many religious groups are composed of people for whom all history has to be compressed in their own. There has to be kind of an instant fabrication of history. That their whole personal histories were formed by a moment nineteen centuries ago is all that matters. And I'm not saying one is a superior and one is an inferior form of faith. We just are that different within the Christian church in America, and that's why a lot of communication is difficult across some of those boundaries.

I don't care quite as much as the speaker does about telling all that he or she went through. On the other hand, judgment certainly would be made in liturgical churches, when to many people nothing seems to have happened at all. That obviously isn't the whole Christian show either. So my scaling isn't who's good and who's bad, just how they're different. But what I would do is ask that speaker, "Why are you telling me this?"

My predecessor in Chicago was Sidney Mead, and he tells a story about a student who came in to him one time and said, "I'd like to be exempted from the History of Christianity comprehensive exam." In Chicago, if you pass the test, you don't have to take the course.

And Mead said, "This is really rare. We can get you out of courses, but not out of tests."

"Well," he said, "I'm an abstract thinker; I'm a conceptualist; I'm a universalizer; I'm a philosopher. I don't really need the details of how this got going and how that emerged. History tells me nothing."

And Mead said, "That's really interesting. I'll have to know more. Make your case."

"I don't want to take the time for it," the guy said. "In order to make my case I'd have to tell you all about who I am, where I came from, what happened to me."

Mead said, "You just lost." In other words, in order for you to give an accounting for me to know how to make up my mind about you, you locate yourself in a history. That's what some people are doing, but they are not knowing it. Now what they are out to protect is probably a valuable thing. They are out to protect the immersion of their identity in some nameless, dead past. What they're failing to do is draw on the incandescent moments of that past that could inform them on future decisions. To illustrate, take the models and images of the church. If you deal with only the recent past, you would have the church you just described—the programmatic, triumphal church. That's not going to remain. The bloom is going to go off the churches that are blooming now. The churches that are prospering today are prospering from the culture as much as the mainline churches profited twenty years ago from a different culture. And that doesn't last. Culture shifts. And that church had better be ready for a long slug. When that happens, if you have only one model, people will drop like flies because what was working won't work. But if you do know something of the history and get an idea from it, you have a range of models. You have Exodus. The exiles. Pilgrims, flock, endless things to draw on. And you can take great courage and cheer from that. I was in Spain last January and had dinner with a Spanish Jesuit friend of ours. We couldn't get over the way in which his Christian faith transcended both Catholicism under Franco and the hope for a new spring after Franco was gone. Simply because he knows there are so many things he can draw on in order for that faith to survive.

People deprive themselves of the models on which they can build when there's a change. I think another thing that they deprive themselves of is the liberating sense of some knowledge of history. I like to use the illustration that everything that is the trouble with the church today—billboard-size trouble—was invented between 1740 and 1840. The denominations are in trouble, and we know it. The Sunday school is in trouble in all but about ten big places. The missionary movement on the old model is in trouble if for no other reason than the governments over there aren't for it. The ecumenical movement. The modern, competitive, non-territorial parish. They aren't on the scene until about the time of Wesley and America's first great awakening. They rise with the beginning of industrialization and the revolutions. And they congeal and take nice shape. They were movements of genius for that period. The church got along for seventeen and a half centuries without them. And for the past century we've been getting messages that they aren't the only thing available. People who get that liberating vision are not less responsible about life in the forms they have, but you don't have to have the ulcer you get about seeing those forms change. This is not to say that I expect every Christian to have a historian's detailed knowledge of history. But

rather an openness to the categories, so that the minister, teacher, or whatever can address this and it will also be the story of their life.

DOOR: There aren't a lot of church historians, are there?

MARTY: No, and it's probably not even the emergent word because outside of the seminaries, there is no field called church history. Most of the students I prepare teach in religion departments, history departments, or in American study departments where the history of Christianity comes closer. But I guess you'd say history of religion in America is what we're about. Because we get into transcendentalism, which I don't think should be called Christianity or church history. We get into religion and nationalism. But I would say fifteen, twenty, twenty-five of us make a full-time living off it. It's a small fraternity on that level. But we're hooked into hundreds of people in college and university religion departments who are not first of all "church historians," but who do religious history as their main theme. So I don't feel lonely there at all. There's a lot of good, quality work coming out. It's a high-morale discipline, although not by nature a big or noisy one.

DOOR: What do you think of Francis Schaeffer?

MARTY: I think he's probably as serious as anybody about articulating a version of an intellectual presupposition for the faith and his positive service is that he's doing that among people who, if he weren't around, probably wouldn't be trying. His limit, I think from my point of view, is a very consistent reformed scholasticism, a very consistent propositional view of the faith, which I think tends to lose the existential dynamism of faith—though not for him personally. Obviously he's a reverent and passionate believer. But I find the people who come to me after his speech quoting him are usually people who are out to settle a score or make a debating point on the basis of a presupposition that isn't widely enough shared for them to get anywhere. That is, if you buy his first point, you buy the whole system. Just as Milton Friedman does in economics at Chicago. If the world were put together the way that Milton Friedman thinks it is, he'd be dead right. There is no place in the argument after he starts.

In looking at Schaeffer, my theme would be that while I cannot prove that the world is not put together the way he sees it, I would rather say he has chosen one of a number of useful handles on the world. That is, the scholastic tradition, Aristotilian logic, the law of contradiction. All the things he uses, whether he calls them that or not, are very respectable, plausible handles. They were the main thing that Catholics thought for 700 years and Protestants thought for 200 years. So I can't say he's invented it. I happen to admire the people who invented it and I think he handles it with some skill. What I resist is the idea that it is the only, or today, the superior mode of grasping that reality.

DOOR: You don't seem to be a big systems person where everything neatly starts and then orderly proceeds from there. You seem to look at a lot of different alternatives and say sometimes it works this way, and sometimes this way, and we can't put it together in a box.

MARTY: I think that's true as long as it's not interpreted to mean that I'm anti-systematic or against the effort for people to process. I frankly can't make my way through Whitehead's process and reality. I haven't the faintest idea what he's talking about. But when the people informed by him relate it to biblical data, I sort of jump to it and say, "Yeah, you are talking about a world I do recognize."

DOOR: In your book, you used the phrase "theological cosa nostra" in describing seminaries. Could you comment on that?

MARTY: I think philosophy of religion is a legitimate discipline untouched by community. But I think theology has no language if it does not have a believing, practicing community to which to relate. And when the theological community forgets that and turns to philosophy of religion, it will under the auspices of the church end up just talking to itself in increasingly remote terms. So without denigrating the value of philosophy of religion—I just defended it in the last question—I think theologians for the church should know something of what the believing people are thinking about and should be responsible to them. And the best theology of our century—best in the sense of the deepest and most consistent—was done by the Bultmann, the Barth types—the giants of the Bible talk about the changelessness of God.

But why do you need changelessness in Christian thought of the scholastic type? You need it because you're Platonic in the sense that you say that if God is perfect, then he cannot change because change could only be for the worst. My wife and I have a very fine relationship. I don't want it to get better, but I want it to be different through the years. God and his people have a good relationship. It can't get better from their comprehension of what he's doing for them. But it can change. So I think when you say that God creates a world, that's different. Any creator is different from creation. But my whole view of this grows more out of reading of what a scholastic would say is the anthropomorphic revelation of Scripture ... than it does from my having started with this neat system that talks about ontology and constructs consistent philosophy. In part, it's my own limit. I'm not trained in philosophy in a formal way. I read a lot, but I'm not trained in it. And in part because I look at what William James calls "The rich thicket of reality" and just say that inside history there's no way I'm going to be pulling these strands together that much that I would be content with the system that came up. I do think it is a valid enterprise for us to ask each other to ground our statements in an even higher or more basic level of discourse until we push it as far as we can. And I guess for me, that would mean finally that I would be pushed closer to a processive view than a being view, or whatever you use if you were a scholastic. By that I don't mean that I equate God and flux. I don't equate God and anything. I'm not a pantheist. As a historian in the faith, I'm naturally very biblically oriented.

Three or four times the Bible says that God does not change. Malachi, James—they are so rare that we really make a lot of them for scholasticism. All it's out to say is God's constant, that his love is steadfast, that you can count on him. I don't see a lot of that in a lot of the formal theologists.

DOOR: You see seminaries as really ingrown?

MARTY: What tends to happen is that we tend to check our credentials with the other people who can check their credentials. And in theology, an author is going to remember the fifteen reviewers and not the fifteen thousand people who are going to be potential readers.

DR. JAMES DAANE

The Sunday morning worship hour has been labeled by some cynical time-management people as the most wasted hour in the American week.

If this observation is even partially true, a great deal of the blame needs to fall on the local pastors who direct that morning worship hour. Sunday after Sunday, mediocrity pours from so many vocal chords.

To find out what good preaching is, and in hopes of motivating those who don't preach well, the Keepers looked at the subject through some respected preachers and teachers of preachers.

We drove to Fuller Theological Seminary in 1977 and talked to the crusty Dr. James Daane. Before his death in 1983, he was director of the doctor of ministry program and professor of pastoral theology. When he wasn't running his huge hands through his shock of gray hair, Daane answered our questions. With his Th.D. from Princeton, post-doctoral study at the Free University of Amsterdam, and experience as pastor at three different churches, he answered most of the questions with confidence.

DOOR: What do you consider the essence of good preaching?

DAANE: The Word. Preaching is by definition preaching the Word. If you want to know what goes into a good preacher beyond that, there are all kinds of things.

DOOR: Could you use some examples of people you think are good preachers?

DAANE: There are many preachers who people think are good preachers that I don't. The popular ones, for the most part, I don't think are good preachers.

DOOR: Why is that?

DAANE: The popular ones are the ones that are chiefly interested in human need, hurts, aches, and religious psychology. They are into developing your religious potential, possibility thinking, and all that kind of thing. That kind of preaching is popular these days, and I think it's widespread. It's interpersonal. But it seems to me in good preaching the relationship is first of all between the church and God. Like "loving God with all your heart and your neighbor as yourself"— the first has to be there and then the second. Right now most preaching deals so much with interpersonal relationships that it degenerates into a man-centered message instead of being God-centered.

DOOR: What about those people who see themselves as pastor/teachers? They spend hours studying, throw out all kinds of Greek and Hebrew, use an overhead projector, and the whole worship service becomes a teaching situation.

DAANE: That's lecturing. That's Bible class stuff, but that's not preaching. Preaching inevitably involves a certain amount of teaching, but it's not a teaching situation. It's a preaching situation. In the pulpit, I have to be able to say, "Thus saith the Lord," and in a teaching situation in a class, I can't say that. I shouldn't say it. In church, I don't preach what I don't know or am not sure about. If you don't know or aren't sure about it, don't preach it. You know what Bruner says about preacher/teacher. Christ was a preacher and not a teacher. You can graduate from a teacher, but you can't graduate from the Christ.

DOOR: This teaching emphasis is a very strong movement today. At churches with this emphasis, you receive notes when you go in. They spend forty-five minutes to an hour versus your twenty-minute sermon. They move through the Scripture usually verse by verse. It's all very biblically oriented.

DAANE: You mean that the service is really an oral commentary?

DOOR: Yes.

DAANE: So when it's 11:00, no matter where you are, you stop there? And you can pick up next week on the next verse? That kind of thing? Well, that's Bible teaching, but I don't call that a sermon. I don't call that preaching. It's the easy way. A lot of people do it. You just go verse by verse and make a few comments, a couple of moral applications, and at 11:00, you stop wherever you happen to be. That's easy. It's a whole lot tougher to take a few verses and construct a sermon where you're bringing home one idea, and all the pieces fit together.

DOOR: How can a person get the confidence to say, "Thus saith the Lord" and be convincing? How can he know that's what the Lord is saying?

DAANE: He needs to have a good biblical theology of preaching. Like Calvin and Luther said, "Preaching the Word of God is the Word of God." If you don't believe that, you don't belong in a pulpit. You're preaching or you aren't.

DOOR: When does a preacher interject examples?

DAANE: Whenever they serve a purpose or throw light on an explanation of whatever point you're trying to make.

DOOR: Suppose a preacher becomes tired of dabbling in religious psychology and says, "I really want to preach this Sunday. I want to get things right." How would you tell him to go about it?

DAANE: Pick a text. Do expository preaching. Basically, I would say all preaching is expository preaching. It might take different forms, different minor points. But you have to bring the message that's found in that Book. And if you don't do that, you're just playing around.

DOOR: What part do you think preaching should play in the total worship service?

DAANE: I hate to get hung up on whether the center of the service is the communion table or the preaching. I don't know. I was brought up in the tradition where the sermon was central and we had communion once in three months. I tend to think that preaching should serve the purpose of a sacramental celebration.

DOOR: How do you deal with personality? There are people who are dynamic communicators, incredible personalities. They are so charismatic that people will listen to them even if they have nothing to say.

DAANE: I see it as religious entertainment. If you have that problem, you should struggle with it, yes. Because then you're getting in the way of the sermon. And when you get in the way of the sermon, it's usually an acquired art. I've noticed some preachers who tended to get in the way of their own message. Many of them have had some kind of dramatic training.

I think the bigger problem is the other kind of problem where the man gets up there and has a good word to say, but his personality is flat. He's so lacking in warmth, fire, excitement. I heard two students like that this morning. One of them is a very good student, but their sermonic delivery is just blah. I can hardly listen to the guy. That's a bigger problem. The other problem I think is largely acquired.

DOOR: The congregation theoretically should be able to say, "I don't care what his personality is, I'm going to listen to what God has to say to me." But people aren't like that. So how do you deal with that tension?

DAANE: Like the students I heard this morning ... one of them didn't project his voice. If he had any excitement about his text, he didn't show it. He was too scared. A lot of that can be eliminated. But at the bottom, I suppose the only cure is to get really excited about what you're saying. If this is really the Almighty speaking through me ... if this is what God really says ... then I'm talking about the biggest thing in the world and in life. And if you can't get excited about that, then it's pretty hopeless. But as life goes along and you see deeper and you live longer, you get more excited. I know I'm a lot more excited about it than I was when I first started. But you have to convey a kind of deep commitment and a little excitement about what you're delivering.

I don't know whether you understand what I mean. A man should be a part of his sermon in the same way that the church is a part of the Apostles' Creed. In the Apostles' Creed, you confess your faith in God, but the church is there. There is such a thing as the "holy catholic church." But you don't go on and give a whole lot of church history. A Christian preacher should be a part of his sermon, just as the church is a part of the creed. And his Christian faith should emerge and become apparent by what he proclaims and how he proclaims it. But his own religious history has no more room in a sermon than church history in the Apostles' Creed. The reality is there. It's obvious. But you don't stand there and talk about it.

DOOR: The idea that the sermon or the preaching is the Word of God ... you teach this to your students?

DAANE: Right. I teach that God is speaking through the preacher.

DOOR: Should the congregation then be taught that the preacher is preaching the Word of God? And where does our fallibility as deliverers of the Word of God come in? How can people be discerning as to whether or not someone is truly teaching the Word of God, because obviously not every preacher is preaching from the same point of view?

DAANE: You mean, how do you convey the idea that what you are hearing is God speaking?

DOOR: It's great in the classroom for a student to take his preaching seriously—to believe that he's preaching the Word of God. But on the other hand, there are a lot of preachers who are preaching the so-called Word of God and it's very questionable whether it's the Word of God. And there are a lot of flocks who believe that their preacher is giving them the Word of God and, therefore, they never question him. He's above any kind of criticism. How do you deal with that?

DAANE: You're asking Harold Lindsell's question in reverse, I guess. The nature of the divine Word is such that it validates itself. It accredits itself. It comes with its own validation. I don't bring external evidence to prove that this is the Word of God. I can't say, "Look, I'm going to prove to you that the word I bring is really the Word of God." It can't be done. And, therefore, all my religious experiences and other people's religious experiences really are not going to prove that it's the Word of God. The Word of God does that itself. And all the attempts to gild the lily are futile.

DOOR: Even though the Word of God comes from the same Scripture ...

there are so many different ways of dealing with it. And different people deal with it in different ways. It's hard for me to reconcile that all of these are the Word of God.

DAANE: Basically we're praising the Word—not Communism or idealism or whatever. It's in that basic stance that you actually preach the Bible. God can overcome my little misinterpretations, misconstructions, and misevaluations. Of course he does. He does it all the time with ordinary Christian witness. A lot of people bear Christian witness that is pretty bad stuff. But somehow God often can break through that. In other words, the Word has power to break through our little obstructions and misinterpretations.

DOOR: You're saying that if a guy bases his whole presentation on Scripture, that even if he blows it in some way, God's going to use him?

DAANE: The Word of God can break through all kinds of opposition, strongholds of evil. That's why I think that if the Bible is used in the public schools, it can be badly mishandled by a lot of teachers, but at the same time, the Word has power to break through all these obstructions and misconstructions and do its work—its thing.

DOOR: Let's take a chapter like Romans 7 where one group of scholars say that Paul is describing his pre-conversion experience, another group says it's a carnal experience, and another group says it's the experience of grace. As a result of this understanding of Romans 7, they interpret it differently and apply it differently. And all three of those positions are held by good folk.

DAANE: But at the same time, all three of them have enough basic, fundamental agreement so that the

Word still comes through. They aren't that far apart. At bottom, they're all trying to say basically the same thing whether you decide that this was pre-conversion Paul or post-conversion Paul. There's no infallibility in the sense that a preacher never makes a mistake, but I think that a man who is committed to the gospel, to the Bible, and preaches it, is essentially infallible. I've heard it said about the church, "Once in a while it drifts around and gets off the street, but for the most part, it goes in one direction." And that's the way I look at it.

DOOR: Where does personal testimony come into play? You negated that in terms of a preaching experience, but when does a person share his story about what God has done?

DAANE: Once in a while when it serves the purpose of the sermon. You can't lay down a cut-and-dried rule about that. But this everlasting reference to personal experience I think is bad preaching. Not only that, it soon becomes very boring. Your religious experience may interest me once, maybe once . . . but after I've heard it once, I don't care to hear it again. It's like yesterday's newspapers. It's not all that important. It's the objective redemptive history of Israel and Christ that's the important thing, not primarily my religious history.

DOOR: Barth said that good preaching is the Bible in one hand and a newspaper in the other. How do you buy that?

DAANE: I guess the way he does. You buy it in terms of relevancy, but you don't let the newspaper dictate how to read the Bible. And you don't go Tillich's route and let the philosophers ask the questions and the theologians have to give answers. Because the question shapes the answer and every question has its direction. You've got to be in the world. You've got to know what's going on. But don't let the newspapers set the substance of the message.

I was brought up in the Christian Reformed Church and preached the Heidelberg Catechism. And early in the catechism comes that question, "Whence knowest thy misery?" The answer is not out of the newspaper or out of your own personal diagnosis. The Bible has to define your needs before it meets them. It has to tell you what you need—the nature of your hurts, pains, aches. In other words, the Bible has got to tell you what sin is, because you don't know.

DOOR: Are there any preachers around preaching like that?

DAANE: Not many.

DOOR: What's happening? Are theological schools supposed to turn out good preachers?

DAANE: Right. Right.

DOOR: Then how come they're not?

DAANE: Well, I guess there are lots of answers to that. A lot of seminary profs never stood in a pulpit or ever had a church. Some of them are bad preachers. Some of them are not interested in preaching. They're more interested in the academic side. By and large, I would guess that somehow we teach theology in a way that doesn't make it relevant to the pulpit. We present systematic theology instead of biblical theology. I don't object to systematics, but a lot of systematics is certainly not what you'd want to hear. It's too academic, too scholastic. I would wish that men in Old Testament and New Testament theology would do a better job of making kids see that there's a powerful lot of beautiful material there for preaching. But somehow they're often so concerned about technical questions, trivial questions. But a seminary exists primarily for preachers. The Ph.D.'s and the profs exist for the sake of the pulpit.

DOOR: A lot of people question whether or not preaching is a valid means of communication for the age that we're living in. Are there other forms of communication that can be used better to communicate the same thing as preaching?

DAANE: Preaching is still the prime medium for the gospel.

DOOR: What about media? Does preaching lose something if it's communicated other than in person, via TV, for example?

DAANE: Sure. The church is part of the creed and you are part of the sermon. When that part gets shadowed out, something essential is lost.

DOOR: You would say that you can't really preach over TV?

DAANE: No, you can preach on the TV. But TV is an entertainment media and preaching isn't very entertaining for most people. So I don't think you're going to see too much of it on TV. You'll see a lot of soloists and spectaculars, but by and large, TV audiences want something else besides straight preaching.

DOOR: What is the purpose of preaching—at least the preaching that you've defined. Is it to learn? Is it to be inspired? Is it to be persuaded to some kind of action or evangelism?

DAANE: The purpose of preaching is, one, to make new converts, and two, to build up the church. To send them out on Monday to serve. To deepen their faith commitments, their love, their service.

There are many evangelicals, I'm

afraid, who have such a low view of the church and low view of the sacraments that the only thing that they think is important is what they call evangelistic preaching. So in many churches you hear an evangelical sermon every Sunday morning. They have different texts, but they always end up in some kind of an altar call.

DOOR: Is it fair to use persuasive devices in preaching to get your message across?

DAANE: You mean like Kennedy does down in Coral Ridge when he gets to some point or other and says, "God says . . . ," and pushes a button and his voice booms through the church? I think that's corny.

DOOR: Is there any way of being objective in your preaching? Or should you be objective?

DAANE: There must be no doubt that the guy up there is a Christian man who believes what he says, etc., etc. But if you're talking about using techniques, that's another thing. Number one, if the Word works its own way and carries its own power through this whole thing, you don't need techniques. You don't need gimmicks. And number two . . . as far as trying to be effective . . . it seems to me about all a minister can do is to try not to be ineffective. Try not to use bad logic, bad English, bad personal habits, poor delivery. All these things can be obstacles that can be put in the way of preaching. And we should do our very best to get rid of all those things. But in the end, the Lord gives the increase.

DOOR: In teaching future preachers, you help them avoid obstacles, but you don't give them a lot of techniques so that they can be more persuasive. Is that how you see the training of preachers?

DAANE: Well, my reason is theological. I cannot impart power to the Word. I can't make that Word effective. I can't convert people. So any ideas I have about making it effective are off base.

You do your duty and your duty is to preach the Word of God and try not to put obstacles in the way. But never get the illusion that it lies within your own power to make it dynamite. It's dynamite in its own right and on its own terms. That's why I don't like altar calls and lowered houselights and "Tell Mother I'll Be There," and all that kind of thing.

DOOR: Do you see a place for apologetics in the church?

DAANE: You only use it when you have to. If you're working with college kids who come off campuses with all kinds of objections to Christianity, then you can say, "Look, man, I can knock all the props out from under your arguments and then you don't have anything to stand on." Then you can use the apologetic approach. But you only do it when you have to, when you're driven to it. You don't use an apologetic approach in the pulpit. Trying to prove it is about the biggest mistake you can make.

DOOR: Obviously you've got to spend time in preparation if you're going to be the preacher you should be. And you've got the demands of your flock. How do you work out this balance between being a preacher and being a pastor?

DAANE: You have to do both. But I would put the emphasis on the sermon, realizing, of course, that you can't be a good preacher if you don't have your feet out in the midst of your people. You've got to be there too. But if I had to sacrifice any place, I'd rather sacrifice on the pastoral bit than on the pulpit bit.

DOOR: When you were pastoring a church, how many hours did you spend preparing for preaching?

DAANE: I didn't spend a lot of time preparing any given sermon. But I did an awful lot of reading. Background reading. Theological stuff. And when you speak out of a background and approach a text out of a background, you don't have to spend forever on each sermon. I don't think it's right to just study for sermons. You're never going to get any place in the long haul. You've got to sit down and read Barth or Calvin or whatever.

DOOR: How can you preach the Word of God without sounding like a super authoritarian figure?

DAANE: You apply your sermon to yourself first of all. I'm judged by that Word just as much as they are— maybe more because of my understanding.

DOOR: How can you help your congregation distinguish between legitimate and illegitimate authority? How can you help your students know when they're preaching with legitimate authority and when they're just being authoritarian on their own?

DAANE: You're being authoritarian in the wrong sense of the term if you think you stand outside that authority—not under Christ's judgment. If you realize that you're under it too, that you're just as much a sinner as the next guy, you're not going to get a big head about being a preacher. If you take seriously that "God speaks through me," that's enough to make me scared.

Remember in *The Robe* when that young priest administered the sacraments for the first time. His hands were sweaty and he trembled. It was the first time he had the Body of the Lord in his hands. I think Protestant preachers ought to have a little of that when they get in the pulpit. When God actually speaks through me, that's kind of a sobering thought.

Are you all preachers?

DOOR: We've all attempted it at one time or another.

DAANE: Are you all seminary students?

DOOR: None of us are.

DAANE: None of you are. How do you preach if you haven't been to seminary?

DOOR: Now you're going to get us angry. Is that one of the criteria for preachers?

DAANE: It's not absolutely necessary. If you're a genius, you don't need it. Like Niebuhr didn't need a doctorate.

But the ordinary fellow, I suspect, needs it. I think congregations suffer enough from preachers without having them suffer more.

DOOR: But you've already admitted that this seminary and other seminaries don't turn out good preachers. So what difference does a seminary make?

DAANE: Just my feeble little efforts. That's all.

DOOR: You give it your best shot and if 3 percent come out better preachers, that's better than 0 percent?

DAANE: Right. In teaching homiletics, I begin with the theology of preaching: what's the nature of the Word; what really goes on in preaching. And it actually grabs hold of a lot of students. They don't all agree with me, of course. And some have never thought of any of these things before.

ANDREW GREELEY

Father Andrew Greeley. Irish. Ph.D. in sociology. Irish. Scholar (professor of sociology, University of Arizona). Irish. Writer (mucho books and articles including *The Cardinal Sins, Thy Brother's Wife*, and *Ascent Into Hell*). Irish. Sociologist (research associate for the National Opinion Research Center, University of Chicago, and adjunct professor of sociology, University of Arizona at Tucson). Irish.

The Keepers of the *Door* traveled to Chicago and interviewed Father Greeley, sans collar, at his apartment in the John Hancock Building (on a clear day he can see Wheaton). He does not speak with an Irish brogue, is definitely not into the latest-style clothing, and never heard of Jack Chick. He's known as some sort of a rebel in the Catholic church, but he sounded very Catholic to us (but what do we know; we're not Catholics). At fifty-four years of age (he didn't look fifty-four, he looked fifty-five, but what do we know, we're not fifty-four either), he turned to writing novels because "if you're Irish, then sometime during your life you have to tell stories." The real reason Greeley says he started writing novels was because "my sociology of religion has taught me that stories are the most effective way to talk about religion." The

Keepers found Father Greeley to be a soft-spoken, articulate, and candid spokesperson for today's Catholic church.

DOOR: We have to ask you this. Do Catholics really play bingo?

GREELEY: The principal use of bingo in the church today is to keep the inner-city black schools open.

DOOR: You're kidding.

GREELEY: No, I'm not. The only parishes that have bingo are the black parishes. They use the money to keep the schools open, and ironically, the majority of the students in those schools are Protestant.

DOOR: Interesting.

GREELEY: Lots of ironies in the fire.

DOOR: We've noticed a resurgence of anti-Catholicism. Could you comment on that?

GREELEY: There are three different kinds. First there is the liberal anti-

Catholicism. It comes from the upper end of the academic and intellectual ladder. These people believe Catholics are people who don't believe for themselves. They believe a Catholic could no more be a good scholar than if they were a card-carrying member of the communist party. In their view, Catholics are all conservative, right-wing, and against the real poor. None of these stereotypes are sustained by the empirical data, but they are quite powerful because they are latent and very pervasive in those parts of the American society where the university and higher media have influence.

The second kind of anti-Catholicism is illustrated by the movie *Monsignor*.

DOOR: It's anti-Catholic to make a film about Vatican corruption?

GREELEY: I don't mind a work of art on Vatican corruption (Andre Gide did it marvelously in *The Caves of the Vatican*), but I consider "Monsignor" a form of bigotry because it is a crude, inaccurate film which portrays what outsiders think the Catholic church is. It reflects people's prejudice. You can make fun of us if you want to, but get the right things to make fun of.

DOOR: Do you think Jack Chick publications had anything to do with the film?

GREELEY: Who?

DOOR: Never mind.

GREELEY: The third kind of anti-Catholicism, of course, is the latent bigotry among the conservative, right-wing fundamentalist strain of Christianity.

DOOR: Speaking of right-wing fundamentalists, it's interesting that groups like the Moral Majority have aligned themselves with Catholics on a number of issues.

GREELEY: Yes, but it doesn't take them long to discover that on most extreme, right-wing views, Catholics are really not on their side. In fact, on most issues, there would be basic disagreement. Take the pornography issue, for example. Catholics may not want their children having access to pornographic magazines, but they wouldn't be in sympathy with anti-porn laws. Catholics are not about to go back to the technique of enforcing morality through laws.

DOOR: Let's talk about the role of the priest.

GREELEY: The priest is the show. As the leadership influence of the Vatican and the bishop diminishes, the most powerful influence in the religious life of a Catholic is the priest. He is the church, and the quality of his preaching is the most important religious influence in the life of the Catholic.

DOOR: Preaching may be the most important influence in the Catholic church, but the last time we checked, there weren't a whole lot of priests who could preach. Catholic preaching isn't very good, is it?

GREELEY: It's terrible.

DOOR: You're so hesitant to state your opinion.

GREELEY: Look, preaching is the most important thing we do, yet only ten percent of the people under thirty rate us as excellent at it. The Catholic priests meet in solemn assembly and condemn injustice all over the world, yet *the* basic violation of injustice is the poor preaching of the gospel. That's never condemned. That's never paid attention to.

DOOR: Why is the preaching of the priests so bad?

GREELEY: There are a lot of reasons, but as the various lay ministerial roles emerge, priests are going through an identity crisis in which they don't think they are important anymore. Certainly, lay ministers are important and necessary, but that doesn't make the priest any less important. The research we've done leaves no doubt that ordinary laypeople still consider their priest to be the church. He is the most important influence in their religious life outside of their own family, and the quality of his preaching is becoming more important rather than less.

DOOR: But in the Catholic church, doesn't the priest have equally important duties? The confessional, for example?

GREELEY: Catholics don't go to confession nearly as much. It is still the preaching which has the effect on people. For the majority of Catholics, the only contact with the priest is the ten-minute homily during mass. If we believe that majority, those homilies are, for the most part, God-awful.

DOOR: We can't believe you're saying this. Those of us who are outside the Catholic church have complimented the Catholic church on its emphasis on worship. We have focused on the fact that good liturgy negates the need for good preaching.

GREELEY: I don't have any data on this, but impressionistically, I think the laity would rate good preaching just a notch under good liturgy, and would link the ability to preach well with the ability to say mass well.

DOOR: In other words, if you can't preach well, then you probably can't do liturgy very well either.

GREELEY: I can't prove it, but I think that's what we would find if we could prove it.

DOOR: The Catholic church has been characterized by its strong church hierarchy. What are your feelings about church hierarchy, both Catholic and Protestant?

GREELEY: The national bureaucracies are becoming more important in the Protestant church and at the same time, the bureaucracies are becoming less important in the Catholic church. Catholics used to listen much more closely to what the bishops and the pope said than they do now. They listen to the parish priest, but they are much more into individual conscience on issues as seemingly diverse as sex and nuclear weapons. They may or may not consider what the church leadership says, but they are not going to be blindly obedient. They'll make their own decisions in conscience. At the level just beneath the Cardinals, the bishops and archbishops of my age down to forty, are the most pragmatic of men. For instance, one bishop said to me about my fiction, "We're not going to make a martyr out of you because if your books should be best-sellers, let them be best-sellers on their own and not because we condemn them." That, I thought, ought to be written in the sky as a sign of the new, very pragmatic, American hierarchy. I mean, there are bishops in the country who now boast that they've never given an order. Everything is settled by consensus. So the next wave of cardinals from this country—St. Louis, Chicago, Detroit, Washington— are going to be much more pragmatic, democratic, and collegiate. Catholicism seems to be rediscovering the importance of the local congregation just at the point when Protestantism, at least in its more liberal manifestations, is becoming terribly suspicious of the local congregation and embarrassed by it.

DOOR: But isn't the church's authority very important in Catholicism?
GREELEY: I don't know that it is so important now. There are still some church people, laity and clergy, for whom authority is important, but there is an ever-increasing number who realize that the Catholic heritage and tradition is much broader and deeper and richer than some sort of rigid, canonical idea about authority.
DOOR: Where does our authority come from? The church? The Bible?
GREELEY: Final authority comes from God in the conscience. The Reformation did not remove the significance of the individual conscience. It may have pushed things in directions that we might not have liked in those days, and maybe in directions that not all Protestants like today. Ironically, we Catholics seem to be returning to the tradition of individual conscience which you Protestants allegedly departed the Reformation with and presently seem to have lost.
DOOR: Many Protestants still criticize the Catholic church for its worship of Mary.
GREELEY: Most of those who do simply don't know what's going on in Catholicism. Mariology has never gone away, but not because the official church has tried to push it. I doubt if there has been a sermon on Mary preached in an American parish in the last twenty years, but that doesn't mean that the Mary-image is not present. It is still very strong in the Catholic imagination ... and, frankly, in the Protestant imagination as well.
DOOR: What do you mean by "strong in the Protestant imagination"?
GREELEY: Mary has a very good image with young Catholics and also with young Protestants. Mary reflects the womanliness of God as Jesus reflects the manliness of God. Mary is an enormous resource in the Catholic tradition and should be in the Protestant as well.
DOOR: Whatever happened to confession in the Catholic church?
GREELEY: People just don't go much anymore. The notion of confessing sins to priests instead of to God doesn't mean much to Catholics any more. I don't hear confessions very often, and when I do (usually during Holy Week in Tucson), I'm impressed with the enormous number of Catholics who now look at confession as a time to discuss their spiritual problems in the context of sacrament. Confession is more and more ceasing to be an impersonal, mechanical encounter and becoming a face-to-face dialogue. Confession is turning into an opportunity to talk about your spiritual problems within the church context.
DOOR: That certainly blows away one stereotype. Let's try another. Can you be a non-Catholic and still be a Christian?
GREELEY: Certainly. God loves all of us and salvation is, therefore, available to everyone.
DOOR: There goes another one. Catholics seem to be rediscovering Scripture. Does that pose any problems for the church?
GREELEY: Well, we certainly have rediscovered the Scripture in the last fifty years, and particularly in the last twenty years. But at least we're not caught in the bind that some of the fundamentalists are.
DOOR: What do you mean?
GREELEY: Well, we simply don't have trouble with modern biblical criticism. There was a little trouble in Rome at the beginning of the century,

but by and large, we're not caught in the literalistic bind that an awful lot of Protestant denominations are.

DOOR: In your articles we've read, and in hearing your comments today, we find you rather optimistic and hopeful about the Catholic church. Yet everyone we talk to says that you are a real critic of the Catholic church, and that you only see the negative.

GREELEY: I don't know where that impression came from. I have criticized the hierarchy in the church, and I've criticized the church's refusal to listen to married people regarding the importance of sex in married life. Anyone who has read my books, and God knows I've written enough of them, could not possibly think I'm negative about Catholicism. In *The Cardinal Sins*, a Jewish psychiatrist says to Kevin, his Irish-Catholic friend, "I can't figure your church out, Kevin. It's both whore and fair bride." And Kevin says, "Well, at least it's alive." The theology that the church is both whore and fair bride comes right out of the second chapter of St. Peter's epistle. So yes, I am utterly aware of the humanity of the church. Anyone who has read fifteen minutes of church history is aware of its humanity. The pretense that the church leaders of today are somehow better than Peter and the apostles is an absurd pretense. Anyone whose faith is dependent on the virtue and wisdom of church leaders has built his house on shifting sand. The pretense that the faithful's Catholicism depends on whitewashing the leadership is, I think, a contemptuous pretense.

DOOR: Uh ... we are beginning to understand why some leadership in the Catholic church might not appreciate your point of view.

GREELEY: The church, indeed, manages to act like a whore all kinds of times.

DOOR: Actually, we're beginning to understand why some of the leadership in the Protestant church might not appreciate your point of view.

GREELEY: But the church also manages to act like a fair bride. Yes, I see the whore dimensions, but I also see the fair bride. You've got to be blind not to see both dimensions of it, and I don't think there is a contradiction, yet I'm afraid an awful lot of Catholics do. They don't want the whore dimensions mentioned because they don't trust people's ability to then see the fair bride. All one has to do is read the New Testament to find out that the church leaders have always been flawed.

DOOR: Have you read any books by Robert Schuller?

GREELEY: Who?

DOOR: Never mind. It's just that it is difficult to find a balance between the beauty of the church and its flaws.

GREELEY: I must say, as someone who also knows the world of the media and the world of the academy, from the inside, the church is better than both of these and infinitely better than the government. Government, media, and the academy are much more cynical and hypocritical than the church.

DOOR: So what do people need to hear from the gospel today? What is the good news of the gospel? What do you preach about?

GREELEY: I preach almost every Sunday, and I think we need to preach what Jesus preached. God loves us. The kingdom of heaven is the kingdom of mercy in which there are all kinds of surprises. The most powerfully effective image of God is God as a lover. People today need to hear that God is a God of overwhelming grace, a God whose grace is so awesome that if humans behaved like God, they'd be thought mad.

DOOR: Knowing God loves us is very comforting, but shouldn't we challenge people as well?

GREELEY: Challenge comes easy; comfort comes hard. Jesus was good at both, but particularly good at comforting.

DOOR: Should the Catholics and Protestants get together and form one church?

GREELEY: No! No! I believe in denominational ecumenism. I believe in closer and closer relationships amongst the denominations rather than the elimination of the denominational tradition. Every time people have tried to put together a super-church in this country, it has meant more denominations rather than less.

DOOR: What would you like to say to Protestants in reference to the Catholic church?

GREELEY: Protestants should be especially aware of the pluralism of the Catholic tradition. Almost any generalization that states "Catholics do this," or "Catholics believe that," is wrong. The genius of Catholicism throughout its history is to define its boundaries as far out as possible. Protestants should try to abandon all of their simplistic notions about Catholics.

DOOR: An ever-increasing amount of people are converting to the Catholic church.

GREELEY: If someone who has been a member of a Protestant church wants to become a Catholic, I say to them, "Don't think you will stop being a Baptist. You are still a Baptist. Now you have become a Catholic *and* a Baptist. While we have something to offer you, you can bring something from your past to offer us." In the novel I'm just finishing, a couple raised in a Missouri-Synod Lutheran church comes to a Catholic priest to have their baby baptized. The priest says to them, "I won't let you stop being Lutheran, but I want you to be Catholic too." I think some Catholics would be uneasy with that, but I'm also sure that it will stand up.

MARK HATFIELD

Senator Mark O. Hatfield is a nice guy ... for a senator. The four-term Republican from Oregon is an evangelical and a liberal. Which makes him the perfect person for evangelical magazines to interview, especially on the nuclear issue, because he's the only anti-nuke evangelical anyone can think of. If people complain about Hatfield's remarks, and they usually do, the magazine can declare "evangelical immunity" (this is the process whereby the publisher denies any agreement with Senator Hatfield's remarks, but emphasizes that he is a fellow evangelical). In fact, when we went to Washington, D.C., to interview Hatfield, we had to take a number and wait behind *Christianity Today* and *Eternity*.

Like we said, Senator Hatfield is a nice guy, but we are not impressed by fancy titles and power, and we certainly were not impressed when he appeared for our interview in designer K-mart jeans. "It's my day off," he said. We felt like saying, "Yeah, sure, so that's what our tax money is going for—K-mart designer jeans." But we didn't. Hatfield opened his remarks by pointing out that he was a subscriber to the *Door*. Big deal! We didn't have the heart to point out that we *gave* him the subscription in the first place (we also didn't have the heart to tell him that the reason we gave him the subscription is so we could tell every-one else that he's a subscriber). Anyway, the Keepers of the *Door* decided that in spite of all Senator Hatfield's flaws, he did have a lot to say about the nuclear issue. We think you will find his remarks as disturbing and thought-provoking as we did.

DOOR: Why have some people been so hesitant to support a nuclear freeze?

HATFIELD: Our government has had a long-standing myopic anti-Soviet perspective.

DOOR: We're talking big words!

HATFIELD: Myopic?

DOOR: Long.

HATFIELD: Why did I agree to do this?

DOOR: We told your secretary this interview was for *Time* magazine. Seriously, you were talking about our government's attitude toward Russia.

HATFIELD: Yes. It seems that everything our government does is a reaction to the Soviet Union—a demonstration of our strength, our macho, and our anti-Communism. We seem to have this need to be assertive, but there is also the factor of fear. People are uncertain of the future. The economic problems people are facing today cause them to turn to authoritarian answers or simplistic notions offered by the government. These "answers" seem to provide people with a security blanket in the time of storm.

DOOR: Isn't much of the opposition to the nuclear freeze based on some basic illusions people have today? For example, the illusion of control—that there is someone in control; the illusion of rationality—that whoever has control of nuclear weapons will act in a rational way; and the illusion of survival—that *if* nuclear weapons were ever used, they could be controlled and the world could survive.

HATFIELD: Let's take a look at the illusions you mentioned first, then I want to add another one. First, the illusion of survival—the idea that you can begin a war with nuclear weapons and keep it limited. If the conditions are so serious that the two superpowers are confronting each other in a battle, what is the restraining force if one side feels they are losing? There is no built-in restraint. There is no check and balance. There is no evidence that once we start the use of nuclear weapons we could somehow halt before we crossed the threshold into global suicide.

Another illusion you mentioned was the illusion of rationality—that those in control of nuclear weapons will act in a rational way. We already have leaders like Khomeini and Kaddafi, and in eighteen years over sixty countries will have the capability of creating and manufacturing a nuclear weapon. Many of these countries are very primitive, have no checks and balances, and are subject to the whims of whatever irrational leaders are in power. Furthermore, the illusion of rationality really breaks down when you realize the potential of accidental launch. Within a twenty-month period our sophisticated advance warning system had over 4000 errors, 147 of which were serious enough to warn us of an impending Soviet attack. Fortunately, we have about a half hour to confirm or deny reports like that, and they were found to be false. The near preemptive weapons that both the United States and Russians are developing will only allow us six minutes to determine if the attack is for real.

DOOR: That's not very long.

HATFIELD: There may be hope for you yet. We also have to recognize that the potential for accidental launch is far greater from the Soviet side because their advance warning system is not as sophisticated as ours. If ours is sending wrong signals that frequently, what in the world is happening on the screens in the command centers of the Soviet Union?

DOOR: That thought is very encouraging. You mentioned an additional illusion.

HATFIELD: Yes. It's the illusion that nuclear weapons are just another weapon in our arsenal. The fact is most of us have little grasp of the magnitude of the weapon we're talking about. The nuclear weapon is totally distinctive from any other weapon because it can trigger the annihilation of all life on the planet. All of these illusions very strongly contribute to the Rip Van Winkle mentality that is so prevalent today, both inside and outside the church. This mentality believes that somehow, some way, all of this will just work out and good will prevail. Somehow the goodwill of the Americans and the Soviets will rise up and prevent this potential mass global suicide. Well, it is *already* beyond control. It is already beyond the control of people of goodwill because, quite frankly, our technology has outstripped our morality.

DOOR: Let's go back to the illusion of rationality. If we cannot be assured that rational minds will prevail, then wouldn't the simple reality that we have more weapons than they do at least keep them in check?

HATFIELD: That's like standing in a room waist-high in gasoline arguing over how many matches you and I have. The only defense is to make a beginning to the total abolition of nuclear weapons. As long as *any* country—superpower or minor power—has nuclear weapons, we are going to be threatened. Humanity is going to be threatened. The only ultimate answer is abolition. But, because that is not going to happen immediately, we are suggesting the freeze. Between the two superpowers we could influence the whole world, if we had but the insight, the vision, and the courage to do so. But first we have to demonstrate to the rest of the world that we are about that business ourselves. The superpowers have the ability, if they took seriously the reality that the world is on the brink of extinction, to pressure anyone who got out of line,

like Libya or Israel, to reduce their arsenals as well. But, as long as we are escalating, we are, in a sense, inviting all of the other countries of the world to imitate. Conversely, if we begin to show some rational judgment to meet this threat of human extinction, then maybe we can cause the other countries to imitate that as well.

DOOR: Ah, but some conservative Christians would say that your hope that the world would voluntarily dispose of its nuclear weapons is a wonderful ideal, but given human sinfulness, given human depravity, you must prepare for the worst.

HATFIELD: I find nothing in Scripture that says Christ died only for Americans. I don't find anything in Scripture which tells me that God's grace is limited. On the contrary, it's limitless. I find nothing in the Scripture which suggests that Christ's power of redemption is in any way circumscribed to certain cultures or certain groups. One of the unique factors of the Christian faith is that Christ died for all humankind. Christ came to redeem all humankind, and God's grace is sufficient to cover all human sin. Now, having that belief in no way blinds me to the reality of the world in which we live, a world where there is obvious sin and obvious depravity, but I am not about to put parameters on the power of spiritual renewal and spiritual rebirth, nor am I going to fall for that Constantinian Doctrine . . .

DOOR: Constantinian Doctrine?

HATFIELD: I should have known you couldn't have been from *Time*. I do not believe in the Constantinian Doctrine which holds that to influence Caesar, we have to imitate Caesar. Nor do I believe that once we Christians get our hands on the power levers of Caesar that somehow we're going to turn the world around. Some of the most heinous crimes in the history of humankind have been committed by those who thought that if they got a hold of Caesar's power, they could regenerate the world. Instead we ended up with things like the Dark Ages ... the Crusades. All I'm saying is this: In this really tough world we live in, if we do not have unlimited confidence, trust, and commitment in the power of redemption and God's grace, what hope is there? Why don't we blow our brains out now and forget about it? If I didn't trust in the power of redemption and God's grace, do you think I would stay in the Senate ten minutes longer? I have been a part of the American political system for a long time now. I know its inadequacies, I know its limitations pretty well, and if my faith were in the American political system, or any political system, for that matter, my faith would be on nothing but shifting sand. Listen, our hope is not in our armaments, nor in our economic system, nor in our technology. Our hope is in the unchangeable, eternal verity of Christ being the Alpha and the Omega of all things. Why can't we believe in the possibility that maybe the power of the gospel can be the greatest weapon of all against the Prince of this world, no matter where he resides?

DOOR: When it comes to nuclear weapons, what is the issue as you see it?

HATFIELD: Life or death. That's what the nuclear issue implies and that's the only question that all humanity faces: life or death. It is the common denominator, the fundamental, the bottom line.

Now, to me, if we choose the road which leads to ultimate extinction, that is the ultimate blasphemy. That is the highest form of obscenity humankind could express. To continue this nuclear madness is to shake our fist in the face of God and say, "We, a nation, have the right to destroy your creation!" We are challenging the Creator. It is a rebellion against God. The issue is not defending ourselves against the Soviet Union; we are rebelling against God; we are destroying God's creation. Spiritually speaking, that is blasphemous and obscene.

DOOR: So, realistically, what can one person do?

HATFIELD: Identify with the People's Movement—which is simply a grassroots reaction against politicians and governments who have lost their ability to recognize what they have created. This could be that moment in history when, as Dwight Eisenhower said, "The people and the politicians have to step aside and let the people have peace."

DOOR: In other words, support the nuclear freeze?

HATFIELD: Yes. The freeze has been misrepresented by critics as a demonstration of weakness, or as evidence of a lack of concern for the defense of America. Supporters of the freeze have been described as black spirits and do-gooders who are being manipulated by Soviet forces. All of those charges represent to me the desperate position that the pro-nuclear development people really find themselves in because they simply cannot rationally and intelligently justify their position. So people need to inform themselves—there's lots of data available, and support referendums and initiatives—and create the kind of public leverage that gets the attention of those in power. Honestly, my hope is not in the government doing something significant on this issue; my hope and trust is in the people. And if the people really want to get involved in the support of human life, then this is really their great opportunity to put their actions where their words are.

MARTIN E. MARTY

I couldn't help myself," exclaimed Ms. Toughie Durango after she slugged Dr. Martin Marty while he was staying at the posh La Jolla Cove Hotel in the wealthy resort community of La Jolla, California. Dr. Marty was being interviewed by the *Door* in the exclusive solarium room when Ms. Durango entered the room with her poodle. "I had just returned from my radical feminist ecology club meeting and was taking my poodle for a stroll when I saw *him* sitting there with that bald head glaring at me. I couldn't believe he would show his head near our beautiful coastline. I was filled with rage and the next thing I knew I was standing behind him yelling, 'James Watt, James Watt, you are ruining our country and our coastline.' The moment he turned around I knew I had made a mistake, but it was too late. My arm was already in motion . . . and I slugged him. The next thing I knew he had me in a full Nelson and was quoting long sections from Tolstoy." While Ms. Durango calmed down Dr. Marty explained, "This happens all the time, so I started watching championship wrestling to learn how to protect myself."

The *Door* was surprised that the University of Chicago Divinity School prof was so physical, but the senior editor of *Christian Century* and editor of his own *Context* newsletter said, "Hey, when you look like James Watt, you had better be physical." The following is the shocking result of our interview with Dr. Martin Marty.

DOOR: First, a personal question. What is the secret of long-lasting hair?
MARTY: I'll answer that question if you will tell me the secret of meeting publication deadlines.
DOOR: So much for personal questions. We'd like to take advantage of your historical perspective. What are some positive trends you've noticed in the church during the last few years?

MARTY: During the last fifteen years, the whole spectrum of religion in the West has experienced a revitalization of piety.

DOOR: You have to start right off with a six-syllable word, don't you?

MARTY: To put it more simply, the church has learned to put more of a premium on religious experience, and it has shown that in the middle of an often sterile, secular world, a significant minority of its people can respond to the sacred, be alert to the transcendent, and experience the love of God in Christ.

DOOR: Would you say that the church is moving from its obsession with a rationalistic, propositional understanding of faith to a more expressive, active, and nonscientific understanding?

MARTY: That was a very well-formulated question.

DOOR: Thank you.

MARTY: Who wrote it?

DOOR: Very funny.

MARTY: The answer to your question is "yes," but what is most interesting is that no social scientist in 1963 would have envisioned this move toward experience and piety.

DOOR: Excuse our ignorance, but why is this revitalization of piety so significant?

MARTY: As a historian, I can say that religion has never existed anywhere with vitality if it didn't put a premium on experience and piety. Merely to talk about the experience of the past or to interpret talking about experience in the past is the beginning of the death of religion.

DOOR: Other trends?

MARTY: We have seen a quiet rebuilding of the patterns of Christian action in the last two years.

DOOR: You see the church moving out of its period of apathy?

MARTY: I believe we overplayed Christian action and its evidences in the early sixties and we have underplayed Christian action in the seventies and eighties. When the model of street demonstrations and pronouncements became ineffective and the media lost interest, then everyone suggested that Christian action had become quiet. But there was a lot of Christian action going on before the media picked it up and there is a lot of Christian action going on now. People have found new ways of social action. There are now little movements where individuals don't worry about whether there is a bureaucracy behind them. These movements are beginning to happen more and more.

DOOR: What are some areas the church needs to work on?

MARTY: Christians need to put their energy into out-*thinking* again.

DOOR: Out-*thinking?*

MARTY: Christian laypeople should begin to bring a passion to their work and to their thought, a passion that would force other people to relate to them.

DOOR: Hasn't Francis Schaeffer called for the same thing?

MARTY: Approaches like Schaeffer's (and the other propositional evangelists) in my opinion, leave most other evangelicals cold ... to be even more honest, I think they leave the rest of the Christian world cold ... and the secular person doesn't know what they're talking about. To paraphrase my evaluation of the propositional movement, it looks like a marvelous edifice on a metaphysically condemned site. It's intricate. It's elaborate and there's an intelligence operative in its people, but they don't allow for ways of looking at reality other than their own.

The Christian investment for endowment in the human story is so deep, so rich, and potentially has so much to say. There are a billion people called by the name Christian; there should be a talent pool of people whom we should be hearing from more and more: We don't need a school or a company, we just need people with an intelligence formed by the Christian faith.

DOOR: What is keeping Christians from evidencing this passion you speak of?

MARTY: I know an awful lot of Christians who are good at what they do. Unfortunately, it doesn't occur to them to put their Christian investment into their vocation. They can't see where it fits into the current acceptable "norms" of spirituality.

DOOR: Norms? What norms?

MARTY: We've given the impression that there is only one game in town, one way to express one's faith, and if we don't have it within us to behave compatibly with those norms, then, supposedly, we are not capable of spirituality.

DOOR: And that is a tragic thing.

MARTY: Yes. We must create a broad scope for other imaginations so that those who don't have it in their gesture pattern or their mannerisms to wave their arms in the air and say, "Praise the Lord!" can express their spirituality in other ways that are just as meaningful.

DOOR: The twentieth century is not over yet, of course, but as a historian, do you have any hunches who will be recognized as having left their mark on the church?

MARTY: I don't think we'd have to stand barehanded and say the twentieth century was a spiritual "slum." Certainly this century has had more martyrdoms than any other, more persecution than any other, and more expansion than any other. We may never know the names of the people who kept something going in China, or those causing the growth of the church in Africa, or the priests in little Latin American villages who fight off oppression. In fact, I hold to the thesis that there is, in a pluralist secular world, a diffusion of talent. Because of the size and nature of the modern world, it's going to be harder to locate the people who are really doing the significant work. If you bump into a Christian down the block and ask them the most significant influence in their life, it will usually not be a book or a theologian; it will be someone they know personally.

Recently, I asked a group of ministers to jot down a code word that would remind them of five significant sermons they had heard in their life. I had them sit there for thirty minutes without anyone being able to remember five. Then I asked them to write the names of five people who had been a significant influence in their lives. It didn't take longer than half a minute for anyone. Then we pooled the names. Very few names were recognized. You see, there are some very heroic Christians out there; we just don't know who they are.

DOOR: You mean the TV evangelists, the nationally known electronic preachers, the builders of Crystal Cathedrals and medical centers that God had ordained to cure cancer . . . you mean, those folk are not the ones history will remember?

MARTY: All I'm saying is that history has a way of sorting those things out. Historians have recognized eccentric evangelists in the past ... and now they're seen as an interesting diversion.

DOOR: A few months ago you suggested in your newsletter, *Context*, that one of the main issues the church will have to deal with in the coming years is fear. Do you still believe that?

MARTY: I believe it more every day. America is finally joining the rest of the human race and is being forced to live with fear. It is not just the poor and the powerless who are experiencing fear, it is also the rich and powerful. The poor know they aren't in control and the rich, who have always lived with the illusion that they were in control, are beginning to see that illusion disintegrate.

DOOR: You mean President Reagan is not in control?

MARTY: All of us need to hear the message that God is in control. Our trust is in that reality.

DOOR: That's easy to say, but at the risk of sounding unspiritual, things are getting kind of scary out there. After all, if you can't trust Social Security, then what can you trust?

MARTY: There are good reasons to be afraid. You can't have your eyes open and not have fears.

DOOR: But there are many who would say that we don't need to be afraid, that if you read the book of Revelation, you know exactly what's going to happen.

MARTY: We cannot render the book of Revelation into a set of spectacles. The book of Revelation is not a timetable of events in the Middle East, and just because we know about Gog and Magog doesn't mean we have a "coup"

that enables us to be one up on all the others out there. I see Revelation as a very current document that can help us get through the bad times, but to make it into a crystal ball is to diminish God and his eternality.

DOOR: Another group of folk would suggest that during these times God wants us to have prosperity and success.

MARTY: We live in a culture of entitlements where people believe that God owes them instant success, instant looks, and instant prosperity. No deferred benefits exist anymore. The new test of faith is how quickly God can come through with a better income. That mentality also leads to a diminishment of God.

DOOR: How can the church counter this diminishment of God?

MARTY: We need to revivify the biblical sense of realism about death.

DOOR: You caught us off guard with that one. What do you mean?

MARTY: When times are tough it does not help to live in a world of illusion and escape. Keeping up false appearances has never been a part of the biblical message. If you gloss over fear, or the depth of evil in the world, or the misery in the world, then you have no sensitivity to the horror of our age. By making death and dying "meaningful" and "beautiful" we minimize our understanding that the new resurrection has already begun. Death is not beautiful. Biblical piety faces the horror of it, and against that background the resurrected life shines more clearly. If you live life in the shades of gray where death isn't bad, then life isn't great. Our faith lives with more radical contrasts.

DOOR: You have been a real spokesperson for the cause of "Christian humanism." Some would say that is a contradiction in terms.

MARTY: I emphatically do not believe there is a "secular humanist conspiracy." It is difficult to get any two secular humanists to agree, let alone get enough to put together a conspiracy. It is foolish to push all the "secular humanists" into a single camp where Satan and Antichrist are the master of everything they do ... because Satan and Antichrist are the masters of one side of everything *we* do. To take everyone, who for some reason or another is not marked by Christian faith, and relegate all that they do as part of Satan is neither honest nor fair.

DOOR: So you don't have any problem with someone calling themselves a humanist?

MARTY: First of all, when you talk about humanism, you have to ask, "What kind?" Humanism is always accompanied by an adjective: religious humanism, Catholic humanism, secular humanism, etc. I have been tracking humanism for the past thirty years. My doctoral dissertation was on "Free Thought and Infidelity in Secular Humanism in America." I support those who say it is worth resuscitating the term "Christian humanism," which means the accent on those elements in the faith that show God's engagement with the human world which he created, cares for, preserves, and calls us to be stewards of. All humanisms are risky, but Christian humanism is necessary to do justice to one aspect of our spiritual work.

DOOR: Is there a "Christian position" on nuclear weapons, abortion, etc.?

MARTY: I do not believe there is a "Christian position," but there is always a Christian motivation. There is no one Christian thing to do, but there

may be a Christian motivation for doing it.

DOOR: If there are no "Christian positions" and only Christian motivations, then can a church ever be prophetic?

MARTY: Two kinds of churches I do not trust: a church that is merely prophetic (one that absolutely knows the answer to everything and knows it is speaking for God) and a church that is content with culture. The church needs to be prophetic in the sense that it self-consciously sets up mechanisms which insure that it can keep hearing the word of judgment spoken against its nation and itself.

I prefer to use the word "critic." People who use the word prophet seem a little too sure they are speaking for God. Critics, on the other hand, are forced to bring their criticism under the judgment of God. Prophets speak the judgment of God, critics face the judgment of God. Prophets burn all their bridges, critics do much more open-field running and shifting of alliances. A prophet stands outside society. Prophets find it difficult to change positions; critics are more able to change and shift.

DOOR: Because you are a historian we feel obligated to ask you this question: Why should laypeople study church history?

MARTY: To get a perspective of our own time. C. S. Lewis said, "If you don't know history, you will be a victim of recent bad history." You cannot use history to predict the future, but a knowledge of history can help you make choices. In other words, if you know that, historically, we have taken a certain path often without success, then you can understand why there is no reason to take that road again.

DOOR: Dr. Marty, one final question. What is it people need to hear today from the gospel?

MARTY: In the midst of a world of cosmic flaws and trivial failures, the God who is in control has not abandoned us. With relentless patience and passion, that same God keeps pursuing us and reconstructing our possibilities, and the result is a new creation that we call the resurrection. How that can be said and greeted by yawns is beyond me. We must continue to find new ways to say that, and wherever it is said and people hear it, it does change their lives, and they change the world.

MR. FRED ROGERS

Each weekday, over seven million households in the United States, American Samoa, Guam, and parts of Canada turn on their television sets and spend thirty minutes with Fred Rogers. No one really calls him Fred. They call him "Mister Rogers," and his program has been enriching the lives of kids and adults for over a dozen years. (The target age of "Mister Rogers' Neighborhood" is three-to-seven-year-olds, but Fred has received letters from a seventy-eight-year-old lady who watches the program daily and from college students who tune in when life seems so impersonal and they need to hear someone who says with sincerity, "I like you just the way you are.") Using the reasoning so many advertisers have used ("seven million households can't be wrong"), the Keepers journeyed to Pittsburgh to interview the man behind the millions.

In his office at station WQED, we met the nicest man in the world. (He was reading the *Door* when we walked in.) Mr. Rogers asked us about our kids, gave us autographed pictures, books, and records for them, and acted like the only thing he had to do all day was talk to us. (The "Today Show" called while we were there, but he told them he couldn't talk now because he was signing pictures for some friends' kids.) He treated us like we were the most important people in the world, just like he does every afternoon on TV.

But behind the soft-spoken nice guy looms a sharp thinker who has a reason for everything he does on the air. Fred—who is now 61, has been married for 36 years, and has two adult sons, one of whom has made him a grandfather—shared these thoughts with us.

DOOR: Why have you devoted your life to helping kids? Did you feel a "call" to work with them through the media of TV?

ROGERS: I don't know whether any of us really knows the genesis of our work identity completely. I'm convinced that it starts very, very young and that it's involved in our own needs.

But I was planning on going to seminary right after college. This was in 1951. And on Easter vacation, I just sat down and looked at television. I'd already been accepted at Western Seminary, but as I looked at television, I thought it was so lamentable that I said to my family, "You know, I think maybe instead of going to seminary this year, I'll go to New York and work in television." They were dumbfounded. My mother and father said, "Why, you've rarely watched television in your life." And I said, "Yes, I know, but I've seen enough to think that this is something I should do in the world before I go to the cloisters again." I think a lot of us have so many years of education that it really is helpful to have some time apart rather than taking all those years in a line.

So I went to New York and got a job at NBC carrying coffee and coke, and I really learned an awful lot about the industry in two years there. I got to be an assistant producer and a network floor manager. I remember such things as working with Gabby Hayes. Do you remember him?

DOOR: Yes.

ROGERS: I once said to him, "Mr. Hayes, what do you think about when you see that camera and you know there are millions of children watching you?" And he said, "Freddy, I just think of one little buckaroo." That helped me immensely to look at a lens and just think of one person. It's an aggregate of all of the children that I have known as well as the child I try to get to know within myself.

People have said, "You use the television like a telephone." And I guess I do try to make it as personal and human as possible. The development of any technology, as you well know, does not insure its being used for human needs. It's only persons who can make something positive out of a new technology.

DOOR: Why did you decide to take this knowledge of television and use it with children instead of adults? And why public television instead of NBC?

ROGERS: I heard that they were going to start a public television station in Pittsburgh, and I came out and talked with the few people who were beginning it. They said, "Would you like to help us out?" And I said, "Yes, I think I would." I went back and talked with my friends at NBC and they thought I was nuts. I was in line for a directorship. My good friend Paul Bogart and I were both film editors together at that time. And Paul said, "Have you just flipped your lid?"

And I said, "No, I really feel that I want to help in this new enterprise"— which was then called educational television.

I don't know why, but practically every weekend while I was in New York, I took time off to visit day-care centers, orphanages, schools. It was probably some sort of a need to understand who I had been as well as who these kids are.

And so I came to Pittsburgh and one of the secretaries at the station and I developed a program called "The Children's Corner." I was the program manager then, but we didn't seem to have anyone around who wanted to do anything with children. So we just got a lot of free film and went on the air at 5:00 to 6:00 every day. The films would break and we would have to fill more and more time.

DOOR: Did you use the same kind of technique then as you do now in "Mr. Rogers' Neighborhood"?

ROGERS: No, I wasn't on camera at all. This girl who was the secretary talked to all these puppets. And the more times the film would break, I'd go home and find another puppet in the attic because I'd say, "We can't use Dan the Tiger for another half hour today."

DOOR: You were into puppets before that time?

ROGERS: Oh yes. I had puppets from when my sister and I were young. She's eleven years younger than I am. And I think in some ways that helped. I was kind of a surrogate father. Certainly a much bigger brother than most kids had.

But the response to "The Children's Corner" was so good that the station had to get somebody else to take care of the other programs. There were times when we would have 750 letters a day, and it was a local program. We had all volunteer help. High school kids would come after school to help us answer letters. And all the people on the air were volunteers. I was scurrying about getting people from the museums and the zoos. Emily Jacobson, a British woman who was in her sixties, became our poetry lady. She did lectures all over this country in Shakespeare and Shaw, but when she was in Pittsburgh, she would come on "The Children's Corner." And little by little, people in this town knew that this was quite a showcase. Anybody

that would come into town would end up on "The Children's Corner": Gertrude Berg, Charles Schulz, and many others.

DOOR: So you decided to go into children's TV full time?

ROGERS: It was more a kind of leading, I believe. Who would have thought that such a tiny seed would grow into such an immense plant and be able to be used by somebody?

DOOR: Everything was live and unrehearsed on the program?

ROGERS: Very live. It was superb training for later when I would have to write the Neighborhoods. But that went on for about seven or eight years. And all during that time I was going to seminary. After a year of working at QED, I decided to take a long lunch hour and take courses. I started with systematic theology and at night I studied Hebrew. And so it went. I don't know when I ever expected to graduate. But I did graduate and was ordained with a very special kind of ordination—to work with families through mass media. It was the only ordination of its kind from Pittsburgh.

And it was then that a friend of ours from Canada called and said, "I'd like you to do a daily program on CBC." So I went to the CBC and developed a fifteen-minute program. It was their idea to call it "Mister Rogers." We had a short opening and a short close and the neighborhood of make-believe in between. It was their idea that I go on camera.

DOOR: What's your strategy at the start of the program? Is there a reason behind everything you do—like putting on your sweater and tennis shoes?

ROGERS: It's a kind of transition from work clothes that says, "We're going to have a comfortable time together." This is my intent. I don't know why at the very beginning I did that. But as I analyze it, I think that's what happened. That sets the tone.

I think of the program as having different parts. The opening is the stuff that dreams are made of. We usually bring something in each day—a recorder or a telephone or a book—and I help the kids to understand the reality of these things. And yet these things invariably turn up in the neighborhood of make-believe in a part of the play. And I use "play" in a large sense of the word. We really try to encourage imaginative play. If a child can play about something, he or she already has a handle on it to deal with it. There are many kids who play doctor and nurse. A lot of that has to do with identification. If I become the doctor or the nurse, I'm the one who's doing the things to others. I don't have to be so passive and have everything done to me. At times it's scary to identify with the aggressor, but other times it's comforting. And kids are put in a good many tough positions in life.

DOOR: Do you see yourself as kind of a surrogate father in the Neighborhood?

ROGERS: I hope that I'm a support to the positive parenting that goes on at home. No electronic image can be as intuitive and as understanding as we can be. It can never take the place of a human being. But I think that we can suggest things in our dialogue with children at home. And I understand it to be dialogue. Many children answer or talk back to the set when they're involved with our program. Many people have said to me, "I wondered what you were about for the longest time till I watched with my kids. And then I began to understand." The kinds of things that we deal with seem to be things parents can take and use. Like our work with a new baby coming to a home. I think it's better not to worry about fancy terms, but instead think about the feelings of the child when the new baby arrives. As we dealt with that on the program, many parents got the notion, "Hey, that's something that can be talked about. That's something that can be dealt with." And they carried it on themselves in their own way. I don't think in any way that my work is as effective as a family's own tradition of using ideas and working them through.

DOOR: But isn't it true that this takes away from the function of the parent when you're talking about the new baby instead of them? "The baby's here; let's make sure our kid is watching this today; then we won't have to talk about it."

ROGERS: Well, I'm hoping that what we're doing is helping them to be equipped to do it, that it is an encouragement rather than a substitute. That's why when you used the word *surrogate*, that really concerned me. To explain, let me talk just a little bit about pathology. There are some children who are very sick emotionally who really cannot communicate with adults or with anybody else except through a machine. They might have to talk to their parents by using a telephone or their play is consistently with trucks. Rather than sleeping with a soft toy, they might sleep with a trike. But it's machines that occupy them.

One such child was at the Kennedy Center, and people discovered that the only time that child would talk would be when our program was on the air and I happened to be on screen. And they were smart enough to use that as a transition. Little by little, that child got over to working with the doctor. But it took a long, long time.

In your family, I would doubt very much that you would be concerned about your children using just our program and not the resources that were in the rest of the family. I don't know anybody who has abdicated their position by using the program instead.

However, I know a lot of families who wouldn't talk about such things with their kids anyway, and some families who wouldn't have been encouraged simply by seeing how a subject was approached. When we talked about babies growing inside the mommy when Prince Tuesday was about to be born, some parents resented my mentioning just that, and that was all that I mentioned. The interesting thing was that the three people who called and complained were all pregnant. They said that they did not want their children to know. And the minute our program was over that day, their children came to them, in all three cases, and said, "Are you going to have a baby?" Here's the mother wanting to hide this from the child, and she was quite angry that we had brought up the subject. Of course, it wasn't our program that did it. All we did was help the child to be more comfortable to talk about it. There are some people who still want their children to think that the stork brings the baby or that the baby grows in a cauliflower patch. But children understand a lot better. And I hope that we're helping people to become more honest and therefore more trustworthy. I feel it's a great responsibility. I always have. And that's why after my work at seminary, I started working on

a master's program in child development. I was taking a course in counseling, and the assignment was to work with one person during the semester, seeing that person once weekly. And I said, "Could I work with a child instead of an adult?" The dean who was teaching the course said, "Yes, so long as you have supervision by Dr. Margaret McFarland," who was then head of the family and children's center over at Pitt. That's how I met Margaret, and she's been our consultant for the last fifteen years. I worked with her once a week as I worked with the child once a week and gave all my observations of the child to her. That was the beginning of working one-to-one with kids in what we call "play interviews." I got so many ideas on how to approach things from that, such things as working with fire. I would never deal with fire on the program until I had dealt a whole week with the control of fluids. Because we know children's fantasies and dreams about fire often have as their root the control of urine. And it's such things as this that form an understandable background. When we dealt in our make-believe world with a factory burning down, we had a father call from Boston who said his little girl was never going to watch our program again because she was so terribly terrified. I said, "Did it have to do with this week dealing with the factory fire?" He said, "Yes." As we talked, very gently, I tried to find out if she had any difficulty with toilet training. I said, "Has your daughter ever had any urinary difficulties?" And he said, "Why would you ask that?" I said, "I'm just very interested in children's concerns." And he said, "Well, as a matter of fact, she's had chronic urinary difficulty since she's been two." I said,

"Well, I bet she's had some mighty painful examinations."

"Yes, she's always talked about how burning they were." We talked two or three times thereafter, and that child, after a few weeks with that family's added understanding about her fluid, came back to watching the Neighborhood again. But what was much more important was how they were in touch with the child.

DOOR: Do you have a lot of contacts like this with people who watch your program?

ROGERS: We do. It happens mostly by mail. But there are people of all ages who write to us. There's a woman in Corvallis, Oregon, who writes once a week. She's seventy-eight years old. There's a woman in Chicago who writes every month. And that's one reason why I'd like to do some work for older people. Grandparents and people of the grandparent generation are so important to kids. And I think kids are important to them.

DOOR: Why is a seventy-eight-year-old attracted to your program?

ROGERS: I think that she feels needed in the kind of thing that we're doing. The first time she wrote to us, she was telling about herself and her days as a teacher. When we responded, we were encouraging to her and supportive of who she was and who she had been and who she continued to be. People long to be needed. And they long to be respected. And this is what I hope comes through in the Neighborhood. I end the program in some form or another with, "You make this day a special day by just being you. There's only one person in the whole world like you. And I like you just the way you are."

DOOR: Your program seems to be vastly different from many other children's programs. It's not so fast paced. It doesn't concentrate on numbers and letters. Would you comment on that?

ROGERS: I don't feel that you can separate affective from cognitive learning. Cognitive learning comes about only through our being able to receive it, and how can we receive "facts" except through a comfortable integrative process? I come through the door every day on the Neighborhood and go from left to right. Every time I show something, it's ordinarily from left to right. That to me is just as much reading readiness as teaching the alphabet. Children pick that up very, very quickly when the time is right.

And I'm not fast paced. A friend of mine once said, "You know, you're the only person in the world who would have dared to take three minutes on television to fill up an aquarium with water." Well, kids are fascinated, and their inner urge at the moment is to control their own body fluids. They are fascinated to see that fluids can stay in a container. You really have to know the developmental needs of your audience. Otherwise, I don't think you're a responsible communicator.

I've done a lot of work on "You Can Never Go Down the Drain." Because at two, many kids are very concerned when whoosh, the water sucks down, that they may go down too. I have seen cartoons that have people going down the drain. These are obviously animators or producers who have not dealt with that concern themselves. What they're doing is spewing out their own unresolved childhood fantasies on millions of kids. That is not funny.

And adults falling down stairs and

dropping things is not funny to kids. They may laugh, but they laugh in a very anxious way because it hasn't been too long since they learned to walk upright themselves. When they see adults falling, they wonder if that's in store for them later. So we really do have to be very serious and understanding of the progressive inner urges of the growing human being as we program for them.

DOOR: What's wrong with children's television today?

ROGERS: I think it's much wider than children's television. I think we have to look at how we present people on television, because children watch much more than children's television and they're looking to see how adults solve problems. And if you take any night of network television and look at it, you'll see what I consider a distorted view of adult problem solving. It's certainly a very unhealthy view, and kids see that.

Television is really part of the extended family now in people's homes. It's right in the living room. Young children don't really know if the family approves or disapproves of what is on that piece of furniture. All they know is that mother and father bought it, brought it in there, and set it in the middle of the living room. And how are they to know that it really does or doesn't reflect the family tradition?

When the hero is faced with a problem on evening television, usually what happens is that he annihilates the problem. It's rarely worked out in a humane way. People rarely talk out their troubles.

The Waltons is a much better example of some people working through difficulties. The world just cannot exist with the overriding view that if you don't agree with somebody, you just finish him off. And that's what a lot of television is telling children. Now there are things on TV that are of immense value. That's why you just can't say that the technology is bad. We're back to the persons who program it.

DOOR: How is the church doing, in your estimation, with the education of kids?

ROGERS: I have a rather limited knowledge. I know what we're doing at Sixth Church, and I think that it is great. Kids come and feel accepted. I don't know how many churches, for instance, have water play for pre-schoolers. But if they're courageous enough to have it, I think it says a great deal to those children about what the church is. I don't know how many churches have times when the children are allowed to play about such themes as the jealousy of the new baby. I don't know how heavy the pounding of the super-ego is for kids. I don't know that because I haven't visited hundreds and hundreds of churches. But those that I do know seem to realize that part of their ministry is to understand what kids are going through. I don't think that that was true a number of years ago. Kids were simply something to be molded.

DOOR: Do you take an active part in the pre-school program at your church?

ROGERS: Sometimes. An old seminary friend of mine who is now a college professor is the head of the group, and sometimes I go with him.

Another thing that we've done together is to set up a facility within some prisons where young children come to visit. We discovered that some very young children were coming with their mothers to visit their fathers at

Western Penitentiary—a maximum security prison. These visits lasted between four and six hours and all the kids had to play with were the vending machines along the one wall of the visiting room. And you know what would happen with that child with that much time? It would be a deterrent to the family's visiting. All the kids would do is get very bad vibrations from the parents because they weren't sitting still. A child of that age can't sit still four to six hours. Who can? So what we did was get the prison to give up one corner of the visiting area. We got it carpeted and put in appropriate child furniture.

Now Jim teaches a child development class there in the prison. His class members have become the monitors for this play area for kids. Now there might be fifteen to twenty children there every day, and they will be with two play monitors who are inmates themselves. And it's had a very interesting effect on the prison. There are some men who have said, "I wouldn't have thought of talking to him (meaning another inmate), but now that he's taken such good care of my kid, we've got something in common." Others have said that their work with children was the most humanizing facet of their entire time in prison. They were able to be in touch with kids in a meaningful way. Those kids are sharing a lot of stuff with them. Because they're not having an easy time of it, as you can well imagine.

DOOR: We know that you don't see yourself as a guru telling parents how to raise children, but could you give us some suggestions you've picked up over the years on how to be more effective as a parent?

ROGERS: The first thing that I'd say is that there isn't anybody more important in a child's life than his or her parents. I think that the experts in many ways have done a disservice to parents. Many parents have been afraid to be who they really are with their kids, and that is the most important thing. The insights that those of us who have studied child development can give are important, I don't deny that. But if a mother or father who's just been delivered a baby can realize that he and she has a supreme chance to grow in a relationship to this new growing human being, and if they can take that opportunity to grow, that to me seems to be the happiest combination of parenting and growing up. Because as your child grows, your own feelings of what it was like to be a child are re-evoked and you have a new chance to deal with them. And in a way, you know your child has an added amount of value for you just by his or her own natural growing in your midst. I think Jesus learned a great deal from children. I certainly know I do.

DOOR: Why do you think you learn more than other people? We listened to Dennis Benson's taped interview with you and it seems that you're able to grab more insights than the average person regarding kids. With Dennis, you talked about why kids love Band-Aids—because "they keep you in." When you have a hole in your skin, you're afraid that you'll run out all over. And as we listened to that tape we said, "Yeah, that's right. That's why kids really like Band-Aids." But how do you pick that up?

ROGERS: I guess it's from hearing over and over and seeing over and over through play what a child's concerns really are. I've watched how children put on one bandage after another on a baby doll, and through their play they tell you so much. I'm afraid we all talk too much. It's hard to listen, but boy, when you listen you learn. That's why I feel frustrated sometimes with interviews, because I would like to learn from you.

HOWARD A. SNYDER

In 1975, Howard A. Snyder (the A. is to distinguish him from all other Howard Snyders who occupy planet Earth) wrote a revolutionary book, *The Problem of Wineskins*. It advocated, of all things, that the church minister to the poor like the Bible tells it to do. The book also contained other specific suggestions regarding ministry and mission and grabbed the attention of evangelical readers. It sold over ten copies.

Before writing the best-seller, Howard A. had served as a pastor in Detroit and a missionary in Brazil for six and a half years. He had also addressed the World Congress on Evangelism at Lausanne, Switzerland, on the nature of the church.

Today he is both associate director of the D. Min. program and associate professor of church renewal at United Theological Seminary in Dayton, Ohio. His recent books include *Liberating the Church: The Ecology of Church and Kingdom* and *Signs of the Spirit: How God Reshapes the Church.*

The *Door* decided to interview Howard A. because of the inflammatory things he had said to the church about mission. The Keepers alerted the San Diego Storm Troopers in 1977 that a radical was about to enter southern California for an interview. But the warning was unnecessary. The then thirty-seven-year-old Snyder arrived with a briefcase, and the establishment-oriented Keepers felt at home.

Here are Howard A.'s thoughts.

DOOR: What is the role of the missionary?

SNYDER: The primary role of a missionary is to build the church. That act involves both evangelism and other kinds of ministry.

DOOR: There is a feeling today that the missionary should be actively involved in changing the political structure of the country. Others say the missionary should stay out of politics.

They say the function of a missionary is to deal with people's lives individually rather than institutionally.

SNYDER: That is obviously a false dichotomy. The role of the missionary is to bring people to a knowledge of Christ and into a functioning body of Christ. This, in particular, leads to an identification with the poor, which lays the groundwork for the church *really* to be the Body of Christ. Identifying with the poor is political action in the sense that it brings people into a new social reality. But identifying with the poor also lays the base for evangelism, political engagement, or other kinds of church ministry.

DOOR: Those results don't seem to be a natural outgrowth of the North American church. What's going to keep the missionary church from being any different from those in North America?

SNYDER: The fault of the missionary church is the same as the fault of the church in North America: we have too superficial a concept of discipleship. We are content merely to see people won to Christ if it's in a conservative evangelical framework. We're concerned only with the faith transaction. The failure of the church here and consequently in lands that have been affected by North American missionary outreach has been a failure to follow through on the commands of Christ, because if we take seriously what Jesus said discipleship means, Christians will be led into the kinds of ministry that are socially transforming.

DOOR: Is it possible for a missionary under the present missionary structure to do what you are talking about?

SNYDER: There are a lot of missionary structures. It would depend on which one you were under. I would say that under the majority of missionary structures as they have grown up in North America or in Western Europe, it is very difficult. But there are exceptions.

DOOR: Why do missionaries from these structures have such a difficult time?

SNYDER: The answer depends on your time frame. I suppose we're basically talking about Protestant missionary agencies that have grown up in the last 100 years. They had a very difficult time distinguishing what the gospel is from a biblical standpoint from the cultural baggage the missionary carries with him. Only recently has that problem been identified in a significant way and it's now being clarified by voices from the Third World as well. Coming with that, of course, is not only changes in missionary structures as we know them in the Western world, but also new missionary structures in the Third World. Now the Third World is even sending missionaries to other lands.

But most missions have been the extension of North American or Western European churches, which grew out of a culture that once adhered to the whole concept of Christendom. The church was allied with culture to the extent that the critical question of distinguishing between the two wasn't raised. The Reformation was incomplete at this point. And I think part of the contemporary revival of interest in the anti-Baptist wing of the church is really saying that only the anti-Baptist wing of the church raised these questions at the time of the Reformation, but were largely smothered.

DOOR: Many people have a view of the missionary as a person out in the middle of the jungle living in a special mission compound. How accurate is that view today?

SNYDER: Well, even if that doesn't exist physically, it still exists in mentality, I'm afraid. Among a good many missionaries from the Western world, there is what I would call a "compound mentality" in which a person has a genuine love for the person of another country, and will profess that love, yet when you probe, you discover that there is still a kind of "we/they" mentality. It takes a real conscious identification of that problem to overcome it, and I don't think it is being overcome nearly to the extent that it ought to be. I could see that even in our work in Brazil. Missionaries were going out from the rather sheltered American subcommunity they were in, ministering to the Brazilians, and then coming back to the subcommunity. It was true in my own experience to the point that I was becoming uncomfortable with that.

DOOR: Was that why you left the mission field after six and a half years?

SNYDER: That was a factor. I had a growing discomfort with my role vis á vis the Brazilians. I also sensed the ministry that God wanted me to have to use my spiritual gifts, and I felt the ministry I was in was not the place to exercise that kind of ministry. There were other factors having to do with further education and so on.

DOOR: What good are missionaries if they have a "compound mentality"?

SNYDER: In the first place there are obviously missionaries who overcome that. Secondly, even if that is not overcome, you still have down through history and even today people who are genuinely touched in some way by the gospel. In the light of that, the church is born and grows, even though it may

not have the fidelity or the authenticity that we would like to see. Beyond that is the fact that these issues are being identified, they are being wrestled with, and here and there we are seeing genuine endeavors to overcome that whole kind of mentality and to minister in more authentic ways.

But let's go back to this idea of the compound mentality. A lot of it has to do with the problem of American racism. If a missionary has not dealt with racism in his own personality before going to the field, he operates in such a way to make the "we/they" mentality almost inevitable. No one can grow up in the U.S. without some degree of racism and racist mentality. If that isn't consciously brought out and consciously dealt with, these same attitudes will be transferred to another culture subconsciously.

DOOR: How do you take racism out of a person? Obviously one week of jungle training is not going to do it.

SNYDER: The first thing to do is to identify racism. It has to be brought out as a problem. We have to be able to recognize that it exists, and that in itself is the biggest part of the battle. We can only do that as we allow Scripture and those who have dealt with this problem to speak to us. Secondly, racism can only be dealt with if we are a part of a community where we are growing spiritually through the actual practice of learning to overcome the barriers that divide us.

DOOR: Besides racism, what other weaknesses do you see?

SNYDER: I think the greatest problem, the greatest weakness, and the greatest danger of the North American missionaries and the North American enterprise in general is the affluence of the Western missionary. The problem with the Western missionary is either he has to commit himself to a lifestyle that is more in keeping with the people he is ministering to (assuming that he is ministering to people who are economically less advantaged, which is normally the case), or else he must find some way of maintaining his old lifestyle and yet authentically communicating the will of Christ. And that means communicating over a barrier which is not a biblical barrier. That points back to one of the basic problems of the North American church: its insensitivity to its own affluence compared to the affluence of other countries.

DOOR: After a church is started and thriving in the Third World, is a missionary still needed?

SNYDER: There is an interesting debate going on about these things. The interesting thing is that we seldom refer back to Scripture in our debate. We may bring in sociological or anthropological insights but we use few biblical insights. When we look into the New Testament we see Paul and others planting a church and staying in that location long enough to help the people not only experience what it is to know Jesus Christ as their personal Savior but some dimensions of the discipleship required by the demands of Christ. That may mean a few weeks or up to a period of two years in the case of Paul. Two primary roles of a missionary in that regard (and really they're all part of one role) are introducing people to Christ and then introducing them to the demands of discipleship. In that process leadership will emerge. Discipleship is the source of leadership, and as leadership emerges there is no further need for

the missionary—at least in that role. Now as a church becomes autonomous and matures, it may need a particular function which a person from another location (whether it is North America or whatever) may bring. But that is a secondary maintenance role.

DOOR: Like what? Give a function.

SNYDER: Technical areas such as helping develop some sort of agriculture specialty. It might be water projects or medical help.

DOOR: But don't many missionaries have a difficult time accepting a secondary maintenance role? They have more of a paternalistic attitude: "These are my people, I started it, and I'm going to stay here until I retire."

SNYDER: Roland Allen identified that precise problem many years ago in some of his books. His argument was that such an attitude is caused essentially by a failure on the part of the missionary to have confidence in the Holy Spirit, to believe that the Holy Spirit can guide that infant church as effectively as he can guide the missionary. It is very easy to have that kind of feeling, because a missionary has prepared for the role and has been used by the Lord to plant a church. A missionary feels indispensable for the ongoing life of that church.

DOOR: What countries are strategic today?

SNYDER: A person could make a case for any number of countries being strategic, but I would start by mentioning China. Obviously the size of population is one reason, but beyond that is the fact that here is a land where the church has been totally severed from its connections with and its dependence upon the Western institutional church and Western models. It has had to develop under the totalitarian regime of Communism. And I think in that process the church has been purified. In the future, if and when the free flow between China and the rest of the world is reopened, this area of the world will teach us a great deal about what it means to be the church today.

Another strategic area is Brazil. I consider Brazil strategic for several reasons. First, economics. There is a large population of over 100 million, but the country has space so they don't feel the problems of overpopulation. From an economic standpoint this is significant because it means here is just about the only country in Latin America with the opportunity or the possibility of becoming a mass market. Rapid economic expansion has produced an economic growth over the past ten years that has been phenomenal. Tie that in with the growing influence of the evangelical church's spiritual renewal and Brazil could produce leadership in the world that would be significant for decades, particularly if the traditional world leaders decline and Brazil acquires nuclear capability.

DOOR: Do you see Communism as a major force to be reckoned with?

SNYDER: The crucial issue before the Third World and almost equally before the rest of the world is what is going to be done with the technological revolution. If Third World countries fall to Communism or are under communist domination, they are essentially going to fall under a communist technological state. If they don't, then they are essentially going to fall under some kind of a Western technological state. In any case it is going to be a state where technology is combined with spiritual forces to produce the

kind of a culture which is to me the very antithesis of the kingdom of God and to a large degree is the embodiment of the kingdom of Satan.

DOOR: Amplify that.

SNYDER: The great challenge confronting the church right now and the strategy of the kingdom of evil is the marriage of technology with the occult or spiritual forces. The paradigm of this is Nazi Germany. Think of how technology was used in Nazi Germany in propaganda, in the elimination of the Jews, in warfare, in the beginning of the missile age. And all this was combined with the whole mythology of racism, Hitler's interest in astrology, and so on. So you have the combination of technology and for lack of better terms spiritism which can happen and is happening in many places. This can have a tremendous impact because you are taking the technological complex and making it sacred, which makes it almost impossible to consider the claims of Christ.

DOOR: One of the big reasons given for Christian missions to move into the Third World is competition with Communism. The Communists have their areas, the Western world has theirs, and the Third World is wide open. We have got to break in there and do the job. How do you respond to that kind of mentality?

SNYDER: I would object to that. The Christian perspective is to see *every* land as a mission land including our own in the sense that there is nowhere in the world where the gospel has penetrated as deeply as it was intended to penetrate. There is infidelity in the church wherever the church is found so that whether we're talking about an area of millions of people who have no contact with the gospel or whether we're talking about Western Europe we are still talking about a missionary situation. Our concern should be to define what kind of a missionary witness we should have in various lands given the realities of each of these situations. It becomes our task to study the reality of any land that we would consider as an actual or a potential location for missionary activity and then ask what is the genuine Christian presence and what is genuine Christian proclamation in that context.

DOOR: Let's take Brazil for example. What would you say would be the genuine Christian presence?

SNYDER: One of the greatest needs of the Brazilian church is the same need of the North American church: to see the true dimensions of Christian citizenship. They must realize that to be a Christian means transcending nationality or adherence to any particular group. Christianity means a commitment to the lordship of Jesus Christ that calls into question our loyalty to any particular political system. The problem with so much of the evangelical church in Brazil as I understand it, is that it is not sufficiently critical of its own culture, which simply reflects the mentality of the churches that have been sending over missionaries. So not only do we have values imported from outside the culture, but those values ally themselves with developments within the country of Brazil. With the growth of the economy and the growth of the middle class, we are in danger of the Protestant church in Brazil simply being a middle-class church taking on middle-class values and therefore not really radically identifying itself with the masses or with the poor. This is happening to a great degree, with the

Pentecostal movement being something of an exception to that. But the pentecostal movement hasn't yet developed sufficient self-consciousness and an attitude of self-criticism to guard itself against the danger of simply growing into this middle-class mentality.

DOOR: What about the political realities of Brazil? If you believe the press, there seems to be a great deal of repression.

SNYDER: You can quite convincingly and truthfully state almost two different cases for the reality in Brazil. If a person is a Brazilian and is leading a "normal life" and doesn't involve himself in politics to any degree, he is not living in a repressed situation. In many ways he can carry on a life which would be very similar to what is going on here, particularly if he is a professional person or if he is involved in education. There is a growing Brazilian middle class that is very similar to what we know here, and as long as a member of that class remains apolitical, he's in very little danger. However, political activity is very carefully scrutinized. The moment a Brazilian person involves himself in political activity he may not be squelched, but he immediately comes under surveillance.

DOOR: Then it seems that a missionary couldn't be honest with the people and say that Christianity means you are going to be involved in changing these structures. Because the minute a missionary does that he is going to be in trouble and the people he talks to are going to be in trouble. Missionaries seem to have their hands tied, don't they?

SNYDER: To go back and reemphasize what I said earlier, if a missionary will identify with the poor, he will be doing something that is of tremendous political significance. As the gospel penetrates, large numbers of people will come into a loyalty to Jesus Christ which will challenge every other loyalty. That becomes political dynamite. I think there is some degree of recognition of this even on the part of the Brazilian government. Witness the fact that some missionaries have been arrested for nothing more than identification with the poor. Such missionaries did no political organizing but worked alongside the poor, spending time with them, helping them with their needs. If a missionary is faithful to the gospel in that sense, he is constantly in danger of running afoul with the authorities. But I don't see the missionary's role as coming from outside the culture to attempt to change social structures directly in political activity. That may be the role of some of the Christians who are citizens of that culture.

DOOR: Then you don't think the missionary is there to agitate?

SNYDER: No.

DOOR: Do you think that if missionaries concentrate on the poor, the upper and middle class will also be reached?

SNYDER: Definitely. As the poor, the masses, come to know Jesus Christ and have loyalty to him, the leaven of the gospel begins to work and transformation takes place within those people.

I would want to avoid any suggestion that we should preach the gospel to these people so that they can come up into the middle class. But I would, on the other hand, call attention to the reality of what the gospel does among people. If we effectively teach the gospel to the poor, we will be affecting

all, permeating the whole culture. There are all kinds of precedents around the world to illustrate the fact that if we concentrate on the upper class or the middle class, we find it very difficult to penetrate to the poor. We see that obviously to a great degree in churches here in this country. The middle-class church incarnates values which they don't see as affecting the poor, but which in fact from the standpoint of the poor, close the door to any effective kind of communication.

DOOR: Why do you feel so strongly about ministering to the poor?

SNYDER: It began to some degree with the influence of Dr. Gilbert James at seminary and of course with my involvement in an urban church in seminary. But that only planted the seeds. The thing that clinched it for me was reading through the whole Scripture, noting every reference concerning the poor. Then I went back and reflected on that, and I was immediately struck by the whole strata of the Scripture that I had never heard. About the same time, others began saying the same things, and that helped me clarify what some of the dimensions of that were.

DOOR: But do you really believe that a missionary who comes from the richest country can identify with the poor? Will they accept him?

SNYDER: A missionary (and of course I speak principally out of my experience in Brazil) even without shedding a lot of the trappings of North American culture can achieve a certain degree of acceptance among the people. But in a sense that is also where the danger lies. A missionary can be very careful not to consciously bring any Western cultural baggage and yet in fact he is living on the same standard that he maintained in the U.S. Whether he realizes it or not, he is communicating the message to those people that somehow becoming a Christian means achieving those kinds of values. It is very difficult to overcome that unless he makes some kind of a conscious decision to identify himself with the poor and live on the same standard as the people he is ministering to. This was exactly the point that I was beginning to come up against in my own experience in Brazil. I guess I took the easy way out because I left rather than following through what the implications of that might have been.

DOOR: If you go with your family to the mission field and try to live at the same standard as the people, doesn't that subject your family to a great deal of strain? Isn't it more effective to have a "short-term missionary style" with a single person or married couple?

SNYDER: I don't know of anyone who has really showed us the answer to that question. It is a question which I am convinced the North American church is going to have to face. However, I think there are two or three things that could be said about that. One is the youth missionary movements. Youth are able to make this adaptation. Maybe many others of us will have to learn how to do that too, but they are ready, willing, and able to do that. This is why I think that this kind of movement is significant. Secondly, Protestantism has so reacted against celibacy in the Roman Catholic church that we have undervalued or underestimated the value of the celibate missionary, and we may need to reaffirm that celibacy is one of the gifts of the Spirit and recognize the fact that many of the most effective missionaries down through history have been celibate.

DOOR: We have heard of a seminary in Costa Rica connected with Latin American missions that is doing an excellent job.

SNYDER: I'm familiar with it only secondhand. I consider it to be probably the most significant center of education and theological reflection within the evangelical fold (realizing that the term "evangelical" doesn't have as much meaning in Latin America as it does here).

DOOR: Why is it so significant?

SNYDER: The Latin American Mission was probably one of the first of the North American mission agencies to say that "the people to whom we are ministering are people who are speaking to us through God, and therefore we need to share leadership and bring people other than from the United States into the whole structure." From that, significant spokesmen and leaders for the church from Latin America in theology and evangelism and theological education have emerged. They are helping the North American church look at issues in missiology and issues in theology from a perspective using different categories than what we have traditionally used in North America. This represents an influence that is going to be helpful for the North American church and the Christian church around the world. The fertility that is there, the intellectual acumen, the education, is speaking to the rest of the church now.

DOOR: What are some of the problems of interpreting the gospel to non-Western cultures?

SNYDER: The basic problem, of course, is distinguishing between what is essentially biblical and what is cultural. The great advantage that we have as Christians and as missionaries is the fact that the Bible is not a product of Western culture. We have tended because of the Western mentality to systematize the Scripture or rather to place a system on the Scripture, to see Scripture basically as a book of doctrines. What we are beginning to learn partly, I think, from the people of the Third World is to look at the Scriptures in a somewhat different way—not so much as a repository of doctrine (although it does contain truths that we can state in propositions), but more in terms of the history of how God has dealt with humanity. We think of the story of the redemptive plan through the people of Israel and culminating in Jesus Christ and the development of the church.

DOOR: Could you list some specific things that the Third World is teaching us?

SNYDER: One thing particularly that we're learning from Latin American theology is that the gospel is inevitably political. We have to learn how to interpret what that means and test what we are hearing on the basis of Scripture just as anyone does. We are also learning more about the nature of the church as community. That is emerging in the Western world too, but I think we're hearing it especially from Third World countries and less in terms of theory and more in terms of practice.

DOOR: What else would you like to say to our readers?

SNYDER: I consider North America to be a very significant land in the whole missionary picture for two reasons. One is because we continue to have in the U.S. thousands of students from other lands who will compose to a large extent the leadership of other countries when they return. This means a missionary opportunity and a missionary responsibility on the part of the church. It provides the opportunity for missionary witness in terms of less expense. The other reason I see North America as being significant is the fact that I think we have a lot to learn from the Third World churches about the dimensions of discipleship. In connection with that, we need to recognize that the leadership of the church is increasingly going to pass from the Western world to the Third World, and we need to be ready for that. There is the new dynamic of the gospel wrestling with the questions raised by a different culture. I think the Western world and the church in the Western world is in decline. In the fourth to tenth centuries, you had the church of Jesus Christ which was principally Roman and Greek passing into the European tribes so that Rome collapsed but the church continued. Now, with the leadership shift, I think something parallel to that is going to happen. We're going to see the eclipse and the decline of Western and traditional communist countries and the rise in the church in the Third World paralleling in some degree the rise in the political sphere of the Third World nations.

DOOR: But as these other countries develop, they become Westernized, don't they? How is Brazil going to be different from the United States in forty years?

SNYDER: This is the danger. This is why the picture in Brazil is not unambiguous. The potential is there either for a great influence for good or for evil and it will depend on how much the church is faithful to the gospel. Much of the church in Brazil is not noticeably more faithful to the gospel than it is in the U.S., but the possibilities for recovery of radical discipleship are more likely in Third World countries than they are here.

DOOR: Can a country moving towards Westernization be radical disciples?

SNYDER: The church will face the same option and the same temptation in the Third World that it faces here: either to baptize technology and say we can use this for the church, or to say that there is something potentially evil in technology, and therefore the church must take a stand that is not dehumanizing but radically biblical, radically incarnational, and builds authentic Christian communities based on the liberating work of the gospel of Jesus Christ. The church has that option. If in the Third World the church is not radically biblical, it will succumb to these forces and it will betray the gospel just as has happened to a large degree in the Western world.

DOOR: Do you feel hopeful about the mission movement?

SNYDER: Depending on what data you want to look at, you can build a very optimistic or a very pessimistic case. In terms of sheer numbers, we are going to see substantial numbers of Third World missionaries being sent to other places in the Third World as well as North America, Western Europe, and communist worlds. While this is encouraging, the fundamental question which doesn't lend itself to as optimistic an answer is: to what degree will these Third World churches as well as the North American churches and the communist world churches be radically and authentically biblical? To what degree are they going to maintain adherence to the authority of Scripture and to what degree are they going to put into practice the demands of discipleship that Jesus Christ teaches? That I think is a very ambiguous situation and one that is thrown back on the total dependence or total confidence in God's sovereignty and the triumph of the kingdom of God. But we don't have too much ground for optimism. We are going to see the emergence of Africa as a Christian continent if present trends continue. Within a few decades, Africa will be more Christian than any continent in the world, if you are talking about people who consider themselves members of the Christian church. Whether that is going to mean authentic Christianity or not in terms of doctrine and even more in terms of practice is really the big question.

DOOR: It seems that when Christianity grows and becomes popular, you lose that authenticity.

SNYDER: The church is always in need of renewal. The church is always in need of missionary work to itself— listening to the Word. Of course, any time the church begins to groan under the weight of institutionalism, the hardening of the wineskins begins to take place and requires a rediscovery of the reality of the wine of the gospel and the attendant new wineskins that have to come with it.

JOHN CLAYPOOL

John Claypool, fifty-eight, is a good old southern boy who doesn't look like your average redneck. His southern roots run deep (his great grandparents owned slaves in Mississippi), he speaks with an occasional agricultural expression ("I had about milked the coconut dry"), he loves country music, he has pastored Southern Baptist churches, but he looks like Wall Street in his gray, pin-striped, three-piece suit.

And he speaks so softly that you're forced to listen— something more people should do. Because John Claypool has a lot to say regarding ministry, fatigue, the church, the South, grief, and probably a host of other subjects the *Door* Keepers did not have time to ask him questions on.

Claypool grew up in Nashville, Tennessee. His heritage was and is Southern Baptist. "My family primarily let that be the cultural endeavor of their lives. Visiting kin folks and going to church were the two things I did besides going to school.... My heritage gave me what I call 'a religious feel' for life."

At the age of ten, he became a doubter when a new boy moved into the neighborhood. John told his new neighbor that he was going to church and the kid answered, "My daddy says that anyone who believes in God is a fool." John says, "I remember very

vividly that night thinking to myself, 'How do you know there is a God? The only reason you know is because your parents say so. And here is this kid doing the very same thing you are— that is, doing what his parents think, and he's coming out on the other end of the conclusion.'"

The church didn't help him deal with his doubts until he attended Southern Baptist Junior College and was exposed to an intellectual interpretation of Christianity. He was also introduced to C. S. Lewis. "And toward the end of my sophomore year, I really did have my first recognizable religious experience. It came in the form of a real flash of insight that Jesus was the clue to the ultimate reality for me. That whatever the mystery was like, that here was a face that really did authenticate itself to me."

From Southern Baptist College, John migrated to Baylor University and then on to the Southern Baptist Seminary in Louisville, Kentucky.

While in seminary, he pastored two smaller churches. After receiving his doctorate, he served as an assistant in Atlanta, where he met and worked with Martin Luther King, Jr. Two years later, he returned to Louisville and pastored Crescent Hill Baptist Church for eleven years. During this time, John took a very active part in civil rights. It was also during this ministry that his eight-year-old daughter died. His book, *Tracks of a Fellow Struggler,* came out of this intensely painful experience.

From Crescent Hill, John moved to Broadway Baptist in Fort Worth, Texas, a congregation of five thousand members. He survived for five and a half years and then did an unheard-of thing in ecclesiastical circles: he voluntarily moved to a smaller church in Jackson, Mississippi.

John added another unheard-of thing to his resumé in 1985: he left the Convention and enrolled in the Episcopal Seminary of the Southwest because, in his words, "the Baptist coat was too narrow a fit." He is now rector of St. Luke's Episcopal Church in Birmingham, Alabama, and author of six books, including *Glad Reunion* and *Opening Blind Eyes.* The Keepers flew to Jackson on a Sunday afternoon back in 1975 and interviewed the good doctor in a rundown hotel room.

DOOR: What pushed you into the ministry?

CLAYPOOL: There were three things I can separate out. First, there was that God-hunger that had always been with me from my Southern Baptist upbringing. Second, the religious experience I had at junior college brought some clarity that Jesus really was the clue. That was very meaningful to me. Third, I was very idealistic; I wanted my life to count for something. I wanted to leave this world a better place.

I had an old doctor who cared for me all my life who would come to our house. And I remember saying to him one time, "I'd really like to be a doctor because you can help people so tangibly." He was not a religious man at all and his reply was, "Hell, what people need is someone to teach them how to live. I've got jillions of patients who are perfectly healthy but are miserable because they don't know what to do with it." And that really did make sense to me—the idea that I could be the most help possible by teaching people how to live. That converged toward my thinking that the ministry was the best avenue to do that.

But there's another factor and this is pretty personal. Like most children, I had always wanted my Mother's blessing more than anything else in the world. But she was not the kind of person that could ever give that kind of blessing because she never did like herself and therefore she had trouble ever liking the way anything was. To her everything should be different or changed. So all my life I grew up with this anxiety that mother was not pleased with me. I wouldn't have put it in those terms then, but I know now that that was what I was looking for.

And I now know that one of the reasons for my going into the ministry was the hope that by doing so I would earn her blessing, because the church was the only thing that mattered to her. She could not have cared less about society, politics, and other areas. I remember writing my folks that I was going to begin to take a pre-ministerial course. I remember very vividly thinking as I sealed the envelope, "Now I've done it; I have at last paid the price that is going to bring me the blessing." To make a long story short, I didn't get it. The minute I went into the ministry my mother then began to dictate to me what kind of minister I'd have to be to be okay, and I never was. I never measured up. The last thing she said to me on the subject about three weeks ago was "You ought to go into the Episcopal Church. You know you're not a Baptist. You're too liberal."

That whole experience has helped clarify for me what grace is and how we are finally accepted. It is either given to us finally, or it doesn't come at all. My mother is not grace to herself; therefore she simply doesn't have it in her to give to anybody else. I have finally let her off the hook; I have finally stopped demanding that she give me something that she doesn't have in her. Once I did that I found that I had been graced by other people. My father has two sisters who were not religious at all, but they were simple, loving, warm, affirming human beings. Whenever I was around them, grace just sloshed out of them without any effort. When I was wanting it from my mother, I was actually getting it from these other sources. When I finally got to the place where I said, "I'll take it wherever I can get it and it doesn't all have to come from one

place," then I found I had been graced. I sensed then that God's acceptance and grace are simply things that he gives out of what he is and not out of what I am or where I am performance-wise. My agony of trying to earn my mother's blessing actually contributed to my coming to understand what grace is and how we come to accept it.

In the sixties when everyone was leaving the ministry for the Peace Corps, I called up all of these questions of God-hunger and idealism. I really came close to going into the Peace Corps at one point because I always struggled with letting other people define reality rather than trusting my own sense of what is real. The culture helped wash me in when I went into the ministry saying, "Hey, that's the greatest thing to do." Then when the tide was out and everybody said, "That is a dumb way to waste your life," I began to say that's probably right. I almost washed out with the tide. I came very, very close to it.

DOOR: How did you feel about seminary?

CLAYPOOL: The Southern Baptist Seminary in Louisville, Kentucky, is the oldest and best in the States. It was a very ecumenical place for Southern Baptists. We were taught that we were part of the larger church and to take whatever we could find. The emphasis there was more on an intellectual and social approach rather than an emotional one.

I'm not conquest oriented; that's just not the way I approach life. I never try to put what I've got on somebody else against their will. That seminary reinforced that. I was there seven years. I did what was called a B.D. and then I did my doctorate in biblical theology. I wish I hadn't done my doctorate there. I had pretty much milked the coconut by then and I wish I had gone somewhere else.

In those seven years I had two student pastorates—one in the country and one in a little town. Then I went to be assistant pastor in the Atlanta area at the First Baptist Church in Decatur. While I was in Atlanta, I got to know Martin Luther King, Jr., very well personally. He had just come back from Montgomery to be with his father. That was before the Southern Christian Leadership Conference was so highly developed. I was in a little luncheon group with him and some others that met once a month. I got to know him and really came to trust what he was all about. I learned a lot from him philosophically. I feel like people have failed to sense that he was a first-rate thinker as well as a preacher and activist. He had really thought through nonviolence as a way of getting it done. In 1960, two years after Atlanta, I went back to Louisville to pastor a church one block from the seminary. King came to give a lecture at our seminary and afterward he said, "Let's go have a cup of coffee." So we walked over to the coffee shop and a reporter took a picture of us sitting together. That picture came out on the front page of the *Louisville Courier* the next day. I don't know how old you were, but you just can't imagine how the South projected on King the blame for the whole racial thing. The idea was that everybody would be happy if this troublemaker would just leave them alone. A lot of that visceral hatred got associated with me because of lunch and the picture. So for the rest of the time I was in Louisville, I was imaged as a civil rights activist, and it was who I was. I was willing to

be that, but it really did shake my ministry because we got all kinds of hate calls and mail and crosses burned in our front yard and threats to our children and the kind of stuff that went with being an activist at that time. And the church got really jumpy.

We also had in the seminary a Nigerian student whom our missionaries had converted. The guy didn't have a car, and our church was the only one you could walk to from the seminary. And a lot of people in the church didn't want him to come. I really went to bat that he should be accepted. A lot of people left and the money dropped off, and that is when I found that institutional success is the functional god of most institutions. That there is hardly any ideal that many people feel is worth enough to sacrifice that success. So the issue shifted from what is right and constructive on the race question to the survival of the church.

DOOR: How did you respond?

CLAYPOOL: I wasn't very ambiguous at that time. I came down flat-footed and said that we were not called to be successful, but called to be faithful. And I must say that the church did hold together. We did lose some strength, but as always we attracted some strength from people seeing that courage modeled.

It really is interesting to me now to go back there. Some of the people who were so opposed to what we did and really were so resistant in the sixties have since said to me, "I'm really glad you did it that way because now we see that there was no avoiding it. It had to be faced."

It was also during that time that my daughter's illness and death took place. Working through the grief with the congregation helped to heal the racial issue. Many of the people that had battled me to the tooth found in this experience a way to reach out and touch. We didn't have to fight with my daughter dying. They could show some compassion and not feel like they were selling out their position. That's also when I first began to learn to preach confessionally—by that I mean, make my own experience a resource of my interpretation. It does have lots of dangers. It can be a subtle form of exhibitionism, but I'm also convinced that it is a very powerful way of saying, "Look, here is what I've found to be the case and here's what is saving me."

DOOR: When did you go to Fort Worth?

CLAYPOOL: I left Louisville in 1971 and went to the downtown church in Fort Worth where I think I went partly to work through my grief. I wanted to get somewhere else since I was having to start all over again. Plus I think that we individuals are so partial in our gifts that the leader of an institution ought not to stay in the same place too long lest the institution take on his strengths and his weaknesses and begin to be his reflection. But institutions instinctively know how to correct themselves. The man that followed me is strong where I was weak and weak where I was strong, which is all right because they can live off the capital for awhile. He is shoring them up in ways that I was not able to help them grow. But I believe that if the minister stays in the church for thirty years, you have really got a monstrosity. You've got something built in the partial image of the pastor.

I went to a church that was bigger, a church that wasn't as academic or tied into a seminary. I went there to see if I could do the gospel with power people in the community, people who had political and financial responsibilities. And I found that to be really tough. I found that these people will like you as a person, but it takes an enormous amount of trust and skill to do what Jesus did with Zaccheus, that is, getting a rich man's attention and trust so that he will let you in on how he decides what he does with his power. That is a delicate, delicate procedure. I think I did it with some, but I found it to be harder than I expected. That is what I went there to learn how to do. Now what I didn't do there was to learn to set my limits. To know where to say, "Here is where I leave off and here's where I begin." So in my years there I really got exhausted. I found the pace of Texas life to be so fast, their willingness to innovate so invigorating that I really didn't know how to pull back. Without realizing it, I got badly fatigued. There were eleven of us on the staff for five thousand members. The sheer quantity of work that went with it was just enormous, and I didn't know how to pace myself.

While I was at Fort Worth, the church in Jackson (with 450 members), which was younger and more innovative, came to me because their founding pastor had gone to another church. They said, "Would you like to do something different? Would you like to opt for quality instead of quantity; would you like to have more time to study, for your people to be responsible and do some things that you want to do rather than react?" (My friends at Fort Worth said I had an affair with this church, that I was seduced at the point of my fatigue.) At first it was so different and I said no; I didn't give it any thought. But they came back to me a second time. The second time I really began to look at myself and saw what was happening. I realized that if I didn't somehow modify my lifestyle, that either I was going to have a heart attack in about five years (which is the way that the super achiever usually legitimates slowing down—by driving himself over the brink) and I didn't want that to happen. Or even worse for me, inch by inch, I would lose what few skills I had so that I would be just an empty drum, having to say something but having nothing to say. The church is filled today with fifty-year-old men who started brilliantly, who worked in places of real prominence, and in the process have lost the very ways of doing their work that give them some insight as to what to do with their power. They are just holding on and frantically trying to survive. I really didn't want that to happen and I saw myself, unless I changed, inch by inch slipping into it. So I decided at forty-six to make the big move and try to simplify and come to a place with fewer demands.

DOOR: Was that the only way out? Could you have stayed and made readjustments? Do you think the church would have been able to handle it?

CLAYPOOL: Yeah. I think I underestimated fatigue and the way that fatigue can distort your perception. What I've learned is that we need to start telling each other that fatigue is a moral category, just like anything else. I didn't know that. I didn't know you could get so tired that you lose your ability to see. I also think that I acted impulsively. I did not call in the community of people that cared for me in Fort Worth and say, "Look, here's what I'm feeling. I'm exhausted; what are my options? Here's one. Here's a chance to do my job differently, but do I have any other options?" Now, I might still have come here. But if I'd shared myself with the Fort Worth community, I think there were options within the situation. In other words, I think the church would have let me take time to study. I think I could even have let the laypeople in the church look at what they were expecting in the ministers and how unworkable it really was. In a way I feel kind of bad because I really and truly had the trust of that church. They might have listened to me, but I was so tired. And when you get so tired, little things look big and distant things look beautiful. The same feeling can lead some men to have affairs out of a sense of personal desperation.

When I left, the church in Fort Worth was astonished, because they didn't want me to leave. What I did was so irregular, you know, to go to a smaller church voluntarily. And I really leveled with the board and with the church as to why I was doing it. I said the job, as it was, was unworkable. And they all agreed, but they turned right around and hired a new minister and didn't change anything. So it made me realize that it really is going to take tough action in a church like that to change the structures at least at the top.

I was also intrigued about coming to a state that has a tremendous growth potential like Mississippi. And I was attracted to what this church here was trying to do and I'm feeling very good about being a part of it. It's just as good a thing to be doing with my life as I would be doing in a big church.

DOOR: What changes have you faced because of your decision?

CLAYPOOL: I had to go through the process of decelerating, learning how to be pro-active instead of reactive. I used to go in and have 10 calls to return, which meant I didn't have to worry about placing any calls myself. Now I have time to take the initiative. At first I was so confused and felt kind of guilty for not having all these demands. I didn't know how to use the freedom, but I'm learning now. I'm studying a whole lot more, going deeper with people than I was able to do in Fort Worth. I also realize that I did have this church over here idealized. I guess we always do. I thought this church was further along than it really was, which says nothing except that I didn't perceive exactly, because they didn't make any attempts to hide where they were. I was so tired, and I was hoping that there were some things that they could be which were not here yet.

DOOR: How long did it take you to realize that it was fatigue that influenced your decision? When did this fatigued feeling end?

CLAYPOOL: One of the things I negotiated in the change was that I take a month off in between churches to study and depressurize. So I went on the payroll and they gave me the first month to do that—which was really a generous thing. I went to the Yale Divinity School as a scholar for a month. I simply rested and went at my own pace. All it took was a month to make me realize how much fatigue had hurt.

I would like to say that you don't really have to take the major surgery solutions that I took just to claim the time that is probably already built in. If you have been at a place for any length of time, ask for a little sabbatical, a refresher. There's nothing the church can do that would be more productive for everybody, I think, than to give a man or a woman who is under this kind of strain some time to replenish. And frankly, what made coming here to Jackson so complicated was that I realized before I ever set foot here how fatigue had played a major part in my decision. Therefore I got here with a measure of self-reproach for having misread myself. And then when I realized I had even misread the situation, I just walked around holding my hands saying, "What am I doing here?" I had gone out here and cut off an arm just to take care of a fingernail. It was a very, very humbling experience to see how far my fatigue had pushed me out of touch with reality.

DOOR: You felt you had made a major mistake?

CLAYPOOL: Oh yes, I thought I had actually jumped out of an airplane with no parachute. I spent the first six months in dismal second-guessing. I had no cultural reinforcement for what I did. I mean everybody else was so shocked when I said I was going to do it and then they began, you know, to concoct a lot of theories. "There really was something wrong and he had to do it." Which of course isn't the case, but you know you're vulnerable to all kinds of gossip. Even the people here in the Jackson church wondered why I came. The great host of folks here are just like anybody else and they think that the better you are the bigger a place you ought to try to go to. So I found a lot of consternation here—why would you do this? Why would you come here? Everybody was confused culturally, and I remembered why I had said I would come, but then I found out that there were a lot of other factors that were important in any situation. I see what happened to me as simply a vocational expression of this middle adult thing that Gail Sheehy was talking about in *Passages.* Around 35-40, the imbalances that have tended to characterize your early days like over-investment in work and underinvestment in relationships really comes home on you. And suddenly what did motivate you, doesn't motivate you. What you've never done begins to cry out, and if we don't have some sense of what that is and some kind of community to help interpret it for us, then we either throw our wives overboard or we throw our careers out the window. Or we do something desperate, dumb, in the midst of this shifting time. And, many times, we buy a solution at a much higher price than it is really worth. To be frank with you, I consider myself very fortunate that I didn't do more damage to the primary realities of my life given the fatigue I was in.

DOOR: You feel you were saved in spite of yourself?

CLAYPOOL: Exactly. I think the goodness and mercy of God washed over me and kept me from an even worse kind of fate. Because although I consciously thought I was finding the shape of my own being, I realize now that there were so many other forces at work on me that I wasn't even conscious of. I was fatigued and tired of doing the same thing that I had been doing over and over. I was in a big church, a church of over three thousand for eighteen years, and I really had worn out those chains—the chains of getting out two sermons and being the crisis intervener for hordes of anonymous people. I'd done funeral after funeral where I had never met anybody that was involved. And there

you are, hoping you're pronouncing the name of the person right. That's urban religion, and I don't claim that I'm all that mature, but that really was not satisfying to me just to be an anonymous functionary with anonymous people. But I would say the major mistake I made was that I didn't call in the community. I acted impulsively and I acted in isolation and I'm convinced that there always are more options in almost any situation than a panicky fear which a tired person is aware of. That's why if we have brothers and sisters who care for us and who will look with steadier eyes and who are not as emotionally threatened, then at least they can make us aware. I could have asked the church in Fort Worth for a study leave and easily gotten it. I could have invoked a restructure program with the staff relations. It could have been done differently.

The crucial thing was that one morning about six months after wrestling with this, I finally forgave myself for the way I had handled the situation. I found that I wasn't blaming anybody; I was mad at myself for not being more perceptive and for having let this happen. I think that's one of the toughest things that grace asks us to do—that is accept forgiveness for our own muddling. And the day that I genuinely forgave myself and took the mercy of God as my medicine, that was the day things began to thaw here. Now I am delighted to be in Jackson, and to be frank, I would not want to be back where I was. There are many possibilities here. Theologically I would say that it's incredible what God can do with our stuff and with our bumblings and our impulsive attempts. I now sense that God is the God of fertilizer, that he can take dung and bring things of beauty out of it. It is incredible what he can still salvage out of what we do.

DOOR: How did your family react to all these decisions you were making abut leaving the church in Fort Worth and going to Jackson?

CLAYPOOL: My wife is really a wise, strong soul. She knows what I am just learning: that the place is really not essential. Doing of life can be done most anywhere, so she doesn't see why we ever moved the first time. She thinks that you waste a lot of time moving around, and it takes two years to get back to where you were. Her sense of rootedness would be that you put your roots down and get that out of the way and then you get on with doing your life. My wife also, and I'm glad for this, is interested in the church, but it is by no means her number-one concern or interest and therefore her attitude is "What's the difference; you've seen one, you've seen 'em all."

DOOR: Do you think that a child can make a commitment to God that's lasting? Can he or she be held to a decision?

CLAYPOOL: Yes, I think as a child you can begin to respond to the delight and warmth of creation as mediated through people and can begin to claim and decide that you have a right to be here and that you are part of the great purpose. I think you can begin to make the belonging, trust stance. I know this is impossible but I wish that we had two rites of inclusion in the church. If I were restructuring, I would let the Lord's Supper come at the time when a child really does sense that they want to belong and they do belong and they have a place at the table. And I would reserve baptism for the time when you have sifted through all the options and have really begun to feel that Christ does put life together the way I want to put it together. And the things Christ affirms are the things that really make sense to me and to commit myself to do my life that way. I think you have to be eighteen or nineteen to at least begin to see all the options and the evidence. But the church has no ritual-ization to celebrate my sense of belonging and then my commitment to live my life a certain way. I honestly think baptism probably ought to be a chosen, almost adult, kind of reality, but you can't wait until that point to give somebody a sense of celebration that they are in creation, that they are here and it's good.

DOOR: Let's address the whole issue of bigness versus smallness. Have you found any qualitative or quantitative advantages in either the big or small church?

CLAYPOOL: The big church does offer the possibility of a variety of programs and activities. You can bring in more expertise and different varieties of things. The smaller church forces you to think more carefully about what you are doing. The quality of in-depth relations can be established easier in a small church than in a big church. In a big church, what we try to do is have churches within the church and have a group that you really feel close to. But it's impossible for the professional staff in a big church to participate in it. Speaking personally, I really like the small church better for me. But I know other men whose gifts are mass gifts—who really thrive on people by the acre and do best in huge arenas. I would not want to go on the record saying that one is a superior form of church. The big church really does have to guard against being just a wholesale warehouse where people are washed through and their individuality is never noted. I never wanted to be that way, but it's hard not to be.

DOOR: So even though you went from big to small, you're not an anti-big man?

CLAYPOOL: No, because I think personalities are different. There are people who like to buy at the big discount store and then there are people who like to go to a specialty shop. I see the church I'm serving as really having a much more narrow appeal and focus. We're trying to do things for the struggler, the downer, the person who doesn't fit easily into the mass answers, the person who really has to struggle to believe. Not everybody does. I find people for whom other people's answers seem to wash right on down. And that sounds like I'm making a snide superiority judgment. I don't mean it that way. Our church is a church that doesn't attempt to have everything for everybody. We do have some limits in our traditioning of the young. This church that I am in was founded to meet adult needs and it is really having to struggle. What do we know and what do we experience that is worth passing on to our young? I'd say one of the real challenges we face is how do we get out from our essentially negative struggle with our heritage that on many points has been found inadequate? How do we sift through that and find that there have been some good things in it? And before we die, how do we gather up what wisdom we

have detected and pass that on to our children?

DOOR: Does any church ever ask that question? I can't imagine many churches asking, "What is valid that we can pass on to our kids?"

CLAYPOOL: I can't speak for any other, but that's what we're trying to do. I remember being so struck by Will Durant's preface. He said the reason he wrote was because he felt that before he died he needed to gather together what he felt was of worth.

DOOR: What is worth passing on in the Southern Baptist church?

CLAYPOOL: The religious zeal for life. The sense that this really isn't just a lonely, secular, meaningless cosmos. That however you want to say it or image it, that reality does come from a Friend. That it really is a gift of grace. And to realize that the source behind it all was joyous and positive though utterly mysterious adds to the journey. I think that is one thing we've got to give. Of course, Baptists historically put heavy emphasis on the individual who has to make his own meaning. Things are not done for us; we really do have to participate in making our own decisions and defining our values. And I take that to be a high value. You know, Baptists were existentialists before that word became popular in the sense that I can't depend on an infant baptism and I can't depend on a church hierarchy. And I can't depend on everything being structured somewhere else and just handed to me without effort. That's not to say that we don't in practicality have many people who let the Baptist tradition do those very things for them. The Baptist way of doing religion is pretty existential; it's been weighted on the activistic line more than the liturgical esthetic line. Southern Baptists are largely a creation of our region. We're lower-middle-class Southerners, still bearing the wounds of the Civil War. And we're just learning now that morality has some corporate dimensions. See, we were poor, tenant farmers—that's where we came from. Which means that we didn't have any power over the community at large. What we did have power over was our bodies, so you could preach to us about adultery. We had power over our mouths, so you could talk to us about drinking whiskey. We had power over private morality, so we could talk about being honest and being upright. But to talk to a tenant farmer about corporate responsibility and all this would have been irrelevant. The tragedy is that the grandsons of these tenant farmers are now bank presidents and chairmen of the boards, making decisions that have vast corporate and social implications. And their tendency is to still think of morality in terms of these individualized concerns and never think that a corporate policy should be viewed as part of their religious responsibility. And that comes out of our heritage.

DOOR: That's an interesting insight into lower-middle-class religion.

CLAYPOOL: You know, the Episcopalians have always had a strong sense of social responsibility, but they had that because they were influential. I mean, if you went to Yale, you were schooled to think that the decisions you make are going to affect a lot of people. But that would really be irrelevant to a tenant farmer. Your family was the only thing you had any control over, so they focused on moral concerns. But the tragedy I see is that things that were very strategic in one situation have a way of living on into

different situations where they are not appropriate. Have you ever heard the story of the groom who was astonished that his wife cut off both ends of the ham and couldn't figure out why she would do that. He asks and she says, "I don't know but that is the way my mother did it." And he traces it on back to the great-grandmother and asks her why she did it. And she says, "It's the only way I could get it to fit in my pan." In other words, she had a reason for doing it; the rest of them didn't. The church has been terrible about getting into certain habits. The 11:00 worship on Sunday morning was a rural creation. It gave them time to milk the cows, do the chores, and get to church—there's not a thing sacred about that time; it was a rural construction. My mother today would say if you had church at any other time that you are being unbiblical.

DOOR: You mentioned the wounds of the Civil War. It's amazing to us Yankees that over 100 years later these wounds still exist. Do you think they will ever go away?

CLAYPOOL: I hope so. You know Vietnam has helped, because now the rest of the country has experienced what we have, and that is defeat. You see, the South was the only part of America that had ever known defeat. The rest of the mythology was that we never lost a war, we never started a war, but there was one exception to that and that was the Southerner and his tragic lost dream of the Confederacy. So the South still festers under the wounds of having lost, of having it ground into them. The Reconstruction did far more damage than the war itself. There's a lot of pride in people that hates to admit that they might have made a mistake. And of course there's the racial thing. Slavery was literally ripped out of the South's hands. They would never have relinquished this. So all the interactions of the country since then around the treatment of the blacks has been a continual thorn in their side.

DOOR: But it hasn't just been the Civil War. It's been that the North came down on the slavery issue and the black issue and everything done was in Selma and Montgomery and parts south.

CLAYPOOL: Yeah, you see the Southerner actually talked about the federal troops "invading" or "intruding" themselves into their territory. Lincoln rightly saw that what he had on his hands was a rebellion, and that he had to put down the insurrectionists. He never saw the Civil War as anything but an attempt to legally constitute authority to maintain itself. But the South saw it as intrusion and invasion. And the civil rights thing reopened all the old memories, and there were all kinds of negative feelings. But Vietnam has universalized this experience in defeat, and what's happening to the blacks today in the northern ghettos is demonstrating that it is not a regional malady, but it's an endemic problem in our whole universal makeup. Of course it's all interlocked. We are all interconnected with it and what's happening in Cleveland today has got roots in the South. It's really not clear to me how much responsibility the dominant white people in this country are going to take for what has happened to the blacks. It's far from clear to me that we're ever going to admit that they represent an exception to the whole ethnic history of this country. Now, Michael Novak, whom I have a lot of

respect for, is on a terror right now as a Catholic ethnic and saying "Let the blacks do it the way the Czechs and the Poles and the Hungarians and everybody else had to do it. They came and they scratched their way up by hard work and adapting to the system." There is a lot to be said for this. And of course Jesse Jackson in Chicago is picking up that line. But I think what Novak is overlooking is that the black did come here with one significant difference, and that is he came here as a slave against his will. The Czech and the Pole, as tough as ethnic conditions were in these big cities, were not slaves and they didn't have a skin color that imaged them wherever they went. So in a sense I think the black is going to have to learn from the ethnic, and yet I also sense that there is one difference—that some kind of compensatory solution is in order, that to treat them equally we have got to treat them differently. I know that is really hard to work out, but I do believe the black represents a special component of the American past.

You know there are those who argue that our country was made up essentially of escapists. The people who came here originally were all trying to get away from something that they didn't like or didn't want. And I remember very clearly back in 1965, a black guy said to me, "This country is never going to face up to the race question or to Vietnam because it's just not in our national heritage. We are a nation of escapists and escapism is going to be the way America is going to try to handle all of her stuff until she is forced to face it." I disagreed with him then because I think another component of our history is that we have a lot of adventuresome, courageous people. I don't think that everybody that came here was a fugitive. I think a lot of them were capable of radicality and rose to the challenge. So my hope is that the strain of our national heritage that was willing to take on an awesome challenge is finally going to win out over the part of our heritage that was just trying to escape.

DOOR: What have you learned about grief since the death of your little girl eight years ago?

CLAYPOOL: One is that grief is a whole lot bigger than we have usually thought of. We usually think of it as bereavement, and that is one of its most intense forms. But any time a loss occurs, grief is going to follow. And not to identify that and not to realize that grief is going to follow certain patterns is to really misread the name of the thing. I'm finding a whole lot more grief now than I used to. By that, I mean I recognize grief. I think I've also learned that the fear of death is very, very pervasive in us and that it comes out in a lot of forms, but at the bottom (and I think this goes back to our early childhood uninterpreted experiences) we get the idea that death annihilates whatever it touches and in a sense death steals from us what rightfully belongs to us. What you have is primordial terror of death and then a seething resentment that death takes from me what is rightfully mine. And therefore the church has responsibility long before experiencing bereavement to help people get at these uninterpreted childlike misconceptions of death and begin to bequeath a different perspective, which is that death doesn't annihilate, but death essentially transforms.

On the physical level, you know, there is no such thing as the destruction of matter; it's just the altering of the form of matter. You burn a piece of paper and it becomes smoke. But the reality in its change of form is that it does not go out of existence. Again, Myron Madden says, take a dead rat and throw it into the swamp and what happens—the living things there gobble it up. That's St. Paul's victory— that death is swallowed up in victory. When something dies, it changes form and then that form is caught back up in the cycle of creativity. So if we can ever get in our heads that death is not annihilation, that it does not extinguish what it touches, but that it does transform into things of life, then some of the terror can be taken out of it and the adventure dimension can get into it. Death is a way of getting on with the great journey of life.

I have learned from my own experience, and a lot of others have helped me, that all of our existence in a sense is a series of deaths/births where we let go of little things and get a bigger thing. I got called out of the sand pile when I was six and told that I had to go to school, which was a death, but a whole world that I didn't even know existed was opened up to me. I had to let something go at some measure of pain to make myself accessible to going to elementary school. You know every move of my life has involved dying so that I could be born to something else. Reul Howell has a great story about going to see an old friend. The friend was dying and he said, "I've always wondered what it was going to be like to die and lo and behold I've discovered it's a new friend in an old garb. I've been doing this all my life and I didn't realize it." I've learned something through all my experiences—that every exit is also an entrance. Every time you walk out of something, you walk into something. I got into this world by dying to the womb—and it must have been painful to get ripped out of that familiar place—but that was the prerequisite of my getting into time and space. You know at the end of my life in history there's going to be a similar kind of transition experience. And if we can get at the terror of death by saying it is a transformer rather than an annihilator, then also we can get rid of the idea that death is a thief and is taking something that is rightfully ours, which is the basis of all the rage that I know—"Why did God take this? He had no right."

And, of course, in my own struggle I began to see life as a gift and to begin to recognize that we are all here not because we deserve it, but because life was given to us. Instead of some possession that we have a right to, it becomes a kind of real dividend that we serendipitously got and don't deserve, and this knowledge changes the cast of life from "It's mine and I have a right to it, and if I lose it I have a right to be mad," into a kind of free flow where I'm always being dealt the cards that I deserve and I've got to hold them and play them and do the best I can. And if the cards are called on, I learn to give thanks.

Is Gettis McGregor a name that rings a bell? The story goes that he is five years old and he goes with his mother to his grandmother's one summer. They don't realize that little Gettis is around and the grandmother says to the mother, "You know, I'm really glad you all decided to have little Gettis. He's been such a joy to us." Well, the kid hears this and his ears perk up because it never occurred to him before that he might not have been born. But the truth was that his parents had been in their forties when he was conceived, and their youngest child was thirteen, and they had read all the books about the older you get, the greater the instances of deformity, etc. So there had been a big family discussion about "should we get a therapeutic abortion" and they had gone so far as to get the medical permission to do it. But at the last minute they had decided not to go ahead so Gettis was born. But Gettis said that when he heard that conversation, his first impression was sheer terror that he could see himself in some anteroom about to be born and this hand reaches out and pulls him aside and says, "You're disqualified." He said, by the way, that that had changed his feelings about abortion. But then he said the second thing he felt after the terror that he might not have been born was the incredible sense of wonder that he had made it. That, in fact, he had been chosen and intended. So he says that beginning at five, he realized that he had just barely made it, that his life had come to him strictly out of gratuitous joy. And that every day from then on he had not taken it for granted; he had really celebrated.

OK, somehow we have to give people a feel for their own existence and the feel for other people's existences that the odds against any of us being here, statistically, are astronomical. That the fact that we ever got here at all is just a lucky fluke in many, many ways, or a gracious intention. Then nothing that we have would take on this sense of possession and "I have a right to it."

So what I've learned about grief since my own grief is that we must get at the terror and rage that is probably born at about three or four when the first puppy gets run over. The child sees that the puppy's not there anymore, and the conclusion is that he was and he wasn't. If we could get at the annihilation fears and the possession fears, then I think we could live with dying and live with grieving a whole lot more comfortably.

DOOR: How does that contrast with the church's approach?

CLAYPOOL: The church has really played a bad role in many times by calling on us to be triumphal. You know, when somebody dies, the way you really prove you're an A-1 Christian is that you don't cry, and you go to that service and kind of wave your banner in the air and thus suppress the enormous pain that ought to go with losing somebody. I wish the church would legitimate our sadness and say when you're broken, when you're cut, you bleed, and it's utterly normal and that all of this is in the context of exit/entrance, death/birth. That everything is part of the great process in which life is given to us in segments, and you always have to die to get out of it to be born to get in. If we could only set it in perspective.

SHELDON VANAUKEN

The Keepers of the *Door* ventured to the rolling green of Lynchburg, Virginia, the home of Jerry Falwell, Thomas Road Baptist Church, and Sheldon Vanauken. As our Avis-provided Granada moved closer to the house on Breckinbridge, we could not help but wonder what Sheldon Vanauken would be like. We wondered if anyone at Thomas Road Baptist had ever heard of *A Severe Mercy*, Sheldon Vanauken, C. S. Lewis, or Oxford. We wondered if Sheldon Vanauken had ever heard of Liberty Baptist College, Jerry Falwell, and Thomas Road Baptist buses.

We had awakened him at 6:00 A.M. to remind him, per his instructions, that we were coming. Our reminder was not received well. "You were to call at 6:15," he mumbled with a sleepy curtness. As usual, the Keepers of the *Door* had not made a positive impression.

There was something absurd about it all, really. The ex–Bob Jones student and ex-Nazarene with briefcases full of *National Lampoons, Bluegrass Unlimited,* and *Ideas* books coming to interview an Oxford-trained college professor whose shelves were full of Shelley, Keats, and the like.

But we, like 100,000 others who have purchased *A Severe Mercy*, felt we needed to see this man, talk to him. As we pulled up in front of the tiny blue-and-white wood framed house that was his, we were surprised. Disarmed would be a better word. After reading of his aristocratic upbringing, especially in the first chapter of his book, we had expected an impeccable mansion rambling over hills surrounded by quiet lakes and ponds. Our minds could not help but compare what we saw with the images conjured up by "Glenmerle" and "Mole Hill." Instead we were affronted by a place badly in need of paint surrounded by a dusty dog pen, unkempt lawn, and a rather sad-looking English Morgan parked in a dilapidated garage. We were already learning something about this mysterious author. We had expected his aristocratic background to be expressed in things, but apparently his was the wealth expressed in ideas.

He told us later, "I have never been very financially uneasy. I think people who come from a poor background sometimes are more uneasy about money . . . but I have always felt something would turn up." In the case of *A Severe Mercy* something definitely turned up. "I think it's odd," he said "There are lots of people who want desperately to write a book . . . to be a success. I didn't write to be a writer or to be a success, but rather to tell this story."

And quite a story it is—a story of two people who fall in love. Nothing new there. But what is new is their conscious attempt to construct a "Shining Barrier"—a sort of walled garden that would protect them from materialism, jealousy, and that insidious "creeping separateness" that seems to break up so many relationships today. As Davy and Sheldon continue their journey, they travel to Oxford where both of them become Christians through a close and life-changing relationship with C. S. Lewis. And then the "deathly snows" fall on Davy, and Sheldon allows us to share with him those last days with her and his pilgrimage through the aftermath of grief. *A Severe Mercy* is a masterpiece, filled with life and majesty, gently bringing all of us to face a quality of life most of us have forgotten is possible. *A Severe Mercy* is more than a book. It is an experience, a truly captivating dialogue between author and reader. Davy died in 1954. More than twenty years later Sheldon Vanauken began to write the book. "I was commanded to do so," he explained. He had donated his C. S. Lewis letters to the Bodleian Library at Oxford, but in late 1975 or early 1976 had decided he wanted to see them again.

He wrote and asked for copies, "lying here on this bed reading them, not without a tear or two at what a friend he really was, I came to the letter that I called the "Severe Mercy Letter" and read that. At that particular moment, I decided that I was going to write a book and I was going to call it *A Severe Mercy*. Just like that. It was settled. And on June 1, I began to write it." For six months he pored over their diaries, the letters and notes they had written, and the book was finished December 30, 1976. He had kept those diaries for over twenty years. "I had a fire in the fireplace and put the diaries in and burned them all. All that had been written. That was that."

So the Keepers of the *Door* wandered up to the front porch wondering if it would hold our combined weight, and we introduced ourselves to Sheldon Vanauken, now in his sixties at the time of this interview, portly, tall, with kindly features and a gravelly voice. He looked so different than we had imagined, a reason, maybe, why he asked that we not photograph him. We entered his house to be greeted by a rather unkempt living room and kitchen and waited while he made us instant coffee. He sat on his bed, which is in the living room, puffing furiously one cigarette after another, while we shared the awkwardness of get-acquainted talk. When the interview was over, we sipped sherry together. Or should we say, he sipped sherry and we gulped it down. (It wasn't until later that Tom Howard informed us that "one must *sip* sherry, you bumbleheads.") Do you suppose he noticed?

DOOR: Your book, *A Severe Mercy*, seems to have a different effect on whoever reads it. Any comments?

VANAUKEN: It seems to me that the book has at least three different audiences. One audience is made up of people who have experienced the loss of a loved one, perhaps recently, and are searching for the meaning of that. There is also a certain audience of people who are near their own death. Then, there is the audience, and a very large one, indeed, of younger people, anywhere up to fifty, who are particularly thinking of the book in terms of their own marriage. I've had letters from ministers who said that from now on their whole life was going to be different . . . as far as their wife is concerned. They've lived for themselves or they've lived for their profession. There are still other audiences, including Oxonians and also England lovers.

DOOR: What has been the general response from the evangelical community to *A Severe Mercy*?

VANAUKEN: Oh, extremely good. I'm told on all sides that I am an evangelical, which I hadn't known up till then. I'm in sympathy with evangelicals, certainly.

As far as I can see, the evangelicals and the catholics (in the broad sense catholic—not Roman Catholic) are allies against the liberals—the waterdowners. So they are brothers. The evangelicals have taken it up, but so have the Roman Catholics, I'm glad to say. It's required reading in some monasteries. Of course, C. S. Lewis always refused to commit himself. You see remarks, now and then, that Lewis was Anglo-Catholic. There is not a word of truth in that. He never said that, never disclosed his position in those matters. He stuck to what he called "mere Christianity." The older meaning of *mere* is "pure," which must

have been on his mind. At any rate, in *A Severe Mercy*, I, generally speaking, adhere to the same "mere" Christianity, which I consider to be the important thing. So no flak. There will be some flak from my new book, *Gateway to Heaven.* There will be some evangelicals who will think I shouldn't write about that awful subject of lesbianism and all that. But it will be good for them if they read it.

DOOR: What did you say your novel was about?

VANAUKEN: It's about a young couple who are very much in love. When the novel opens there is a crisis when Richard, the hero, receives a letter from Mary, the heroine (she is on a visit to Georgetown to see her father), saying that she has fallen in love with another woman and that she must have at least a month to work this thing through in her mind. Of course Richard is shocked, but he abides by her wish for a month. So he decides to go through the past few years and see if he can find clues to the meaning of what has happened.

DOOR: What happens?

VANAUKEN: I ain't goin' to tell you.

DOOR: Okay, back to *A Severe Mercy*. Your book is about a love affair, really about love itself. You and your wife discussed at length what you wanted out of marriage, but you never define it. When is a couple married?

VANAUKEN: Theologically, they are married when they genuinely and sincerely intend to be married forever. If two people intended to be together only three years, that would not be a marriage. There must be the intention to form a union that is for life. Of course, the other part is the consummation, the physical consummation. My particular image of marriage is based on eyes. It is only because we have two eyes looking from slightly different angles that we can see depth at all. And the feminine and the masculine combine two different angles (and they *are* two different angles regardless of the feminists) and that gives fullness of vision.

DOOR: When you talk about your relationship with Davy, you talk a lot about the problem of "creeping separateness." What suggestions do you have for couples who have to fight living two separate lives?

VANAUKEN: The first suggestion is to be aware that there is such a thing as creeping separateness. What do young people who are freshly married do? They can't rest when they're apart. They want to be together all the time. But they develop separate interests, especially if they have separate jobs and some separate friends. So they drift apart. Pretty soon they have little in common except, maybe, the children. So the stage is set for one of them to fall in love with someone else. Later they'll say that the reason for the divorce was that he/she fell in love with someone else, but it wasn't that at all. It was because they let themselves grow apart.

DOOR: There is a significant movement in our culture toward "doing your own thing." Doesn't this narcissistic trend in our culture make it more difficult for marriages to stay together?

VANAUKEN: Obviously "doing your own thing" is a part of our present-day culture and not in the past, although in the past people did their own thing all the same. They were expected to. In the past, men lived in a world of men and were expected to. Women lived in a world of women, which meant babies and household chores, and were ex-

pected to. There wasn't so much "creeping separateness" as there was built-in separateness. But today it is perfectly possible for people to be closer than they were in the past.

DOOR: You say that, but can all of us work at the "creeping separateness," or is that really only the privilege of middle- or upper-class people who have the time? What about families where both people have to work?

VANAUKEN: Most people—middle class, upper class, lower class—have to work. It is still largely the men who work, and if the women work, they are simply substituting the work they used to do in the household (where the husband wasn't there anyway) for work in the office. That is one of the givens in life for most people, including the middle class. But the will to stay close, the will to do all you can together, that is the thing that makes the difference. It certainly did with Davy and me.

DOOR: In your book you talk about making a choice early on to go for the heights and depths rather than for sameness?

VANAUKEN: When you stop to think about it, which would you rather have? Wouldn't you rather have the heights of joy even if it does entail pain? I made the deliberate choice, and somehow I never quite forgot it. Lots of decisions made later were made in the light of that. For instance, when I came back from the war, and we weren't wealthy by any means, we chose to take our little boat and amble down around the Florida Keys and Bahamas. Everyone else coming back madly tried to get a job and make up for the lost years. That was a choice we made in light of creeping separateness and heights and depths.

DOOR: But all of us can't take a year or two off to cruise the Bahamas.

VANAUKEN: If you did take a year or two off to do anything you like, in the long run it wouldn't make any difference . . . in the sense of career. You'd come back and get a different job. It would all work out. My father used to say, "It doesn't make a damn bit of difference what a man does until he's forty-five. It's what he does after that." But if you took a year off you would have a year that you would never forget. It would be one of the high years in your whole life. If you keep working at your job, in retrospect it would all be a blur. So why don't you do it?

DOOR: We had better change the subject or we'll quit! In your book, when Davy christens your schooner and breaks the bottle of wine on the bow, she says, "Keep us out of the set ways of life." What did she mean?

VANAUKEN: We did not want to have the same pattern of life that our fathers and the people we knew were in. We wanted to go our own way and that tied up with beauty, with love, and with staying close. It tied up with the saying "we would rather sell apples on the street together than be apart with lots of money." All of our choices were made on that basis. (My word, look at that red bird on the wire out there; can you see it? Flash of color. There it goes . . . it's gone now. Anyway, what was I saying?) A poem was more important to us than a job. Poetry and beauty in general. Love was a form of beauty.

DOOR: Here's another quote from your book. "We long for things that in the long run do not bring us jobs . . . because what we're really longing for is God." Can you explain?

VANAUKEN: That is one of the underlying but overriding thoughts in my life (which C. S. Lewis was also always thinking and talking about). I think we've all had that experience. Maybe it's more so in youth, though, I'm not sure about that. But some moment when we're not especially hurried and we see something or hear something, we feel a longing but don't really know what we're longing for. We long to climb over the mountain or up the mountain and we believe that somehow the joy will be fulfilled. We fix on all sorts of things. We decide if we only owned the Mona Lisa and could look at it everyday, that would be happiness, so we steal it. But if we do steal the Mona Lisa, it's never the magic we thought it would be. If we get to the top of the mountain it's just a bunch of rocks after all. So nothing is ever quite that magic that we sometimes feel in our longing. We almost always fix on something earthly, but it is never enough when we get it.

DOOR: You mention C. S. Lewis a lot in your book. What do you think of all this C. S. Lewis fadism that is going around?

VANAUKEN: It has a little of the cult feeling to it. Still, though, if it persuades people to read Lewis, that's good. His own reasonableness and logic cuts through a lot of that cult thing.

DOOR: Did you happen to see "The Lion, the Witch and the Wardrobe" on CBS?

VANAUKEN: I wouldn't see it under any circumstances. I'm so much afraid that we're going to raise a generation with an atrophied imagination, and if there is anything that should not be put on television, it's any kind of fairy story. I couldn't be paid to see it and have their images substituted for my own.

DOOR: You don't have a television?

VANAUKEN: No. I have a radio though. I listen to the six o'clock news. I did have until a month ago an enormous stereo. But I've got a lot of the things I want to listen to on tape and it isn't quite as good but it's good enough. I don't suppose in my entire life I've looked at television more than say fifteen to twenty hours. How about that?

DOOR: Do you know Walter Hooper, the executor of C. S. Lewis's estate?

VANAUKEN: I've never met him actually. We've had some correspondence. I know that some of the things that are in Major Warren Lewis's diary would contradict some of the things that Walter Hooper says. And Clyde Kilby, who I do know at Wheaton, is talking to Harper & Row now about the publication of the diary. So I know a bit about the controversy and I have not taken sides in this. But I have some thoughts.

DOOR: Are you going to share them?

VANAUKEN: No.

DOOR: Well, then, let's talk about C. S. Lewis himself. You must have been asked this a million times, but what are the things about Lewis that made you feel so close? What were the things about him that made him so magnetic?

VANAUKEN: I don't know if I can say anything that goes beyond what I said in the book. The physical description. The understanding and the sympathy—you see the letters. The mind that cut through anything that was not well thought out. And the unfailing intelligence. He was obviously one of the most brilliant men of this century as far as his mind alone was con-

cerned. He was, by the way, a triple first at Oxford, which is no mean accomplishment. One first is a good deal better than a Phi Beta Kappa key and much harder to get. For him to be a triple first in philosophy, classics, and English literature . . . well . . . I suppose he knew more about English literature than any man alive. Yet he wore that learning lightly. Very human.

After his death I heard that J. B. Phillips, the chap that wrote *Letters to Young Christians*, had this uncanny experience, and I believe it, of looking up one evening and in a chair across the room Lewis's apparition was sitting. Lewis simply smiled and disappeared. I would have given anything to have had that experience. But I didn't. Just to see him again. Even just to see him grin.

DOOR: How does anyone from Oxford decide to live in Lynchburg? The only thing we've ever heard about Lynchburg, Virginia, is Jerry Falwell and the Thomas Road Baptist Church.

VANAUKEN: If anyone in Jerry Falwell's church has read my book, I don't know about it. Even Virginia Baptists I've talked to from other churches are extremely unhappy and tense about the whole Falwell thing and don't want to have anything to do with it. They do not claim it as a Baptist phenomenon even though he calls himself a Baptist.

DOOR: You mention in your book that one of the strongest arguments for Christianity is Christians. But isn't one of the strongest arguments against Christianity also Christians? How do you view the fundamentalists who would condemn you for being liberal in your lifestyle, smoking and drinking, etc.?

VANAUKEN: I've had one or two letters where somebody says, "I love the book, but how could you have a drink?"

DOOR: What do you do with those people? Write them off?

VANAUKEN: No. No, in their own way ... a dim way, perhaps ... they are groping towards the light. If they talk to me and if they are willing to listen (which they often aren't), then of course, I'm willing to explain whatever their question is.

DOOR: How have you changed since you and your wife studied at Oxford? How have your perceptions of Christianity changed with time?

VANAUKEN: It's deepened, of course. That would be an obvious thing to say. Probably the simplest thing I could say and yet the truest is that I have learned to put first the kingdom, to put first Christ. At Oxford, as my book says, and until after Davy's death even, I did not put it first. It was an intellectual adventure. It was challenging and I believed it intellectually, but not with my whole being, as Davy did. But now I know, and I don't know when I learned this for sure, but I really do put Christ first now as best I can and wish nothing more than to die unto self. My deepest prayer is always that Christ will be in me, thinking through my brain, speaking through my lips, loving through me. I drifted away in the sixties because of the movement. I don't mean I ceased to be a Christian, but I did drift away into the anti-war movement. I went into it for Christian reasons, but like others, I tended to put movement goals ahead.

DOOR: Do you think your own perception of the events that took place in the book have become glorified or exaggerated?

VANAUKEN: All I can say is I don't think so. If I had written this book right after Davy's death, where I wouldn't have had any power of selection (that's one reason it would have been a bad book if I'd written it then), emotions would have played such a big part in it. I would have glorified events, no doubt. But with the passage of the years, as you draw away sitting on the observation platform of the train—to use that analogy—the hills that the train has been going through sink and you see the mountains far behind which were originally obscured. I think I have a clearer view now of that event which I didn't have earlier.

DOOR: Your wife's last words ...

VANAUKEN: "Oh, darling, look"?

DOOR: Yes, like she could see into the other side. Do you believe that is what happened?

VANAUKEN: I don't disbelieve it. I read something the other day from some doctor who was saying that people who come back from the brink of death don't always report wonderful, good things. Sometimes they come back with a sense of horror; they've seen something terrible. That is interesting, although it is not an answer to your question. As for Davy, I'd give the world to know what she meant when she said that. It could have been that she was saying in her frail voice, "Oh darling, look ... I understand." I knew, absolutely knew, that if I said, "What? Tell me," she would have made an effort, but I didn't. I don't know why I didn't.

That whole chapter of the dying was extremely accurate, by the way. Every word she uttered. There is nothing that is any different to what really happened. Most astonishing was that I knew the second she died. My face was close to hers and I heard the last breath. I knew it was the last breath. I knew she was gone, and I stood there in that empty room, no nurse, no nothing, and I absolutely knew—it wasn't a matter of faith. It was a matter of knowing that she still existed. I don't have that knowing now; I have the memory, but then it was just an absolute certainty.

DOOR: You talk about the second death. Can you explain what that means?

VANAUKEN: This is all speculation, but I did feel her with me in some sense and I was able to write letters to her, which I couldn't do now. I've tried sometimes and it's very artificial and unreal. She did seem to be with me, and I wept a lot at the loss and grief. But then there came a time when suddenly all that was gone. My eyes were dry. I might have summoned up tears by playing a familiar record or something, but it wasn't happening by itself. The world was simply empty. Empty of that sense of her, and that's what I mean by the second death. It's the time that comes in any grief when your tears are dried.

DOOR: It seems like what you're talking about is the natural process of repression.

VANAUKEN: Repression, you say?

DOOR: Yes.

VANAUKEN: I'm not aware that I ever repressed the grief. It simply ended.

DOOR: It seems like when you went back and read all of your diaries that you were consciously trying to keep alive the grief and pain rather than allowing it to fade naturally.

VANAUKEN: I don't think it made any difference. Remember what I said in my book, that each thing, each memory, each physical object, even the coat she had worn, the old MG, each of those things called forth tears *once*, but never again. That's the key to the whole thing as I see it. The first day I went back to teaching, when I came out of class, there was the MG— little and lonely. All of a sudden I was pervaded by that loss and I could scarcely get off the campus before the tears were running down my face. But the MG never again called forth any emotion.

When I went through the diaries, playing the records and reading the books, each of them called forth tears. Each of them had to be seen for one minute alive and smiling . . . calling forth tears. But, then, that particular Davy was dead and each one of them had to die. I did it all at once instead of spreading it over the years as some people do. They get haunted by grief and picture ghosts walking with them. I've never had any sense that Davy is here in the room since those days. In other words, I did it in a concentrated fashion, going as deep into grief as I could.

DOOR: Can the common person experience the kinds of things you are talking about—the insights, the quality of life that you allude to in your book?

VANAUKEN: I don't quite know how to answer that. If you keep on reading poetry, whatever poetry you like (keep on reading it aloud to somebody), at first you'll like poems that seem to express your own philosophy of life. You'll be caught up, of course, by the beauty of the words and language. Don't read very much modern poetry. (So much of it is not poetry at all— just prose arranged as poetry.) Your taste will develop. You will find you are living on a constantly higher plane, and you'll also find that you are somewhat more isolated from others by doing so, but it's worth it all the same. It's simply your own will to move upward.

DOOR: Can you describe with some succinct adjectives the American culture today?

VANAUKEN: Heavens! In some ways, becoming ever more monotonous in the sense that it's the same everywhere. There isn't very much difference in going from New York to San Francisco. It's the same culture, the same motor cars, and the same films. Everybody has the same TV programs. Individual differences are being ironed out. There is far less difference in going from Virginia to Indiana than there is in going from England to France, where they each have a very different culture and tradition. I'm sorry that this whole bloody continent is becoming so monotonous. I'm extremely sorry to see our culture—any one culture—pervading the whole universe. I don't feel prepared to sum it all up in a few well-chosen words, but there is an immense variety in human beings despite the sameness of our culture. That's encouraging. I don't see everything all black as some people do, because love exists and Christ is stronger than we even think he is. . . .

LEWIS SMEDES

Divorce is no longer an isolated occurrence that one hears about occasionally. It is no longer something that happens to that anonymous crowd "out there" that makes up statistics.

Divorce is an epidemic. It has become an uncontrollable swell of destructiveness smashing what remains of marriage, family, and permanence. None of us has remained unscathed. No one around us seems safe. Our friends, family, ministers, authors, counselors, parents ... even our own marriages. Divorce has affected us all.

It no longer shocks us. Numbed by the sheer size of the divorce rate, our sensitivities have been eroded by its reputation. We wake up each new day with an increasing acceptance of divorce as "normal."

Because of that, the *Door* had no choice, really. We had to talk about divorce.

So many of our friends have become the victims of divorce, and the reality of our faith makes it so difficult to know just what to do. So we decided to interview Dr. Lewis Smedes, professor of theology and ethics at Fuller Seminary.

We had no choice about him, either. He was the unanimous suggestion from everyone we talked to. Dr. Smedes does provide an answer to the age-old question, "Can anything good come out of Moody Bible Institute?" He did attend Calvin College and Seminary, however, and eventually received his doctorate in systematic theology from the Free University of Amsterdam (of course, we would have attended there too, if we would have known it was free). We asked Dr. Smedes why he went to Amsterdam after all his Bible training and seminary training. "I didn't think I knew anything when I finished seminary," he replied. Frankly, we were impressed with a man who is so willing to admit he doesn't know it all.

Unfortunately, but not surprisingly, Dr. Smedes was not impressed with us. "I had expected you to be quite different ... you know ... someone a little more ... er ... sophisticated, if you know what I mean?"

We didn't know what he meant.

Dr. Smedes came to Fuller Seminary in 1968 as professor of religion and later switched to ethics. He has managed not to switch his wife of thirty years, however, and lives with Doris in Sierra Madre (just outside Pasadena). They have three adult children.

The Keepers of the *Door* traveled in July to the smog-infested campus of Fuller Seminary to interview Dr. Smedes in his typically professor-decorated office (i.e., lots of books, lots of papers, very little space, with a view of the campus furnace).

DOOR: Is divorce wrong?

SMEDES: Yes. I believe that strongly. So do you. But you have to ask what *kind* of wrong it is.

DOOR: O.K. What kind of wrong is it?

SMEDES: It's many kinds. I've never met a divorced person who afterwards said, "I can't wait to go through that again." I've known divorced people who said, "I had to get it and I'm glad I got it. Life is better now." But it is still a wrong. Divorce is wrong in the sense that it is a rupture. It is a break, a sadness, a wound, a pain. It's a wrong of which people are a victim, but it is also a wrong for which people are responsible. Divorce is a moral wrong, but I don't mean by that that everybody who gets a divorce is equally morally culpable. Do you know what I mean by that distinction?

DOOR: No.

SMEDES: I am not saying that every person who gets a divorce is equally morally in the wrong, but divorce is always a moral wrong. It ought not to be. It is against God's will. God hates divorce. It goes against the very way that life is meant to be put together.

DOOR: If God hates divorce, you would never know it by the incidence of divorce amongst religious people, would you?

SMEDES: I've gotten to feel angry about that, to be honest with you, yet I'm ambivalent. I've had a growing anger, but also I've had a growing sorrow because I think that people who get divorced are people in mass, and each case is different. Each person has a different degree of personal involvement in a divorce ... but I am still angry at what's happening. I am particularly angry at the easy ways that religious people are getting divorced. I'm angry because a real distortion is going on—a distortion of life. It's my conviction that life together has two sides—a structural side and a personal side. The structural side is covenantal. I make a commitment, for example, to be a citizen of this country, and as long as I take its goodies and I'm involved in this country, I make a covenant to participate, to be responsible and to be identified as "Lou Smedes, American." I think marriage is the same way, only the marriage covenant is explicit. That is, nobody has to get married and nobody has to marry the person they do, but once they do there is a covenantal structure. We've come to think of marriage simply as a relationship, and I'm angry that people are breaking covenants thinking that they're just breaking up a relationship.

DOOR: Does your anger bother you?

SMEDES: I search my soul about that anger and wonder if I'm getting angry because I'm jealous about the freedom that other people have who get a divorce. Maybe there is some jealousy of people who are liberated from my old-fashioned notion of covenants, I don't know. When I meet real people who are divorced or people who are going through a divorce, I realize, "Hey, they're not just guilty people who have broken a covenant—they're victims of a million things that went into their inability to keep the marriage covenant." So I'm sorry about that. I have compassion for that. I feel angry and sorry at the same time. I don't know how to resolve my ambivalence, but I think there is moral justification for my anger.

DOOR: When we do come across real people who have been involved in divorce, what should be the Christian response? Can we condemn the sin without condemning the sinner?

SMEDES: People want to believe that unconditional acceptance means unconditional approval, but it is practically impossible to disapprove of the act and accept the person. I don't know how to accomplish that myself. Divorced people sometimes get angry with me for saying things like this, but I think that most people who have willed to be divorced need forgiveness. The church that simply says, "We accept you" without saying "We forgive you" is ignoring the reality of what's happened. A covenant has been violated. Someone has been hurt.

Now, being forgiven is an awful thing. In fact, few of us know what it means. What is this thing called forgiveness? What do you do when you forgive somebody? What are you when you are forgiven? That's a great mystery, but one thing is involved, and that is the awareness that a wrong has been done. A wrong has been done with some degree of personal responsibility involved, and the community thereby

has been injured (subtly, perhaps, but it has been injured). Don't tell me that the city of L.A. is not injured by the problem of divorce. People need forgiveness from God and from the community. The church has to say that. It's wrong in our compassion and our eagerness to heal to avoid any hint of judgment, as the church has been doing. Damn it . . . a wrong has been done. Why should we who are involved in the church evade that?

DOOR: If the church doesn't evade its responsibility . . . then what does it do?

SMEDES: The pulpit has to go back to preaching moral law and moral responsibility. We've gone overboard with marriage encounter, marriage therapy, and marriage enrichment. We can't really correct divorce until we get out of this confusion we've created in the pulpit between psychic therapy and redemption, between relational theology and covenantal theology. I recognize the biblical word to divorced people is not limited to what the Bible says on divorce. The biblical word to divorced people is the biblical word to anybody who looks back on yesterday's failures—there is the possibility of beginning new, the possibility of new life, or better things for the future, no matter how bad the past was. That word has to be there . . . but in company with the other.

The evangelical church has psychologized its way out of sturdy theology. I don't like the way they do it at all, but the hardline fundamentalist churches have kept something that the mainline churches lost.

DOOR: You mentioned a couple's inability to keep the marriage covenant. Is it really true that people are unable to keep their commitment?

SMEDES: I'm not in a position to know when someone is unable, but my suspicion is that most people jump to the conclusion that they are unable when they are, in fact, unwilling. They jump to the conclusion that the pain is too great when, in fact, it isn't. They don't know yet. Love suffers long. That doesn't tell us how long, but it suggests that it might be longer than we imagine. Yes, there comes a time when the destructiveness of a marriage is so great that the evil of staying with it is worse than the evil of getting out of it. But that's not saying very much. It's parallel to the notion of a "just war." There are awful times when the hell of war might be worse than the hell of peace, but that doesn't say a good word for war. A basic decision has got to be made by a religious person. Are there tracks of human associations that are meant to be kept and is marriage one of those tracks? I think it is.

DOOR: Does divorce disqualify a Christian leader from leading?

SMEDES: Not necessarily. Not divorce per se. Two or three divorces might show that a person is not capable of maintaining credibility, but I'm not saying that someone who gets a divorce shouldn't hold a marriage seminar. Or that a divorced person should never preach anymore than anyone else should refrain from Christian ministry for other failures. But it shouldn't be so easy. It's still my conviction that what has happened is not simply a failure; what has happened is an offense ... and for that reason the Christian community has got to have some opportunity to say to the offender, "Forgiven! Absolvete!" The offender has to have some sense that he's been forgiven.

DOOR: What about the leader who wants acceptance without forgiveness? The leader who gets divorced and never misses a step in his or her ministry?

SMEDES: If you mean the person who represents the church of Jesus Christ officially, where the church commends this person to the public as its spokesman, then it isn't just a matter of whether he can still preach or whether he is still smart enough to teach or if he is competent to counsel ... the issue is, does he have moral credibility?

I don't think divorce per se robs him of that moral credibility, but if he divorces simply so he can marry the organist, then I'd say he is no longer competent to be a spokesman of the church. Or if he divorces after a history of marital indifference and abuse, and his wife says she can't take it anymore and he concurs; even though she initiates the divorce, I think his competence might be questioned.

I don't know. It just strikes me that while this is the time for the church to be compassionate, I think compassion has become synonymous with moral indifference in the churches today. In a mad dash to replace judgment with healing, we've forgotten that Jesus says, "God doesn't want you to get a divorce ever." And the church has to say that in our time and has to say it with a lot of credibility and power.

DOOR: Years ago in the Nazarene church, for example, anyone who was divorced couldn't be a member of the church, let alone preach in the pulpit. As a result of that, when the church stood up and said divorce was wrong, you believed it. Today it seems like many of our Christian superstars are divorced. How can the church possibly say divorce is wrong when so many of them are divorced?

SMEDES: I was at a huge church in the Midwest this spring with ten ministers on its staff. Six of those ten ministers were divorced. The Nazarene prophetic word against divorce and for permanent marriage is being damaged at that church. I'm sure divorced people feel a lot more comfortable in a church like that, but it just may be that the total community as symbolized by that Nazarene church might be healthier than the total community life that was symbolized by the church in the Midwest.

DOOR: What about this argument, "Look we've all sinned, so if you're going to make divorce an issue, then why don't you make pride an issue? If you're going to speak the hard word about divorce, then why don't you speak the hard word about other things?"

SMEDES: Well, why not. Let's speak a lot of damned hard words about a lot of things.

I'm almost shocked to hear myself talking this strongly because I didn't grow up as a Nazarene, but the church of which I am a member does have a history of being grotesquely compassionless when it comes to the matter of divorce ... particularly in respect to remarriage. Our church prevented people from being members if they were divorced and remarried. If they said that they had repented, then they had to show the sincerity of their repentance by divorcing their present wife or husband and going back to their original spouse. There were many Christians who could never join the church because they were asked by the church to destroy their second marriage by going back to the first marriage ... which was impossible because the original partner had also remarried. So you were destroying that marriage also.

My word within my own communion has been the word compassion—new beginnings, new possibilities and healing. But I hear only the pop-religious psychology coming from these people who speak around southern California ... not a prophetic word. I suspect that the prophetic word doesn't come about divorce because it doesn't come about injustice and all the other wrong as well.

DOOR: You mentioned the word compassion. Isn't real compassion difficult for all of us?

SMEDES: I think so. Compassion and forgiveness have real meaning only in accompaniment with law. You can have pity without law, but true compassion is saved from being cheap grace only if it is accompanied with law. I don't know that the church has done all that great with its emphasis on compassion. The pain of divorce is so deep and full of shame that most divorced people feel a sense of failure even when there is no judgment and no forgiveness. I don't think the church does all that great at healing, either. People are not helped that much by the most accommodating church. Divorce just hurts too much.

DOOR: Would you say that in many churches divorce is coped with by ignorance?

SMEDES: I think so. I don't know how the church can really do a job of healing when it tries to make believe that there isn't a deep disturbance that's taking place.

DOOR: What about the abundance of divorce recovery books now being written by those recovering from their own divorces?

SMEDES: It's better that those books exist and that people can get some help after having had a divorce. That's better than just resigning yourself to your own devices and your own guilt. The trouble is that those books are in harmony with the church's voice and that is only a voice of therapy, only a voice of helpfulness. Forgiveness is out of the picture. I'll bet not one of those books deals with coming to terms with forgiveness.

DOOR: Is divorce the worst sin?

SMEDES: Let me keep my answer somewhat within the jargon of my own job. It strikes me that we have, as evangelical Christians, bought into the hedonism of our time, we've religicized it. Today the most important thing is to be "happy" and then to interpret happiness as pleasure. In the last ten years I have felt more dissatisfaction with my marriage than I have in the first twenty years. I think it is because of where I live and the times that I live in. I'm affected by a desire to get more pleasure in my marriage and I'm less satisfied when it's not there. If an old curmudgeon like me senses that in himself, I'm sure that it happens to people who are less Calvinistic and more hedonistic by nature than I am. Of course, people would never call it hedonism, but what they are doing is nothing more than an escape from pain to pleasure.

Another factor is the new legitimacy of eros. Erotic love. Sexuality. We have become far more tuned to our erotic needs and desires, and we have let our fantasies come out in the form of demands for erotic fulfillment. Look at the glut of books on sex. I've written one myself on sexuality. It indicates that we're involved and thinking about the adventure, excitement, and passion of eros, and that makes us dissatisfied with what often is the boring routine of a marriage when the flame has gone down.

The third thing that has contributed to the trouble of divorce in the evangelical circle is theology, a theology that has been dominated by psychology. We emphasize relationship at the cost of covenant. We emphasize fulfillment at the cost of fidelity. We emphasize one's personal future over against one's personal history. We emphasize pleasure over character. Today, it's become more important for people to be happy than for people to be good. These are theological categories.

These things have happened, plus there's the fact that evangelicals, like everybody else, have become victims of the loss of supportive communities. We don't have neighbors. Most of our neighbors could not care less if we got a divorce because they don't know us. We're not neighbors at all ... just people who happen to have houses next to each other. We're not a neighborhood. We don't have an ethos in which divorce is looked on as a tragedy or a shock.

DOOR: Where does the church go from here?

SMEDES: I think the Christian community has got to examine what goes into fidelity. I don't mean by fidelity not sleeping with somebody else. I mean fidelity to love. Fidelity to marriage. Fidelity to make a marriage on what's good, compassionate, loving, kind, and honest. Fidelity to the genuine good of the partner.

DOOR: What produces fidelity in people? How can the church help in the nurture of this kind of character?

SMEDES: Our characters have been affected by the world we live in. The church might, therefore, ask again about the function of preaching. How does preaching affect character? I suspect that old-fashioned, puritan preaching affected character, that old-fashioned preaching had a character productive power. In short, I think the church has to preach the law as well as grace . . . even though I like to preach grace better than the law.

DOOR: Can the church do anything to stop the increasing incidence of divorce in the American culture?

SMEDES: Maybe Bertrand Russell had a point in 1921 when he said that the basic cause of divorce was marriage. He meant that the only cure for divorce is to do away with marriage . . . have only families. Then, if you do have a family, make divorce almost impossible to get. In other words, until you have a family, don't have a marriage. Let people have friends, live together, let them do what they wish, but the moment there is a child then the law enters. That was really wild in 1921, but it's not so wild anymore because it's practically that way now. When Bertrand Russell said that, the church people only heard the part about marriage—they didn't hear what he said about the family. He wanted to make the law really rigid when it came to breaking up a family. Maybe that's the way the church will have to go in terms of what it seeks from the law. I don't think we're ever going back to making divorce harder to get, and I doubt if we'll go back to making divorce less frequent.

RON SIDER

Ronald J. Sider is an evangelical, radical, social activist, professor of theology and culture at Eastern Baptist Seminary in a suburb of Philadelphia. He is also fairly short, married to Arbutus Lichti Sider, has three children, a Volkswagen, a Volvo, and has one vice—books.

Ron received his B.A. at Waterloo Lutheran University, then went to Yale where he received a B.A., M.A., and Ph.D. His dissertation was entitled "The Life and Thoughts of Andreas Bodenstein von Karlstadt Through 1524." (He was a fellow theologian with Martin Luther at the University of Wittenberg.)

Ron Sider, author of *Rich Christians in a Hungry World* and numerous other writings on social justice (including the recent *Nonviolence: An Invincible Weapon?* and *Completely Pro-Life*) remains one of the primary spokespersons on social issues in the church. He is executive director for Evangelicals for Social Action as well as for Just Life, not to mention president of the Andreas Bodenstein von Karlstadt Fan Club, of which H. Winfield Tutte is a charter member.

The Keepers of the *Door* traveled to Philadelphia in 1979 to a mutually agreed upon location where we were blindfolded and driven to Eastern Baptist Seminary. The blindfolds were taken off and we were led down a large hall to a room full of books where we met Ronald Sider in person. We found Ron Sider to be soft-spoken, personable, and deeply committed. We left his office with the feeling that we had met someone significant. He shared his ideas and his passions with us, and we are the richer for it. The church is richer because of his presence, and after you read this interview, we think you will agree.

DOOR: What is the difference between Christian social action and other kinds of social action?

SIDER: Social action is Christian when it begins with the assumption that Christ is Lord and then tries to reshape the structures of our society on the basis of God's revelation about the nature of justice. A profoundly biblical movement immerses its activity in prayer, is guided by the Holy Spirit, and involves a lot of direct evangelism as well.

DOOR: So far you sound like Campus Crusade. Somehow we don't think there is much similarity. How would those assumptions you mentioned look in practice?

SIDER: Suppose we have a multinational corporation that is acting in an unjust manner. We would start by having a whole group of people pray for several weeks as we plan our strategy. We would then approach the corporation and say, "We come in the name of Jesus Christ. He wills justice for the poor and your operations are simply not just. You go to church and confess him as Lord so we come to you as brothers." (There aren't many sisters at the top of multi-national corporations.) We would have a group of people praying as that happened. And we'd believe that sometimes the Holy Spirit would be so present that a person would say, "I see what you are saying. I must make Christ Lord of my activities with this company." We wouldn't in any way assume that that would always be the case. If anything is clear from the Bible it is that people resist God's will and may say no to the call to repent.

DOOR: If the corporation didn't respond to your "call," what would you do then?

SIDER: We wouldn't stop at that point. We would then go on to organize stockowners' options, boycotts, demonstrations, etc. But all the way through we'd immerse it in prayer and expect the Holy Spirit to act. We'd even expect people to be converted.

DOOR: It has been said that Christian social activism is nothing more than the political activism of the sixties twenty years too late.

SIDER: The kinds of movements I dream about are significantly different than the social justice activities of the sixties. The social action of the last decades (some of it very excellent and very costly) was inadequate at several points. The activists didn't do a very good job explaining when their positions were grounded in Scripture. I don't think it was rooted in prayer or rooted in the Holy Spirit. It was too secular. That doesn't mean that you don't try to change structure. I want to change structures, but I want to do it in the power of the Spirit. I want to do it in a way that doesn't exclude evangelism. God may want some governmental and business structures to change because the people at the top become Christians. But I know very well that you don't change whole structures just by converting the person at the top. In fact, in many cases, the person at the top will be kicked out if he starts to operate a company based on biblical norms rather than on profit.

DOOR: Are the biblical norms you speak of the same for a conservative Republican?

SIDER: The Bible does not have an economic blueprint for the modern economy or a political platform for the next presidential candidate. But Scriptures do give us some fundamental clues about what justice should look like in society, and some fundamental principles.

DOOR: What are those fundamental principles?

SIDER: That God is on the side of the poor. That God wills structural mechanisms which tend to reduce the extremes of wealth and poverty—both among the people of God and society at large. The Bible tells us about the fundamental value of every person. But it is a big jump from biblical principles to a specific public policy option. It's not a simplistic jump. There is a lot more room for honest disagreement between Christians regarding public policy options that are a faithful implementation of biblical norms than there is regarding the biblical norms themselves. But that doesn't mean the whole thing is totally wide open either. If we were all willing to try as faithfully as we could to be shaped by biblical norms about justice and God's concern for the poor, then we would be pointed in one direction rather than another.

DOOR: Do you mean that two congressmen could then come to different conclusions on a piece of legislation?

SIDER: There must be freedom for evangelicals in Congress to have different viewpoints. There isn't just one faithful move from biblical principles to public policy. But what would happen if all the people who claimed to be biblical Christians in Congress would say, "We're going to get together once a week. We believe that Christ is Lord and he has to be Lord of our politics. Therefore, we want our political action to reflect that. We are going to explain to each other why we voted the way we did and explain that in terms of how we understand Scripture." I'd be willing to bet that would change the way people voted in a short period of time because they would have to give account to each other. The tragedy is that we assume that somehow our faith has very little to do with that area. So people end up getting their political direction from society, from a secular source, from their political party rather than from their faith.

DOOR: Is it possible for biblical Christians to come to different conclusions about issues?

SIDER: Well, it was kind of startling when Senator Hatfield joined with a very conservative Senator Buckley to cosponsor the "Right to Life" amendment. Senator Hatfield felt that grew out of his biblical faith. He's seen as a liberal, but he joined with a conservative. That sort of thing might happen more often if people were really trying to let Scripture inform their politics.

DOOR: But the fact that you just said "it was kind of startling" implies that even *you* were surprised by Hatfield's actions. It implies that you would have expected Hatfield to come to a different conclusion. So isn't it true that social activists expect certain conclusions to be made about what is biblical and what isn't? Can Christian social activists tolerate significant differences in opinion?

SIDER: I have to ask what you mean. We all must be committed to the basic things that Scripture says God's people must be committed to. You wouldn't want to say that a whole block of the church can be faithful and have no interest in evangelism. That is not acceptable. It is equally true in the case of justice. It is *not* true what liberation theologians are saying that knowing God is nothing *but* seeking justice. But you can't know God without seeking justice.

DOOR: Are you saying then that justice is a concern for all Christians?

SIDER: The evangelical church has virtually ignored the whole question of justice in society and God's special concern for the poor for decades. The fact that we have ignored those issues means that we've really fallen into theological liberalism. The essence of theological liberalism is to let surrounding society, rather than biblical faith, provide the norms for our thinking and action. Evangelicals know the bodily resurrection of Jesus is absolutely crucial to our faith, but then they turn around and allow our materialistic society, rather than Scripture, to be our norm.

DOOR: So to be an evangelical and be only concerned with evangelism is not enough?

SIDER: No. It is not acceptable to have groups of evangelicals who are not concerned with justice in society and justice for the poor. That is a fundamental denial of our confession that Christ is Lord of every area of life and a fundamental denial that all of Scripture is normative. That doesn't mean that every individual has to be as active as every other individual in politics or justice. There are different callings. Billy Graham should do evangelism and Mark Hatfield should do politics. But there is a fundamental kind of unfaithfulness in a lot of our churches. Pastors are preaching what the people want to hear, and people want to hear about the comfort and meaning the Christian faith brings. They want to hear about forgiveness and the alleviation of guilt. That's important. It is a crucial part of biblical faith. They are less interested in hearing about unjust economic structures. And if we're really going to be biblical people, then what God's Word says, rather than what our people want to hear, must be decisive.

DOOR: But are issues of social concern the only things that make Christians uncomfortable?

SIDER: No. They don't want to hear the biblical norms about sexual faithfulness, the family, or homosexuality. What I am pleading for is biblical balance. I want to see churches that are doing only evangelism doing social justice; churches that are concerned only with worship more concerned about community. The people who are concerned with social justice can't let people who are not concerned with it off the hook. Tolerance just won't do. But the people who are concerned with evangelism dare not let certain evangelical social activities ignore evangelism either.

DOOR: It is easy to feel guilty when you are around a social activist. Many social activists seem to have an air of "one-upmanship."

SIDER: There is undoubtedly a powerful temptation to self-righteousness and arrogance among people who are concerned with social justice in a passionate way. That's too bad. It shouldn't be there. It's not justified.

The other side, though, is that at one level the gospel is bad news to unjust rich folk. God wills justice for the poor so if one is rich in the context of systems that make one rich by oppression, then coming to Jesus is going to mean repenting of that sinful involvement in structural injustice and making changes that are going to be costly. Of course, it's actually not bad news at all. The biblical call to repentance, change, and joining Jesus in the new messianic community is a call to the deepest kind of joy, peace, reconciliation, and fulfillment. But at one level the kind of tension (feelings of guilt) you mention is inherent in the message but is sometimes complicated by the self-righteous, harsh legalism that people like myself can too easily fall into.

DOOR: Throughout the interview you have used the term "biblical norms." You have suggested that everything we do must be evaluated by "biblical norms." Are your "biblical norms" our plumb line or is Jesus Christ?

SIDER: I sure don't want to develop some dichotomy between Jesus Christ and biblical norms. I'm committed to biblical norms because Jesus Christ my Lord calls me to biblical norms.

DOOR: But calling people to "biblical norms" and attempting to legislate these norms into structural changes sounds a lot like "legislating morality."

SIDER: I am certainly opposed to a situation where the state has civil penalties for religious stances. We must have separation of church and state. People must be free to sin. I don't want to have secular penalties exercised by the state for people who commit adultery or homosexual sins. People need to be free to make their own choices in that area and suffer the consequences. But I believe that one should legislate on issues that affect not just the person involved, but whole classes of people. So it would be appropriate to have open housing legislation that makes it illegal to refuse to sell housing to Jews or blacks.

DOOR: But there are well-meaning people on all sides of an issue, biblical people as well. The nuclear arms issue, for example.

SIDER: I'd want to ask the brother who thinks the biblically faithful response to the nuclear threat is to defeat Salt II and build more missiles, if he thinks that in the name of Jesus Christ it is being faithful to destroy a quarter of the world's people and

make the planet uninhabitable for a few millenniums.

DOOR: That's a loaded question.

SIDER: But responsible scientists say that there is at least a fifty-fifty chance there will be nuclear war in the next twenty years. People in Washington are even less optimistic.

DOOR: But there are Christians who would respond by asking if you as a biblically faithful Christian can stand by and watch atheistic nations slaughter unarmed, defenseless nations because they would not protect themselves.

SIDER: I want to ask of all people, "Are you willing to submit your position unconditionally to Christ as Lord and the biblical norms? Are you willing to go on talking about that in the Body of Christ with other folk who are equally committed to Jesus Christ?" It seems to me that if we did that, then we'd make significant progress ... although we'd never arrive at one common position on everything.

DOOR: But what we're saying is that biblical norms means different things to different people. Robert Schuller can build a beautiful glass cathedral in the name of Jesus Christ and as much as we disagree with him, we think he means it. Would you be willing to accept that he is sincere?

SIDER: I would love to sit down with Brother Schuller (and I'm quite happy to call him a brother in the Lord Jesus) and look at what the Bible says about justice and poor people. Let's look at the world and let's develop a process for trying to decide what and when church construction should happen. Let's include biblical analysis and the study of the world. Let's include major input from evangelistic, relief, and development agencies. Let's go to inner-city congregations and share our plans with them. And by all means, let's talk with evangelical artists and architects. (I'm in favor of beauty too. Look at the creation; it's a gorgeous place.) But it's not clear to me at this point in time that the only way to affirm and announce that beauty is to build a ten-million-dollar cathedral. I am open to discussion to be more informed. I accept Robert Schuller as a brother with whom I want to go on talking and by whom I want to be corrected. What I am unwilling to do is to simply say that whatever he decides is okay for him, and whatever I decide is okay for me, and we each do our own things.

To be brothers and sisters means to be accountable to each other. One of the serious disasters in the evangelical community is unbiblical organizational individualism that has infiltrated the church. Everyone does what is right in his own eyes and nobody consults with anyone else.

DOOR: Okay. It sounds good to have "brothers and sisters" accountable to each other, but for some reason we can't visualize Bill Bright being accountable to Jim Wallis or vice versa. Aren't you being naive to believe a community like that is possible?

SIDER: Am I naive to talk about Jesus' new messianic community where economic relations are fundamentally transformed? My answer is no. Not if, in fact, Jesus rose from the dead and the Holy Spirit has indeed been given. Right at the heart of the expectations for the Messiah was the hope that the Messiah would come and usher in a new age of peace and justice for all. Jesus came, said he was the Messiah, and said that two of the clearest signs that he was the Messiah

were that the blind received their sight and the Good News was preached to the poor.

I don't know why anybody finds it a surprise that Jesus' first new community in Jerusalem did radical economic sharing. They did it because Jesus said he called them to that and the gift of the Holy Spirit was just overwhelming evidence that the new age had really begun. If that is naive then so be it. I think the new messianic age has broken into the present and it's now possible to live the values of Jesus' new kingdom.

It's true that the old age continues and that the kingdom will not reach its fulfillment until Jesus returns. Until that happens there will be all kinds of sinfulness and evil, and the church will be far from perfect. But the basic affirmation is that the Messiah has come, that the new messianic age has begun, and that his new messianic community is here now and with the power of the Spirit can live according to his values.

DOOR: When you said earlier that God was on the side of the poor, did you mean it is unjust to be rich? Is there such a thing as a just rich person?

SIDER: I don't mean that poverty is the ideal. It's not. I don't mean that the poor are automatically saved because they are poor. And I don't mean that God cares more about the salvation of the poor than the rich. God cares about all equally. To say that God is concerned for the poor or that God has a special concern for the poor just doesn't capture the strength of the biblical teaching at that point. When I say that God is on the side of the poor I mean that over and over again God's at work in history, casting down the unjust rich and exalting the poor. So if you apply it to the current context, it would mean that it's not necessarily wrong to make a lot of money, if one makes it within a structure that's just.

DOOR: What does that mean?

SIDER: It means that if someone makes a lot of money, he should do it in the context of fair employment practices; he should pay his employees a good wage; he should have good working conditions; he should not discriminate against women and blacks. He should be producing something that, in fact, we need in our kind of world rather than more elaborate gadgets or products that cater to the taste of the affluent upper class. Then it's okay to make a lot of money on that needed product. But then the question is, what are you going to do with that money? What would be a faithful lifestyle then?

DOOR: That list of qualifications certainly sounds like legalism.

SIDER: You think that's legalism?

DOOR: Yes.

SIDER: Good grief! You surely don't deny that any of the qualifications I've mentioned are relevant, do you?

DOOR: No, not at all. But are they the only ones?

SIDER: No. But I'm talking about a handful of crucial ones.

DOOR: That's where we would disagree.

SIDER: Do you really?

DOOR: Yes. What about the questions that need to be asked to the workers? To the poor? Are you being honest? Are you putting in a day's work for a day's pay? Are you showing love and concern for other people? We could go on and on.

SIDER: No. Not on and on. Things aren't that complex. But I agree that

the questions you raised are also important.

DOOR: And that is our point. When you start making lists of qualifications, then we're very close to radical fundamentalist legalism.

SIDER: Not at all. We must strive in very concrete and specific ways to make Christ Lord. The fact that I mentioned specific qualifications does not mean that I think they are automatic three-second answers, but I was trying to answer your question which dealt with how one could make a lot of money justly.

DOOR: But who decides the criteria for being a kingdom person? Who settles on what is a biblical norm? Who decides what constitutes a messianic community? In other words, how do we decide whether affluence or intellectual arrogance is the primary sin?

SIDER: I just can't categorize sins and say that one group is primary and some group is secondary. You run into trouble when you do that sort of thing. The only thing we can do is let the whole biblical message inform us, go on dialoguing within the Body, and hope we'll make progress. The tragedy is that we infrequently really sit down and talk with people we fundamentally disagree with.

But let me come back to the issue you raised about legalism. I felt you weren't just playing the devil's advocate at that point.

DOOR: We weren't.

SIDER: I really believe I am not a legalist. But somehow I'm coming across that way. I want to allow room for individual diversity. I want individuals rather than communities to finally decide individual questions of where to spend their money. There is no *one* faithful lifestyle.

DOOR: But?

SIDER: But that doesn't mean there aren't very important biblical norms that are relevant or that one can simply decide these questions on their own. There is a need to ask what the biblical principles are on these questions, and then you need to talk about that in the context of the church. That is not legalism at all. It is a community-oriented, Spirit-oriented, biblically oriented way of trying to make decisions. And each piece of those—the Scriptures, the needs of the contemporary world, discussion in community, dependence on prayer and the Holy Spirit—are all crucial pieces.

DOOR: Is that kind of biblical soul-searching and discussion possible in the church?

SIDER: Yes, it is. Take the issue of lifestyle. If a local congregation would take the next three years and make it a top agenda item, they would start out with very different points of view. I don't think they would arrive at one uniform position ultimately, but I'm thoroughly convinced that the Spirit would give them a sense of direction as they looked at the world's situation together, and that the more well-to-do people would want to live more simply than they do now.

DOOR: You mentioned a number of times that evangelism ought to be just as important as social action. Do you really believe that?

SIDER: Theoretically I'm committed to evangelism as well as social justice. They are equally important. That doesn't mean that each individual must do equal amounts of each. But practically, in my personal life, I have not been satisfied in that I really wasn't sharing my faith in any direct or frequent way. Recently I was in Africa lecturing on social justice, and I was approached by a Jewish university student who is deeply involved in social justice in Africa. We talked about politics for hours, and then he said to me, "Ron, I'm burned out. God told me if I came to this conference, I'd learn something about his Son." I gulped, my heart skipped a beat, and I shared my faith and invited him to accept Christ. He struggled. He didn't want to be like the white Christians he had met who loved Jesus but didn't care about injustice. He was afraid to come to Christ and lose his commitment to social justice. I said that he didn't have to lose his commitment to social justice and again invited him to come to Christ. We prayed together and he did! It was very renewing for me. I hope it happens scores of times in the next decade.

FREDERICK BUECHNER

It is my name. It is pronounced Beekner. If somebody mispronounces it in some foolish way, I have the feeling that what's foolish is me. If somebody forgets it, I feel that it's I who am forgotten. There's something about it that embarrasses me in just the same way that there's something about me that embarrasses me. I can't imagine myself with any other name—Held, say, or Merrill, or Hlavacek. If my name were different, I would be different. When I tell somebody my name, I have given him a hold over me that he didn't have before. If he calls it out, I stop, look, and listen whether I want to or not.

In the book of Exodus, God tells Moses that his name is Yahweh, and God hasn't had a peaceful moment since.
Wishful Thinking, p. 12

Buech-ner, Fred-er-ick (Beek'ner), n. 1. A twentieth-century writer/minister. 2. Location: Vermont—as in rambling New England farm complete with rambling New England house.

Background (bak'ground), n. 1. One's training and experience. 2. Union Seminary. 3. Teacher at Exeter (Eastern Prep School). 4. Writer—more than two dozen books; a 1980 Pulitzer Prize nominee for his novel *Godric*. 5. Married. Three children. All girls.

Books (books), n. 1. Printed works on sheets of paper bound together, sometimes between hard covers. 2. *Whistling in the Dark* . 3. *A Room Called Remember* . 4. *Peculiar Treasures* 5. *The Book of Bebb*.

Pho-bi-a (fo' bee-ah), n. 1. An irrational, excessive, and persistent fear of something. Example: Frederick Buechner refuses to fly anywhere.

Pig (pig), n. 1. A domesticated animal with broad snout and fat body; swine, hog. 2. Enormous black-and-white pet of Buechner family. 3. Name: Piggy.

Gift (gift), n. 1. A natural ability; i.e., makes gospel new and alive while using the unfamiliar, the unexpected. 2. Ability to give new insight by not speaking in cliches.

Worthwhile (wurth whil), adj. 1. Worth the time or effort spent; of true value, as in the statement, "This interview is worthwhile."

DOOR: It is kind of refreshing to meet someone who speaks about the Christian faith in a new way, at least a new way to us. What is your connection with the church?

BUECHNER: To be honest, I grew up without any real church connection. When I was young, I was nominally an Episcopalian. I was confirmed, but had no strong connection.

DOOR: But you are Presbyterian. How did that come about?

BUECHNER: It was really almost a matter of tossing a coin. When it came time to be ordained (I had to be ordained in some particular church), I chose Presbyterian, basically because of George Buttrick. It was in his church that the whole thing came alive.

DOOR: What happened?

BUECHNER: Years ago I had decided to move to New York and become a writer. While I was there, I drifted into George Buttrick's church on a Sunday morning—for no good reason, really, except it was there and I had nothing else to do. Buttrick preached the sermon, and he was talking about coronations. (He was a marvelous preacher because he had no finesse. He plucked at his robes and mumbled his words, which made him all the more powerful.) This was at the time of the present Queen's coronation, and he was talking about Jesus at the time of his temptation. He said that Jesus was offered a crown, like Queen Elizabeth's, if he would kneel down and worship Satan, but he turned it down. Then Buttrick said, "But now Jesus is crowned in the heart of the believer," and he used this phrase, "among tears and confession and great laughter." For reasons I've never been able to explain, that phrase "great laughter" absolutely decimated me. I found tears spouting from my eyes. If one were looking for the "born-again" experience, in some funny way, this was it. I couldn't have told you then, nor can I tell you now, why the phrase "great laughter" did it. Maybe it was the laughter of incredulity that perhaps it was true, or the laughter of relief that all the things that might have been true, instead weren't.

DOOR: Is it the thought that the gospel is really true that overwhelms you?

BUECHNER: It's sort of a continuing dim spectacle of the subterranean presence of grace in the world that haunts me. If you look deeply enough into yourself or into the *New York Times*, there are many mysteries. And the mystery of the mysteries at the bottom of the well, at the far reach of the road, is the mystery of God, of Christ. This is what I explore as a novelist—the incredibleness of it, the spectrum of it. It seems as if maybe it isn't true . . . but, yes, maybe it is true! And the moments when it seems to be true are just staggering moments.

DOOR: You are an ordained Presbyterian minister?

BUECHNER: Yes, but I'm afraid I'm a bad Presbyterian. Just the other day I was invited to give a talk on "Why I Am a Presbyterian." I told them I couldn't possibly, because I don't know why I'm a Presbyterian.

DOOR: That probably doesn't make the Presbyterian fathers very happy, does it?

BUECHNER: In fact, I keep getting letters from the Presbyterian church asking how I justify my ordination. It is a question that absolutely makes my scalp go cold. How can anybody "justify" his ministry? Is the ministry or priesthood something you can put on and take off? What they are saying to me is, "You've taken off your coat of ministry, so let us take you off the rolls." Something in me just rises up in horror. I was ordained an evangelist. If an evangelist is one who preaches the Christian faith as best he can, then that's what I've spent my life doing.

DOOR: Being an evangelist, you must have heard of the four spiritual laws?

BUECHNER: I don't know that I have.

DOOR: And you call yourself an evangelist? Bill Bright would not be happy.

BUECHNER: Who is Bill Bright?

DOOR: Seriously? You have never heard of the founder and president of Campus Crusade, an evangelical organization committed to reaching the world by 1984? An organization that is in the process of raising one billion dollars to reach the world for Christ?

BUECHNER: He hasn't reached me.

DOOR: Your religious books don't seem very religious, which is a compliment, by the way.

BUECHNER: Well, I've never learned to talk about the Christian faith in the accustomed way. I've talked about it in the only way I can. In some ways it has created a dilemma for me as a writer, because my religious books are too colloquial and too secular for church people, yet too churchy for secular people.

DOOR: So are you primarily a writer who happens to be a minister, or a minister who happens to be a writer?

BUECHNER: People sometimes say to me, "Why did you get out of the ministry?" I find that deeply upsetting, because I don't, in any sense, think of myself as giving up the ministry. But I do think of writing as a ministry.

DOOR: The Bible is very important in the evangelical church. There is a lot of discussion about the inerrancy issue. In your books, you seem to approach the Bible in a very unique way. How do you read the Bible?

BUECHNER: How many ways are there to read the Bible? You can read it devotionally, and I suppose I do that somewhat, St. Paul especially. But I don't want to give the impression I'm a great Bible reader. I don't sit down every day and read for an hour through the Bible. But I really do read it with a great deal of pleasure ... which is the last thing I would have suspected. It's fun to read. So I read it sometimes as a devotional, but really more, not for fun, but because it's fascinating.

DOOR: Is the Bible truth?

BUECHNER: There is a wonderful piece by Karl Barth in a book called *The Word of God, the Word of Man.* He says that reading the Bible is like looking down from a building onto the street and seeing everyone looking up, pointing at something. Because of the way the window is situated, you can't see what they're seeing but you realize they are seeing something of extraordinary importance. That is what it is like to read the Bible. It's full of people, all pointing up at some extraordinary event. All those different fingers are pointing at truth; all those different voices are babbling about truth in all the Bible's different forms.

DOOR: But what is the truth the fingers are pointing to?

BUECHNER: Well, the truth has to do basically with the presence of God in history, the presence of God in the tangled history of Israel, of all places, and the tangled histories of all of us. The truth is very hard to verbalize without making it sound like a platitude framed on a minister's wall. It is a living truth in the sense that it is better experienced than explained. Not even the Bible can contain it finally, but only point to it.

DOOR: You mentioned in your book *Wishful Thinking* that reading the Bible as literature is like reading *Moby Dick* as a whaling manual. As evangelicals, our problem seems to be the opposite—an extreme literalism that reads the Bible as a whaling manual rather than literature.

BUECHNER: You can't listen to some of the more blood-curdling psalms without feeling they've got something basically wrong. The one I always think of is Psalm 137:9, "Happy shall he be, that taketh and dasheth thy little ones against the stones." Something has gone wrong. That must be an imperfect expression of the majesty of God. But I would want to be very careful with the one who does take the Bible literally. We had a baby-sitter once who was very fundamentalistic. She became a Jehovah's Witness later on. She would say to me, "Mr. Buechner, I will not allow my children to take the Salk vaccine because the Bible says you are not to eat blood, and everyone knows there is blood in the Salk vaccine. What do you think?" Part of me wanted to say that such a response was a travesty, and suggest that, of course, her children should have the Salk vaccine. But I always drew back from saying that, because I was afraid that if I destroyed that way of reading the Bible, I might destroy all sorts of other things. But I have always had the feeling that to take things literally may be closer to the truth than some of the more sophisticated ways of looking at the Bible. If you want to talk of being literally washed in the blood of the lamb, there is something in me that recoils from that. Yet, in another sense, I'd rather have that kind of language used as an expression of the experience of Christ than whatever it might be watered down to.

DOOR: What does the Bible tell you about Jesus Christ?

BUECHNER: He's central. I mean, he's there even when he's not being talked about. I never felt that so much as I did while reading the book of Job, the other day—Christ in Job, the innocent sufferer. Christ is an enormously moving figure. I never cease to be moved to the roots of my being. (I'm even moved now thinking about him.) It is only his friends who make him boring. You'd think he'd grow stale after a while. Certainly, the Bible can grow stale, but I've never found him to grow stale. I've never been bored by him.

DOOR: Is the Bible primarily a book of rules, principles, and norms set down for us to follow?

BUECHNER: I don't feel that. At least that's not what I hear. To me, the most precious words of his are, "Come unto me, all who labor and are heavy laden." I can hardly speak those words without getting a lump in my throat. It is as though the Jesus that comes through to me is less a lawgiver, for all his giving of laws, than the speaker of a stern and loving word. What I hear is his great openness. What I experience is the opening up of a whole new range of possibilities. Jesus has the invitation. He's the inviter, the opener of doors. Falling back on biblical images, he opens the door, and a light floods through that you never dreamed possible.

DOOR: Your book *Telling the Truth* is subtitled *The Gospel as Tragedy, Comedy, and Fairy Tale.* Of course, the most intriguing part of that is your concept of the gospel as fairy tale. What do you mean?

BUECHNER: I mean the idea of preaching the gospel in all its preposterousness and not trying to water it down. The gospel does have many of the earmarks of a fairy tale. In fairy tales you have the poor boy who becomes rich, the leaden cabinet which turns out to have the treasure in it, the ugly duckling who turns out to be a swan, the frog who becomes a prince. Then we come to the gospel, where it's the Pharisees, the good ones, who turn out to be the villains. It's the whores and tax collectors who turn out to be the good ones. Just as in fairy tales, there is the impossible happy ending when Cinderella does marry the prince, and the ugly duckling is transformed into a swan, so Jesus is not, in the end, defeated. He rises again. In all these ways there is a kind of fairy-tale quality to the gospel, with the extraordinary difference, of course, that this is the fairy tale that claims to be true. The difference is that this time it's not just a story being told—it's an event. It did happen! Here's a fairy tale come true.

DOOR: It seems that many of us have tried to squeeze the fairy-tale quality out of the gospel. We have taken the peace that passes understanding and made it the peace everyone can understand.

BUECHNER: One of the greatest temptations, of course, in trying to sell something is to put it in terms that people will find palatable and swallowable. To reduce it to something that others will find in their powers to believe. But maybe the best apologetics is to present the truth as it really is. Why not present the gospel in all its madness? Why not say things like, "Yes, you will be given your life back again. Yes, it doesn't end with death. Yes, the kingdom will come. Yes, Christ will come down from heaven." Maybe people are hungry for these wild and mad things which some preachers attempt to pull down to earth.

DOOR: How do we keep our eyes open to the fairy-tale quality of the gospel?

BUECHNER: There has always been a certain mystery to me about Jesus' saying that we must become like children. I think that is the answer to your question. A lot of what I'm trying to do as a preacher and writer is to reawaken the child in people. The child is the one who trusts. The child will at least go and look for the magic place. The child is the one who is not ashamed of not knowing the answers, because he's not expected to know the answers. Maybe this is part of calling the gospel a fairy tale. Who believes more in fairy tales than a child? Therefore, maybe we need to speak to the child in people, who can indeed believe.

DOOR: You are invited to speak to ministers a great deal. What do you tell them?

BUECHNER: I tell them that a minister has only two stories to tell. One is the story of Jesus. The other is his own story. Most ministers don't dare tell their own stories—the ups and downs, the darks and lights. In a sense, the two stories are the same story. The parallels are not exact . . . Jesus is tempted and resists; we are tempted and don't resist. Of course, all ministers draw some stories from their lives—what somebody said or something that happened, but I mean more than that. If you want to talk about grace, if you want to talk about revelation, talk about your life with some depth (which doesn't mean lurid revelations as much as simply looking to your own deep experiences and describing them as they are). Many ministers agree that this is the way they should bear witness to their faith, but instead of drawing on their lives for truth, they draw on it only for anecdote.

HAROLD LINDSELL

In the next two interviews, Harold Lindsell and Jack Rogers battle it out. The issue? Biblical inerrancy. The stakes? Evangelicalism itself, says Harold Lindsell.

Yep, there were fierce battles ahead for Hurricane Harold at the time of this interview, including a book defending capitalism as a biblical view (*Free Enterprise: A Judeo-Christian Defense*) and another about the Second Coming (*The Gathering Storm*).

Now seventy-six years old, Harold weighed in for this interview at one-hundred-eighty pounds and is 6'3". He is married, and rooting for him in this bout are four children and lots of grandchildren.

In preparation for this level of competition, Lindsell began his training with a B.A. at Wheaton, then his M.A. at U.C. Berkeley, his Ph.D. at N.Y.U., and an honorary D.D. from Fuller Seminary. He's taught at Columbia Bible College, Northwestern Baptist Seminary, Fuller, and spent ten of thirteen years at *Christianity Today* as editor.

Harold's book *Battle for the Bible*, however, brings us to the present controversy, whereby tonight's bout with Jack "The Ripper" Rogers could well make any future confrontations seem comparatively pleasant.

DOOR: Why did you decide the issue of inerrancy was crucial at this moment—crucial enough to write a book about it and to put yourself out on a limb?

LINDSELL: I had become convinced that something was taking place which I thought to be of singular significance—namely that people who were normally called evangelicals had been deeply infiltrated by a view of Scripture which has not been common to evangelical theology. In other words, there were now substantial numbers disbelieving that the Bible is without error. They were saying, one way or another, that the Bible has errors in it. You can say that in a number of ways. You can say that inerrancy is limited to matters of faith and practice. You can adopt the JEPD hypothesis; you can raise questions about the dual authorship of Isaiah, or suggest that Daniel was written after the prophetic events occurred. Whatever, I sensed erosion in the view of Scripture that had been maintained historically by evangelicals.

DOOR: Why did you decide to personalize the issue, rather than deal with the issue in general?

LINDSELL: If I had written the book in a general framework, there would have been no repercussions of any significance.

DOOR: You have certainly had significant repercussions.

LINDSELL: Remember we are dealing within the scholarly context. And the first question anybody's going to ask when you write a book like this is, "What is your substantiation for the serious allegations you've made?" If I had not named names I would have been derelict in my duty as a scholar. I had to name names.

DOOR: You have been accused of using the issue of inerrancy as a camouflage for personal attack on Fuller Seminary.

LINDSELL: The book was not written with Fuller in view. Fuller Seminary is only one small part of the total picture, and a far less significant part than they themselves imagine. The Southern Baptist Convention is a far more significant part of this problem because there are thirteen and a half million Southern Baptists. We're talking about approximately 40,000 churches. The Southern Baptists are, perhaps, the most alive denomination, from the vantage point of evangelism. By the way, it is my conviction as a historian, that once you lose Scripture you also lose evangelism. Secondly, the Lutheran Church-Missouri Synod is far more significant than Fuller Theological Seminary. I'm speaking of size and

importance and significance to the total world picture. Look at the Evangelical Theological Society which has a thousand or more members in it. That society was established with one point in its doctrinal statement, and that was inerrancy. Yet you have scholars representing institutions all around America and Canada in this organization who do not believe in inerrancy. These men are saying things contrary to the doctrinal statement which they signed. That's not only a theological question; that's an ethical question. The ultimate question is this: Did I tell the truth? All that any person or institution needs to do is come out and say that Harold Lindsell is mistaken. All any of these people need to do is publicly say, "We believe, as we always have believed, that the Bible is free from all error in the whole and in the part." Fuller never said that. Bernie Ramm hasn't said that. Clark Pinnock hasn't said that. Nobody has said that.

DOOR: What difference does inerrancy make to the layperson?

LINDSELL: The answer depends upon how much he knows and how much he thinks. From a theological perspective it becomes very significant. Once you say the Bible has error you immediately have three very severe theological problems. The first problem has to do with your Christology, your theology about the person of Jesus. Jesus taught that the Scripture cannot be broken. If I don't believe what Jesus said about Scripture, why should I believe what Jesus said about salvation? Secondly, the Holy Spirit is the author of Scripture, and he is the one who made the Scripture errorless. So when I deny what Jesus taught, I'm also denying the witness of the Holy Spirit. Thirdly, you have a bibliological error. If you don't believe what the prophets and the apostles taught, you have a bibliological error. When you discount the person of Jesus, the Holy Spirit, and the prophets in Scriptures, it's serious.

DOOR: Do you have to believe in inerrancy to be a Christian?

LINDSELL: Belief in Jesus Christ is salvational. I have never said that if a person doesn't hold to biblical inerrancy he cannot be saved. I have asked the question, "If a man does not believe in inerrancy, can he truly be an evangelical?"

DOOR: The critics of inerrancy say that the Bible nowhere claims inerrancy. Do you disagree with that?

LINDSELL: The Bible claims the doctrine of the Trinity. The word *Trinity* does not appear in Scripture. But the Trinity, Trinitarianism, is a basic concept of systematic theology. The word *inerrancy* doesn't appear in Scripture, but the Bible definitely claims inerrancy.

DOOR: What do you mean by the word *inerrant*?

LINDSELL: All of the Bible and each part of it is free from error. It was St. Augustine who wrote a letter to Jerome which said that once you open up the Scripture to one error in principle, you can open up the Scripture to all kinds of errors at all points. He says this: "Freely do I admit to you, my friend, that I have learned to ascribe to those books which are canonical work. (Now notice that word *canonical*. He's talking about the canon of Scripture.) And only to them such reverence and honor that I firmly believe that no single error due to the author is found in any one of them. And when I am confronted in these books with anything that seems to be at variance

with truth, I do not hesitate to put it down either to the use of an incorrect text or to the failure of a commentator rightly to explain the word or to my own mistaken understanding of the passage."

I would buy St. Augustine's definition. He goes on, "That it is one question whether it may be at any time the duty of a man to deceive, but it is another question whether it can have been the duty of the writer of the Holy Scripture to deceive. Nay, it is not another question, it is no question at all. For if you once admit into such a high sanctuary of authority, one false statement as made in the way of duty, there will not be left a single sentence of those books which if appearing to anyone difficult in practice or hard to believe, may not by the same fatal rule be explained away as a statement in which intentionally and under sense of duty the author declared what was not true."

People have said that inerrancy is Lindsell's view of the Scripture. It's not *my* view of the Scripture. It's the view of the church, of Augustine, of Jesus. Not my view.

DOOR: What is without error? The King James Version? The original autographs?

LINDSELL: The answer is the autographs as they were given in the Hebrew and the Greek. Of course you can translate from one language to another and you can make mistakes in translation.

DOOR: So what version do we trust?

LINDSELL: Any translation is a trustworthy translation to the extent that it's a correct rendering of the Greek or the Hebrew. There are problems, of course. But that isn't the question. The question is, "When God gave the autographs, did he tell us what isn't true?"

DOOR: Isn't the issue of inerrancy inconsequential and divisive?

LINDSELL: Let's go back in the history of the Christian church. The issues were always divisive. You had your Christological controversies about the person of Jesus. The Reformation was highly divisive. Read Martin Luther's book on the bondage of the will. If you think that the things I have written were mean, nasty, and unloving, let me tell you, Martin Luther's got me beat by a wide margin. He was as tough and rough as anyone could be. He not only named names, he used horrible names. I'm not defending him. I'm just saying that great controversial issues always result in division. The truth unites and the truth divides. The Christian faith is a divisive faith intrinsically because it rules out the Buddhist, the Hindu, the Muslim, and the cults—everyone else. We could have peace with them all if we wanted to. All we have to do is give up those things we think intrinsic to the Christian faith.

DOOR: But is the issue of inerrancy absolutely integral to faith, or is it peripheral, like the issue of baptism?

LINDSELL: The issue of baptism is inconsequential. It is an open question, just like the issue of church government. I wouldn't divide over those things even though churches are divided over them. But the reason I think inerrancy is of such significance is that, from a historical viewpoint, once you take that step it is a fatal step. It inevitably leads you down the primrose path until you deny the other great fundamentals of the faith.

DOOR: That's what has been called . . .

LINDSELL: The domino theology?

DOOR: Yes.

LINDSELL: You can call it anything you want; it is the progress of unbelief.

DOOR: Can you give some specific examples?

LINDSELL: The United Methodist Church lost a million members in ten years. The missionary task force overseas has been reduced by seventy percent. Evangelism in the Methodist church is virtually dead except for a few churches where they still are orthodox or evangelical. The United Presbyterian church has lost 700,000 members in ten years. Their missionary task force has been cut back two-thirds. This is the progress of disease. If you give up your belief in Scripture it inevitably leads to other things.

DOOR: Jack Rogers and Don McKim say in their new book, *The Authority and Interpretation of the Bible*, that inerrancy is not the traditional view of the church. They suggest that Calvin, Luther, Augustine, and others did not hold to a belief in inerrancy. They say you are wrong to claim that inerrancy is the traditional position of the church.

LINDSELL: There is nothing that I can do to change Dr. Rogers if Dr. Rogers refuses to look facts in the face. Let me give you a statement from the new *Catholic Encyclopedia*: "The inerrancy of Scripture has been the constant teaching of the fathers, the theologians, and the recent Popes in their encyclicals. It is nonetheless obvious that many biblical statements are simply not true." The author of that statement doesn't believe in inerrancy, but he acknowledges the honest historical fact that the church has always believed in inerrancy. All I can say is this: In my first book I tracked down the fathers and I gave their statements. I gave the confessions, I gave both the Roman Catholic statements and the Protestant statements. If Rogers and others don't want to believe them, there is nothing I can do about it.

DOOR: Why did you choose to call your book *The Battle for the Bible*?

LINDSELL: Titles oftentimes are different from the content of a book. There *is* a battle going on. As a Baptist I believe everybody is entitled to believe as he/she chooses. I believe in the freedom of religion. But you have no right to be deceptive. When you are hypocritical, when you profess that which you don't believe, then you are off base and you are not walking in obedience. Let's use the illustration of Fuller Seminary. Teachers were signing the creed of the seminary when they didn't believe it. I have no objection to Fuller's changing its creed, but when you sign something you don't believe, you're being dishonest.

DOOR: We agree.

LINDSELL: *Now* Fuller Seminary has changed its creed. But Paul Jewett still doesn't believe the present creed that he signs and he's still around. That's dishonest. Look, Fuller Seminary—or any institution, for that matter—has a right to change their creed or anything else they want to change as long as they're honest. But when they're deceptive, then that's where the problem lies.

DOOR: A lot of people are very angry with you and your book and have publicly said so. Have you been able to handle the criticism?

LINDSELL: When you take a stand which is not pleasing to the academic fraternity, the academic fraternity will let you have it. And, yes, the academic fraternity is not happy. That's to be understood. They're going to get mad at you. But I think I have been led to do what I did by the Holy Spirit of God, and if I don't get plaudits and approval, that's just too bad. Now, on the other hand, I have received hundreds of letters. I can only remember one that was critical. The people who write to me, they're all happy. The people who write *about* me, they're all unhappy.

DOOR: What about the danger of worshiping the Bible? Of the Bible becoming a focal point rather than the Christ of the Bible, *the God* of the Bible?

LINDSELL: There are two basic epistemological questions. The first one is this: Where do you go to get your answers to religious questions? You can go to the Koran, you can go to Mary Baker Eddy. All religions and all cults have places where you can go to get answers to questions. I start off by saying I go to the Bible to get answers to my religious questions, questions like, where do I come from? Who am I? Why am I here? What happens to me when I die? The second epistemological question is equally significant. If the source from which you get your answers is not trustworthy, you're dead. You ask me about worshiping the Bible. The function of the Bible is to lead me to Jesus Christ, but I cannot know Jesus except from Scripture. There is no other Jesus than the Jesus in the Bible. I worship Jesus. But the Word of God written and the Word of God incarnate are inextricably linked together, so that if you destroy one, you destroy the other. The Bible is the only place in which I get my knowledge of Jesus. We don't worship the Word written, we worship the Word incarnate, but it is the Word written that leads me to the Word incarnate.

DOOR: Let's talk about some of the criticisms of Scripture. There are a number of scholars now saying that Peter didn't write Peter, that Paul didn't write books attributed to him.

LINDSELL: If I look at Peter on the basis of the Scripture itself, Peter is the author of Peter. But we have people saying Peter didn't write Peter. It was written after Peter was dead in the second century. Somebody borrowed his name. If another man wrote to make me believe it was Peter writing, that's plain rank deception. Why should I believe anything else about him when he's deceiving me at that point? Usually the response is that this was the custom used in that day. My response is, are you saying that the Holy Spirit resorted to this process? Why did he write this way if he wasn't Peter? What was the purpose of his saying this—to make what he said acceptable? To make it canonical?

Well, there are lots of books in the Bible for whom the Scripture doesn't say who the author is. Hebrews doesn't say who the author is. Lots of the Old Testament books don't specify an author. The Holy Spirit doesn't have to descend to that kind of fraud and chicanery to get a book in the canon of Scripture. If I have to come to the scholars to find out what parts of Matthew, Mark, and Luke were written by them when the scholars are not even sure that Matthew, Mark, and Luke wrote the books in the first place, if I have to go to them to find out which sayings I read in the Bible Jesus really said ... well, I'm simplistic, and if it says in the Bible that Jesus said it, I think he said it. If it says that Jesus did it, I believe Jesus did it. It makes a great deal of difference whether Jesus did or didn't say these things. If it takes a scholar to tell me, then I'm trusting the scholar more than I'm trusting Matthew, and Mark, and Luke.

JACK ROGERS

In an early-round decision Jack gave up his aspirations in law and politics to pursue the ministry. After graduating from Nebraska State he went on to seminary at Pittsburgh Xenia, graduating from there in 1959.

For his doctoral work he went to the Free University of Amsterdam to study under Gene C. Berkhouwer as a philosophy of religion major. While in the Netherlands (for four years), he also taught at Westminster College.

Next stop, London. There Jack spent a great deal of time in the museum, researching the *Westminster Divines*. These huge books played an important part in Jack's physical training as well as in the writing of his dissertation on "Scripture in the Westminster Confession."

He wound up a professor philosophical theology at Fuller Seminary from 1971 to 1988, during which time he wrote *Confessions of a Conservative Evangelical*, and at the request of Fuller president Dave Hubbard, *Authority and Interpretation of the Bible: An Historical Approach.* He is currently director of theology and worship for the Presbyterian Church of the U.S.A. in Louisville, Kentucky.

Thus, Jack "The Ripper" Rogers is fully qualified to meet what may be his match, Hurricane Harold Lindsell, in tonight's BOUT FOR THE BIBLE!

DOOR: Harold Lindsell says that the church has always believed in the inerrancy of Scripture. How do you respond?

ROGERS: First of all, Lindsell begins with a definition of inerrancy which no one ever thought of until the seventeenth century. When you look historically, to find out what is the earliest exposition of Lindsell's point of view, it turns out to be the seventeenth, eighteenth, and nineteenth centuries that hold his view. Lindsell begins with the notion that the Scriptures are inerrant—accurate by what we know to be true. In other words, by the standards of modern science (but just in the original autographs). Lindsell quotes Augustine, amongst others, and finds one quote where Augustine uses the word error. Augustine said that the Scriptures do not err.

DOOR: Then you agree with Lindsell that Augustine said that.

ROGERS: The issue is, what does it mean when Augustine says the Scriptures do not err? Lindsell says the way you understand the meaning of a word is to look it up in the dictionary. But that doesn't tell you what a person who lived in the fifth century A.D. meant by a word. He didn't have the same dictionary. You have to go to his historical context to understand ... and we did.

DOOR: And what did you find?

ROGERS: Jerome translated the Old Testament from Hebrew into Latin. (This was the first time you had a Latin translation that ordinary people could read.) Augustine chews Jerome out for translating the Bible directly from the Hebrew into the Latin because Jerome should have translated from the Septuagint, the Greek translation, because it was authoritative. That's a little peculiar for a guy who would believe in the inerrancy of the original autographs. His beef with Jerome was that he was following a tradition that was started by Origen, who was the first systematic theologian of the Christian faith. Origen was getting hassled by a pagan philosopher named Porphyry. And Porphyry pointed to the place in Galatians where Peter and Paul are having a fight about whether or not Peter should eat meat when the Jews were around, and Peter was giving way to the Jews. Paul chews him out for it. Porphyry, the pagan philosopher, made a big deal of this and asked how can you believe a Bible when even the apostles who wrote it can't agree with each other. Origen responded by saying they didn't really disagree with each other. They really agreed, and that was just a little charade they put on for the benefit of the simple people who did not understand. Now that's the context and in that context, Augustine writes to Jerome and says, "I believe the Scriptures do not err."

DOOR: What you mean is that Lindsell is correct?

ROGERS: Wait a minute. What's Augustine talking about? Is he talking about technical information? Is he talking about science and astronomy, as Lindsell is? Absolutely not. Augustine says the biblical authors never intentionally told anybody a lie about a moral issue. The context is moral, not scientific.

DOOR: Then Augustine did not believe that the Scriptures were inerrant?

ROGERS: Augustine specifically denies that theory by saying you shouldn't use the Bible in matters of science. Here's a quote from Augustine: "Many non-Christians happen to be well-versed in the knowledge of the earth, the heaven and all other elements of the world, etc., etc., etc. It is therefore deplorable that Christians, even though they ostensibly base their dicta on the Bible, should utter so much nonsense that they expose themselves to ridicule. Ridicule is all they deserve, but they give the impression that the biblical authors are responsible for their mutterings, thus discrediting Christianity before the world, which is led to assume that the authors of the Scripture were ignorant fools also. Whenever any Christian is confounded and shown to be an idle chatterer, his chatter is attributed to our holy books. No wonder the critics refuse to believe what the Scripture has to say on the Resurrection, life eternal, and the kingdom of heaven, when they can point out the Bible is ostensibly wrong about facts which they can see or determine for themselves. Hence these idle boasters cause untold grief to our more thoughtful brethren."

Augustine says when you try to use the Bible to prove things about science which people can find out on their own, all you're going to do is bring the Bible into disrepute. Tell them what the Bible says about the resurrection; that's where you ought to start.

DOOR: Don't you also say Calvin did not believe in inerrancy?

ROGERS: Ken Kantzer wrote an article in *Christianity Today* where he said it's incredible that people should act as if Calvin wasn't an inerrantist. If you should need to prove this, Kantzer said, Calvin had Servetus burned because Servetus denied a minor historical detail in the Old Testament. We traced back to the sources.

DOOR: Here we go again.

ROGERS: We found what Servetus was talking about and it turned out again the issue was a moral one, not technical. Servetus had written a geography. (Actually, he'd kind of rewritten one that somebody else had done.) Calvin thought that Servetus made the claim that Moses knew that the land of Palestine was a barren and sterile land, but he lied to the children of Israel and told them it was flowing with milk and honey in order to get them to go there. He knew they wouldn't go if they knew it was a worthless place. That's what Calvin thought Servetus had said. Calvin was furious because he said the biblical authors do not lie and Moses didn't tell a lie. So, you see, it had nothing to do with geography; it had to

do with whether Moses would deliberately lie to the children of Israel.

DOOR: But doesn't Lindsell say exactly what you're saying and that is, that Moses didn't lie. Peter didn't lie. Jesus didn't lie. The Bible doesn't lie. And if you allow the view that portions of Scripture are open to an error or a mistake, that's a very serious problem.

ROGERS: That is certainly Lindsell's intent. But he confuses two things. He confuses the moral issue of lying with people speaking in a way that is suitable in another historical and cultural context. Let's get the record straight. I have never said, verbally or in print, that the Bible has mistakes in it. The inerrancy people think anybody who doesn't believe in inerrancy must believe that there are mistakes in the Bible. Those are not the only two choices. The choice is, whether you believe that the biblical writers somehow were lifted out of their own historical, cultural setting and spoke truth as if they were speaking it in the twentieth century, or whether you are willing to let them be who they were in their own historical and cultural setting and talk like first-century Jews in Palestine. That's what is at issue for me.

DOOR: Okay for willful mistakes, but what about mistake mistakes?

ROGERS: The inerrancy people want to add another dimension. They say, "But if someone was mistaken about something (mistaken as judged from our twentieth-century point of view), then you're saying he made a mistake and that mistake is an error." No, it isn't at all. The issue is did they deliberately lie to us? No. Let me give you an example. The Middle East notion of time is different from the Western notion of time. They may say noon, but to them noon is anytime between twelve and four. When we say noon we mean 12:00. Is it a mistake or an error when they say something happened at noon and they mean 3:00? No.

DOOR: Okay, let's take another issue. Suppose the book of Peter says that Peter is the author, but he wasn't. Isn't that a serious mistake?

ROGERS: I'm not a New Testament scholar, but I would be willing to think along these lines. Did people living in the first century have the same notion of copyright laws that we do? My hunch is that they didn't. Would it have been legitimate in an earlier day for a person to use the name of a well-known figure to set forth a writing that he believed was really in the spirit of this person and put forth this person's ideas? I know that as a matter of fact that was done in the ancient world. Whether it was done in the biblical times, I don't know. The point is, if that practice was understood in that context, then it would not be a lie, it would not be an error. All that's the matter is that we don't understand their way of doing things. Whether what is said in Peter is true or not, the truth does not depend upon whether Peter wrote it, but on whether whoever wrote it knew the material to be true from his own experience, however it's represented.

DOOR: Isn't a lie a lie? Isn't a lie in the first century a lie in the twentieth century?

ROGERS: Some kinds would be, but there are things . . .

DOOR: Let's suppose, for example, that in certain cultures adultery is acceptable; isn't adultery wrong whether or not a culture believes it is?

ROGERS: There are going to be things in every culture that are wrong.

It turns out that, among the Old Testament patriarchs, you can sleep with a whole bunch of women regularly, but that's not adultery. But it sure would be adultery to us, because for us adultery is sleeping with anybody except your own wife. With them it's adultery if you sleep with anybody except your own whole bunch of wives and whole bunch of concubines. If we're really going to be serious about the Bible, we cannot impose our twentieth-century notions on it. We have to look for the fact that God revealed things that were true for all people and all time, but he did reveal them in the first instance in a setting and a context that made a lot of sense to those people in that time. And some of that context no longer makes the same kind of sense to us.

DOOR: But wasn't God's intent in giving the commandment about adultery that having more than one wife is wrong?

ROGERS: I don't think you can find anything in the Old Testament that suggests that at that time God revealed to those people that polygamy was wrong. I think, as you do, that God's best will for mankind is monogamy.

DOOR: Those who believe in the inerrancy of Scripture say that once you allow for errors in Scripture eventually it will affect your Christology, your evangelism, and you will have no faith at all. Historically, they say that's what has happened.

ROGERS: That is an absolutely false statement historically. They are actually building on some very narrow historical examples, like Unitarians in New England. You can only make the statement that once you give up inerrancy, you give up everything else if you can prove that the early church theologians and reformers were inerrantists, and they were not.

DOOR: The inerrancy people name names. They mention G. C. Berkouwer.

ROGERS: He writes fourteen volumes of theology that all the inerrantists praise as probably the finest theological work from an evangelical. Then his book, *Holy Scripture*, comes out, and he doesn't say inerrancy and they say Berkouwer's changed. He hasn't changed. He has the same view of Scripture that informed all those other thirteen volumes. That is simply a false statement and they should not get away with it.

DOOR: Lindsell talks a lot about Fuller Seminary.

ROGERS: Fights among brothers or cousins are always the worst, aren't they? The fact that Lindsell was on the Fuller faculty at one time is, of course, one of the reasons why he feels exceptionally bitter toward the fact that people at Fuller do not share his point of view.

DOOR: He says that the Fuller Seminary Statement of Faith has been changed—specifically the part regarding Scripture.

ROGERS: Sure. What Fuller has done is try to make the Statement of Faith more in accord with the mainstream of historic tradition instead of allowing it only to represent this minor side tributary that got started with the old Princeton theologians in the nineteenth century. That's why I think history is really what's at stake here. The whole approach to the thing depends upon what you think the central Christian tradition, and especially the Reformed tradition, has been. We deduced an awful lot of evidence here to show that the Hodge-Warfield tradition

is really a side stream which owes its vitality to the Middle Ages and Thomas Aquinas, not to Calvin and Luther, and not to the early church theologians. So far, nobody's given us any evidence to the contrary. All they do is say that if you would just realize that Warfield knew best, you know you wouldn't raise these awkward questions.

DOOR: People like yourself disagree with what Lindsell's done, but according to him, no one has ever said he was wrong.

ROGERS: Everything he says isn't wrong, but he certainly says a lot of things that are absolutely wrong.

DOOR: Lindsell says that no one has said that anything he has written in the book is wrong.

ROGERS: Listen, his statement that all Christians for 2000 years have always held to inerrancy is a flat, false statement. He's wrong. He can put one on the record. That's just false. It's untrue. We've got 480 pages as evidence to show that it's not true.

DOOR: He also says that his statements about Fuller have not been proven untrue.

ROGERS: The example of Fuller is absolutely false. Fuller isn't out of step with any of the Reformation confessions or ancient creeds. It's just out of step with Lindsell. If you let Lindsell define the norms then most everybody's out of step.

DOOR: One question that's always raised by those who hold to inerrancy is if you allow the possibility that maybe something in the Bible may be in error, who's going to tell you what's true and what's not true?

ROGERS: That's really a question not about authority but about interpretation, and the question applies equally to everybody. Everybody has to decide what it means in any given text. If they claim to take everything in the Bible literally, that's a theory about what it means, and as a matter of fact, nobody does that. Even the Chicago statement on Biblical Inerrancy where they keep saying, "God chose the very words," and then they say when the Bible says women should be veiled, you shouldn't take that seriously. The Chicago Statement on Biblical Inerrancy has drawn the line. They've picked and chosen. They've decided that when the Bible says women should be silent, that is normative for everybody, but "women wearing veils" is only for that time. I can't for the life of me see how they can make that distinction. It looks to me as if it ought to be both ways or neither.

DOOR: So what does a layperson do?

ROGERS: Read the Bible. Understand it as any sensible, ordinary layperson would, by trying to understand it in its own context. The Bible really functions at two levels. The first level is what does it mean? Creation, Fall, redemption. How to get right with God and your neighbor. That's what laypeople read the Bible to understand. A seminary education is not required to get that in the Bible. The Westminster Confession says, "But in matters of controversy in religion you should resort to scholarship." So when we deal with difficult matters, praying about it doesn't solve that. Taking it literally doesn't help. The only way to understand what something means is to go back and study and try to figure it out.

DOOR: But what about the issue of truth? How do you know if a Scripture is true or false?

ROGERS: I've never said that there are parts of the Bible that are true and parts are false, but I'm certainly willing to say there are parts that are central and parts that are just surrounding that central message. It's more important that Christ died for my sins than it is how many guys happened to come down a certain valley during a certain battle. And John 3:16 does not depend on if I understand the accuracy of that other business. I'm very upset with this whole inerrancy debate because moral and ethical spin-off is setting Christians against Christians, setting brothers against brothers, and dividing people who should be working together on things.

DOOR: We agree. So why do you and Lindsell continue to debate the issue of inerrancy? What are the issues that keep you from working together?

ROGERS: The basic problem is that the inerrancy people have confused function and form. They are trying to make the literary form of the Bible what carries authority. That's impossible. Why? Because none of us have the original autographs and the Bible has been translated in over 1,500 different languages in different cultural settings. So the form is infinitely variable. The authority lies in the basic meaning that is conveyed. I can tell you everything the Bible's about in the next ten seconds. God made a good world. Human beings messed it and themselves up, and God came in Jesus Christ to put the world and us back together again. That's all the Bible's about. That's the most important thing in the whole world that we could learn. The Bible's about how to get back in right relation to God and to your fellow human beings.

TIM LAHAYE

When we talked with him in 1980, he looked fifty-four, but he looked good at fifty-four. Maybe it was that he'd been married thirty-three years (now forty-two years) to the same woman (Beverly LaHaye, founder and president of Concerned Women of America); maybe it was his four kids (and, now, a herd of grandkids); maybe it was living in San Diego for twenty-five years or writing as many books (count 'em). Whatever it was, Tim LaHaye has certainly come a long way from his impoverished Detroit background.

He's opinionated ("After fifty-four years, I've got opinions about everything."), he talks a lot ("I'm prone to be windy."), and he's not afraid to admit to his gifts ("If I have a writing gift, I have the gift of simplicity where I can put things down so the common man can understand.").

Now the president of the Washington, D.C.-based Family Life Seminars, Tim LaHaye was influential in the Moral Majority at the time of this conversation and had just published *The Battle for the Mind* about humanism. "It's the best book I've written," he said modestly. He has since published several more, including the recent *Faith of Our Founding Fathers* and *Finding the Will of God in a Crazy, Mixed-Up World.* Anyway, the *Door* traveled a few miles down the road from its World Headquarters to east El Cajon, where we met then-Baptist

pastor Tim LaHaye in his modestly appointed office on the campus of Christian Heritage College, which he cofounded in 1970, and asked him some modestly appointed questions. We found Tim LaHaye to be warm, personable, very confident, and one who knows what he believes and why. And he's deeply committed to "saving our country."

DOOR: What is the Moral Majority?

LAHAYE: We are a group of ministers who see an enormous number of Christians who need to be motivated. These Christians can't be motivated unless they are informed, and ministers are the ones who can inform them. So the Moral Majority is trying to organize and educate ministers to see the issues and give them the tools to educate their people.

DOOR: Why do you call your group the Moral Majority?

LAHAYE: We believe we represent the overwhelming majority of the American people. More importantly, we represent the minimum moral desires of the majority of the people.

DOOR: Do you really believe that you represent the minimum moral desires of the majority?

LAHAYE: Look. Gallup says there are 60,000,000 born-again believers. There are another 60,000,000 who are what I call "pro-moralists" (Catholics, Mormons, etc.). Then there are another 50,000,000 "idealistic moralists." That represents the 84 percent of the people in this country who still believe the Ten Commandments are valid.

DOOR: What, then, do you think are the crucial moral issues today?

LAHAYE: We think that abortion, homosexuality, pornography, prayer in the schools, and family protection from government interference are among the most crucial issues.

DOOR: The obvious question is, of course, if the majority of Americans have minimum moral desires that agree with the ones you represent, then why do we need an organization like yours to "educate" them?

LAHAYE: We have been led to Sodom and Gomorrah by a hard-core group of committed humanists who set out over a hundred years ago to control the masses. They have us in a stranglehold. There are only 275,000 of them, but they control everything—the mass media, government, and even the Supreme Court.

DOOR: So the masses have been duped by these 275,000 humanists?

LAHAYE: Yes. Humanists believe in the evolutionary flow of history. They believe that everything is changing, so they feel required to change whatever is in existence. They attack the status quo simply because it's the status quo. They have taken the time-honored principles that have been good for the family and a moral society and changed them, and they've changed them for the worse. They have changed the divorce laws. Abortion has been made legal. Homosexuality was once illegal; now that's been changed. These humanists won't be happy until they've torn down all the laws against incest. Humanists feel they are the elite gods. They feel they need to run the masses because they are too dumb to know what's good for them.

DOOR: So you advocate instead an elite group of ministers who tell the masses what to do?

LAHAYE: I don't see any comparison at all. We have a biblical precedent for advocating a moral society.

DOOR: But aren't you really advocating a legislated morality?

LAHAYE: Morality has always been legislated in our country. We have laws concerning murder, rape, marriage, pornography, prostitution . . . areas of morality. The question is not whether to legislate morality but where to draw the line. The government today is legislating immorality. It is making it easy for people to sin. The humanists in government are moving that line away from the biblical standards originally established by our founding fathers. America needs to return to those biblically based moral standards.

DOOR: Let's turn to politics. Your organization and others like it are concerned with electing the "right kind of person" to public office. Does that mean a Christian votes Republican or Democrat?

LAHAYE: The day is past when we can indulge the luxury of voting Republican or Democrat or Independent. Nor can we simply vote on the basis of economic or social policy. We have to vote for the person who is the most aggressive at bringing about moral reform in our country.

DOOR: In other words, we should vote for the born-again candidate?

LAHAYE: Ideally, I'd like to have a born-again Christian who is committed aggressively to morality. But the present occupant of the White House proves to us that claiming to be born again is not adequate assurance that one will do born-again things. So what I say is this, if you can't have a born-again Christian or a Spirit-filled Christian, then take the committed moralist.

DOOR: A committed moralist who happens to be a Mormon?

LAHAYE: If I had to choose between Garne or Hatch from Utah and an anti-moralist, I would vote for them because of their past voting records and their commitment to morality.

DOOR: Are you saying you would support anyone whose commitment to morality agrees with yours whether he/she is a Christian or not?

LAHAYE: Absolutely.

DOOR: Martin Marty in a recent *Christian Century* pointed out that on the basis of your evaluating scale (past voting record and commitment to your stands on abortion, etc.) that Congressman Paul Simon would re-

ceive a zero rating—even though he publicly admits to being a Christian, is well respected for his ethical behavior, and was cofounder of Bread for the World. But shockingly, that same rating scale gave Congressman Richard Kelly from Florida a 100 rating, and Richard Kelly has admitted pocketing $25,000 in the Abscam scandal. Is Martin Marty exaggerating? You wouldn't vote, in this case, for Kelly over Simon, would you?

LAHAYE: Well, I don't condone Kelly's moral actions. Bribing a congressman is deplorable. What it boils down to is we must make a choice even if the only option is the lesser of two evils. But if I had to choose between a rascal like Kelly and an anti-moralist, I would be inclined to vote for the rascal, with misgivings. But I would rather do that than send someone to Congress to vote for the murder of human life. Kelly's vote on an issue like that will have far greater impact on society than a $25,000 bribe.

DOOR: You can't be serious.

LAHAYE: I'm dead serious.

DOOR: Could you support someone who says he is born again but has arrived at different "minimum-moral requirements" than you have? Someone like Mark Hatfield, for example.

LAHAYE: Mark Hatfield and others of his persuasion are a real enigma to us. You laud him for his Christian position (and I don't know anyone who questions that) but almost every time he opens his mouth on political issues, I find myself disagreeing with him. He must be a melancholy temperament. Melancholy temperaments are such supersonic idealists that they are often highly impractical.

DOOR: But could you support a born-again melancholy temperament who disagreed with you?

LAHAYE: A Mark Hatfield type might have been indulged thirty years ago because of his Christian commitment, but now he is a danger to the Christian community *if* he votes against what we consider to be basic morality. And I don't care if it's Mark Hatfield, Jimmy Carter, or Barry Goldwater. If they vote in support of abortion, for example, then they should be removed from office.

DOOR: Removed from office?

LAHAYE: I feel so strongly about the mass murder of 8,000,000 unborn creatures of God, that, in my opinion, every individual who votes in support of abortion should be removed from office by whatever legal means are available.

DOOR: But don't you think the Holy Spirit can bring two born-again Christians to different conclusions?

LAHAYE: The Holy Spirit is never going to lead us in things contrary to the Bible. He wrote it. No one is living in the Holy Spirit when he violates the Word of God, so if a congressman doesn't vote right on the issue of homosexuality, then he is in violation of the Bible.

DOOR: There is only one correct interpretation of the Bible?

LAHAYE: On homosexuality? Yes. Pornographic literature? Sure.

DOOR: But aren't there other moral issues that are equally or even more important than the ones you emphasize? Could a Christian be against war?

LAHAYE: It's possible, but it is safe to say that the overwhelming majority of committed Christians are not pacifistic.

DOOR: Why do you say that?

LAHAYE: Because you don't find pacifism in the Bible.

DOOR: What about the issue of the nuclear arms buildup?

LAHAYE: I don't think it's appropriate to use that issue as a measure of a politician's qualifications, although, personally, a man who isn't committed to a strong military posture is gambling with America.

The rule of thumb is that boxers and linebackers never get mugged. I just have to believe that the country that is militarily superior is not going to be attacked. I'm not worried about America attacking anybody else. We never have. We have to face the fact that we are living in a culture where the Communists are dedicated, unswerving, and committed to controlling the world. To naively say that we should not invest in nuclear defense is not realistically facing the enemy.

DOOR: Surely you believe that world hunger is a much more important moral issue than prayer in schools?

LAHAYE: That is an individual issue. The real question is are you helping people most by giving them bread to eat or by leading them to a vital life-changing experience with Jesus Christ and then showing them how to become self-sufficient?

I have visited the Setewel Indians on the southern tip of Mexico. They were a vanishing group until some missionaries went there twenty-five years ago. Today, as a result, they are the most productive Indian tribe in Mexico. They have been transformed by the power of Christ. Here were a people who were starving and now they are self-respecting, productive, and effective.

DOOR: That is admirable, but that is not the issue we are raising. What we are asking is whether the immorality of a society that squanders its abundance is more important than the immorality of not allowing kids to pray in school?

LAHAYE: If our country does not return to the path of moral sanity we will not have an abundance to worry about. Our children need to be taught proper values and protected from the evils of our culture.

DOOR: How about rating the presidential candidates for us. Let's start with President Carter.

LAHAYE: I shook hands with him twice and got absolutely no spiritual response.

DOOR: We don't quite understand that . . . but . . . go ahead.

LAHAYE: I think Carter set out to be governor of Georgia by way of the Plains Baptist Church. He learned the jargon and identified with the liberal branch of the Southern Baptist Georgians. It worked to get him into the governor's mansion, so he used the same jargon to get himself into the White House.

DOOR: But he does claim to be born again.

LAHAYE: Yes, but he has not appointed one single person of a born-again committment to any position of government leadership on a highly visible basis. When I accosted him with that, his response was, "Well, I'm not sure that's a fair appraisal of my administration. I've brought several religious people into government. I've brought Fritz Mondale, and he's a very religious man. His grandfather was a minister. His father and brother are ministers." Carter was right. They are Unitarians, and a Unitarian is a humanist. Carter also mentioned Ann Wexler. We'd already met her, and she's a

feminist Jew. She won't use her husband's name because of her feminism.

DOOR: Has Carter done anything right?

LAHAYE: The one thing Carter has done that I admire is not allow Americans to participate in the Olympic Games.

DOOR: How about John Anderson?

LAHAYE: Anderson is a first class opportunist. He was so fearful he wouldn't win his own congressional campaign that he dropped out of the race and went for president. On moral issues he is to the left of Carter. He's aggressively anti-moral. I commend his own church—the Evangelical Free Church—for publicly censoring him for his persistence in voting for abortion.

DOOR: And Ronald Reagan?

LAHAYE: Reagan has the strongest moral position. He is aggressively opposed to ERA. He has spoken out positively for voluntary prayer in the public schools, and he's in favor of the pro-life amendment. He is also in favor of getting the government bureaucrats out of the family.

DOOR: What do you think the future holds?

LAHAYE: Either the church is going to become morally active and set moral issues as the dominant standard for its elected officials or we will be overrun by humanist thought by 1990. The humanist overlords are determined to stamp out religious rights. The Christian has become the number-one enemy. We are in a war, but only one side is fighting.

I'm not saying that we should drive the humanists out of the country. This is a free country. Humanists ought to be free to live here, but I don't think they should be our leaders and make our policy because they misrepresent the majority.

DOOR: So what do we have to do?

LAHAYE: Look, government isn't bad. It is bad people in it that make it bad. So we have to replace the bad people with people who are committed to a lifetime of moral surveillance and principle.

DOOR: Do you really think that will make a difference? Isn't it naive to believe that if we get a group of "morally right" politicians, that significant changes will occur?

LAHAYE: If I gave up that ideal, I don't think I could live with the alternative. I pray to God you are wrong.

JUAN CARLOS ORTIZ

Author, evangelist, Argentinean, former pastor of the largest Assembly of God church in Latin America, Juan Carlos Ortiz has very definite ideas about God, the Bible, and the church and how it ought to work. Not everyone agrees with him. The Keepers of the *Door* think he's our kind of guy! So in 1980 we traveled to San Jose, California, (just north of the Argentine border) to talk (his English is better than our Spanish) with "Johnny" in his home. His wife, sixteen kids (it sounded like), and pet llama were not interviewed. We found him unique, fascinating, engaging, and short. We are sorry we can only give you his words, for his ability to communicate was as impressive as his thoughts.

DOOR: You make a startling point in your book. You suggest that when we are talking about the significance of the Bible, in practice, evangelicals believe that God speaks, then the church, and then the Bible. Wouldn't most evangelicals strongly disagree with that?

ORTIZ: Sure they would. That viewpoint has upset many people, but they are only getting upset at themselves. Look at history. It was not the Bible that made the church; it was the church that made the Bible. It was not the Bible who chose the members of the church, but the members of the church who chose the canon of the Bible.

DOOR: Your viewpoint sounds very Roman Catholic.

ORTIZ: The only difference between Catholics and Protestants is that the Catholics are honest and say it.

DOOR: Say what?

ORTIZ: That the church is before the Bible and that what the church magistrates and councils decide is what you have to accept. Protestants say they don't believe that, but they do.

DOOR: For example?

ORTIZ: For example, if you came to a Southern Baptist church and said you would like to dance in their meetings because the Bible says "Dance unto the Lord," they would tell you they didn't care; their church doesn't dance. Now, what is first, the Bible or the church?

DOOR: The church.

ORTIZ: You guys are extremely bright. The point is that every denomination believes that the church is before the Bible, and what they decide the Bible means is what you have to accept.

DOOR: You are going to make some Southern Baptists and others real upset.

ORTIZ: In effect, the church fathers said, after the canon was formed, we don't need the Holy Spirit to give us any more revelation. That is not scriptural. The Bible says that the Spirit which the Father sent in his name will abide with us forever. He didn't say abide with us until the end of the canon in the first century. Jesus is still alive, I believe, and we cannot say to him, "Shut up, we have the Bible."

DOOR: Are you suggesting that for some the Bible actually keeps them from hearing anything new or fresh from God?

ORTIZ: I am suggesting that many evangelicals use the Bible like the Koran. The Islamic people believe that Muhammad died and left the Koran. The evangelical church is saying the same thing about Jesus. Jesus died and left the Bible. That isn't what Jesus said. He said he would not leave us completely. Yet many evangelicals are actually denying the resurrection of Christ because they don't let Jesus do or say anything more. He is in our midst but in a casket. Jesus can't talk today because we have the Bible.

DOOR: There goes our mail.

ORTIZ: The Bible is like a light unto our path. But it is not the path. The path is the living Christ. We walk in Jesus, we live in him, and the Bible sheds light on him. The Bible is a lamp unto our feet. I believe the liberals have put the lamp on their backs, so they don't see the way, and the fundamentalists have put the lamp in their eyes, so they don't see the way either. Both extremes are dangerous and heretical.

DOOR: In your books you also talk a lot about church renewal. You were a pastor in Argentina for a number of years. Can you describe the renewal that went on in your own church?

ORTIZ: We had experienced tremendous numerical growth in our church. But the assistant minister and I were concerned that the so-called "success" of our church was solely dependent upon our effort. We noticed that if we relaxed, the church slowed down. If we worked hard, things picked up. We were deeply disturbed by this. So we asked God to show us what we were doing wrong.

DOOR: And?

ORTIZ: We discovered three things. First of all, we were running the church like a business. We were promoting Christ like we would promote a product, like we would promote Coca-Cola.

Secondly, we realized that our church was not growing at all. We were just getting fat. First we had two hundred without love, then we had four hundred without love, and then a thousand without love. We were not increasing the quality along with the quantity. We realized that simply increasing the number of people that attend church is not growth . . . cemeteries grow that way, too.

DOOR: You said you discovered three things.

ORTIZ: Yes. The third thing we discovered was that our church was more like an orphanage than the family of God. We had all of these people with no spiritual fathers and I, as a minister, was simply functioning as the director of the orphanage.

DOOR: The three problems you have mentioned sound similar to the problems faced by many churches in America. What did you do about them?

ORTIZ: One of the things we did right away was to change the focus of our message. Instead of urging people to come to Christ for all the blessings they would receive, we began to talk about Christ as Lord. We began to preach that people should come to Christ for Christ alone, not for a miracle, a blessing, or even for heaven. We simply went back to preaching the person of Christ.

DOOR: You must have noticed that in America many churches have done the opposite. They would suggest that if you come to Christ, you will have financial prosperity, physical healing, and personal success.

ORTIZ: If that is done then you have people coming to Christ to get, not to give. You have people who expect God to serve *them*. From the very beginning they will expect the Lord to take care of their house while they are away, heal their mother in the hospital, and help their children. That becomes the way they view their relationship with God. They call him Lord, but treat him as a servant.

DOOR: Aren't there blessings people receive from serving Christ?

ORTIZ: Of course, but those blessings are for those who "seek first the kingdom."

DOOR: Do you see this "getting-things-from-God" attitude permeating all aspects of the church?

ORTIZ: Yes. Take worship, for example. People come to be blessed rather than to bless. They come for self-service rather than his service. They come to take from the Lord instead of presenting themselves to the Lord as Paul talks about in Romans 12.

DOOR: What is your concept of church structure? Biblically, are there any principles that tell us how the church should look in this day and age?

ORTIZ: I don't believe there is a biblical model for church structure. The "biblical model" was created by the circumstances. Deacons and elders met the needs of that day, but I don't believe we have to copy that again. Jesus did not come to start an institution. He never intended to buy a piece of land and build a headquarters. We have to ask the Spirit today how to meet the needs of today.

DOOR: Then what kind of structures should the church have today?

ORTIZ: I must say that all structures are a hindrance to people in their search for God. If people have to accept Christ plus the pipe organ, the piano, the program, and the television ministry, millions will reject Christ. The more things we add to Christ, the more things people have to accept with Christ, the more difficult it is for them to respond. Let me give you a personal example.

DOOR: Please do.

ORTIZ: My wife asked a friend of hers why she wasn't attending church any more. Her response went something like this: "I started attending a church I liked very much. I went to the Sunday evening service. The people were very nice. They prayed for me and visited me. After awhile they suggested that I attend prayer meeting on Tuesday nights. Then they wanted me to come to Bible study on Thursday night, choir on Wednesday night, and Ladies' Circle on Friday night. All of a sudden, I was at church every night. I neglected my family, my relatives. Soon everyone thought I was a fanatic. Finally, I told the church that I was only going to attend on Sundays, and the pastor said I was a 'Sunday-Christian.' Now I don't go any more."

That lady was right. So often when a person comes into the church structure, it alienates them from their family and friends. Who is it that brings new converts into the church? Usually, it's the new converts, because they still have friends in the world. But it doesn't take long before the new converts will lose all connection with those outside the church.

DOOR: So you end up serving the structure rather than the Lord?

ORTIZ: Anything that takes the place of the Lord is wrong. For lots of people the structure takes the place of Jesus. They become meeting-centered instead of Christ-centered.

DOOR: So should churches cancel all their meetings?

ORTIZ: It isn't quite that simple. If you release people from meetings, they will stay home and watch television or go to a movie and not use their life for the kingdom of God. We have to help people improve the quality of their faith. That is the reason for discipleship. Teach them what they can do with their time to further the kingdom of God, and then you can cancel your meetings.

DOOR: When you talk about a church that emphasizes discipleship, what does that mean in terms of structure?

ORTIZ: Rather than having deacons and elders, who function like the members of a board, and a minister, who functions like the president of the board, you strive for a group of people who become friends. Just like the disciples—they work together, love one another, and take care of one another. Discipleship means a committed group of people meeting each other's needs, while together they perform the necessary tasks of the church.

DOOR: When we hear of the word *discipleship* we think of a strong authority figure who becomes the discipler while exercising control over the disciplee, if there is such a word.

ORTIZ: I would not use the word *authority*. That could be dangerous. I would use the word *love*. In my house, for instance, there is authority, but we never use the word. Authority is like soap, the more you use it, the less you have. The more you say you are the boss, the less authority you have. There is a kind of authority that lives in love, but we're talking about a love relationship, not a military relationship.

DOOR: There exists in the church today increasing polarization amongst denominations. There must be very strong feelings between denominations in South America, between Catholics and Protestants, for example. How did you deal with the problem of unity?

ORTIZ: I believe in unity through relationship. If I invite a Baptist minister to my meetings, he won't come because he is anti-charismatic, and I am charismatic. But if I invite him over for ice cream, he is not anti-ice cream, so he would come. It does much more for the unity of the church to play golf with a priest than it would to invite him to a meeting. So, in Argentina, we would go backpacking with four or five other ministers. When we came back, we were old friends. After you are friends, the barriers can be ignored.

DOOR: We have to admit that is a new approach. Ecumenical unity through ice cream.

ORTIZ: All I know is if you play a soccer game with a group of ministers, you will have more of a united church than you ever would by meeting together.

DOOR: You aren't bothered, then, by denominational differences? Don't you think denominations are what divide the church?

ORTIZ: Denominations are not what divide us. What divides us is our flesh. Our ego. Every one of us wants to build our own kingdom, to be king in our own kingdom instead of in the kingdom of God.

DOOR: Now you're starting to meddle. So how do we deal with our ego?

ORTIZ: Most of us do not have an understanding of what it means to be crucified with Christ. We must crucify ourselves, not tobacco or adultery, etc. When Jesus was on the cross, he was not taking my sins with him. He was taking me. Too many of us crucify our sins, but keep ourselves very much alive. *We* have to die. We should be teaching that we are to be dead to everything. Even to our denominations. Even to our own little kingdoms.

DOOR: Nice words, but do you really believe that unity can happen?

ORTIZ: In Argentina I visited an Anglican minister. His church was about twenty blocks from mine. He only knew a little Spanish and only had seven English-speaking members left in his church. Our church had one thousand members. I called my elders together and suggested that if we believed in unity, our actions ought to be consistent. So I asked who would like to become members of the Anglican church. Fifty members of our church became members of the Anglican church—full members. They adopted the new structure complete with bishops, processional, the garments, candles ... everything. Even paid their tithes. It wasn't long until the Church of England found out about it, so they invited me to England to have meetings with the Archbishop of Canterbury and then to Australia to preach on unity in Anglican churches all over the country.

DOOR: Incredible.

ORTIZ: I am telling you, it works. I was invited by a Catholic priest to preach in a Catholic church in Montevideo, and thousands came to the Lord. They didn't even know I was a Protestant, and I realized then that our main thrust should not be to make Catholics into Protestants. I went back to my church and told them we were not going to baptize Catholics or bring them into our church. As a result, we simply formed a Catholic branch of our evangelical Protestant church. We had a group of 200 Catholics discipling Catholics. One day a Catholic priest came to the Lord, and we told him, "We have been waiting for you. We have 200 that belong to you." So we gave them to him and that opened the door of the Catholic church to us.

DOOR: If every church started giving away their members like that, they probably would flunk the church growth contest.

ORTIZ: That is true. With that approach to unity you have to understand that your church will probably not grow much. It requires an ability to die to the idea of a large church.

DOOR: You have classified yourself as charismatic, yet we haven't heard you talk much about the Holy Spirit.

ORTIZ: That is where the unity we've been talking about comes from: the Holy Spirit. If I have Christ in me, and you have Christ in you, we do not have two Christs. We have the same Christ in us. So, though we are two with Christ, we are one. The Spirit makes us one. Any number and Christ is equal to one. Doctrines make us many. Doctrines divide us.

DOOR: Even the doctrine of speaking in tongues?

ORTIZ: Jesus never said, "By this shall all men know that you are my disciples, that you all speak in tongues." The test is clear. The fruit of the Spirit is love, joy, peace, long-suffering, gentleness, goodness, faith, meekness, and self-control. How will people know that we are his disciples? Because we have love for the brethren.

DOOR: There is tremendous poverty in South America. There is great social unrest. There are many who believe that the focal point of the gospel is identification with the poor and concentrated effort to alleviate social injustice. How did your church in South America deal with the problem of the poor?

ORTIZ: Are you from *Sojourners*?

DOOR: Why did you ask that?

ORTIZ: Your question was longer than my answer is going to be.

DOOR: Sorry.

ORTIZ: In answer to your question, I believe that the gospel of the kingdom of God involves spiritual and social dimensions. If we stress just social concerns, we are preaching just part of the gospel. If we only stress spiritual blessings, we preach another gospel. We cannot be spiritual without being socially concerned and we cannot be socially concerned without being spiritual.

DOOR: Okay. But how did your church handle that tension in a practical way?

ORTIZ: The Bible says to sell your possessions and give them to the poor. In our church, for example, we changed the way we handled our money. See, people give money to the church for their own luxuries—buildings, organs, carpets, etc. But in the early church the people put their money at the feet of the apostles. The apostles gave it to the deacons who gave it to the people. In other words, the deacons did not receive the money from the people to put in the church's account; they received it from the church's account to give it to the poor people. So in our church we began to give the income from the church to the poor. Our deacons received the money from the church and gave it to the people.

DOOR: What else did your church do?

ORTIZ: We gathered all the members of the church together and asked them to choose just one neighbor and love them completely. Not just in words, but in a complete way. I chose a neighbor who did not have a house, a car, or anything, and I helped him buy a house and a car.

DOOR: Did you just give him a house and a car?

ORTIZ: Help has to be done with wisdom. You can't just give money to people. You have to maintain their dignity. If you help someone who is a plumber, for example, you ask them why they are not working. If they reply that they don't have any tools, then you buy them the tools so they can earn their own living. We asked our neighbor what they needed, and they said they needed a roof. So we bought the materials and they built the roof. They built it themselves.

DOOR: What are the signs of immaturity in the church today?

ORTIZ: One sign of immaturity is a lack of a sense of values.

DOOR: Materialism?

ORTIZ: It is more than that. Have you ever watched children play? They can play with diamond rings as if they were marbles and not know the difference. The same thing is true with immature Christians. They invest in things that have no value and do not invest in things that have value.

DOOR: Other signs of immaturity?

ORTIZ: Another evidence of immaturity in the church is the need for rules and laws. Children live by rules. They take a bath or brush their teeth because they are told to do it. They walk by rules until they grow to be ruled by their own common sense. Christians should grow to the point where they know what is right and what is wrong and act accordingly.

DOOR: The natural question is what suggestions do you have to help immature Christians grow?

ORTIZ: Frankly, one of the reasons we have so much immaturity in the church today is because the leaders of the church don't want anyone to challenge or question them.

When our children become teenagers they start to question us as parents; they start to form their own values and establish their individuality. Is that rebellion or growth? In the church system, we often label as rebellion what is actually growth.

DOOR: Are you suggesting that the reason we have so much immaturity in the church today is because the church is afraid to change, afraid to allow questions that might result in new ideas?

ORTIZ: Suppose the Lord tells me to eat an orange. So I eat the orange and sincerely believe that God has led me. Tomorrow, the Lord tells me to eat an orange again. So what happens? The next day I write down a rule to eat an orange every day. And do you see what that does? Now I don't need the Spirit anymore. I have a law instead. Laws kill life. Laws stop growth. You end up staying with a concept, a principle, or a doctrine rather than life. What we did yesterday in the Spirit, we do today in the flesh.

DOOR: Can you summarize your suggestions for helping the church become a healthy and viable expression of Christ today?

ORTIZ: We need to clean the church of all that is not essential or necessary. Hebrews says that everything shall be shaken, and only the unshakable will remain. So we don't need to waste our time on shakable things like buildings. Buildings are just monuments to the people that build them. They are a symbol of the division in the church. They are a symbol of the church's self-centeredness.

DOOR: So much for buildings.

ORTIZ: Secondly, we should strive toward a very simple structure of the church that could go underground any minute. Nobody on the payroll. No secretaries. No letters to write. We should create a church that can live through relationships so that we are connected person to person. And we can attain that by dividing our churches into small cell groups where people can build each other up.

DOOR: In other words, the structure of the church must be simple, flexible, and constantly changing.

ORTIZ: If the church is always singing the same hymns, saying the same prayers, performing the same liturgy, and giving the same messages, it is because there is no growth. The wineskins of the church have to be elastic so we can always put in new wine.

J. RODMAN WILLIAMS

This may come as quite a shock, but the *Door* is not known for its charismatic leanings. That is why the Keepers were somewhat apprehensive when we traveled in 1980 to what was then the Melodyland School of Theology in Anaheim, California. It was there that we ended up in the office of a real charismatic who happened to be the president of the seminary, J. Rodman Williams.

To our surprise, not once during the interview did Dr. Williams speak in tongues, lay on hands, or fall on the floor. But he did answer our questions, sipped coffee, and periodically tossed John McArthur tapes into the shredder. Dr. J. looked quite preserved for his then sixty-two years. Married forty-one years with three grown children, J. Rodman Williams completely shattered our stereotype of charismatics. We, in turn, shattered his stereotype of professional magazine publishers. His credentials are impressive: B.A. at the ever-popular Davidson College in North Carolina, M.A. at Union Theological Seminary, doctorate in religion and ethics at Columbia University. Before coming to Melodyland in the fall of 1972, Dr. Williams pastored a church in Rockford, Illinois, served as chaplain at Beloit College in Wisconsin, and taught for thirteen years at

Austin Presbyterian Seminary. In 1982 he left Melodyland for Virginia Beach, Virginia, where he still teaches in the theology department of C.B.N. (Christian Broadcasting Network) University. Dr. Williams has written and lectured extensively. His book *The Gift of the Holy Spirit Today* is a well-written apologetic for the modern charismatic movement.

WILLIAMS: Biblically speaking, every Christian is a charismatic. The word *charisma* simply means "gift." So in the New Testament where Paul speaks about the the gift of eternal life, it's the charisma of eternal life. So every Christian is a charismatic in that sense.

DOOR: But we all know that ain't the sense most people talk about. *Charismatic* usually describes a person who speaks in tongues, etc.

WILLIAMS: O.K. Here's one way to describe it. Noncharismatics tend to accept some of the gifts—let's label them gifts A-P. Charismatics, in the more defined sense, accept all the gifts, A-Z. So, in answer to your question, one distinctive of the charismatic movement is an openness to all of the gifts.

DOOR: Are charismatics better Christians than noncharismatics?

WILLIAMS: I wouldn't use the word "better." A Christian is a Christian. The charismatic dimension has much more to do with openness to the whole variety of things God is doing.

DOOR: One common criticism of charismatics is the role of experience. Do charismatics start with their experience and then go to the Word, or do they allow the Bible to interpret all experience?

WILLIAMS: Biblical truth must stand in judgment on all experience. I would admit that charismatics have sometimes allowed experience to carry them far from biblical teaching and have fallen into error, but I would not agree that the charismatic movement is based on experience. The basis remains the Word of God. To put it in theological terms, we believe in the normativity and priority of Scripture over any and all experience.

DOOR: If the charismatic experience isn't the issue, then what is?

WILLIAMS: The real issue is the way the Bible is read and understood.

DOOR: Explain.

WILLIAMS: It is not that the noncharismatics place the Word first whereas charismatics place it second. We believe the order is like this: The reading and study of God's Word, followed by a life-changing experience. Martin Luther, for example, rediscovered the message of God's free grace and justification. He described his ex-

perience this way, "I felt myself to be reborn and gone through open doors into paradise."

DOOR: What we hear you saying is that you believe that the Word is first and experience is second, and noncharismatics believe the Word is first and experience is second. So what are we talking about?

WILLIAMS: But I was also saying that the issue is the way the Bible is read and understood. In other words, we believe many noncharismatics read the Scriptures, especially in relation to the Holy Spirit, with blinders on. They do not see—perhaps do not want to see—what is really in the biblical text. They shut themselves off from charismatic experience and criticize charismatics for being experience oriented.

DOOR: So noncharismatics read the Bible with a built-in bias?

WILLIAMS: From my own experience, I vividly recall my early, strong biases against matters like prophecy, tongues, and fits of healing. As an evangelical theology professor, I spoke out rather vehemently against such things, and when I went to the Scriptures, it was with a determination to prove these phenomena to be wrongly understood. So ... totally inexperienced in the charismata, but on the whole, knowledgeable in Bible and theology, it was not to difficult for me to find ways to attack charismatic understanding. I was actually operating out of a nonexperiential, anticharismatic bias.

DOOR: It sounds like you are implying that experience must precede understanding.

WILLIAMS: No. I am saying that although experience is not primary, lack of experience can affect the way one reads the Bible.

DOOR: But you are saying that your lack of experience kept you from understanding the Word correctly. In other words, you had to have an experience *first*—then go back and study the Word.

WILLIAMS: No. I am saying that it was reading the Word—especially Acts, Romans, and First Corinthians—which resulted, with much reflection and prayer, in my deepened spiritual experience. Note the order again. Word first, experience second.

DOOR: You mentioned the book of Acts. One of the criticisms of charismatics is the primacy of the book of Acts. I think anyone with any sense of objectivity has to admit that the book of Acts certainly is pivotal to charismatic theology. But critics suggest that too much emphasis is given to the book of Acts—that all the Bible must bear on the meaning of Acts. One critic put it this way, "The only teachings in the book of Acts that can be called normative (absolute) for the church are those that are doctrinally confirmed elsewhere in Scripture." How would you respond to that?

WILLIAMS: Who told this author that? The book of Acts doesn't say so. Would he say the same thing about Romans? Why are the Epistles considered a guide for our Christian experience today, but not Acts? Could it not be that what happened in the earliest recorded history of the church can also be an invaluable guide to help us reexamine the situation of the church in our time? One other thing. . . .

DOOR: Yes?

WILLIAMS: Even if the criticism you just recounted was true, even if we were guilty of putting a lot of weight on the book of Acts, Acts is the Word of God. Again, Word first, experience second.

DOOR: Do charismatics have less problems? If you took a survey of charismatics, would you find less illness, less marriage difficulties, or less nerds?

WILLIAMS: Nerds?

DOOR: Forget that example.

WILLIAMS: Well, less problems? I think charismatic people have resources to draw on if the Holy Spirit has become real in their lives and if the gifts are operating, but as far as charismatics being insulated from the problems you've just mentioned, I don't think we have a monopoly on being free from them.

DOOR: Often we feel that what charismatics are saying is that they have the Holy Spirit and we don't.

WILLIAMS: We do not have a monopoly on the Holy Spirit. It is not a matter of whether or not you have the Holy Spirit dwelling in you. That is true of every child of God. A popular way of putting it is like this: Every Christian has the Holy Spirit, but does the Holy Spirit have the Christian? In other words, the reality is there, but are you living in the reality?

DOOR: So what you are really saying is that it is not enough to have the Holy Spirit dwelling in you, you . . .

WILLIAMS: Please. I never try to draw circles around people and suggest that we charismatics are the only ones who have the Holy Spirit. I know some charismatics do suggest that, but they are only the most arbitrary and opinionated kind. What I *am* saying is that all Christians should investigate the Word of God, including Acts and Ephesians, without bias. The very fact that Paul came to the Ephesians in Acts 19 and asked, "Did you receive the Holy Spirit when you believed?" raises, at least, the question that a person may believe and not yet have received the Holy Spirit.

DOOR: An issue that is often raised is the legitimacy of all the gifts today. Your critics would say that some gifts were only temporary sign gifts, given to the church for a specific age and a specific purpose.

WILLIAMS: My response is quite simply, "Who says the gifts are temporary?" Paul does not say this. He does not so much as suggest that some are only temporary or that others are permanent. How could that be when Paul *insists* that all gifts are the work of the same Spirit, and all are needed for the body to function properly?

DOOR: But what about First Corinthians, where Paul says that "tongues will cease"?

WILLIAMS: No one can question that Paul does speak of a cessation of tongues, but any unbiased reading of the text would surely suggest that such a cessation of tongues will only occur when "the perfect comes," namely, the perfection that occurs when we see the Lord "face to face."

DOOR: But weren't some gifts given as signs, and others for edification?

WILLIAMS: Again, this is an impossible distinction, exegetically and practically. *All* the gifts, according to Paul, are meant for edification—"To each is given the manifestation of the Spirit for the common good (to profit withal)" (1 Cor. 12:7). The gifts may indeed serve as signs, but that does not mean that they are not also, even primarily, for edification.

DOOR: Speaking in tongues is not exclusively a Christian experience, is it? Doesn't it occur amongst Buddhists and others?

WILLIAMS: That is true. In fact, you can go all the way back to the Greeks in Delphi. The prophetess would speak in tongues when she gave the oracles. What is interesting about that is that she was completely out of her mind when she did it. She'd inhale deeply of some fumes from a pit below, and was often intoxicated.

DOOR: Hmm. Then you are implying that what other groups call speaking in tongues is not really speaking in tongues?

WILLIAMS: To be honest, I don't know how to evaluate what other groups are doing when they say they are speaking in tongues.

DOOR: Well, what characterizes or differentiates Christians speaking in tongues?

WILLIAMS: One of the unique features about Christians speaking in tongues is that there's nothing irrational about it.

DOOR: You are kidding. We've seen many charismatics that seemed like they were in some kind of ecstasy land when they were "in the Spirit."

WILLIAMS: Well, I don't like the word *ecstasy*. That means getting out of yourself, going into orbit so you don't know where you are.

DOOR: Yeah, that's it.

WILLIAMS: The testimony amongst the charismatics I talk to is that their speaking in tongues is not a transirrational experience at all. Rather, it's a penetration into a more vivid sense of reality.

DOOR: Can tongues be learned behavior?

WILLIAMS: Some claim that it is. But I've never known anyone who claims to speak in tongues and say they learned how to do it. Some suggest that when you speak in tongues, it is the unconscious surfacing, that it's the language of the unconscious. That could be possible. But speaking in tongues is not a learned behavior if the Holy Spirit is inducing it. Speaking in tongues is a spiritually formed behavior of the Holy Spirit.

DOOR: Charismatics refer a lot to the New Testament. Is there any evidence of charismatic activity in the Old Testament?

WILLIAMS: There are charismatic judges in the Old Testament. The Spirit comes down upon a judge, and Israel is judged. Or the Spirit comes upon an artisan, who is filled with the Spirit and designs artistic designs for the tabernacle. The Spirit comes upon David, Elijah, and others. There is a charismatic line throughout the Bible.

DOOR: Why is it that the charismatic element in the church, more often than not, appears to be more divisive than unifying?

WILLIAMS: Let's be frank. In some instances churches feel threatened by people who talk too much about God. It sometimes turns them off. Charismatics feel it's very difficult, because they want to talk freely about Jesus. They want to talk about what has happened to them, but people are fearful of hearing it. They feel they are being judged, so even with the best intentions in some churches, charismatics have felt shut out. Sometimes the pastor is not open to them. Often, a minister feels threatened by something that hasn't happened to him. So, yes. Sometimes charismatics leave a church. They want to stay, but they are not welcome.

DOOR: You have described one kind of charismatic, but we both know there are other kinds. . . .

WILLIAMS: Yes. I call them the "pushy" charismatics. They are so convinced they have the "real thing" and that nobody else has it, that they become a nuisance in the church.

DOOR: So how does a church deal with the problem?

WILLIAMS: First of all, you have to decide which of the situations you have—a group of pushy charismatics or a group of threatened Christians. Then you go from there. It is a difficult issue, and it certainly isn't as simple as saying that charismatics bring disunity, but I think it is very important to point out something that is often overlooked.

DOOR: Feel free.

WILLIAMS: Though there are cases of division, as you have mentioned, there has been a movement of unity across denominations amongst charismatics that is rather significant. This unity in the Holy Spirit transcends many of the old denominational distinctives that used to keep us apart. So, from the larger perspective, I believe the charismatic movement is, in fact, a movement of renewal and unity.

DOOR: Earl Palmer, pastor of First Presbyterian Church in Berkeley, has a diagram which he uses to point out the dilemma in the church today over which gifts to emphasize. He draws a wheel. At the center of the wheel is Christ. Each of the spokes on the wheel represents a different gift or emphasis. The Holy Spirit is the rim. Earl says that the problem in the church occurs when people take a spoke or rim and try to make that emphasis or gift the center of the wheel instead of Christ. Are charismatics guilty of that?

WILLIAMS: That can easily happen.

DOOR: But isn't the fact that you are president of a "charismatic seminary" evidence that you are emphasizing charismatics instead of Christ?

WILLIAMS: That doesn't mean we only talk about charismatic things. Lutheran seminaries don't teach exclusively about justification by faith. Methodist seminaries don't talk exclusively about sanctification. I would agree with Earl Palmer that Jesus is at the center, but we still need all the different emphases (spokes) for the wheel to run. We need the Roman Catholic Church and their sense of the sacraments; we need the Greek Orthodox Church and their tremendous sense of tradition. You don't object to a seminary being called a Lutheran seminary do you? So why would you object to a charismatic seminary?

DOOR: That's a good point, but are you suggesting that being charismatic is almost like being a separate denomination?

WILLIAMS: I would fight against that.

DOOR: You have a Presbyterian background, and now you are the president of a charismatic seminary. Are there any teachings in the charismatic movement that you have difficulty with?

WILLIAMS: Some teachings in the charismatic movement I think are abhorrent.

DOOR: Such as?

WILLIAMS: The so-called "name-it-and-claim-it" teaching.

DOOR: You mean the idea that your prayer has already been answered—that all we have to do is claim what's been promised, and we've got it?

WILLIAMS: Yes. That is putting pressure on God. It's saying he is no longer the sovereign God. Here's my Calvinism coming out, but you have to give God his sovereignty. But that is

why we have this seminary—to provide balance. Yes, we believe that God is sovereign, but we also believe in doctors and nurses. We believe that God can and does intervene . . . when he decides to.

DOOR: Doesn't the presence of charismatics in a noncharismatic church, or noncharismatics in a charismatic church, create tension?

WILLIAMS: There are two kinds of tension. One is disruptive, and the other is creative. We need the creative tension brought about by the dialogue between two different emphases.

DOOR: Why do you think there has been such a worldwide explosion of the charismatic movement?

WILLIAMS: I think God is doing something for the whole church. I believe that what is going on in our day is a preparation for increasing evil in the world. There's very definitely an eschatological dimension of God's power. We need more power today to stand against the powers of darkness, and I believe God is stepping up his spiritual power in the church to meet these forces before we come to a head-on collision. God is preparing his church for the end times. It's similar to Pentecost, when God poured out his Spirit.

DOOR: To summarize, what are the most important things you as a charismatic would like to say to noncharismatics?

WILLIAMS: I would start by saying, "Is Christ real to you?" Then I would want to press on to the whole matter of the Holy Spirit. I would share with you about the dimension of the Holy Spirit. I would want to be sure that you understand that I am not talking about something I am a possessor of, and you are not. Surely as we know the Lord, we're on the same level. The Holy Spirit is at work in you just as he is in me. But I would want to ask, could it be that there are promises of God in the Bible that we have not actualized or received? There is always something out there that God is offering. As charismatics, we certainly haven't received everything God has to give, but we do have some things to share that others may not have discovered.

DOOR: Isn't the charismatic movement with its emphasis on "what God has done for me" an extension of the narcissism of an age where the ultimate value is, "what am I getting out of it?"

WILLIAMS: A gospel of salvation alone reflects the inwardness you are talking about. Frankly, I think the charismatic movement is a breaking-away from a self-centered evangelicalism. We believe the Bible is not a book of salvation exclusively; rather it is a book of God's glory. He wants his glory to be made manifest in our lives and throughout the world. God wants to give us more so he can deliver us from ourselves into a fuller kind of ministry under his glory.

DOOR: There seems to be a real lack of action.

WILLIAMS: I would say the primary thrust of the charismatic is not toward social involvement; rather the primary thrust is spiritual. The primary concern, as with most evangelicals, is that of changing people's lives so that the social order can be changed. With the charismatic, we focus on a renewal of life so that we can minister more effectively. But having said that, it is a mistake to assume that there is not a social consciousness amongst charismatics. Charismatics are deeply involved in inner-city ministries, drug addiction, and alcoholism. There are many places where works of mercy are being done by charismatics, but I would have to say that very much like evangelicals, it is in the background more than in the foreground.

REINHOLD NIEBUHR

The *Door* has long been known for its innovation in the field of religious journalism: the cover as statement, the prominence of the interview, humor and satire, the elimination of the proofreader, the disregard for deadlines. Always in the pursuit of journalistic excellence, the Keepers of the *Door* have perfected still another creative technique . . . interview the dead. Necro-interviewing is definitely new, but the *Door* has never shied away from controversy.

The interview is with Reinhold Niebuhr (1892–1971), who was quite controversial himself while he was alive. He taught at Union Theological Seminary (a little to the left of Wheaton) for thirty-two years, and was an ethicist, theologian, and political philosopher. From 1915 until 1928, Niebuhr was the minister of Detroit's Bethel Evangelical Church—the setting of that which follows. (At the end of this interview you will discover the shocking technique that was used to "interview" Reinhold Niebuhr.)

DOOR: Should ministers subscribe to magazines critical of the church like the *Door?*

NIEBUHR: Every preacher ought to take several radical journals, preferably the ones which are extremely inimical to religion.

DOOR: We have been accused of being in . . . in . . . er . . . inamclab . . . uh . . . hostile to religion.

NIEBUHR: See, the ethical ideals of Christianity are so high and the compromises which the average church and the average minister have made between these ideals and the economic necessities of society are so great, and self-deception is so easy, that we need the corrective of a critical and perhaps cynical evaluation of religion in modern life.

DOOR: But ministers don't like criticism, especially "successful" ones.

NIEBUHR: I would recommend this kind of reading *particularly* to successful ministers who are so easily obsessed by messianic complex because of the compliments they receive. Let them remind themselves that there are astute observers who think that all their preaching is superficial and never touches the fundamental defects of modern society, and that these critics are at least as near the truth as their too-generous devotees.

DOOR: But many ministers already have difficulty with cynicism and disillusionment and don't need a magazine or anything else making it worse.

NIEBUHR: A spiritual leader who has too many illusions is useless. One who has lost his illusions about mankind and retains his illusions about himself is insufferable. Let the process of disillusionment continue until the self is included. At that point, of course, only religion can save from the enervation of despair. But it is at that point that true religion is born.

DOOR: But aren't ministers afraid to admit they are human?

NIEBUHR: I think we ministers like to strike heroic poses. We are astute rather than heroic and cautious rather than courageous in practice. Thus we are in the dangerous position of being committed to the cross in principle, but escaping it in practice.

DOOR: Are ministers paid too much?

NIEBUHR: "A man must live," and it is promised that if we seek first the kingdom and its righteousness "all these things shall be added unto us."

DOOR: You sound like Rev. Ike.

NIEBUHR: But I doubt whether Jesus had a $45,000* salary in mind.

DOOR: Now you don't sound like Rev. Ike.

NIEBUHR: If the things that are added become too numerous they distract your attention terribly. To try to keep your eye on the main purpose may only result in making you squint-eyed. I hope the new $45,000* prophet won't begin his pastorate with a ser-mon on the text, "I count all things but loss."

DOOR: So you do not think the amount of money a minister makes is relevant?

NIEBUHR: The modest stipend which the small church can afford makes for simple living and the absence of social pride. If more young fellows would be willing to go into churches like that and not suffer from inferiority complexes because they had not landed one of the "big pulpits," we might put new power into the church.

DOOR: You mention "social pride." What contributes to arrogance in the ministry?

NIEBUHR: We ministers maintain our sense of importance only through a vast and inclusive ignorance. If we knew the world in which we live a little better we would perish in shame or be overcome by a sense of futility.

DOOR: What do you mean by ignorance? Ignorance of what?

NIEBUHR: There is something ludicrous about a shallow young fool like myself standing up to preach a sermon to these good folks. I talk wisely about life and know little about life's problems. I tell them of the need of sacrifice, although most of them could tell me something about what that really means.

DOOR: Do ministers find it difficult to speak the truth to their congregations?

NIEBUHR: To speak the truth in love is a difficult, and sometimes an almost impossible, achievement. If you speak the truth unqualifiedly, that is usually because your ire has been aroused or because you have no personal attachment to the object of your strictures. Once personal contact is established you are very prone to temper your wind to the shorn sheep. It is certainly difficult to be human and honest at the same time.

DOOR: Why?

NIEBUHR: Well, it isn't easy to mix the business of preaching with the business of making a living and maintain your honesty and self-respect.

DOOR: So do most just end up preaching nice, safe sermons?

NIEBUHR: The whole weakness of the professional ministry is striving each Sunday to make an interesting speech. It simply can't be denied that the business of furnishing inspiration twice each week on a regular schedule by a person who is paid to do just that and whose success is judged by the amount of "pep" he can concentrate on his homilies is full of moral and spiritual dangers. To follow such a program without running into spiritual bankruptcy requires the resources of a saint. I am not surprised that most budding prophets are tamed in time to become harmless parish priests.

DOOR: Ministers do not have much respect today; would you care to discuss why?

NIEBUHR: There are too many men in the pulpit who look and act for all the world like cute little altar boys who have no idea that the mass in which they are participating is a dramatization of a tragedy.

DOOR: The result is ministers who expect people to come to church out of duty?

NIEBUHR: What is worse is to identify church attendance with moral heroism. Do we not realize that faithful church attendance develops and reveals the virtue of patience much more than the virtue of courage?

DOOR: But ministers need an audience.

NIEBUHR: I have urged people to come to church myself as a matter of duty. But I can do so no longer. The church service is not an end in itself. If the church service does not attract people by the comfort and challenge it brings to them, we only postpone the evil day if we compel attendance by appealing to their sense of duty. It may not be wrong to appeal to their sense of loyalty to the institution and tell them that if they have identified themselves with the institution as members, they owe it to the strangers to be there. But even that is dangerous. The church is already too much an end in itself. These appeals make it appear that we regard religious devotion as a service to God, a very dangerous idea. Of course a modern preacher doesn't really believe that. What is really in his mind, consciously or unconsciously, is that the people owe him the duty to hear him preach. That is perhaps a natural glorification of his own function, but it cannot be denied that there is something pathetic about it.

DOOR: How would you define the church?

NIEBUHR: The church is like the Red Cross service in war time. It keeps life from degenerating into a consistent inhumanity, but it does not materially alter the fact of the struggle itself. The Red Cross neither wins the war nor abolishes it. Since the struggle between those who have and those who have not is a never-ending one, society will always be, in a sense, a battleground. It is therefore of some importance that human loveliness be preserved outside of the battle lines. But those who are engaged in this task ought to realize that the brutalities of the conflict may easily negate the most painstaking humanizing efforts behind the lines, and that those efforts may become a method for evading the dangers and risks of the battlefield.

DOOR: Isn't the battlefield especially brutal in the city?

NIEBUHR: A big city is not a society held together by a productive process. Its people are spiritually isolated even though they are mechanically dependent upon one another. In such a situation it is difficult to create and preserve the moral and cultural traditions which each individual needs to save his life from anarchy.

DOOR: There is a trend in the church today toward calling society back to certain moral absolutes.

NIEBUHR: You may be able to compel people to maintain certain minimum standards by stressing duty, but the highest moral and spiritual achievements depend not upon a push but upon a pull. People must be charmed into righteousness. The language of aspiration rather than that of criticism and command is the proper pulpit language.

DOOR: What do you think of evangelism?

NIEBUHR: I passed one of our big churches today and I ran across this significant slogan calculated to impress the passing wayfarer: "We Will Go Out of Business. When? When Every Man in Detroit Has Been Won to Christ." Of course it is just a slogan and not to be taken seriously, but the whole weakness of Protestantism is in it. Here we are living in a complex world in which thousands who have been "won to Christ" haven't the slightest notion how to live a happy life or how to live together with other people without making each other miserable. Yet the church goes about the business of winning people to Christ—that is,

pulling them through some kind of emotional or social experience in which they are made to commit themselves to the good life as it is symbolized in Christ, and imagining that this is the end of the task. I do not say that such commitments do not have their value. But surely one must be very blind to live under the illusion that the desire or even the will to live a Christ-life is automatically fulfilled in present-day society or in any society. The church which conceived that slogan is really better than the silly advertisement might lead one to suppose. I think people receive some light and leading there. Nevertheless, most of its energies go into the business of "winning others." The saddest part about these highly evangelistic churches who put everything into the recruiting task is that they generally tempt those who are already "won" to imagine themselves perfect, or at least "saved." I know one lawyer in that church, and not a bad man either, who needs to be "won" to several ideas in the gospel of Christ about which he hasn't the faintest glimmer of light. But he is too sure of himself to get a new idea.

DOOR: What about evangelists?

NIEBUHR: Evangelists are not necessarily consciously dishonest; they just don't know enough about life and history to present the problem of the Christian life in its full meaning. They are always assuming that nothing but an emotional commitment to Christ is needed to save the soul from its sin and chaos. They seem never to realize how many of the miseries of mankind are due not to malice but to misdirected zeal and unbalanced virtue.

DOOR: In the time we have left we would like your short comments on a potpourri of subjects, if you don't mind.

NIEBUHR: I don't mind.*

DOOR: Fundamentalists?

NIEBUHR: What about them?*

DOOR: What do you think of them?

NIEBUHR: Fundamentalists have at least one characteristic in common with most scientists. Neither can understand that poetic and religious imagination has a way of arriving at truth by giving a clue to the total meaning of things without being in any sense an analytic description of detailed facts. The fundamentalists insist that religion is science, and thus they prompt those who know that this is not true to declare that all religious truth is contrary to scientific fact.

DOOR: There is very little emphasis today on church history. Evangelicals seem more interested in the present and future.

NIEBUHR: A wise architect observed that you could break the laws of architectural art provided you had mastered them first. That would apply to religion as well. Ignorance of the past does not guarantee freedom from its imperfections. More probably it assures the repetition of past errors. We ought, of course, to cultivate a wholesome skepticism in our young people so that they will not accept the ideas of the past too slavishly. But appreciation must come before criticism.

DOOR: Can there be such a thing as wholesome cynicism? Doesn't cynicism cause you to lose the ability to trust people?

NIEBUHR: Cynics sometimes insinuate that you can love people only if you don't know them too well; that a too-intimate contact with the foibles and idiosyncrasies of men will tempt one to be a misanthrope.

DOOR: Misanthrope? Can't those be surgically removed? Oh ... misanthrope ... as in one who hates and mistrusts all people.

NIEBUHR: I have not found it so. I save myself from cynicism by knowing individuals and knowing them intimately. If I viewed humanity only from some distant and high perspective, I could not save myself from misanthropy. We have a lady in our church who has had a hard life, raised a large family under great difficulties, is revered by her children, and is respected by her friends, and she has learned to view the difficult future with quiet courage as she surveys the painful and yet happy past with sincere gratitude. She thanks me for praying with her and imagines that I am doing her a favor to come to see her. But I really come for selfish reasons—because I leave that home with a more radiant faith of my own.

DOOR: What do you think of the social concern of the modern church?

NIEBUHR: It seems to me rather unfortunate that we must depend upon the "publicans" for our social conscience to so great a degree while the "saints" develop their private virtues and let the city as such fry in its iniquities.

DOOR: But so often the church professes to "love" the poor.

NIEBUHR: They love like the person I heard tell a story about how much he loved his Negro mammy. Someday he ought to have a lesson in ethics and learn how much easier it is to love those who acknowledge their inferiority than those who challenge our superiority.

DOOR: There is a lot of talk today about church unity.

NIEBUHR: What we accomplish in the way of church unity ought to be accepted with humility and not hailed with pride. We are not creating. We are merely catching up with creation.

DOOR: Worship?

NIEBUHR: A religion which never goes beyond a sense of awe is not more complete (though perhaps less perceivable) than one which has reduced life's ultimate and ineffable truth to a pat little formula which a proud little man expounds before a comfortable and complacent congregation. I am sorry that there is no more ethically vital preaching in the cathedral. I am sorry that the sense of awe and reverence has departed from so many of our churches.

DOOR: You have such a way with words, could you wrap up this interview with a homily or two that we can remember?

NIEBUHR: How about this one?* It is so easy to repent of other people's sins.

DOOR: Not bad. How about one more?

NIEBUHR: How much easier it is to adore an ideal character than to emulate it.

DOOR: Thank you.

NIEBUHR: You're welcome.*

The "interview" with Reinhold Niebuhr was done by taking direct quotes from his book, Leaves from the Notebook of a Tamed Cynic. *The book is a journal of Niebuhr's thirteen years in the ministry in Detroit. All of his words in the interview are as they appeared in the book, except for a couple of minor instances when the introduction to his words had to be changed to conform to the interview mode. The questions are, of course, fabricated. The Keepers of the* Door *recognize that lifting his words out of context, and combining them with questions that we never asked, is very risky. We realize that the entire meaning of his statements could have been changed. We did our best to keep that from happening, and we felt that what Niebuhr had to say was so significant it was worth the risk.*

Two other things: Niebuhr's statement regarding ministers' salary originally used the figure $15,000. We adjusted it to $45,000. Secondly, there are a number of places where dialogue was added for comic relief, or simply to define words we didn't understand. These places are marked with an asterisk (*).

We hope you enjoyed the "interview" as much as we enjoyed "conducting" it, and we encourage you to purchase the book from which the "interview" was constructed.

Quotes from Leaves from the Notebook of a Tamed Cynic *were used with permission from Harper and Row.*

RICHARD OSTLING

Richard Ostling (those of us in the publishing business call him Dick) is the religion editor of *Time* magazine (the magazine evangelicals quote when it agrees with them). Ostling looks like a high school band teacher. He attended the University of Michigan and Northwestern University (no degrees, simply attended . . . just kidding), and then received a masters in religion at that well-known evangelical college, George Washington University in Washington, D.C. Ostling admits to being an evangelical (although he whispers when he says that) and worked with *Christianity Today* before coming to *Time* magazine in 1969. He subscribes to the *Door*, reads it even, and has his own ideas about what is happening and what ought to be happening in religion today. We couldn't think of a better person to interview for our tenth-anniversary issue.

DOOR: How do you view the religious press?

OSTLING: Potentially, the religious press should have intensive influence on their audience, and often they don't because they don't deal with the things people are talking about. They're not close enough to the event. There are too many sacred cows. Denominationally owned or organizational magazines are not too helpful for the most part, and generally don't cover the newsy things that people are talking about.

DOOR: Why is that?

OSTLING: They are a little too cautious. They don't really cover the hot issues. I look at this from a newsman's point of view, of course.

DOOR: Do you see any room for a magazine like the *Door*?

OSTLING: No.

DOOR: Seriously, though . . .

OSTLING: I am being serious.

DOOR: This is going to be a very short interview.

OSTLING: Well, humor is a valuable commodity in religion. The good thing about the *Door* is that it is partly journalistic and partly reportorial. Some of your humor does bear directly on things that people are talking about. There isn't too much humor in the religious field. The former art and production director at *Christianity Today* used to say that you could judge the integrity of a movement or group firstly on their sense of humor and only secondarily on their theology. If someone came along who was humorless, he would immediately distrust them theologically. He might come to trust them later, but his first criterion was whether they had a certain gentleness and humor about themselves.

DOOR: What issues do you think are most significant right now?

OSTLING: Hmm. One is the authority of the Bible. That comes up in a lot of denominations. It is an important question. How do Protestants deal with biblical authority? They don't have a magisterium and they don't have a pope.

The role of women is an issue facing Protestants, Catholics, and Jews alike. Homosexuality, and more broadly, the new morality are other issues, as well as sexual mores—the attack on sexual absolutes.

Personally, I think the biological engineering of the human race is a very important question. When you are talking about genetic engineering and manipulation of genes, potentially you are talking about mankind designing himself. C. Everett Koop is the object of a very strong campaign to keep him out of the surgeon general's chair. I'm not particularly happy with all of his rhetoric, but I think he is a moral man who sees that there are big problems which everyone is skating over. He's particularly concerned about the deformed child, because that's what he's given his life to. He contends that infanticide, in fact, is a regular procedure in U.S. medicine, and that his fellow doctors are purposely passing by on the other side (like the Good Samaritan story), thereby allowing deformed infants to die when surgery could remove the deformity in some cases or preserve the life in other cases.

DOOR: Most religious publications don't talk much about biological engineering.

OSTLING: There's some awareness of it. *Christianity Today* has been fairly on top of genetic engineering, euthanasia, and abortion. They quoted Helmut of the University of Hamburg on tying abortion and euthanasia to the Nazis. The L.A. *Times* charged that Koop's logic was incomprehensible when he suggested in an article that abortion leads to infanticide, then to euthanasia, and "indeed to the very beginnings of the political climate that led to Auschwitz." Yet here you have one of the grand anti-Nazi theologians suggesting the same thing. It just shows that Koop is not a nincompoop. That rhymes, doesn't it?

DOOR: Er . . . yes it does, Dick.

OSTLING: My point is that I think Koop needs to be listened to rather than just be dismissed.

DOOR: Is the Moral Majority still a story?

OSTLING: Religion and politics is an important story, but I wouldn't limit it to the Moral Majority. You must talk about both the left and the right because a generation ago, the left was saying the church should meddle in every conceivable political issue and raise its voice. It should put the gospel in the streets. The right was saying that the church should stay out of politics and ministers had no business lobbying in Sacramento or Washington. Now, a full generation later, it's a 179-degree flip.

DOOR: A 179-degree flip?

OSTLING: Well, you know what I mean. Edit it so it sounds better.

DOOR: Of course we will, Dick. We wouldn't want the religion editor of *Time* magazine to look bad. . . .

OSTLING: Anyway, now suddenly the left is very upset about ministers becoming involved in politics.

DOOR: Aren't you impressed with the new surge of evangelicals? Does the evangelical church really have a lot of influence?

OSTLING: It's surprising how little impact the whole evangelical upsurge seems to have. It doesn't have much staying power. Christians of non-evangelical views or so-called liberal views probably feel correctly that they can bide their time and outlast the evangelical thing because it doesn't have influence in the key sectors of the American society, which would include commercial television, the general press, the academic world, public education, military, and corporate business. Even as a religious movement, the evangelicals do not have a strong seminary network. They don't have much power in the Protestant seminary world right now. In spite of that, a lot of people have been genuinely surprised at how much staying power it has and how many people are involved in evangelicalism in this country. It hit the secular media as a surprise, too, and they're not quite sure what to make of it.

DOOR: So what you are saying is that for some reason evangelicals seem to

have kept the attention of the larger populace and have given the image that they have power, but in fact, in any major institution in this country where real decisions are made, they really don't?

OSTLING: Yes. At least that's the general feeling I have. That's putting it more sharply than I did, but I guess I would have to go along with that. Certainly the evangelical church does not seem to have cultural staying power.

DOOR: What are your biggest concerns about the evangelical church?

OSTLING: There are several things. First, there isn't enough good thought in the church. There isn't enough good education. I have a hunch that a farmer with a sixth-grade education 100 years ago knew the Bible much better than a college graduate churchgoer today. People seem to be shaky in terms of what's in the Bible—even people from the so-called "biblical churches." The ignorance about the Scripture is amazing sometimes. Look at religious television. It's largely a failure. You could watch all of the programs that are on in a week and you'd get a thimbleful of biblical teaching. If you would listen to all the top evangelists for a year you would get very little Bible teaching.

DOOR: But you'd sure learn how to take an offering.

OSTLING: You need the local church not only because we need to relate to people who are difficult and cantankerous (like us), but you need the local church for the Sunday school class and the pulpit ministry. A lot of good teaching is going on in the pulpits.

DOOR: You said you had several concerns?

OSTLING: I am very worried about the success syndrome in the church, because if you tie Christianity to success, the Cross is left out. I mean, God the Son did have to die on the cross. You can't understand the Christian faith on a success basis. There's a lot of "failure." There has to be faithfulness to Christian teaching, and it's easy to forget that. Evangelicals are aping their liberal opponents of a generation ago when they judged the validity of their gospel by how many bills they got through Congress.

ROBERT WEBBER

We hate to admit it, but once in a while the *Door*, open-minded as we are, forms a stereotype of people and places. Places like Wheaton, Illinois, for example, the holy land of the West. Places like Wheaton College, the citadel of all truths. People like professors at Wheaton College, especially theology professors.

When we discovered that Robert Webber not only taught theology at Wheaton College but had done so for thirteen years, we were convinced we knew what to expect. We assumed he would be into Greek, Hebrew, Bill Gothard, Amway, and the Baptist church. Frankly, we expected a kind of midwestern theological nerd. It turns out that Robert Webber is a prolific writer of more than respectable books (*Common Roots*, *The Secular Saint*, *God Still Speaks*, and *The Moral Majority, Right or Wrong?*), a political activist, an Episcopalian, and smart (which made us feel real uncomfortable). The *Door* sent their Wheaton correspondent, Isabell Ericson (yes, we have correspondents, all one of them), to Robert Webber's office, actually located in Wheaton College's Blanchard Hall (named after Ed Hall). We think you'll find Dr. Webber's comments very intriguing.

DOOR: One gets the feeling reading your books that you have known fundamentalism personally.

WEBBER: I grew up with a fundamentalism which said that the church should be basically obscurantist. It said that a person's piety should be individualistic, privatistic, subjectivistic, and existentialist.

DOOR: Shouldn't that be existential*istic*?

WEBBER: I don't think so.

DOOR: But you said individualistic, privatistic, and—

WEBBER: I don't believe this.

DOOR: Go on.

WEBBER: As I was saying, our faith was not to be involved in the public domain. It was not to encounter the mud and dirt and filth of life itself. But the more I understand the life of the church, the more I understand that faith has to be lived out in the life of the world. There is a constant interaction and tension between the church and the world.

DOOR: Of course, the Moral Majority would agree with you.

WEBBER: That is somewhat true. The Moral Majority does recognize that faith must be lived out in the life of the world, but they have chosen to do that by restoring civil religion. They want to restore morality to government by supporting legislation that will produce a moral country . . . at least externally.

DOOR: We have the feeling you don't think civil religion is a good idea.

WEBBER: True Christianity is not moralistic. Moralism is do-goodism simply for the sake of doing good. Christianity, on the other hand, is rooted in a radical regeneration in Jesus Christ—out of which one's morality flows. But if you try to legislate a morality on a nation and set morality above regeneration, then you've fallen into the position of pure moralism. That is exactly what the Moral Majority has done. The Moral Majority is trying to transform this country into a "moral country" with the belief that then American will be a "Christian country." That's a wrong notion of transformation because it's not rooted in the death and resurrection of Jesus Christ. It hopes in what man can do in America, instead of what God is going to do in all of his creation as a result of the Incarnation and the Resurrection.

DOOR: Maybe we are simple minded, but we are confused. On one hand you seem to suggest that the Moral Majority believes in moralism. You also suggest they believe in civil religion. Then you say that what the Moral Majority needs to do is recognize that radical regeneration in Jesus Christ must happen first and then good mo-

rality will flow from that. But isn't that exactly what the Moral Majority says they believe? And, in fact, isn't that what they have been criticized about in the past? For example, the problem of poverty. They have always contended that you need to lead poor people to Christ first and then worry about feeding them; that all major social problems stem from not having Christ at the center of life. So, here's the question—

WEBBER: I was beginning to wonder . . .

DOOR: What specifically do you disagree with about the Moral Majority?

WEBBER: OK. First of all, I do not believe that the free enterprise economic system is biblical. I do not believe that the free enterprise system is "clearly outlined in Proverbs," or that Jesus has something to say about the "work ethic," or that "competition in business is biblical," or that "successful business management is part of God's plan." Anyone who says that is doing nothing more than Christianizing secular humanism.

DOOR: Jerry would not be thrilled with that conclusion.

WEBBER: I do not think the Moral Majority takes the fall of humanity seriously enough, either.

DOOR: The *Moral Majority* doesn't take sin seriously enough? Are you kidding?

WEBBER: I wish I were. But to suggest that the basic reason this country is in a moral mess is because we have departed from a conservative economic and political viewpoint fails to recognize the pervasive influence of evil. Considering the abuses of capitalism and republicanism by sinful people, it is hard to believe that a return to these systems run by Christians is the road to morality and peace.

DOOR: That address, folks, is Robert Webber, Wheaton, Illinois. That's all the address you need.

WEBBER: You might as well wait until I'm done. I also object to the view that America is a special nation raised up by God for a specific mission to the world. That is a poor reading of the facts and an unwarranted elevation of America.

DOOR: Want to keep going?

WEBBER: Yes. I really disagree with the Moral Majority and their tactics, which are a sort of single-issue approach to evaluating issues and results in legalism and inconsistency. So you end up rejecting a man like Senator Hatfield and supporting a man like Representative Robert Bauman, who is a confessed alcoholic and admitted sex-offender. I also disagree with the tactics of Jerry Falwell, personally.

DOOR: What tactics?

WEBBER: Jerry Falwell believes in the "mighty man" philosophy of leadership. He goes back into the Old Testament and refers to Gideon and all the "mighty men" who rose up to lead Israel into spiritual renewal.

DOOR: We have the feeling you don't think that is a good idea either.

WEBBER: The church does not need "mighty men." What the church needs instead are mighty ideas that will capture the thinking of its people. If the average pastor, elder, deacon, and person in the pew could recover the central ideas of the Christian faith, then they wouldn't hang on the coattails of some "mighty man" and create another cult of personality that ultimately damages the impact of the Christian faith.

DOOR: But the fact is that the cult of personality worship is gaining amongst Christians. Jerry Falwell, Oral Roberts, Jim Bakker, James Robison, Rex Humbard, Robert Schuller, and others have even more influence today.

WEBBER: The problem is that if a cult figure with his power can use that power politically to destroy his opponents, then it's a power game. When that happens then the church is called apostate. That's why I say that the leaders of the church have to be very, very careful when they take political stances, because to tie the church in with a political stance is to tie it in with political power from which emerges messianic complexes and political structures that destroy the opponents. Then the whole thing ceases to be Christian.

DOOR: Why are religious people so susceptible to personalities?

WEBBER: Most people are uninformed. They don't think. They are products of a television era where they see and act without thoroughgoing reflection. What they want is for somebody to tell them how to think and what to believe. That is very dangerous.

DOOR: OK. The church needs to be wary of the cult of personality and they have to be wary of civil religion and moralism. We are still somewhat hazy regarding what exactly you think Christians and the church should do. What is the specific role of the church in the world?

WEBBER: First of all, the focus of God's work in the world is in the church, not in a particular nation or in any other group. God has not raised up America or the Marxist revolution to save the world. He only saves the world through Jesus Christ, who is manifested in the history of the church. Therefore, the true meaning of history is not dependent on a nation, nor will God's kingdom be brought to the world through moral betterment or social liberation. Rather, the instrument of God's kingdom, the focus of his activity for the salvation of the world, is the church alone.

Furthermore, the church is the source of Christian values. God has revealed himself and his values to the church, especially in the incarnation of his Son, who by his life, example, and teaching imaged the way his church is to live. Thus, the revelation of God's values has been given to the church, and the church is called to guard, preserve, and pass on these values.

DOOR: You're on a roll now.

WEBBER: The church exists as a prophetic witness in the world. That means that the church acts as a social critic. It denounces the powers and their evil effects in society and calls on people who are under the powers to renounce them and turn to Jesus Christ.

DOOR: That sounds wonderful, but the last time we checked, the church didn't seem to be cooperating too well amongst themselves. Frankly, the conservatives don't seem to trust anyone else.

WEBBER: When I went to Bob Jones, it was implied that only the people who went to Bob Jones University were true Christians. When I went to the Reformed Episcopal Seminary, the impression was that only Calvinists were true Christians. Covenant Seminary gave me the impression that only those who separated from mainline denominations were true Christians. Then I went to Concordia Seminary and became involved in an ecumenical

group, half of whom were Roman Catholics studying for the ministry. I was shocked to discover: (1) They knew more about the Bible than I did; (2) they knew a lot more about church history and theology than I did; (3) they were much more pious than I was; and (4) they really cared about the world in which they lived. I discovered then that we have to get off our high-hat view that we evangelicals are the apple of God's eye. That is pure unadulterated pride that results in apostasy. It leads to the kind of thinking which would suggest that America is God's new Israel, and therefore we have to have military might and we have to be able to dominate the rest of the world. When we start believing that we have all truth, that we are the only ones who can preserve liberty and that God is on our side, we are in trouble. It's just plain sloppy thinking.

The biggest fear I have of both the left and the right is that they do not tolerate another point of view. Both groups are legalistic. There is no freedom. We need to be able to walk into both of those groups and say, "I belong to the church of Jesus Christ and I am wrestling with an understanding of what it means for the church to be in the world. As I seek to understand the Scripture and know how the church has functioned historically regarding this particular issue, I have come to a conclusion . . . But I don't say that this is God's only conclusion."

DOOR: Again, your concept of the church is a noble one, but we all know it doesn't operate that way.

WEBBER: I understand your cynicism, but I am afraid we all have to answer to the same question, and that is, "What is our relationship with the church?" Because, like it or not, that's where Jesus is in the world today.

DOOR: Are there any issues you can think of where there is only one true point of view? Can a Christian be dogmatic about anything?

WEBBER: There is a place for dogmatism. In some ways I appreciate what the Moral Majority has done because, while I don't think they are as thoroughly biblical as they should be, by taking a dogmatic stand they have pointed out to all of us the moral decadence of this country. And they have reminded us that we do need to do something about it.

DOOR: You surprise us.

WEBBER: I do not believe Christians should be so moderate and flexible that they have no point of view. If you have no point of view you'll have no enemies and no friends. You'll simply be a blob. I much prefer someone like Jerry Falwell who has a point of view.

DOOR: You still surprise us.

WEBBER: Well, don't pin a "Jesus First" pin on me yet. I am simply saying that it is valid to point out issues dogmatically. But the difficulty arises when we suggest that only one response is valid.

DOOR: You mentioned earlier that many evangelicals think they are the only true Christians and that worried you. Is there anything else about evangelicalism that worries you?

WEBBER: One of the main things that worries me about evangelicalism is that it seems characterized by amnesia. Evangelicals have forgotten, for the most part, their past. The historical roots of some evangelicals go back as deep as Dwight L. Moody, for others, as far back as the Reformation. Some act like Pentecost occurred on October 31, 1517, the day Martin Luther tacked his Ninety-five Theses to the Wittenberg door. It is as though nothing had happened for fifteen hundred years. That is positively absurd. What we need to do is to recover the whole life of the church in the world, just as we need today to recover our ecumenical global unity as a community of communities. So, we need to know what Ignatius and Tertullian and Irenaeus and Athanasius and St. John Chrysostom said. They are our great-great-great-great-great-great-grand-fathers, and we belong to the same family that they belong to. They and others have passed down a rich and glorious heritage for us, and unless we have the benefit of that heritage today, we miss the fullness of the church as it can be in the world.

DOOR: All right. Let's just pretend that the church will get it all together. It has listened to all of your suggestions. It has remembered its history and its roots. What should the church look like?

WEBBER: If there is any point at which the church in America has truly failed, it has been her inability to express a "corporate otherness." For the most part, the church's corporate life has become secularized by the values of American culture. But the church ought to be characterized by a set of values which is distinctly over against the values of society. In other words, the church recognizes that it is part of culture, but it isn't part of culture. It is "in the world but not of the world." The second-century epistle of Diognetus describes this tension much better than I can:

"They dwell in their own countries, but simply as sojourners. As citizens, they share in all

things as if foreigners. Every foreign land is to them as their native country, and every land of their birth as land of strangers. They marry, as do all others; they beget children; but they do not destroy their offspring. They have a common table, but not a common bed. They are in the flesh but they do not live after the flesh. They pass their days on earth, but they are citizens of heaven. They obey the prescribed laws, and at the same time surpass the laws by their lives. They love all men, and are persecuted by all. They are unknown and condemned; they are put to death, and restored to life. They are poor, yet make many rich; they are in lack of all things, and yet abound in all; they are dishonoured, and yet in their very dishonour are glorified. They are evil spoken of, and yet are justified; they are reviled, and bless; they are insulted, and repay the insult with honour; they do good, yet are punished as evil-doers. When punished, they rejoice as if quickened into life; they are assailed by the Jews as foreigners, and are persecuted by the Greeks; yet those who hate them are unable to assign any reason for their hatred."

TOM SINE

First of all, the Keepers of the *Door* don't like to interview people with Ph.D.s . . . they know too much. Secondly, if we do find a Ph.D., we don't like to do an interview with them if their Ph.D. is in a subject we've never heard of . . . like American intellectual history. Thirdly, we don't like to interview people who are older than we are . . . but look younger. We interviewed Tom Sine anyway . . . we felt sorry for him. After all, somebody has to interview intelligent Ph.D.s from Idaho. As it turns out, Tom Sine is a lot more than a futurist, a lot more than a research and planning consultant for corporations, government agencies, and Christian organizations. He wrote *The Mustard Seed Conspiracy* (and, more recently, *Why Settle for More and Miss the Best?*). *The Mustard Seed Conspiracy* is a book that actually has something to say. It is definitely Christian and definitely threatening, no matter what your present lifestyle is.

Now don't get us wrong. Tom Sine did not completely fool us. His dress is sort of 1960s Berkeley professor (minus the pipe); he only likes his picture taken from one side ("otherwise I look like I'm stoned"), and he's into health foods (he offered us some kind of carrot concoction and herb tea . . . we politely declined and ate at McDonald's after the interview). However, Tom Sine does have a lot to say, and what he says not only has the ring of truth; it has the uncomfortable ring of prophetic truth.

DOOR: You are a futurist. . . .?

SINE: I go under that label.

DOOR: What do you see as the significant issues of the next few years?

SINE: One of the most significant issues is whether or not the *Door* will be published on time in the next decade.

DOOR: Real funny.

SINE: The most disturbing issue to face the church is the widening gap between the rich and the poor. The urban explosion in the Third World is mind-boggling. Thirty-two million people in Mexico City by the end of the century; twenty-five million in Sao Paulo, Brazil; nineteen million in Bombay and Calcutta. There are already one million people living permanently on the streets of Calcutta. That means families fixing meals on dirty sidewalks, kids going to the bathroom in gutters, washing themselves in sewer water. The filth and squalor there is indescribable. And it is getting worse every day.

DOOR: Church people don't like to face the ugly facts that you have just described.

SINE: Well, the church had better begin to pay attention to these conditions . . . now. We blew it in the sixties and seventies. We missed an enormous opportunity to minister. But we don't have to blow it again. We can begin now to anticipate the implications of the urban explosion and get a jump on the problem. We've got ten years. We have the resources to move now. We know what to do . . . we just need to start doing it.

DOOR: Where does the church . . . where do *we* start?

SINE: We need a whole concept of stewardship that starts with the biblical premise that "the earth is the Lord's." If we buy into that, then it's no longer a question of how much I have to give up; rather, it's how much of God's do I get to keep in relationship to all the other brothers and sisters with whom I share this planet? If I try to answer that question, maybe it will cause other questions like, can we add a third building to our suburban southern California church when the church in Bolivia can't afford to build a badly needed roof, or do we need a new RV

when a family in Haiti doesn't have enough antibiotics to keep their family alive for a week?

DOOR: Now you've started to make us uncomfortable. Other issues?

SINE: The arms race. We spent something like $500 billion last year on arms and we are committed to spend $1.5 trillion to try to get the edge on the Russians. We now have the capability to kill one another fifteen times over.

DOOR: That's certainly reassuring.

SINE: What is reassuring is the emergence of a peace movement in Western Europe and the United States led by Christians.

DOOR: That may not be so reassuring to a certain group in Lynchburg, Virginia, but moving right along . . . what are some other issues?

SINE: Economics. The fact is the party is over.

DOOR: The party's over?

SINE: There is a growing polarization between the haves and the have-nots. The decade of the seventies was the me-first decade, but the decade of the eighties is much more ominous; it is fast becoming the decade of "us vs. them." That's because the kinds of things that we've come to expect are not going to be there anymore because the party was made possible by vast availability of relatively inexpensive resources—not the least of which was cheap oil. And there are no more cheap resources.

Technology is another important issue. Jacques Ellul makes a very strong point that technology not only reflects the darkness within us; it magnifies it. We can see that not only in our nuclear missiles and arms but in the Love Canal. Christians had better wake up to the ethical ramifications of our new technology from genetic manipulation to patenting life forms. There are some in the scientific community today who are suggesting that we should try to achieve human immortality through science and technology by interbasing man and machine. The quest for immortality is nothing more than the quest to be like God. That is science at its root, the drive toward omniscience, omnipotence, and immortality.

DOOR: It seems incredible that we can send a man to the moon, yet we can't even get a *Door* out free of typographical errors.

SINE: There are some things even technology cannot help. But the point is that the advances in technology far surpass our ability to cope with its implications. For example, the computer. We now have the marriage of the computer to cable TV. This is going to create whole new problems. The TV will stop being a passive entertainment device and become an interactive communication system. That means that we will be able to interact through the television by having access to virtually unlimited information. We will be able to respond to surveys, pay our bills, deposit and withdraw money, make purchases from video catalogs, and interact with people across town. This will create a number of serious problems. One is that there is no way to keep anyone from monitoring the kinds of choices we make. That means that the government and any organization that wants to will be able to collect the most comprehensive information about us. Ethically, the potential for the invasion of privacy is massive. And, frankly, I don't think anyone is going to be able to stop these technological advances.

Already advertisers are salivating all over the floor. The potential is incredible. They are already designing ways to narrow-cast commercials. That means an advertiser (from soap suds to politicians) can gain access to a profile of a potential customer and then design a commercial that will appeal to that profile. In other words, they will be able to say what you want them to say. You will be manipulated without being aware of it. In terms of the demonic use of technology, the possibilities of mind control are remarkable.

DOOR: So, in the face of all those issues, how do you think Christians are doing?

SINE: There is a great deal of reinforcement of the narcissism of our culture within Christian homes. We teach our kids to look out for themselves, get to the top of the heap as fast as they can, look out for number one, make it to the best college, and don't let Johnny play with your trike. As a result, much of our youth ministry today seems oriented toward keeping kids distracted until they settle down rather than preparing them to be servants for Jesus Christ. I know very few Christian homes or youth ministries where young people are challenged and enabled to be servants or to look outside themselves toward the needs of others. I know very few situations where families are involved in ministry together.

DOOR: Most families are involved in accumulating things for their children and themselves.

SINE: That's so tragic because there's no way young people are going to have what their mother and father have.

DOOR: You mean God doesn't want American children to have more than their parents . . . or at least as much? That sounds almost blasphemous.

SINE: The middle-class expectation that everyone can expect to move from a cottage and an old Chevy to a split-level, ranch-style home and a new Pontiac is just not going to happen in the eighties and nineties. That's shattering because the church and the home have been reinforcing that expectation with our children.

DOOR: How do we begin to counter that?

SINE: By helping our children and ourselves fundamentally redefine what the good life is. We need to let people in on the secret that the good life doesn't have anything to do with materialism or consumerism. The good life is a life given away.

DOOR: What can the organized church do?

SINE: The primary job in the church is cultural formation. It's not just getting people saved and getting them to abstain from a few things and hang around the church buildings. It's getting them to incarnate a whole new culture, to become new people.

DOOR: What about Christian colleges? What can they do?

SINE: I wish they would do something, but typically what I find happening in Christian colleges is a little game called "finding-the-will-of-God." It is a game which begins with the question, "What do I want? What do I want for a job, house, and spouse?" Then you find something that approximates what you want, a foxy girl, neat job, nice-looking Porsche, and you start negotiating (sometimes called prayer). In other words, you try to talk God into letting you have what you want.

We are taught that once we get all of our ducks in a row (great job, house, spouse), then if we have some extra time left over, we will be glad to usher once in awhile, and if the ski slopes aren't good, we'll be there. Ironically, the last question we are taught to ask is the ministry question.

DOOR: Of course, you are not speaking of Christian colleges like Wheaton, Seattle Pacific, or Biola.

SINE: No comment. The first questions shouldn't be what do I want, or, better yet, what will God let me have. The first question should be "What does God want? What is God doing in society, and how does he want me to use my life, gifts, and time to be a part of what he's doing in history?" If we seek first the kingdom (Matthew 6:33), if we discover our role in being a part of the advance of God's kingdom, if we find out how God wants us to minister, then we can decide what job to take, when and who we are to marry. Everything is done within the context of our calling.

DOOR: But does it really matter what your vocation is as long as you do the best things you can and try to witness for Christ?

SINE: We have a distorted notion of Christian vocation. Out of Reformed teaching, we have taught that essentially every job is as good as every other job as long as you work hard and say a little word for Jesus. That is not true. In the New Testament a lot of folks just left their jobs to follow Christ.

DOOR: Are you suggesting that all jobs are not neutral?

SINE: There is no such thing as neutrality in occupations. Some occupations are going to reinforce what the kingdom is all about and others are going to be destructive, or even worse, just plain irrelevant. So many in the church today are teaching that all you need to do is confess your sins, accept Christ, and continue to do what you are doing ... just do it a little more honestly. Well, I don't believe that. There is a radical character to the call of Christ in our lives, and helping IBM increase their corporate profits is not the same as working for the kingdom of God. Frankly, many of us are investing in occupations that have nothing to do with the kingdom of God.

DOOR: How do we find the right occupation?

SINE: Quit asking how can I do what I want. Instead ask how God wants us to minister in the world and how we can help that happen. Once we've answered those questions, then we can choose an occupation compatible with our answers to those questions.

DOOR: But in all honesty, don't most of us think that if we do what you are suggesting, we'll all end up in a Christian commune or in the mission field?

SINE: All I am saying is that the first question we ask must be the ministry question. Once you decide what your ministry is, then you may end up doing the ministry one evening a week, or you may decide to work twenty hours a week so you can minister thirty hours a week. Let me give you an example. Some friends of mine in Seattle decided that God's call in their lives was to work with international students. The best they could swing was four hours a week because they were both working full time. They were convinced they needed the two incomes to live adequately. But they weren't satisfied that they were really fulfilling God's ministry call in their lives, so they quit their jobs. They discovered they could live on one-half of one income instead of two full

incomes by living in community. As a consequence, instead of spending four hours a week in ministry, they are now able to spend thirty hours a week in ministry. You see, every Christian has a ministry vocation in life, and that can be the same as or different from our occupation, but our kingdom vocation has to have number-one priority in our lives. We simply have not challenged people with the radical discipleship we find in the New Testament, which definitely requires a radical reprioritization of our time.

DOOR: This all sounds great. In fact, we middle-class folks have been hearing stuff just like you're talking about for years now. We end up feeling very guilty for a few days ... but we make no significant changes.

SINE: I'm not after the feeling of guilt; I'm after a feeling of opportunity.

DOOR: Do you sell Amway?

SINE: Look, I believe, as a historian, that the God of Abraham, Isaac, and Jacob is alive and well. He is the Lord of history. Contrary to what things appear to be, things are not out of control. The powers of darkness are not calling the shots. God is moving us into a new age beyond anything we can imagine. And we have the opportunity to join with God in bringing about this new age.

DOOR: A lot of dedicated materialists would agree with you. They would suggest that God is bringing in his kingdom any minute now so we need to get our personal act together, lead all our friends to Christ, and watch the signs signaling Christ's return.

SINE: That is what I call the eschatology of escape that has so captured the evangelical consciousness. In actuality, it is the eschatology of despair. Spending so much time trying to figure out how Ezekiel 38 fits in with the common market is like writing a birth pamphlet for expectant mothers and focusing on the pain, the agony, and the trauma of the birth process. Our call is to be captured by the imagery and power of God's new age. God is saying, "I invite you to join me in being the presence of the future now."

Churches need to be captured by the same imagery. I don't find churches with a strong sense of vision, instead I find them equipped with "chronic randomness," which means they are doing thirteen different things with no sense of how any of it fits together. They have a potluck once a year where they congratulate themselves, but they are still doing the same thirteen things with no sense of what they are doing. So much of our activity in the church does no more than serve ourselves. Tom Skinner said, "Let's quit kidding ourselves; we even tithe to ourselves."

DOOR: Tithe to ourselves?

SINE: He's right. Everything we put into our churches we take back. We give to build more comfortable buildings, softer pews, nicer carpet, better air conditioning. We are not, as Bonhoeffer said, "the church for others"; we are the church for ourselves. The tithe is not a New Testament concept anyway. We don't sing, "Ten percent to Jesus I surrender, ten percent to him I freely give," We are to be totally available to Jesus Christ.

DOOR: But a lot of tithers would say that everything they have is God's. All God has to do is ask.

SINE: That is what I call the "doctrine of passive availability." The doctrine of passive availability says that everything I have is God's and anytime he shows me a vision and hits me with

white lightning, he can have it; but until then I am going to enjoy all of my possessions. But nowhere in the New Testament does it say that. In fact, we've already been asked. We've already received our marching orders. The marching orders are to work, use our lives and resources for the kingdom now.

DOOR: You are starting to make us uncomfortable again.

SINE: John Alexander says that the problem with Jesus is that Jesus is a radical and we're all moderates. I think he's right. Jesus comes to every culture and makes us all very uncomfortable because he calls us to put the kingdom first. We are not called to look out for number one. We are called to be the mustard seed that falls to the ground and dies.

DOOR: Does that mean (horrors) to give up the good life?

SINE: A lot of lifestyle literature gives the impression that working for the kingdom means giving up the good life. That's balderdash.

DOOR: Balderdash?

SINE: Balderdash.

DOOR: Strong words, Tom. Surprising, too. We would have expected someone like you to ask us to give up the good life.

SINE: I believe God does better than that. It is time we understood that we are not called to give up a chunk of the good life; what we are called to do is fundamentally redefine what the good life is. We are the ones that should be teaching the world to sing and dance and know what the good life is all about.

DOOR: And how would you define the good life?

SINE: One thing for sure, the good life has nothing to do with consumption. If it did, then Americans would be the happiest people in the world because we've been conditioned to believe that what we throw in our garbage cans and store in our garages and ring up in our charge accounts has something to do with happiness. Actually, Americans are really a miserable group of folks. They aren't very happy. We all need to understand that. The good life is the celebration of our relationship with our Father, with one another, and with his creation. It is the joy found when we give our lives away.

DOOR: So, realistically, how do we help the people in our churches discover this good life?

SINE: You find the people who are ready. I find there is normally a handful of people in any church who have reached a level of readiness. They've heard God's voice and are ready to move. I would encourage pastors to focus on that handful and equip that handful to start living differently. You can't try to get everyone on board—that's a hopeless task—but you can find a handful.

DOOR: What do you mean, live differently?

SINE: We need to move away from the splendid isolation of every lone-ranger family out there on their own with no contact. The church needs to start being a family.

DOOR: Many futurists are very pessimistic about the future. Do you really believe the church can begin living like a family? Do you really think there is any basis for optimism?

SINE: When I first got into futures back in the early seventies, I became very depressed and cynical. I was forced back into the Scriptures, and as I reread the Old Testament, I began to see the imagery there of the future of God. I realized that God really is in control. He *is* going to create a new heaven and a new earth. God *is* going to wipe away all tears. He is going to be in the midst of his people reigning forever. No more children born for destruction, no more oppression, no more sickness and illness. Praise the Lord, the future of God is come in the life, death, and resurrection of Christ, and all of us can participate in the future of God now! And so, in answer to your question, I am an optimist.

ED DOBSON

Ed Dobson doesn't look like a fundamentalist. He looks like an Amway salesman ... er ... wait a minute ... that's worse. Okay, so he looks like a nice fundamentalist ... and he is. He used to work at some college in Lynchburg, Virginia, that is associated with the inventor of the "Jesus First" pin. In fact, he was vice-president of student affairs at Liberty Baptist College, but he's still nice. In fact, when we interviewed him in 1982, we thought he'd be wearing white shoes and he thought we'd be wearing Levis. Turns out he wore the Levis and we wore the white shoes.

The point is Ed Dobson is not only a fundamentalist, but he and a fellow named Jerry Falwell wrote a book about them, *The Fundamentalist Phenomenon.* Believe it or not, it was actually controversial amongst fundamentalists. Before arriving in Grand Rapids to pastor Calvary Church in 1987, Dr. Dobson was also senior editor of *Fundamentalist Journal.* And he graduated from Bob Jones University. If that doesn't make him a fundamentalist, then nothing does.

DOOR: What are fundamentalists?

DOBSON: Fundamentalists, first of all, are characterized by a commitment to the basic fundamentals of faith. The inerrancy of Scripture, the Virgin Birth of Christ and his deity, his substitutionary atonement, and so on. Funda-

mentalists have a strong emphasis on truth.

DOOR: What are the differences between an evangelical and a fundamentalist?

DOBSON: One of the differences is that an evangelical is "concerned" and a fundamentalist is mad. In other words, evangelicals have a great deal of "concern for issues"; they just never do anything about them. Fundamentalists, on the other hand, right or wrong, are never satisfied until they confront an issue and change it. In fact, I can give you an illustration that points out the differences between a liberal, an evangelical, and a fundamentalist.

DOOR: Oh no, we feel a joke coming on.

DOBSON: If you ask a liberal if he believes there are literal flames in hell, he will tell you, "Hell, no!" If you ask an evangelical, he'll begin a lengthy dissertation on eternal retribution in light of the implicit goodness of God and after thirty minutes you still won't know whether he believes there are flames in hell or not. Ask a fundamentalist if there are flames in hell and he will say, "Hell, yes . . . and hot ones."

DOOR: Can a person be a Christian and not hold to the "fundamentals"?

DOBSON: Each person can only answer for himself what is or is not a Christian. However, of all the fundamentals, it would be very difficult to be a Christian and deny the deity of Christ, which is the very heart of the gospel.

DOOR: So you are saying that as long as one believed in the deity of Christ, one would not necessarily have to believe in the other "fundamentals," say, for example, the Virgin Birth?

DOBSON: I believe that particular issue is an absolute essential. To me, the Virgin Birth is an issue which dovetails on the deity of Christ. You don't go through the Virgin Birth to establish the deity. The deity of Christ is clearly established in Scripture, and the logical consequence of that is to ask how he became man. How was he the God-man? The answer to that is the deity of Christ.

DOOR: The Virgin Birth, then, would be another of the "fundamentals" that a person would have to hold to in order to be a Christian?

DOBSON: I would say so, yes.

DOOR: The Philipian jailer asked, "What must I do to be saved?" and the answer was, "Believe in the Lord Jesus Christ." Why then would you insist that someone has to believe in the Virgin Birth to be a Christian? Did the Philipian jailer or the primitive Chris-

tians in Greece and Rome believe in the Virgin Birth or even know about it?

DOBSON: I don't believe you have to fully comprehend all the theological implications of the gospel in order to accept the gospel. To say that you have to understand all the implications of this or that to benefit from the gospel is not necessarily true. Most people who are saved, especially most of a very secular background, certainly don't understand the entire picture.

I cannot, on the basis of someone's writing, or even on the basis of what they say, be absolutely sure that they are or are not a Christian. I wouldn't want to put myself in that kind of position. Certainly, people can disagree with us and be Christians.

DOOR: So what you are really saying is that people don't have to believe in all the fundamentals to be a Christian?

DOBSON: Hold it, guys. What you're asking is if we can negotiate on the fundamentals?

DOOR: Why didn't we think of that?

DOBSON: The difficulty when you start renegotiating the fundamentals is that you open up Pandora's box, and I'm not sure when or how you can shut it. Once you allow yourself to get to first base, it's much easier to steal second, and once you get there, it's much easier to get to third, and maybe you end up in the outfield somewhere. The basis of Christianity, of course, centers around the person who represents it—that's Christ—and faith in his death, burial, and resurrection, which is the gospel. To say that the gospel is less than that is to say that it isn't the gospel at all.

DOOR: What about the Second Coming?

DOBSON: There's negotiation there. There's amillennial people, premillennial people . . . personally, I believe in the premillennial, pretribulation rapture of the church, but I wouldn't die for that. All of us genuinely believe that somehow, some way, Jesus is coming. Now what that means and how that is interpreted, there's a vast difference among Christians.

DOOR: You seem pretty open to different understandings of future events. How open are you about charismatic?

DOBSON: In general, the charismatic movement is doctrinally unpredictable and fundamentalists, historically, are very doctrinally oriented. Philosophically, I have trouble with their emphasis on personal experience and theologically, I object to the whole idea of the baptism of the Spirit and speaking in tongues.

DOOR: But, other than those objections, they're okay guys?

DOBSON: Frankly, we went further than fundamentalists have gone in our book by saying that there are some things we can learn from the charismatic movement.

DOOR: Such as?

DOBSON: That orthodoxy alone is not meeting people's needs. Charismatics do emphasize the personal relationship and they emphasize love, which are things we could emphasize more, but we must not do that to the exclusion of doctrinal criteria.

DOOR: Frankly, you are disappointing us. We had hoped for a raving, finger-pointing, white-shoed evangelist.

DOBSON: Well, your hair is much shorter than I thought it would be . . . and neither one of you is wearing blue jeans.

DOOR: Sorry. Aren't you going to make a lot of fundamentalists mad? You almost seem . . . er . . . sensible.

DOBSON: Our book is sort of like a manifesto, and in our movement people will either like it or hate it. The people we lost are not truly mainline fundamentalists . . . but the lunatic fringe.

DOOR: All this time we thought of *fundamentalists* as the lunatic fringe.

DOBSON: In our book we call this "lunatic fringe" hyper-fundamentalists. A hyper-fundamentalist is one characterized by negativism, pessimism, extreme separatism, and an exclusivism that rarely extends beyond their immediate circle (which is usually rather small).

DOOR: Now the hyper-fundamentalists are going to be mad at you.

DOBSON: I doubt it, since most hypers rarely read books, let alone satirical magazines. I have written some satire myself.

DOOR: You're kidding.

DOBSON: It was called *When the Roll is Called Up Yonder, We'll Be First: An Irrelevant Look at the Fundamentalist Movement*. We had all kinds of interesting chapter headings: "Deacons and Other Endangered Species," "Women and Other Missing Links in the Chain of Command . . ."

DOOR: Did you try to get it published?

DOBSON: It was rejected by eight different publishers.

DOOR: Why don't you let us publish it?

DOBSON: Uh . . . I'll have to think about it.

DOOR: Why did you write the book?

DOBSON: I had almost finished my doctor's degree at the University of Virginia, and because of my schedule it looked like I might not be able to finish it. I couldn't be a legitimate fundamentalist without a doctor's degree, so I wrote the book in hopes that someone would offer me an honorary degree.

DOOR: Oh yes, honorary degrees. Fundamentalists and Campus Life directors have a corner on those.

DOBSON: Yes. Fundamentalists like to hide behind their honorary doctorates.

DOOR: You've written a book about fundamentalism. Why? To list the criteria for being a true fundamental Christian?

DOBSON: The one thing we have tried to do in the book is not argue theology, but rather record a history, and try to evaluate where we are today. We do something in the book that fundamentalists have never done and that is admit our weaknesses.

DOOR: For instance?

DOBSON: We are a pragmatic, action-oriented people, and thinking is considered almost a sin. We're saying it is time for fundamentalists to reflect and to think.

DOOR: Often, when fundamentalists say, "Let's think," they mean something different . . .

DOBSON: They mean, "Let's think like us."

DOOR: Right. Are you suggesting that the fundamentalist church needs to admit that they may not have all the answers?

DOBSON: Yes. If we don't, we're going to end up out in left field somewhere, isolated from the real needs of man, the real questions that are being asked. We may get a lot of people baptized, but it will be the revolving door, in and out, and the question is have we really helped them?

DOOR: It seems that fundamentalists make a big deal about labels. They constantly want to make sure your credentials are sound. Isn't the whole label thing a waste of energy? Does anyone really care? And does it really make any difference?

DOBSON: I was interviewed awhile back by *Newsweek* magazine. I was trying to explain the difference between an evangelical and a fundamentalist and all of a sudden the interviewer asked, "Could you tell me what a Christian is?" I think that sometimes the unsaved world just couldn't care less whether we are an evangelical or a fundamentalist.

DOOR: But fundamentalists not only seem to care; they seem to have come up with a big list of distinguishing characteristics.

DOBSON: I look at it this way. There are convictions we can substantiate from Scripture like the deity of Christ. These are both absolute and non-negotiable. Then there are personal convictions that we infer from Scripture, like our beliefs on baptism. Our personal convictions about baptism, etc., are important for each of us, but certainly not worth dying for, fighting for, or arguing for. Then there are personal preferences, and what fundamentalists have done is to throw all three categories together as absolutes. So that not only is the deity of Christ an absolute, so is our particular form of baptism, and so is hating long hair and rock music. And that is a tragic mistake. Fundamentalists need to be honest enough to start distinguishing the categories.

DOOR: To be quite blunt, one image many people have of fundamentalists is not only their total unwillingness to cooperate with anyone who disagrees with them, but to admit that anyone outside the fundamentalist camp is worthwhile.

DOBSON: I spoke at Harvard quite awhile back and met Harvey Cox. We had a long conversation, and I came back with a whole new perspective.

DOOR: You're kidding. It's hard to imagine Jerry Falwell and Harvey Cox having a revival together.

DOBSON: Don't misunderstand. You have to let down the anchor of truth somewhere; you can't pretend that truth doesn't matter, but that doesn't mean that you're unwilling to invite everybody aboard your vessel . . . or that you're unwilling to get aboard someone else's vessel. What we're trying to emphasize is that the anchor has to be there, but that does not preclude me from talking with and learning from other people.

DOOR: Uh . . . oh . . . you're starting to sound like a liberal.

DOBSON: I want to point out something else. Maybe we won't see that day when Harvey Cox and Jerry Falwell will put on a crusade together, but five years ago if anyone would have said that Francis Schaeffer and Jerry Falwell with his "Jesus First" pin would work together, they would have been laughed at . . . but that is exactly what has happened.

DOOR: Why do fundamentalists make such a big deal about national defense?

DOBSON: Because in America the freedom of our country is dependent upon our national defense, and we need a free country to preach the gospel and to evangelize the world.

DOOR: But aren't there many countries where the opposite has happened? That, in spite of extreme repression, the church has grown and is full of life?

DOBSON: From God's perspective, I suppose one could say that he doesn't need a free society in order for the church to survive, but from a human perspective, we must try to accomplish what we think God wants us to do, and we can do so much more in a free society. I mean, what are you suggesting, that we allow totalitarian governments to survive because it fosters a vital church?

DOOR: Wait a minute. We're asking the questions!

DOBSON: The point is that if you carried my argument out logically, then you could argue that God doesn't need any of us, so why try? But I believe God wants us to do all we can do yet recognize his ultimate providence in world affairs.

You could make an argument that the times of greatest growth in God's kingdom have been the times of greatest adversity and suffering. All that we are saying is that in a time of freedom, the opportunities are even greater, but the church doesn't seize the opportunity, historically, until it's really tested.

DOOR: As a fundamentalist, what do you struggle with most?

DOBSON: As a fundamentalist, the thing that grieves me the most is the fact that we are so isolationist and separatist, and consequently we are a fragmented, polarized movement around people and personalities. We are the only army that kills its wounded. As a movement, generally speaking, we have very little mutual appreciation for each other. We have elevated minor issues into major issues. We have made absolutist statements without thinking, and then for fear of looking like we didn't know what we were talking about, we didn't back down and forced ourselves into a "stand."

Personally, I struggle most with the suffering in the world. There is so much pain and suffering and hurting. There is so much that needs to be done that is of far greater significance than whether we are fundamentalists or evangelicals or not. We get so consumed with little things that we miss the important things.

DOOR: Aren't fundamentalists adamant that the *King James Version* is the only version inspired by God?

DOBSON: Most mainline fundamentalists believe that the *King James Version* is the most true to the original autographs. We do have the group of hypers who, reacting out of a sincere desire to defend the Bible, violently defend not only the King James but the Authorized *KJV* with italicized words. However sincere people like that may be, their position is based upon almost complete ignorance. The integrity of the Bible is vital, but when its defenders deteriorate to quoting bus drivers as authorities, their integrity must be questioned.

ROBERT CAPON

Whoever heard of Robert Farrar Capon? We never had. Oh, sure, Frederick Buechner talked a lot about Capon's *The Supper of the Lamb*, and some obscure Catholics mention his book *Hunting the Divine Fox*, but Buechner lives in Pawlett, Vermont, and most Catholics who know Capon are in seminary and we're not allowed to talk to them. As a matter of fact, we're not allowed to talk to a lot of people. Now, where were we? Oh. Robert Farrar Capon. Well, if you haven't heard of him, you should have. That's why we decided to interview him. He's Episcopal (an ordained one, at that), prolific writer (more than a dozen books), columnist for *The New York Times*, and a heck of a cook. He's not a bad theologian, either. In 1983 the *Door* traveled to Shelter Island, New York, to talk to Father Capon. After reading his interview, we think you'll agree it was well worth the trip.

DOOR: You used to teach theology?

CAPON: Someone had to do it.

DOOR: We're glad it was you and not us.

CAPON: So is the theological community.

DOOR: We were going to be easy on you, but now you have forced us to ask the difficult questions. Here's our first: What is theology?

CAPON: That's the difficult question?

DOOR: Quit stalling.

CAPON: Theology is a funny kind of knowledge. Unfortunately, most theologians don't know that.

DOOR: Most theologians we've met are sort of funny.

CAPON: Most theologians are too deadpan, too literal, too straitlaced. Theology is not a scientific study in which we say this is "a" and that is "b." Theology does not deal with concepts; it deals with images.

DOOR: Images?

CAPON: The great thing about Scripture is the images it gives you. Scripture delivers us a thousand images or flashlights of different colors and intensities. Scripture is a box full of flashlights, and the role of theology is to take these flashlights or images and play with them.

DOOR: Play with them?

CAPON: Is there an echo in here? My point is that theologians must stay with the images or, rather, the interplay of images, otherwise they end up shrinking the faith down to a system of theology. But the images of Scripture are always very large and demand that you go beyond the limits of your system.

DOOR: We take it you are not a "systematic theologian"?

CAPON: I distrust the idea of systematic theology. I like the name "dogmatic theology" because at least the word "dogma" has some give to it. The only rule in dogmatic theology is that you mustn't sweep any evidence under the rug. In other words, you must never lose a single image. The mystics did this. They said that God is both father and not father, God is both good and not good. The theologian must not lose any of these images and must work to keep all the images in front of the church so that the mystery is opened as wide as it can be.

DOOR: Have you ever heard of a person named Francis Schaeffer?

CAPON: I don't believe I have.

DOOR: Well, anyway, he and others suggest that the gospel is propositional, that it must be understood by discovering the propositions it is built upon.

CAPON: Propositions are a dangerous thing. To reduce the mystery of faith to a series of propositions is something that can't be done. Jesus doesn't make propositional good sense. He is rude. He is nice. He is patient and long-suffering, yet he was one nasty arguer. Even the parables contradict each other right and left. But that is not the point. If you are making wine, the concern is not how many grapes to put into the crusher, because they all contribute to the wine. It's the wine that counts and it is the total impression of Scripture that matters.

DOOR: We have a hunch that you aren't one of those people that believes in the inerrancy of Scripture.

CAPON: That is where you are wrong. I stand firmly behind the inerrancy of Scripture. But what's Scripture? Scripture is a book written by people, and if it is an inspired book, then it should be inspired as a book is inspired. It will follow the rules of a book. Therefore it will contain literal statements, metaphors, etc. If Scripture is inspired, it's inspired as a written thing and also as a spoken thing. And words have their rules, but to say that only one little tiny set of rules—namely, literal, straight-line, one-meaning interpretation—is possible is totally crazy.

DOOR: We knew you were a raving liberal. Do you believe that all parts of the Bible are inspired?

CAPON: I do not buy this business of taking out bits of Scripture and then saying that I believe the whole of Scripture except the parts I don't believe. No one can take out the gospel of John and get rid of the Old Testament. That's silly. That's not playing the game and that's not accepting the box of flashlights. If you are going to play this game called theology, then you have to accept the whole thing. But to expect that the gospel will all be propositional truth is nonsense. For example, the beauty of the parables is not discovering the propositional truth behind them. The parables are mysteries aimed at greater mysteries. The

Scriptures are full of mysteries aimed at the great mystery. We can grasp a little bit of that mystery, but there should always be a greater deepening.

DOOR: Let's talk about the gospel a minute. What do you think the average layperson today needs to hear from the gospel?

CAPON: You can judge what people need to hear by what they're most afraid of hearing. And what people seem to be most afraid of hearing is the notion of unqualified forgiveness—grace. When I preach a sermon on grace I see the people in the congregation smiling and nodding their heads. It is like 200-proof whiskey to people to understand that they are forgiven and loved and the fuss is all over. But by the time the service is over and they arrive at coffee hour, the smiles are gone and the people are full of qualifying questions. People want to hear the Good News, but they dread the Good News. I don't know why they dread it so much, but they do. We all do. We are afraid of it. We are afraid of really being forgiven and being free. It's very strange.

DOOR: The subtitle of your book *Between Noon and Three* says that you are writing about "the outrage of grace." We must admit, deep inside there is a voice that keeps saying that you can't allow people to be forgiven without repentance or some kind of cost. Otherwise people will go crazy. They will sin openly without remorse.

CAPON: But grace is outrageous. Remember the parable of the laborers in the vineyard?

DOOR: Where everyone gets paid the same, even those who only worked an hour?

CAPON: Yes. That is not a parable about labor relations, by the way; it is a parable about goodness. It is a parable about the fact that there is no proportion between the grace given and the earning of it. All you have to do is be there and you receive grace, the whole day's pay. That's outrageous and there is no way to mute it.

But the most outrageous of all parables is the Pharisee and the Publican. The Pharisee says, "I thank God I am not as other men. . . ." He tells God that he is a good man. And he is. There's no question about it. The Pharisee is the kind of person that every church would be happy to welcome as a member. He tithes, he's not a womanizer, and he honors his contracts. He does everything he's supposed to do. He is an honest-to-goodness-no-sham-no-fake-good-man. And not only that, he's coming to thank God for being that way; he's not thanking himself. Then comes this other bozo, a tax collector who is bleeding his own countrymen dry on a franchise from the Roman government. He's been skimming the cream off the people's milk money for years. Outside is his Cadillac, with a case of Chivas Regal in the back and two whores in the front. He looks at his shoe tips and says, "God be merciful to me a sinner." And Jesus announces that this man goes down to his house justified rather than the Pharisee. Why? The other man is a good man. It is not because the Publican is humble. That is a cheap interpretation. The Pharisee has religion, and Jesus is trying to point to the futility of religion. He is trying to point out that no one is bound to God because they have a series of chips that can be traded to God or a deck of cards that can be dealt to God, because God says, "Look, don't play with me because you haven't got a full deck.

There's a free drink on the house for both of you." That is the real point. They both have no cards to play with God, but the Pharisee doesn't know it and the Publican does.

DOOR: But....

CAPON: But you don't like this scenario? Okay. Let's rewrite the parable a little. Let's bring the Publican back a week later. Let's suppose he's made no change in his behavior. He has continued to skim money from his neighbors. He has continued to drive around with flashy whores and drink high-priced scotch. What do you think God is going to say to him? On what basis can you say that God is going to say anything different this week than he did the week before?

DOOR: Wait a min ...

CAPON: You still don't like the scenario? Okay, change it again. Bring the Publican back after one week of reform. Let's say he has stopped drinking expensive scotch and donated his drinking money to the heart fund. Let's say he only has one girl instead of two. What do you want God to do with him? Do you want God to look at this Publican and say that he's a good guy? Why are you so intent on sending the Publican back with the Pharisee's speech in his pocket?

DOOR: Well, we ...

CAPON: It's because you don't understand the parable. The point is that both the Publican and the Pharisee are invited to the reconciliation with the only difference being the Publican knew he was dead and said so. Jesus came to raise the dead. The only qualification for the gift of the gospel is to be dead. You don't have to be smart.

DOOR: That's good news for us.

CAPON: You don't have to be good. You don't have to be wise. You don't have to be wonderful. You don't have to be anything ... you just have to be dead. That's it. You see, the whole problem with the church is that the church does not want to die. None of us wants to die. But that is the one qualification and that is what is outrageous. There can be only one requirement and it's got to be low enough to include all of us ... and it is. All you have to do is die.

DOOR: You mentioned that the church does not want to die. What else do you think about the church?

CAPON: The first thing the church has to realize is that it is not in the religion business; it's in the gospel-proclaiming business. So often (and it doesn't matter whether it's the Catholic notion of the church or the Protestant notion) the basic impression given is that the church is kind of a divine panel board that goes through the world with a lot of slots in it, and the role of the church is to persuade people to plug their little jacks into the panel board and then they'll be okay. Depending on the particular ecclesiastical model, you can plug it in sacramentally or plug it in by being born again, etc., but for the church to give that impression is fatal. It's fatal because the church is in the world primarily to announce that God has gathered up every human being's jack and plugged it into himself by his death and resurrection.

DOOR: You are starting to make some conservatives nervous.

CAPON: Oh, I know. I always have to apologize for saying what the gospel says. I have reassured people that I don't mean salvation is automatic. If someone is nasty and rotten, they really can go to hell. But that is not the gospel; that's the theological tinkering, which is legitimate, but it's still tinkering. The Good News is that God has done the plugging in for us, and what the church should be doing is running around saying, "Do you realize that he has plugged you in? Would you like to believe that? That's terrific, isn't it?"

DOOR: Okay. You've forced us to ask you this. Are you a universalist?

CAPON: If by universalist you mean that the forgiving grace in Jesus has been universally given to all human beings, yes, I am. You cannot sing in church, "Oh Lamb of God that takes away the sins of the world . . . except for this list of sins."

DOOR: It wrecks the music for one thing. . . .

CAPON: The point is you can't do that. Every Christian who believes that the Lamb of God takes away the sins of the world believes that he took them all. But if you ask if the universal gift of forgiveness and grace is refusable by people, then obviously, yes. Of course. But acceptance of grace is a tricky phrase because in one sense you don't have to accept it; you've got it, but the enjoyment of it and the acceptance of it can be refused. "Oh, taste and see how great is the Lord." In other words, you've got a whole cellar full of it. If you want to sit there and drink Pepsi for the rest of your life with a cellar full of that stuff down there, you can do it. You can go to hell. But that is not the point. The point is you already have the gift.

DOOR: Here's one of those nagging questions you mentioned earlier, but one can't help but wonder about sin. Doesn't sin matter? Doesn't it make a difference?

CAPON: Sure it does. It has tremendous consequences. It screws up everything. No one needs to cheer for it. It's doing very nicely, thank you. It's winning hands down.

DOOR: We . . . uh . . . can see you don't exactly have a low view of sin, but the point is that if you talk only of forgiveness and unqualified grace, doesn't that, in effect, give people permission to sin?

CAPON: There are two kinds of people. First, there are those who sin boldly. They do exactly what they want to do and wouldn't think of asking anyone's permission. Then there are those people who need permission for anything they do, good or bad. Those people will always be shopping for permission and they will find it somewhere . . . even in the gospel. But that doesn't constitute a flaw in the gospel. That constitutes a flaw in personalities. You can't soft-pedal the proclamation of the gospel because people like that are around.

The point is that God gave permission to sin. The cross itself is God's answer to that. If you sin, God isn't going to do anything to you except die for you. He's not going to bop you on the head; he's not going to belt you in the chops.

DOOR: This sounds like the Living New Yorker's translation. . . .

CAPON: It's not the role of the church to tell people not to sin and to devise lists. The world knows perfectly what sin is. The world knows what morality is. The world knows what's right. Morality is the world's cup of tea. What the world doesn't know is forgiveness, and that's what the world needs to be told. People confuse forgiveness and permission. Forgiveness is what you do with the impermissible. Life is full of the impermissible and that's what sin is. But God has died for us and he's risen, and in the consummation of that mystery he's going to vanish into thin air and leave an even deeper mystery, leaving behind only the word of forgiveness.

DOOR: How do you view the role of the clergy?

CAPON: The clergy ought to be a sacrament to the church of its priestliness, just as the church ought to be a sacrament to the world. The clergy have a sacramental significance, not an essential significance. The fact that I am a priest does not make me any better or holier, nor does it demand that I be better or holier than any other Christian. (We all should be perfect, but we're not, so that's the end of that subject.) Therefore I am not to be a moral hotshot compared to you. My function is to be a mirror of the church's priesthood. That's the end of that subject.

DOOR: But what does the clergy *do*?

CAPON: Very few things, really. I come from an Anglican-Catholic priestly tradition, and what I do that nobody else does is celebrate communion and hold a few sacraments. I also happen to preach, but good laypeople preach as well. So the ordained priesthood is a very narrow thing that has strictly a sacramental function. Historically, however, and by tradition, we have lumped a lot of other expectations on the clergy. We are stuck with that lumping, so clergy are also expected to be good preachers.

DOOR: There is a movement today in the evangelical church to define the role of the pastor as a "pastor-teacher." The primary role of the pastor becomes one of studying thirty hours a week and teaching the other ten. What do you think of that concept?

CAPON: Just as the church is a grab bag that brings in all kinds of strays to be a sign to the world of the Word of God, so the ministry brings in all kinds of strays. There will be those in the ministry who spend thirty hours a week perusing the Greek and Hebrew and there will be others who couldn't read Greek or Hebrew if you paid them. There will be other strays who spend thirty hours a week visiting the sick or hitting golf balls around. It is perfectly obvious that someone who spends thirty hours a week producing something really worth listening to is a great person, but to define that as the only role for ministry is nuts.

DOOR: What do you think about people's passion for eschatology, for figuring out the times and seasons?

CAPON: First of all, eschatology shouldn't be about the time and seasons.

DOOR: Why?

CAPON: Because the signs of the end, as they're proclaimed in Scripture, are signs that have always been present. There is no age that could not read itself as having been foretold in Scripture. So either Scripture is a big hoax when it talks about eschatology, or it's talking about the end goal, the final wrap-up of the world as something present to every age. When I preach on eschatology I often try to illustrate this by stopping in the middle of my sermon and saying, "Excuse me a minute; I forgot something." I then walk out to the sacristy and come back to the pulpit. Then I say, "Did any of you have any theological problems with that? Did it change any of your lives? No. My Second Coming was present to you all this time because it was simply a promise from me personally to be back in this interchange that we now have." The early church didn't get hung up on the literalism. When he didn't come back, why didn't the church fall apart? Because they understood that eschatology was a relationship of expectation, not a literal date. Then I say to the congregation, "Why didn't you all go home when I stepped out for a while? Because you were still involved with me while I was preaching, and you assumed I would be back."

The point is that the second coming is not only a future event, it is a finality of fulfillment, a consummation promised under the terms of the future event ... but experienced now. Predicting dates is only important when the immediacy of a present relationship is lost. When people start haggling about whether Jesus meant ten minutes or fifteen, they have lost the connection with the person they are expecting. The promise of his return is what counts. We'll all know he's back when he's back. That's all. End of subject. He is going to be who he has been in relationship to us all along. The last day will not manifest anything that we have not known already. It will manifest Jesus, the Lamb of God who takes away the sins of the world.

DOOR: Okay. You made it very clear throughout this interview that the Good News has to do with what God has done for us through Jesus Christ. But once people have understood that, once they have become part of the church, what then? What is it that distinguishes Christians from non-Christians? What does it mean when the church is described as salt and as light? Shouldn't there be more than just an awareness that we need to be dead. Shouldn't there be fruits or visible behavior that others can see?

CAPON: The idea that there is a formula of warm toastiness or other wonderfulness that you can judge Christians by is false. The issue is not goodness or badness. We witness to Christ in our death. That's it. When we are not willing to die to ourselves, that's when we don't witness to Christ. But when we are willing to die, that's when we do witness. If Christ came to raise the dead, what witness does he need to the world except a bunch of people who say that it's safe to die because Jesus will raise you. Christians are people who speak to the world that it's okay for them to die.

DOOR: Somehow we keep thinking there must be more to the Christian witness than that.

CAPON: People can't stand it when you say that the final ticket to heaven is a ticket that everybody has ... you've got to be dead.

DOOR: But we keep thinking that the local church, those who understand the meaning of forgiveness in Christ, ought somehow to look better than those who don't understand grace.

CAPON: The church is a sacramental community, but it is still a sacrament made out of people, which is neither unfortunate nor fortunate; that's just the way it is and God's to blame for that. But he did choose to make the church out of people, and therefore they're not going to behave like anything other than people. Therefore the church will be rotten, but that's okay. If you take a piece of bread that's been consecrated for communion and leave it in a damp closet long enough, it will turn moldy. Why? Because it was consecrated? No, because it's bread. The church is made up of a sacramentally human nature and given enough damp closets, it will become moldy and rotten and crummy.

DOOR: That is not a very optimistic view of the church.

CAPON: But don't you see that not only do we have hope in God, but God has hope in us. He really didn't offer us forgiveness for no purpose at all. He does have a very great hope that we will say "Yes."

ROBERTA HESTENES

There are a lot of reasons we wanted to interview Roberta Hestenes. The fact that she has subscribed to the *Door* since the beginning days had nothing to do with it. Of course, it does show how bright and astute she is . . . and what good company she keeps.

Actually, Roberta is president of Eastern College. Before she came to this Pennsylvania school in 1987, she spent several years in southern California as professor at Fuller Seminary and as associate pastor for La (pronounced La) Canada Presbyterian Church. She has written a book *How to Whip Men into Submission During Bible Study* . . . er . . . no . . . that was written by Estelle "Crusher" Morgan, sister of Marabelle Morgan—actually she has written, among other books, *Using the Bible in Groups* and *Ministry of Women in a Changing Church*. Roberta is the mother of three grown children and lectures extensively. As a feminist she considers herself a moderate (even though she is not an extremist, she credits them with making it possible for her to have the opportunity to state her moderate views). But as a former pastor and professor, and now as a college president and chairman of World Vision, Roberta Hestenes has some very important insights into the meaning of the Christian faith in the American culture. We think you will be glad we interviewed Roberta Hestenes . . . we are.

HESTENES: Why are you doing a feminist issue?

DOOR: Wait a minute! We're supposed to ask the questions.

HESTENES: Oh.

DOOR: Would you like to know why we're doing a feminist issue?

HESTENES: Yes.

DOOR: Well, to be blunt about it, we thought it was about time someone had some fun with the extreme feminists. They manage to "out-obnoxious" even men, and basically alienate almost everyone, even fun guys like us, and we figured it was about time we had a surge of cancellations again. It cleans out our files.

HESTENES: It's a red herring.

DOOR: Pardon?

HESTENES: It's a red herring.

235

DOOR: What does fish have to do with the women's issue?

HESTENES: If we can make fun of libbers, bra-burners, and women who are obviously ridiculous, then we don't have to take women's issues seriously. It's a cheap shot.

DOOR: But is it those who make *fun* of the obviously ridiculous, or is it the obviously ridiculous, who cause us not to take the women's issue seriously?

HESTENES: In the whole spectrum of the Christian women's movement, are you talking about more than thirty people who are extremists? You ridicule the easy target and ignore the thousands, or should I say millions, of men in the church who do not take women seriously. So there are thirty or so women out there asking you to de-sex your God language. Is that where the struggle is in the church, or is the struggle still in the hundreds and hundreds of churches where women cannot have any significant role? That's not funny, but that's where the struggle is.

DOOR: But our point is that it is the extremists in the women's movement that cloud the issue, not those who satirize the extremes.

HESTENES: First of all, you have to define what you mean by the women's movement. You cannot treat it as though it were a monolithic movement. The tendency is to let the extreme talk for the center, but the center is much larger than the extremes. One of the foundation stones of the biblical feminist movement is the recognition that the strident, militant, anti, hostile posture gets you almost nothing.

DOOR: So you would agree with us.

HESTENES: I would agree that it is easier to make fun of the extremes,

but you are missing the point entirely. I am a pastor and pastorally I have dealt with hundreds of women who have been forbidden ministry. They have been denied the very basic Christian freedoms, and very often that denial has been done in the name of anti-extremism. And these women who have been denied ministry are not extremists; they are simply Christians who want to serve the Lord. But the fact is there are hundreds of women moving into the significant ordinary places of ministry that were not open to women a hundred years ago. We have seven hundred ordained women in the United Presbyterian church now. The church is changing whether people know it or not, and it is in the middle where that change is occurring.

DOOR: There are a lot of very vocal critics of the women's movement in the church, and they seem very aware of the inroads women are making. That's why they are so vocal. Do you try to confront those critics?

HESTENES: I don't. My own personal philosophy of ministry is that a person should study the Bible, pray, decide what needs to be done, and get out and do it. Let the critics do what critics do; in the meantime we need to go out and do what needs to be done. There is a needy world and a needy church, and women ought to be out filling those needs. We just need to do what God has called us to do.

DOOR: As far as feminism goes, you do sound like you're somewhere in the middle yourself. We would guess you are not invited to the latest "Death to the Chauvinist Pigs" rally.

HESTENES: Well, the right is convinced that I'm not a Christian and the left is convinced I've sold out to John McArthur, but that is the price of leadership. You wish people would understand. You wish people would not impugn your motives, but if I spent all my time trying to help the fifteen people that misunderstand me understand, then I would have no time to spend articulating a better philosophy of discipleship, which is what I believe God has called me to do.

DOOR: Let's broaden the discussion a bit. You are a minister, and every day you come in contact with the people in your congregation. What part of the Good News do people need to hear today?

HESTENES: They need to discover the availability of the transforming love and power of Jesus. They need to understand that the gospel is true, that God's love is not just an abstraction, and that love can be known in ways that change persons and change worlds.

DOOR: You're talking about evangelism.

HESTENES: Yes. Authentic evangelism. Evangelism based on words but not backed up with authentic models of community and service is bankrupt evangelism. It is just not enough to have orthodox words if the community is not there.

DOOR: What you are really saying is that there are a lot of churches that are not practicing evangelism.

HESTENES: I am convinced that a great many church members simply do not believe in the transforming power of God. As a result there are a lot of Christians who have been captured by the culture.

DOOR: Sounds like a new movie.

HESTENES: What does?

DOOR: *Captured by the Culture* . . .

HESTENES: I don't believe it. May I go on?

DOOR: Sure.

HESTENES: In the eighteenth and nineteenth centuries, we had deism. Deism simply portrayed a God who wound up the universe and then stood back like a clockmaker and watched it run. So people believed in God but not in his presence and work in the world. There are a lot of modern Christians who are functional deists when it comes to their personal lives. They will acknowledge that God has made them and saved them, but they do not really believe that the power of God is available to them and through them to make a real difference in the world. The Christian life, then, is not following a list of do's and don'ts; the real challenge of the Christian life is, how does my life count? I believe that in Christ everyone's life can count. And I think people need to know that.

DOOR: And people don't know that?

HESTENES: No. People need to know that there is hope in the gospel, and it isn't just the hope of heaven. It is hope of a meaningful life.

DOOR: We think you're right. We think the gospel does give us hope of a meaningful life, but how did you come to that conclusion? It seems everywhere you turn these days someone is promising something new from the gospel. Prosperity. Success. Health. What do you base your philosophy of ministry on?

HESTENES: It may seem too simple, but I believe you have to come back to the authority of Scripture. If you believe, as I do, that God has disclosed himself and his will for us, then the path to sorting that out is found in interaction with Scripture, not in Christian philosophy or programs. That is how you keep your balance.

When you move away from Scripture you get unbalanced and lopsided.

Let me give you an example. I am on an advisory board for a service organization. It is very fashionable for them to talk about God's preference for the poor. You can certainly make a good biblical case for that. But I've been reading Paul's letters recently and noticed Paul's instructions to the rich. He does not suggest that the rich become poor, but he *does* suggest that the rich use their riches responsibly and remember that before God they were poor. So when dealing with the issue of the rich and poor, it is Scripture that gives us a balanced perspective.

One of the reasons I am committed to the church is because the church historically has tried to keep its balance by finding its authority in Scripture.

DOOR: But every new theological fad is based on Scripture.

HESTENES: Evangelical movements are faddish. We move from one to another as if we had done something about the last issue. The evangelical attention span is about two years, and if we haven't solved the problem by then, we get tired and move on. We work on the women's movement for two years, and if nothing seems to be accomplished yet, we move on to the next hot issue.

DOOR: Why do evangelicals have such short attention spans? Are we victims of TV, computers, and technology?

HESTENES: In most contemporary Christian churches, the amount of Christian teaching that we are exposed to has shrunk from multiple hours per week to a one-hour worship service where the sermon lasts fifteen to twenty minutes. The average church-goer, then, is exposed to fifteen minutes a week of religious input in contrast to 167 hours of outside input. Fifteen minutes a week is not enough to give us a Christian mindset. And even *that* fifteen minutes, if it is a sermon, consists of three jokes and two things to think about. Evangelicals are simply not getting any food. You have hundreds of starved congregations, and they don't even know it.

DOOR: People must be getting something. Evangelical churches are growing and no one is complaining.

HESTENES: It is much easier to eat a Twinkie than chew on a steak. We are a Twinkies culture of predigested, processed, instant nourishment. But if you keep eating Twinkies, you will end up with one bad case of malnourishment. If everyone is malnourished, then no one can tell the difference. That, in my opinion, is what's happened to the Bible. We have not learned what nourishment really is. People ought to know but they don't. That's what happened in the Reformation. People were malnourished, they were starving, so they rediscovered the Word of God.

DOOR: Don't you think the role of the church ought to be to help its people think? Isn't much of the problem the fact that churches are spoon-feeding their people and giving them formulas without encouraging them to think?

HESTENES: We were made to think. People don't feel very good when they can't think. I just don't buy the hypothesis that people don't want to think. They do, but they get discouraged. In most churches we underestimate people's capacity.

DOOR: That sounds wonderful in theory, but try preaching a one-hour sermon and see how many people hang around.

HESTENES: You have to have a different kind of church. You have to have a different dynamic going on. The church has to become a community that is related to each other more than on Sunday. There must be a network of relationships where people matter to each other. There must be teaching . . .

DOOR: Again, that sounds wonderful, but . . .

HESTENES: I see lots of opportunity for that to happen, even in a traditional congregation.

DOOR: We sincerely wish you were right, but we don't see much relationship ministry going on. We do see more and more superstar preachers bring in large crowds.

HESTENES: I see Christian superstars in trouble all over the country because they are not accountable to anyone. You must have a center, and if you don't, then you are in trouble with this culture. You will be pushed from fad to fad. We must rediscover the spiritual life, the spiritual disciplines including confession of sins, repentance, and prayer. American Christianity doesn't repent. We need to repent more often than we do. We need to be more humble than we are.

DOOR: How do we straighten the church out and get it on track again?

HESTENES: It's not my role to straighten out every Christian. My goodness.

DOOR: My goodness?

HESTENES: An old Latin proverb. Look, I've got all I can do to deal with the beam in my own eye. Of course we are responsible for each other, we should bear one another's burdens, but that is a different thing than tearing

people down. C. S. Lewis said that we should not tear people down unless we have the ability to raise people up. We do need an accountable community, but we don't need to go around and tell others what they need to do. That isn't very helpful.

DOOR: So what do we do?

HESTENES: One of the biggest challenges in my own Christian life has been to take seriously Jesus' command to love not only within the Christian community but our enemies as well. That means that there shouldn't be anyone outside the circle of that love.

DOOR: Even Amway salesmen?

HESTENES: I know what you mean. But that challenge to love includes the strident feminist who really gives me a bad time and doesn't try to understand the kind of tension I labor under. That challenge to love includes the person who hates me because I am from Fuller. It includes loving those who make assumptions about me without any effort to understand. That's the only option Scripture gives us. We have to love even those whose view of Scripture is different from ours, or whose world view is different from ours. I once went to Thailand for World Vision, and we were feeding people in the refugee camps. Some of those we were feeding were Khmer Rouge. Probably some of them were murderers. What do you do? Feed only the non-murderers? You can't do that. Believe me, it isn't easy.

DOOR: That kind of loving seems almost impossible.

HESTENES: Frankly, we are quite willing to hate in American Christianity. We think it's our right to judge, to belittle, to exclude. We draw circles that become smaller and smaller.

DOOR: That's not just a trait of Americans, is it?

HESTENES: No. We're not the only ones that do that. In Africa, Cambodia. I am afraid it is a most human trait.

DOOR: Okay, Roberta, we keep asking this question and we'll try once more. How do we pull this off? How do we create the kind of loving Christian community you've talked about? What's your magic formula?

HESTENES: I do not have a "Roberta Hestenes Spirituality Kit." We don't need any more programs or gimmicks. We just need to rediscover what every generation needs to rediscover on their own . . . that we need each other. We need to laugh and cry with each other, and we need to realize that almost any way we find each other is better than all the ways we miss each other.

I am more a reformer than a revolutionary. I believe in calling people back to their roots rather than chopping things down and starting over. Those of us in the church must quit trying to live our lives individualistically, shallowly, and on the surface of culture. Instead, we must try to find ways to go in deeper. The deeper one goes the more pain one encounters. There is no way around the facing of that pain, but there's a joy in that. We need to quit running from the cost of pain. We really have to learn that for every pain there is a joy, but the pain has to be chosen, accepted, and dealt with.

OS GUINNESS

Guinness beer. It's stout actually, but it doesn't matter . . . it tastes terrible. Os Guinness has the same name (his middle name is Beer), and he is related to the Guinness beer fortune (we understand from reliable sources that Os's inheritance is already worth something in the neighborhood of three kegs). So not only can Os Guinness have all the beer he can drink (if his relatives would return his phone calls), he is also good-looking (sort of an Omar Sharif with brains), English (complete with accent), and holds a Ph.D. from some obscure university in England, and is the executive director of the Williamsburg Charter Foundation in Washington, D.C.

The *Door* sent its Washington, D.C. correspondent, Mike Cromartie (who looks like Yassar Arafat and talks like Tammy Faye Bakker), to interview Os in 1983 while he was in the States promoting his new book, *How to Stay Slim and Trim While Writing Your Doctoral Dissertation*. He has also written another book, *The Gravedigger File*, which is an exposé of the funeral business. In this interview Os Guinness's penetrating analysis of culture and prophetic understanding of the role of the church combined into a powerful and challenging call to all of us to take our faith seriously.

DOOR: You have a new book out called *The Gravedigger File*. What is the significance of that title?

GUINNESS: There is a thesis in the social sciences which says that Christianity contributed to the rise of the modern world and now is being undermined by the very world it helped to create. As a result it is becoming its own gravedigger.

DOOR: You agree with that, we presume.

GUINNESS: I believe that the church, rather than being transformed by Christ, is becoming conformed by its culture. The church is being distorted by the shape of the demands and priorities of the capitalist market just as civil religion is the church being shaped by the demands and priorities of the American political system.

DOOR: Is "secular humanism" one of the forces shaping the church?

GUINNESS: Certainly the dedicated secular humanists such as the ACLU and Madeline Murray O'Hare are important to notice. I wouldn't minimize the damage they can do, but they are a tiny minority. The real problem the church faces today is not secularism, but secularization. Secularism is a philosophy of a very small number of people, but secularization is a process that has happened in the American society which has affected us all, including the church. Too many Christians have been guilty of creating a bogeyman out of "secular humanism" and have failed to see the far deeper problem of secularization.

DOOR: Of course we know exactly what you mean by seculari—secular—uh—we know what you mean, but just in case some of our readers don't, what is seculari—.

GUINNESS: Secularization.

DOOR: Uh ... yeah.

GUINNESS: Secularization, put simply, is the process through which the central areas of modern societies such as science, technology, economics, business, and politics have become mutual territories with religion. As a result, you have individual Christian believers who work in those areas, but their influence is purely private and personal. Their faith flourishes only in the private world. Let me give you an example: The president of McDonald's was recently interviewed by the *New York Times* and was asked what he believed in. He said, "I believe in God, and the family, and McDonald's, but when I get to the office I reverse the order." Let's hope he was being facetious, but whether he was or not he was describing what millions of Chris-

tians do every day without realizing it. As one commentator put it, "Christianity today is privately engaging but socially irrelevant."

DOOR: In the past the church separated itself from the world, but now it seems to have decided that Christians can be in the world, not of it, and use technology, for example, to communicate the Christian faith. Is there anything wrong with that?

GUINNESS: People who are using today's modern technologies, techniques, and philosophies often have the right motives, but many of them have gone to the world's methods uncritically. They have tried to use the world's ways to do the Lord's work. This is often called bureaucratization.

DOOR: We often use that term ourselves.

GUINNESS: The clearest example is the denomination which is so heavily shaped by modern bureaucracy that it is almost a pale ecclesiastical version of a multinational corporation. An even better example is many of the evangelical para-church ministries. Many of them are rushing to use the latest tools from the American Management Association or whatever and they use them uncritically.

DOOR: What is wrong with that?

GUINNESS: It is not that technology is wrong, but when technology is used uncritically, it ends up being used for things which are not appropriate. For example, in some para-church ministries the computer has almost made the Holy Spirit redundant. God could fail to speak to these ministries for ten years, and they would run on cheerfully without ever noticing it. Another example is evangelistic training methods. If you look closely at the Scriptures, you will notice that the deepest knowledge cannot be taught in words. Some things can only be learned under a master, or from experience, or under authority. Discipleship means apprenticeship, and yet the "how-to-training-methods" are profoundly rationalistic, based on an engineering type of mentality that is thoroughly inappropriate and shallow.

DOOR: Many in the electronic church today seem to be implying that prosperity is a direct result of the gospel.

GUINNESS: It is fascinating to see the difference between the early Puritans and the present-day American evangelicals. For the early Puritans, prosperity was not necessarily a sign of God's blessing. For them, it could just as easily have been a sign of God's judgment. Today, American evangelicalism has changed the Puritan way of looking at the gospel. The Puritans saw the master sin as covetousness (the lust of the spirit). Today we have almost no master sin at all. The gospel has been shaped by the mark of monetary gain.

DOOR: The evangelical church today seems fascinated with the celebrity.

GUINNESS: The power of television is such that instant, fabricated famousness is now possible. People can be famous without genuine achievement or genuine worth. We live in an image society. As Daniel Boston put it, "The celebrity is the person who is well-known for his well-knownness." You would think that of all people Christians would be wary of that kind of celebrity, but instead Christians today seem enamored by celebritism. You can see the devastating impact of such an attitude on the church. It shifts the focus from reality of character to image; from genuine spiritual gifts to glamor; from true followers, who are disciples, to fans. All of this is very destructive, not only to the celebrities themselves, but to many of the people who look up to celebrities. Many Christian celebrities have become role models of sanctification, yet personally they are hollow, lonely, and inconsistent.

DOOR: What do you think of the rise of the Christian right, the resurgence of fundamentalism?

GUINNESS: First of all, much of the Christian right has been unfairly criticized. They are brothers and sisters in Christ and have every right to apply their faith to public policy. Frankly, I think that is much healthier than the pietism they practiced in the past. Many of their critics are simply being hypocritical. However, having said that, there are weaknesses. One is that some of them, not all, confuse Christian principles and conservative politics. Secondly, they often romanticize and idealize American history, exaggerating the Christian influence and ignoring the influence of other sources. The third problem is that they do not have deeply coherent, biblical Christian minds, so they can only be turned on by single issues—the so-called "hot-button" issues. This means that not only do they not have a full biblical coherence to their thinking, but they are also open to manipulation not by the left, but by the right. Another problem the Christian Right has evidenced is its tactics: They have sometimes resorted to lies and vilified their opponents in ways that have been extremely unfortunate. While in some instances they have genuinely had a case (the bias of the press, for example), often the Right has replied in kind rather than standing for integrity even in their response to opponents.

DOOR: We hesitate to ask you this.

GUINNESS: Well, then you don't . . .

DOOR: But we'll ask you anyway. It has to do with someone whose name rhymes with wafer.

GUINNESS: Hmm.

DOOR: To be quite honest, we have been surprised to see Dr. Schaeffer aligning himself with people like Jerry Falwell. Is Schaeffer moving to the right?

GUINNESS: Three things come to mind. First of all, I believe Schaeffer is actually a deeply moderating influence on the conservative right. For example, he's challenged them to fight the issue of prayer in schools on the basis of freedom of speech rather than many other things they have done. The second thing I would like to say is that maybe it isn't Schaeffer who is moving, but evangelicalism. Maybe evangelicalism is not so critical and clear about its distinctives as it used to be. For example, look at a sample of reviews of *Ghandi*, the film. Most of them contain the most amazing, naive uncritical statements ranging from a mildly uncritical one from *Christianity Today*, to a review which was grossly uncritical and thoroughly anti-biblical like the one in *Sojourners*. The evangelical reaction to *Ghandi* tells you more about where evangelicalism is than it tells you about Ghandi, the man or the film. The third thing I would say is that Schaeffer has always made a clear distinction between being a cobelligerent and being an ally, so there may be many people whom he is fighting alongside of (abortionists, fundamentalists, atheists); however, he is not an ally of these people, but a cobelligerent.

DOOR: That is a very positive evaluation of Dr. Schaeffer. Does that mean there are no areas where you would disagree with him?

GUINNESS: I haven't been with him recently, but from the times I have been with him and from all I have read of him, I would rather say that he and I emphasize different points.

DOOR: Such as?

GUINNESS: He is focusing on secularism, which I think is important, but I would put much more weight on secularization, which he often ignores. We just differ in emphasis. I see a stronger danger than perhaps he does in the current swing to the right. I recently did a series for the BBC on the religious dimensions of the 1980 presidential election and I was surprised at how many secular right people openly admitted their attempt to woo evangelists and pastors so that they could manipulate conservative Christianity for their own political ends, not because conservatism was true, but because it was useful as a social glue. That is dangerous.

DOOR: We have to be honest and say that we are surprised that you would have anything to do with the *Door*. After all, you are a graduate of Oxford and you do use big words once in a while. Do you actually think that humor has a role in the church? Most intellectuals we know (both of them) wouldn't dream of slipping a poo-poo cushion under the seat of a guest.

GUINNESS: To my own shame I, like many other modern evangelicals, have allowed my view of faith to become too prosaic, too linear, too rationalistic. In the Scriptures, whenever there was complacency or hostility, God himself and his prophets always used indirect, creative, subversive styles of communication in drama, parables, questions, and so on. In other words, imagination and humor is absolutely vital to Christian communication. The *Door* does this instinctively, which is tremendous, but there is a danger. The goal of persuasion is always to win the other person. Often in satire, the goal is the put-down. Satire is not interested in persuasion. It can put the other person down and dismiss them savagely. Sometimes that kind of humor can become destructive and dismissive and occasionally the *Door* has had to watch for that.

DOOR: Us?

GUINNESS: No comment.

DOOR: Every time we hear your critique of the modern church, we are overcome with a chilling realization that you are more right than you are wrong. After reading your books or hearing you lecture, we also begin to wonder what the ordinary, unOxfordian, basic nerd Christian can do.

GUINNESS: The same thing that an Oxfordian nerd Christian can do.

DOOR: What's that?

GUINNESS: The deepest problems are answered by the most basic biblical beliefs. What is at stake today is what has always been at stake: the lordship of Christ, the kingdom of God, obedience. We need to recover the simple things.

DOOR: Where do we start?

GUINNESS: Many Christians today, if they know what they believe, don't know why they believe it. They don't have a solid sense of theological foundation.

DOOR: In other words, we should be intellectuals?

GUINNESS: It is intriguing to me that you would ask that question. For some reason many people today think that having a good theological foundation is nothing more than academic

and intellectual elitism when the simplest Puritan plowman would have been expected to have a basic theological knowledge. It was basic to discipleship then as it should be now.

DOOR: We seem to have hit a sensitive area.

GUINNESS: Yes. Sometimes I think that if the letter to the Romans was written to the average church today they would dismiss it as being overly intellectual.

DOOR: What else can people do?

GUINNESS: We need to have a "biblical reformation" sense of individual calling that is an expression of our identity and an exercise of our gifts. In other words, when we are *called*, these things are given a direction and a dynamic because they are done as unto the Lord. Another thing we can do is develop a Christian world view. We not only need to read the Bible, but we need to think Christianly about everything—our reading, our voting, our vocation. Everything we do needs to be shaped by biblical truth. One more thing: Christians need to be members of a fellowship group that is a genuine core group. Many groups focus only on fellowship and prayer and Bible study . . . but they don't go far enough. They are spiritual, but they must also be *intimate* biblical fellowships where the members can discuss the professional issues and questions they have in the public world. This way, a doctor who is wrestling with a huge ethical dilemma can be supported by a group which can help him live and act Christianly in the hospital. The same is true, of course, of the politician, the scientist, or the person working at McDonalds. These are comparatively simple things, but if people would practice them, the lordship of

Christ would start being a practical thing applied to every area of life.

DOOR: In other words, it is not the sophisticated things we need.

GUINNESS: No. We don't need a new movement; we don't need to rally around a banner declaring our intentions to win the world by 1984; we just need to start fleshing out many of the simple things we say we believe but don't practice.

M. SCOTT PECK

The first time we heard of Scott Peck was when he contacted us to ask if we would be interested in reviewing his then-new book, *The Road Less Traveled*. We looked it over and explained as subtly as we could that his book would never sell. That was over a million copies ago. He's written more books since then—*People of the Lie* and *Community Making and Peace*, among others. We decided to contact Scott Peck and ask if he would be interested in talking with *us*. It turned out he actually subscribes to the *Door* and, in spite of that, was willing to talk. M. Scott Peck was interviewed in 1983 by our Keeper of the Shrinks, W. "Bill" McNabb. W. "Bill" traveled to New Preston, Connecticut, where he found Dr. Peck in an old rambling house that he shares with his wife Lily (also a psychotherapist), three children, and two passive/aggressive cats.

Dr. Peck is recognized as a leader in the current movement toward the integration of psychology and spirituality (whatever that means). He was educated at Harvard University and Case Western Reserve University and conducted a private practice in psychiatry from 1972 to 1984.

The interview took place in his cluttered home/office complete with books, papers, and a motorcycle (parked in the living room). After the interview, Dr. Peck suggested that the Keepers of the *Door* (especially W. "Bill") seek therapy immediately.

DOOR: Before we jump into the subject of evil, we've noticed after talking with you and reading your books that your Christian faith doesn't fit into any categories we're familiar with ... which is very refreshing, by the way. How did you come to embrace Christianity?

PECK: I have always been interested in religious things. At the age of seventeen, I encountered the mystical Hindu and Buddhist thought and became avidly interested in Zen Buddhism. But gradually over the years I became convinced that there were certain flaws with Oriental religions, which are a kind of bloodless, abstract religion, whereas I was being attracted to a much more carnal and bloody religion. I found that in Jesus hanging on a cross. That was real.

DOOR: But how did that come about?

PECK: I had just finished the first draft of *The Road Less Traveled.* I am one of these people who writes first and does his research afterward. Having written this book, which was sort of religious, I thought I ought to check out the Gospels, so I read them for the first time at the age of thirty-nine. I had always believed in an historical Jesus who was a pretty wise cat.

DOOR: Cat? Cat? What is this, the fifties?

PECK: Do I have to take this kind of abuse?

DOOR: Yes.

PECK: Anyway, that is pretty much where I left Jesus. A nice guy who got shafted in the standard manner of the day.

DOOR: And then you read the Gospels?

PECK: Yes. And when I finally read them, I had already experienced a dozen years of trying in my own small way to be a teacher and a healer. I knew something about teaching and healing and with this knowledge under my belt, I was absolutely thunderstruck by the reality of the man I found in the Gospels. I found a man who was continually frustrated. It leaks out of every page. He says, "What do I have to say to you? How many times do I have to say it? What do I have to *do* to get through to you?" I found a man who was frequently angry, a man who was scared, a man who was terribly lonely. I realized that

this Jesus was so real that no one could have made him up. If the gospel writers had been into mythmaking and embellishing, as I had assumed they had, they certainly would not have tried to create the kind of Jesus that my wife calls the "wimpy Jesus."

DOOR: The "wimpy Jesus"? Sounds like a horror film. What does your wife mean by the "wimpy Jesus"?

PECK: The Jesus who goes around with his sweet sickening smile that never leaves his face while he does nothing but pat little children on the head. The Jesus with his own highly developed Christ consciousness which causes him to achieve a mellow-yellow sort of nirvana and peace of mind. But the Jesus of the Gospels did not have peace of mind, and I began to suspect that the gospel writers, instead of being mythmakers and embellishers, were in fact extremely accurate and conservative reporters.

DOOR: You were recently baptized. What brought you from the place where you were struck with the authenticity of Jesus to becoming a baptized believer?

PECK: It was just a gradual process. God kept tugging, pushing, kicking, prodding, and pulling. From the time I first toyed with the notion of my baptism until the actual event two and one-half years passed.

DOOR: Why so long?

PECK: My baptism represented a real death for me. No one likes to die, so I dragged my feet. But an Episcopal priest of mine said, "Well, Scotty, we all have to die sooner or later; why don't you get it over with?" But I continued to use every rationalization I could use to drag my feet. The one that worked the best was trying to decide whether I should be baptized as a Catholic, Lutheran, Presbyterian, Methodist, or whatever. I figured that decision would take at least twenty-five to thirty years to make. After a while, though, I realized that decision was just a cop-out, that baptism was not a denominational celebration. I was finally baptized on the ninth of March, 1980.

DOOR: We are dying to know which denomination you settled on—not that it's important, of course.

PECK: Well, I'll let you figure it out. I was baptized by a North Carolina Methodist minister in the chapel of an Episcopal convent.

DOOR: Oh.

PECK: You can pin me wriggling to the wall as a card-carrying Christian, but you cannot pin me down any further than that.

DOOR: Why did you write a book about evil?

PECK: I wanted to say that there is such a thing as human evil.

DOOR: Isn't that obvious? Is there anyone who doesn't believe in human evil?

PECK: Oh yes. There are many who do not believe in human evil. Some major religions regard evil as an illusion. Many who consider themselves Christians also do not believe in the reality of evil, which I suppose is a heresy, but please remember that the persecution of heresy is, itself, heresy. What I am trying to say in this book is that evil not only exists, it exists in such a way that people can be evil. There really are evil people in the world.

DOOR: We assume you've met some of these people.

PECK: In my psychiatric practice, I have encountered a number of evil people, but very rarely are they en-countered as patients. Usually, they have been the parents or relatives of my patients. These people have, through their chronic and subtle destructiveness, wreaked havoc upon their children or relatives. In my book I not only have tried to say that there is such a thing as human evil and that there are truly evil people, but I have tried to give people some understanding of what characterizes truly evil people to help people more accurately identify the bad guys.

DOOR: So what does characterize the bad guys?

PECK: One of the most significant characteristics of bad people is they are liars.

DOOR: That's why the book is called *People of the Lie.*

PECK: That's very good. Evil people lie, and their lying tends to be repetitive and accumulative.

DOOR: You are making us paranoid. We have told a lie or two.

PECK: You mean like telling people you're going to get the *Door* out on time?

DOOR: Very funny.

PECK: I want to underline what I just said. What distinguishes evil people is the persistence and constancy of their sin. Their destructiveness is often subtle, but it's constant and continuous. So, it's not that evil people occasionally do destructive things; they *consistently* do destructive things. They have a genius for doing what is destructive.

DOOR: Do they feel guilt or remorse?

PECK: Never. The key thing is that these people who I call evil deny their own sinfulness. They deny their potential for sinfulness. All sins can be overcome except the sin of believing that you do not sin. The people I am calling evil suffer from a certain kind of narcissism which is somewhat analogous to pride. It's no accident that pride is so often designated as the number-one sin. With evil people, we're talking about an overwhelming kind of pride where the individual thinks he is perfect. Evil people are often extremely sophisticated. They will say, "Oh, of course I have my faults . . . just like everyone else." But deep down inside of them they believe that they are without fault, without stain, and that everything they do is good.

As a result, the people of the lie are continually running away from their own conscience. The way they do this is by disguising their evil from themselves and others. And because they are engaged in this effort to disguise, it is not unusual to find evil people in greater than normal concentrations in the church.

DOOR: I suppose we shouldn't be surprised?

PECK: No, because if your guiding motive is to disguise your evil from yourself and others, what better way than to be a highly visible Christian or Muslim or other emptily pious person?

DOOR: A pillar of the faith?

PECK: A pillar of the faith.

DOOR: What is so chilling about what you've just said is these people's willing, deliberate, conscious denial of their sinfulness and their refusal to do anything about it.

PECK: There seems to be a line which people cross, not a clear arbitrary line, but a line where a person becomes so convinced that he cannot sin and so utterly unwilling to look at his faults that he becomes utterly impenetrable and uncorrectable.

DOOR: That sounds so hopeless. Doesn't the reality of Jesus Christ leave room for hope? Surely Jesus can cure anything.

PECK: A lot of people have the illusion that Jesus went around healing everybody. He didn't. Jesus healed only those people who wanted to be healed. A person's free will is the absolute basic. It takes precedence to everything.

DOOR: Including healing?

PECK: Including healing. Neither Jesus nor God can heal someone who does not want to be healed. Evil people, whose whole being is dedicated to denying that there might be anything wrong with them, do not want to be healed because they do not believe they have anything to be healed of.

DOOR: It is difficult to know how to react to people like that.

PECK: I have met a lot of them and, frankly, they are easy people to hate. But, if you understand them, they are ultimately more to be pitied than hated because they live their lives with a terror that the rest of us simply have not experienced. This is hard to appreciate because on the surface they look like people who have it all together. Calm. Cool. They may be deacons in the church, pillars of the community, but underneath, they are terrified that their image of respectability might be shattered.

DOOR: What a horrible way to live.

PECK: An old book published in 1947, written by Gerald Vann, describes just how horrible it is: "There can be a state of soul against which love itself is powerless because it has hardened itself against love. Hell is essentially a state of being which we fashion for ourselves—a state of final separateness from God which is the result not of God's repudiation of man, but of man's repudiation of God, and the repudiation which is eternal precisely because it has become in itself immovable. There are analogies in human experience—the hate which is so blind, so dark, that love only makes it the more violent, the pride which is so stony that humility only makes it the more scornful, the inertia, last but not least, the inertia, which has so taken possession of the personality that no crisis, no appeal, no inducement whatsoever can stir it into activity, but on the contrary makes it bury itself the more deeply in its immobility. So with the soul then gone, pride can become hardened into hell. Hatred can become hardened into hell. Any of the seven root forms of wrongdoing can harden into hell and not least that slough which is boredom with divine things. The inertia that cannot be troubled to repent even though it sees the abyss it has accustomed itself to refuse whatever might cost it an effort. May God in his mercy save us from that."

Once you and I, instead of fighting against our sin, start fighting for it, and we do it long enough, we end up fighting for all our sins, and that is when our sinfulness becomes uncorrectable.

DOOR: We find it very unusual that a psychiatrist from Harvard would not only believe in the Devil, but write a book about it.

PECK: When I started this book, in common with 99.99 percent of my fellow psychiatrists and the vast majority of clergy, I really did not believe that the Devil was real or existed. But I felt that if I was to write a book on evil, I at least ought to explore the evidence for the Devil. I decided that if I could see one good, old-fashioned case of

possession, I might change my mind. Of course, I didn't think I would ever see a real case of demon possession since I didn't believe that demons existed. So I started reading on the subject. Most of the books seemed shoddy, sensational, and not terribly responsible. But I did come across a couple of books that seemed to be quite responsible.

DOOR: What were those?

PECK: The most notable would be *Hostage to the Devil* by Malachi Martin.

DOOR: And what did it say?

PECK: It suggested that genuine demon possession was a very rare phenomenon. If it was a rare phenomenon, the fact that I had never seen a case didn't mean that it didn't exist. So I made friends with some of the people that were involved in this area.

DOOR: Exorcists?

PECK: People like exorcists. The first couple of cases I saw had standard psychiatric disorders so I made two marks on my scientific pistol ... but the third case turned out to be the real thing.

DOOR: By "the real thing" you mean someone who was possessed by an evil spirit?

PECK: Someone who was indeed possessed of an evil spirit.

DOOR: Sounds spooky.

PECK: It was more than spooky. I have had the experience, twice now, of seeing people who were genuinely possessed. In both cases, I was privileged to be a part of a team where we encountered the evil spirit incarnate. They were very dramatic, frightening, and dangerous experiences.

DOOR: Can you tell us the specifics of the exorcisms you witnessed?

PECK: I can, but I choose not to. For two reasons. The first is I do not want this interview (or my book) to be unbalanced. Secondly, there is no way I could adequately describe what goes on in an exorcism. It's like trying to describe the taste of artichokes to someone who's never had one.

DOOR: But, surely, you must be able to tell us something.

PECK: I can tell you that exorcism ends ultimately with a choice on the part of the patient. During the exorcism there is a final stripping away, an exposure of the demonic as demonic, and then the patient has to decide whether he is going to cast his lot with God. Both the possessions I witnessed ended successfully with each patient making a relatively clear choice to cast his lot with Christ at considerable risk rather than continuing to follow Satan's laws. It's by his faith that a person is healed, believe it or not. The primary exorcist, ultimately, is the possessed person himself. It is his free will and his free choice which casts out the demon. The process of the exorcism simply makes that choice very clear to him.

DOOR: That must have been quite an experience for you.

PECK: The most exciting thing about my participation in these two exorcisms was not meeting the Devil; instead it was sensing the palpable presence of God. That presence of God was not an accident, because in both cases there were teams of people (seven in one and nine in another) that came to work with the patient. When you get seven people in a room at considerable personal sacrifice and risk who have come in love for the purpose of healing, it's not an accident that God is present in the room.

DOOR: How do people become possessed? Do people play with Ouija boards and then suddenly an evil spirit moves in?

PECK: Demon possession should really be called partial or imperfect possession because in these two patients there was clearly a struggle going on between the demonic and the human soul. These two "possessed" people were not evil people. There are evil people, but these two were not evil. They had evil in them, but in some ways they were unusually good people.

DOOR: What does that mean?

PECK: One of my theories is that good people are more prone to possession than bad people precisely because Satan, in accord with traditional Christian theology, is on the run and is trying to put out fires, so he goes where the threat is. Possession is not an accident. It is very important for your readers to realize this. You don't go walking down the street one day and all of a sudden a demon jumps out at you from behind a bush and penetrates you. Both patients that I saw had very, very difficult childhoods. They were terribly lonely and in one way or another, both of them repeatedly sold out to unreality. Their possession was a gradual phenomenon for which the individual had a considerable amount of responsibility. In some ways they invited this spirit in. They made various compromises with reality and at some later date decided that this spirit which had portrayed itself as being a friend really wasn't a friend so they decided to begin the very long fight against it.

DOOR: How would you define evil?

PECK: There are many definitions, of course, but the best I have ever heard came from my son when he was eight years old, believe it or not. I asked him what evil was and he said, "That's easy, Daddy; evil is live spelled backward."

DOOR: Not bad.

PECK: No, because evil is very much an anti-life force. And when I say anti-life, I'm not talking about things like natural death; I am talking about murder. Not only the murder of one's physical body, but the murder of one's spirit.

DOOR: Where do you think evil comes from?

PECK: I have lots of theories, but my main theory is centered around the concept of the free will.

DOOR: Are you saying that evil is more a function of our choice than the results of some outside force?

PECK: Yes and no. There is no doubt in my mind that there is an evil spirit in the world just as there is the Spirit of God, but what role this evil spirit plays in human affairs beyond occasional very rare cases of genuine possession, I don't have any idea. But my own suspicion is that people do not need Satan to recruit them to evil. They are quite capable of recruiting themselves.

DOOR: Do you believe in the concept of original sin?

PECK: For the purposes of understanding human evil, I don't think it is necessary to discuss original sin. We can talk about certain ways in which evil does tend to be passed down across the generations, but the key thing is that all of us have the capacity to sin. All of us do sin. One of the virtues of Christian doctrine is the acknowledgment that we are all sinners and that anyone who thinks he is not a sinner, yet calls himself a Christian, is lying. To be a Christian is to know that you are a sinner. Christian-

ity holds not only that we are all sinners, but there is the possibility of instant forgiveness as long as there is repentance and contrition. Here again the problem with the evil person surfaces because, for them, there is not repentance or contrition.

DOOR: Is there anything else you would like to point out about evil people?

PECK: There is a Brazilian psychiatrist, Keppe, who defines the basic human disorder as theomania, the desire to be God ... in other words, the desire to be the playwright instead of an actor in the drama. That desire is what characterizes most people who are immature. It is the immature person who moans, complains, and bitches when life doesn't meet his demands. But real adults, mature people, don't try to get life to meet their demands; they try to meet life's demands.

DOOR: We would guess that evil people have similar characteristics?

PECK: Evil people are enamored with their own will. When there is a conflict between their conscience and their will, it is the conscience which has to go. They are extraordinarily willful people and extraordinarily controlling people.

DOOR: What do you mean by controlling?

PECK: Erich Fromm described a certain kind of person as a necrophilic personality type. He described them as the type of people that want to control other people. They want to destroy others' initiative, independence, creativity, and unpredictability. They want to make people into very orderly automatons or robots. He contrasted those kind of personalities—necrophilic—with the biophilic personality, which, of course, is the kind of person who tries to encourage independence, creativity, and initiative in others. Evil people are necrophilic. They want to control the drama. But look at the contrast in Jesus Christ. I kind of like the Mormon's story regarding Christ's decision to come to earth.

DOOR: Oh, oh. Here goes our mail again.

PECK: What?

DOOR: Never mind.

PECK: Anyway, the way the Mormons tell it is that God asked his two sons, Christ and Satan, to work on a plan to deal with the problem of human evil. Satan came up with a plan which most of our corporation executives would love. It was very simple. Satan suggested that God give each of his angels a submachine gun and assign one angel to each human being. For some of the more difficult cases, Satan suggested some concentration camps, with more angels, machine guns, and barbed wire. Satan suggested that this plan was fail-safe for keeping human beings in line and would insure that human beings would do exactly what God wanted.

DOOR: This is the Mormon version?

PECK: Sort of a loose translation.

DOOR: Go on.

PECK: Christ's plan was, of course, by most of our worldly standards, bananas. Jesus told God, "What you want to do, God, is not try to control people but let them go. Why don't you let me go down and live and die as one of them and give them an example of how they ought to live and also an example of how much you love them. So God settled on Christ's plan, which was unpredictable, creative, and allowed people to show initiative.

DOOR: With evil as a reality, do you see any hope? Is evil winning?

PECK: People always ask me why there is evil in the world, but no one has ever asked me, "Why is there good in the world?" We assume this is a naturally good world which has been contaminated by evil.

DOOR: You don't agree with that?

PECK: I am not sure it is that simple. If you want me to be honest, I am more attracted to the notion that this is a naturally evil world which has somehow been contaminated with goodness. I believe that the good bugs are growing and that the infections of goodness will win the day. One of the reasons I believe this is that if you look at young children, while they still have a sweet, innocent quality to them occasionally, they are also born liars, cheaters, thieves, and manipulators. The fact that many of them grow up to be adult liars, cheaters, thieves, and manipulators is not surprising, nor is it difficult to explain. What is difficult to explain is why some of them grow up to be honest and self-sacrificing people. One of the dangers with focusing on the subject of evil is that you can lose your bearings. Perhaps the mystery of human evil isn't as great or magnificent as the extraordinary mystery of human goodness.

DOOR: What do you hope to accomplish by the writing of this book? What do you hope will happen to the people who read it?

PECK: I hope people will take God, Christ, and themselves far more seriously than they have done. We all leave our mark on history, yet people have a hard time believing they are that important. But the fact is, in this drama we play terribly important roles. We *do* leave our mark on history. We have a choice. We have the freedom to choose whether we are going to submit to God or to what God represents—truth and love and light—or refuse to submit our will in any way, which means we are choosing to be enslaved to the powers of darkness and evil. We have to choose one kind of enslavement or another—either the enslavement to God or the refusal to be submitted which is automatically, although unconsciously, to become enslaved to Satan. As C. S. Lewis said, "There is no neutral ground in the universe."

R. C. SPROUL

R. C. Sproul is scared to death someone will think he is a fundamentalist. We've always had that same fear. R. C. Sproul had never read an issue of the *Door* until we wanted to interview him. Okay, so the Keepers aren't very good judges of character. Of course, after R. C. read a couple of issues of the *Door*, he wasn't so sure he wanted us to interview him. Well, *we* weren't so sure we wanted to interview him *either*. But we decided to risk everything and do it anyway.

You are probably wondering who the heck R. C. Sproul is. Frankly, we wondered ourselves. R. C. came, as he describes it, from a "higher critical, radical leftist environment" (which, we assume, was not anywhere near Grand Rapids, Michigan). Sproul is known for his work at the Ligonier Valley Study Center located in the exciting town of Stahlstown, Pennsylvania. Ligonier (pronounced Ligonier) is a place where laypeople can get training that is somewhere between a Sunday school and a seminary education. People have an image of Sproul as a Bible-thumping-right-wing-orthodox apologist. Not true. R. C. says he is a classicist (we assume that means he is a classy guy).

R. C. travels six months out of the year speaking, teaching, and preaching all over the world . . . er . . . all over the U.S. . . . uh . . . all around the Pennsylvania area. Besides a novel entitled *Johnny Come Home*, he has written the popular *Holiness of God.* The Keepers of the *Door* found R. C. to be candid, personable—and a funny talker.

Editor's note: You will notice that, throughout the interview, R. C. occasionally falls into the use of such terms as "da," "dis," and "dat." These are localized, Philadelphia-ized, theological abbreviations of words we commonly know as "the," "this," and "that."

DOOR: What does the church need today?

SPROUL: I am passionately convinced dat da biggest need of the church is to develop a deeper understanding of da character of God. People need to know, cognitively and intellectually, who God is.

DOOR: Why do you believe understanding the character of God is so important?

SPROUL: The character of God encompasses three basic realities: the true, the good, and the beautiful. Those three facets, collectively, make all the difference to me. My dad died when I was a young boy and, ever since then, I had a passion to understand the truth. Life is often filled with difficulty and confusion. In the midst of that difficulty and confusion, whom can we trust? Who will tell us the truth? I have always wanted to know these things, and I think others do too. I am a needy person. So whatever fills that need has to be true because, if it isn't true, then it isn't going to help. That is why the truth of God's character is so vital.

DOOR: And what do you mean by the goodness of God's character?

SPROUL: The goodness or righteousness of God is not simply a neutral description of God. His goodness affects you and me. Goodness has to do with behavior. Goodness affects our relationships with other people because, when I sin against you, I hurt you and I violate you. I don't like to have someone violate me, I don't like to be the victim of sin, and I definitely don't want to be a perpetrator of sin. But I am a perpetrator of sin, and that is the struggle for all of us, isn't it? We are part of the very evil that we're trying to deal with in the world. Then we come face-to-face with the goodness of God, the grace of God. That is what happened when I was converted. My conversion was an overwhelming experience of forgiveness. I was simply blown away by the grace of God.

DOOR: That's one of the more theological descriptions of grace that we have heard.

SPROUL: What?

DOOR: Blown away.

SPROUL: But I *was* blown away.

DOOR: Tell us about it.

SPROUL: I was in college, and I began talking to a friend of mine whom I respected. He didn't tell me the gospel, exactly—at least, he didn't go through any sort of evangelistic spiel. He just talked to me, very conversationally, about being a Christian. But it was clear that this guy took his Christianity seriously. It wasn't so much *what* he said—I just saw it in his eyes. Somehow, I sensed that Jesus was real. After our conversation, I went up to my room and prayed to a Jesus who, I now knew, was really there. After that, I knew I needed to read the Bible—so I read the whole thing from cover to cover in two weeks. Something came through those pages that said to me, "Whatever this is, pal, this is for keeps." And right then, I surrendered to the hound of heaven. I poured out my life to God. My shallowness, my sinfulness, my pride—all of it was exposed, and I was devastated. I felt like my soul had been raped. But, at the same time, there was a tenderness, a sweetness, and a beauty which said that God loved me in spite of all the garbage in my life. I couldn't get over the fact that I was really forgiven. That is why I believe that ethics and behavior are motivated by gratitude. And that is why I've always wanted to have a high standard of ethics—not so I can impose my ethics on others, but so I—

DOOR: —But isn't that what Christians are supposed to do—impose their ethics on society?

SPROUL: Well, let's put it this way. Authentic Christian virtues are very difficult to attain. If I'm honest, *I* certainly have a struggle trying to attain them. All of us do. Therefore, we Christians need to learn to be tolerant of others. That doesn't mean we *condone* others' imperfections, but it does mean we recognize our constant need for forgiveness. After all, we are called to be salt and light—not bulldozers.

DOOR: You mentioned beauty. You don't often hear people talk about beauty.

SPROUL: I am moved by beauty. I am moved by order, by coherence, by excellence. I think God must be exquisitely beautiful. That is why it concerns me when I look at the conservative churches with their anti-art, anti-aesthetic attitudes.

DOOR: We take it that certain denominations' worship services would not exactly turn you on.

SPROUL: Like what denominations?

DOOR: We certainly wouldn't want to cast aspersions, but we have the feeling that the denomination which rhymes with "Flaptist" might be one.

SPROUL: Well, let's put it this way, I love the Episcopal Church. I love their liturgy. But it is still difficult to find one church that emphasizes truth, goodness, *and* beauty. Even though Episcopal churches have quality liturgy, many of them tend to be as loose as a goose regarding truth.

DOOR: That's another interesting way to describe things, R. C.

SPROUL: Then we have my own Presbyterian tradition. We Presbyterians fight like cats and dogs over the finest points of theology. Yet our worship tends to be bland and flat. Our image as Presbyterians is one of austerity—having little concern for beauty. And I can't figure dat out; except that we're so preoccupied with truth.

DOOR: We can't figure dat out either.

SPROUL: Then there are the Baptists.

DOOR: Don't you mean "den dere are da Baptists"?

SPROUL: Cute. In my opinion, Baptists give the impression that their central concern is morality. There is almost a hostility toward the aesthetic. And I think, "Jeez, isn't it possible to integrate goodness or morality, *and* truth *and* beauty?" Maybe I am reading history through rose-colored classes, but I think classical Christianity tried to do that. I find it in Augustine, Aquinas, and many other giants of the past.

DOOR: Let's change gears just a little. You mentioned the grace of God. Forgiveness and the grace of God have been discussed many times in the *Wittenburg Door*. How do you view the grace of God? Is everyone forgiven—period?

SPROUL: Are you asking whether or not I believe in a universal atonement in which, because of Christ, everyone's sins have been paid for, and all we have to do is tell people they are forgiven, with no call for repentance?

DOOR: Yes.

SPROUL: No.

DOOR: Uh . . . could you elaborate just a little?

SPROUL: I believe dat repentance *is* a biblical requirement. I also think dat repentance is one of the most painful, excruciating experiences a person can go through. One of the best examples I can give you is Isaiah. He gets one glimpse of God, and it wipes the sucker out. He's crawlin' around sayin',

"Woe is me," and he is hurtin'—really hurtin'—

DOOR: —this sounds like the original Philly translation of the Old Testament—

SPROUL: —and then what does God say? Does he say, "Hey, Isaiah, don't be so neurotic. I've already forgiven you"? No. What God does is send a seraph over with a red hot coal to put in Isaiah's mouth. *Then* God says, "Behold, thy sins are forgiven and thine iniquity is taken away." God doesn't have to put coals in our mouths today, because there is a sense in which the ultimate coal was put in Christ's mouth for us. But I must acknowledge my sin before God. I must realize that my being able to stand blameless before God is not the result of God's indulgence. Rather, it is because God has taken my sin seriously enough to lay it on Christ. That is grace. I don't get the punishment for my crime. That is a whole lotta grace. I can't make up for it. I can't atone for it. The hardest thing in the world for me, as a prideful creature, is to flatly say, "The only way I can stand before God is on the basis of somebody else's righteousness."

DOOR: What happens when we sin, and then we sin again?

SPROUL: First of all, God tells us that he doesn't *want* us to sin. He doesn't want us to sin today or tomorrow. That's what he told the woman caught in adultery. But, understanding that, if we *do* sin tomorrow, he is dere to forgive us. However, we must never take the grace of God for granted. If we really are sensitive to this God who forgives us so readily, then there ought to be a sense in which we are surprised every time we are forgiven.

DOOR: Practically, then, what does the grace of God mean? How do we live ethically? Do we do what we want and not worry because we can count on the forgiveness of God? Or do we come up with a list of acceptable behaviors and look over our shoulder for God's wrath if we blow it?

SPROUL: Ultimate goodness is based on the character of God himself. I am supposed to be an imitator of God. That is a big deal, you know. We are supposed to reflect and mirror who God is. The trouble is, I'm not a very good mirror. So, how do I decide what to do? How do I decide what is good or bad?

DOOR: That's a good question. Why didn't we think of it?

SPROUL: I have some pretty good clues to the answer. I don't think dat da minute I'm converted, God drills a hole in my head and pours in all the information I'll ever need to automatically know what is right. Once I am converted, I have two basic problems when it comes to doing what is right: First, I need to know what is right. Second, I must find the moral courage to do what is right once I know what right is.

DOOR: So, how does the Christian decide what is right? The Bible?

SPROUL: Principally, yes—but not exclusively. I am a big advocate of natural theology and general revelation. Still, the Scriptures have to be studied—and I mean studied. The Bible is a profoundly complex book. It is not simplistic. It is not pharisaical. It is not moralistic. If I am to know what righteousness is, if I am to know the mind of Christ, if I am to know what to do, I must *study* the Scriptures.

DOOR: That really sounds great, R. C., but the facts are that most of us do not have the time or the resources to "really study" the Bible. And, oftentimes, we need to know the right thing to do in a crisis situation when there simply isn't time to study.

SPROUL: First of all, you try to find someone who knows more than you do about the Scriptures. Someone you trust. Then you ask them their opinion.

DOOR: That sounds okay if you're talking about whether to attend X college instead of Y college. But what if a person needs advice regarding a very tough moral issue? For example, what if a couple has a thirteen-year-old daughter, and they want to know what to do now that she is pregnant?

SPROUL: I'll give you a better example than that. Some parents called me because they were facing a very difficult decision. Their baby had been injured in a car accident and was castrated. The doctors said that they could spend *years* attempting to reconstruct the male organs, or that they could put him on hormones and change him into a girl. Furthermore, the doctors indicated that, from the child's perspective, the adjustment in his life would be much easier if he were to develop into a girl.

DOOR: Uh . . . you weren't kidding. That is a fairly complex problem . . . um . . . weren't you concerned that you might tell them the wrong thing?

SPROUL: Sure I was concerned, but here's my philosophy. As a pastor, teacher, counselor, or leader in the church, we are not only supposed to know the Scripture, but we are also supposed to accept the responsibility that goes along with it. That is why there is such a heavy burden on the pastor, the teacher, or the counselor. So I tell people, "Listen, here is what I think you should do. If you run into trouble on the Judgment Day, you can blame me, and I'll take the flak."

DOOR: That sounds sort of flippant.

SPROUL: I don't mean it that way. My point is that, if I am going to be a leader in the church, I must be willing to take responsibility for helping others make decisions. It is a frightening responsibility, and the Bible warns us about it. It says, "Don't let many be teachers because with the teacher comes greater judgment."

DOOR: Okay. Fine. But what about the majority of us who are not teachers or preachers?

SPROUL: In the Psalms it says, "Blessed is the man who walks not in the counsel of the ungodly . . . but his delight is in the law of the LORD and on his law he meditates day and night." Who wrote the Psalm? The king. Even though he was a leader and was making decisions that affected many people, the same principle applies to all of us. The more we know about the Law of God, the more we'll be like a tree that's planted by living waters. We won't be blown about with every wind of doctrine.

DOOR: Someone once said, if we have to make a decision, we should take as much as we know of God and as much as we know of ourselves, weigh what we know, then do what we think is right based on what we know—and that if we do this, we will never make a wrong choice. It might *later* prove to be wrong, but based on what we knew at the time, it was the right choice.

SPROUL: I'm not sure about that. I don't think God can accuse you, in the instance you described, of making a *malicious* decision. But I would say that a person could make a *wrong* decision for which he or she is somewhat accountable. In other words, there may be decisions we make out of ignorance, but often that ignorance exists because we didn't do our homework. We were lazy or slothful. We didn't pay attention to what we should have. Had we paid attention, we would have known better and would have been able to make the right decision. That is why, in the Old Testament, you have offerings for sins committed in ignorance, and that is why the Catholic church makes a distinction regarding sins of ignorance.

DOOR: Okay. Let's take the person who *does* study the Bible. Even among great scholars, there is legitimate disagreement regarding the ethical implications of the Christian faith. So how does one resolve those differences?

SPROUL: With great difficulty. But, I will tell you what *I* do, as a classicist. On an issue where I am confused, I try to find what Augustine, Aquinas, Luther, Calvin, and Edwards said.

DOOR: Douglas Edwards?

SPROUL: Jonathan. For me, those five are the most impressive teachers in the church, historically. Their stuff has stood the test of time.

DOOR: They could be wrong.

SPROUL: Of course. But when I come across an issue where they all agree, it does make me think they might be on to something. That doesn't mean I don't try to understand *why* they say what they do. Where I really get into trouble, though, is when I find them all disagreeing.

DOOR: Then you call Bill Gothard.

SPROUL: Right.

DOOR: It seems as though people in the church today want leaders to do all of the thinking for them. Doesn't that bother you?

SPROUL: Of course that bothers me. I have been on a soapbox for years warning the Christian community that we are in the most anti-intellectual period in the history of the church. People don't want to hear that stuff. They want to be entertained. They want the quick and easy answer. Thinking is work. It's hard work. But the good news is that we can improve our ability to think.

DOOR: How do you feel about the church in America?

SPROUL: The church is the most important institution on earth and the most corrupt institution on the earth. The reason it is the most corrupt institution is that it *is* the most important institution. The church is very weak today. Weak liturgically. Weak in its preaching. We are supposed to have sixty million people trained and nurtured in the church. Tell me why sixty million people are having no impact on this culture? Why doesn't the church have any influence on art and on the intellectual community? How can sixty million born-again people, who have been trained and nurtured to be light to a dying world, have no demonstrable impact on the culture? I don't often agree with Harvey Cox, but he made a statement I agree with: "The church should be God's avant-garde. It should function much like a floating crap game."

DOOR: Uh ... we agree too, we think—even though we don't have a clue as to what he's saying.

SPROUL: I think what he is saying is that the church needs to be where the action is. When things get hot, we move. As transformed people, we should be radically sensitive to the pain of this world. We should be there first—like the Salvation Army.

T-BONE BURNETT

T-Bone Burnett. Musician. Record producer. Songwriter. Cowboy. Texan. Christian. His grandfather, J. Henry (J-Bone?) Burnett, was secretary of the Southern Baptist Convention for twenty-five years. His father, J. Henry (H-Bone?) Burnett II, was an Episcopalian. J. Henry (T-Bone) Burnett III probably will not be secretary of the Southern Baptist Convention (he calls himself a mild-mannered Episcopalian).

When you first meet T-Bone, you are stunned by his appearance. At the sight of his baggy white T-shirt (not-so-carefully-wrinkled), and his baggy Levis (a little-more-carefully-wrinkled), you immediately want to ask the question, "Uh . . . are things that bad?"

T-Bone Burnett is kind of a cult figure. Loyal T-Bone Burnett fans probably have every one of his albums (which include *Truth Decay*, *Trap Door*, *Proof Through the Night*, *T-Bone Burnett*, and *The Talking Animals*). They hear him every time he goes on tour. They usually like Bruce Cockburn too. In summary, most of his fans are a little strange.

Oh sure, you won't find T-Bone Burnett's songs in the Maranatha Songbook, but you will find a significant group of people who think T-Bone's songs sound like . . . well . . . T-Bone's songs.

We were lucky enough to find him in Los Angeles. He was wandering down Sunset Boulevard looking for someplace in L.A. that served beer in a long-necked bottle. We did manage to help him find a bartender with a long neck who served root beer.

We also managed to find T-Bone Burnett to be bright, witty, and fun to be around. We know he found us to be good for a lot of laughs, too, because he kept saying "Boy, you guys are a bunch of bozos." What a guy.

DOOR: Are you a Christian artist?

T-BONE: Are you a Christian magazine?

DOOR: Are you kidding?

T-BONE: I am not proud of my Christianity and I'm not ashamed of it. But I think it is dehumanizing to be called a "Christian artist." It's demeaning.

DOOR: What do you mean by dehumanizing and demeaning?

T-BONE: To pigeonhole someone is to take away that person's humanity. A lot of "Christian" artists make it seem as though all they do is sit around and read the Bible all day long and go to church. They give the impression that they never go to a baseball game or play with the dog. That's demeaning. The proper question is, "What is the relationship between a performer and his audience?"

DOOR: It is? Uh, of course it is. So what is the relationship between a performer and his audience?

T-BONE: A person's faith comes in *between* a performer and his audience.

DOOR: What does that mean?

T-BONE: Let me put it this way. What difference does it make to the audience whether I'm a Christian or not? Is somebody in the audience going to say, "Well, this guy's a Christian so I'm going to be a Christian"? And even if someone did, would that be a good thing?

DOOR: Is it a bad thing for a performer to speak outright about his or her faith?

T-BONE: That's a perfectly fine thing to do. It's just not what I do.

DOOR: Why not?

T-BONE: Because art does not instruct people or inform people or teach people. As soon as art does that it becomes resistible. One of the prerequisites of art is that it is irresistible—or it is not art. It's something else, but it's not art. It may be propaganda, rhetoric, or a hundred other things, but it's not art.

DOOR: What do you think of what is called "Christian music"?

T-BONE: Most "Christian music" is just some kind of rehash. It simply has nothing to do with today. It has to do with the status quo of 1972 and 1973 and, because of that, it's impotent.

DOOR: So, we assume that you view yourself as an artist and a musician. . . .

T-BONE: I see myself as a man standing up trying to give my point of view as clearly as I can. I want people to understand that life is worth living. That this world is an incredible place to live, and that it's wilder than anyone's fantasy. I don't think I have to be perfect to say those things. I am a mass of contradictions myself.

DOOR: Funny you should mention your contradictions. In spite of your optimistic appraisal of your point of view, you are often portrayed as a brooding person.

T-BONE: Because I am. I don't want to be brooding, but I am.

One thing that really upsets me about "Christian" musicians is that they tell people that they used to take a lot of dope, then they became a Christian, now everything is rosy, and you people in the audience are screwed up so why don't you become like me. I haven't found it to be that way at all. I've found that being a Christian makes life 100,000 times more difficult than just being a sort of standard, run-of-the-mill hedonist. I would like someone to get on the "700 Club" sometime and say "Hey, life is rough!"

DOOR: Let's change the subject for a minute. What do you think of the church?

T-BONE: Organized religion is a really good thing—the more organized the better. Organization is important. Hierarchy is important. I agree with C. S. Lewis when he says that everything in nature speaks to us of hierarchy.

DOOR: Hmm. We would have expected you to rip organized religion and praise individual piety.

T-BONE: Individual piety is a good thing too. I mean, it's like being a saint, right? I think Mother Teresa probably really is a saint—an honest-to-God, twentieth-century saint. I mean, I don't know how pious she is, but she just gets down and helps people. That's one of the problems today. By that I mean that if somebody's starving, we pray for them instead of giving them some food.

DOOR: Can you merchandise your music and still maintain your integrity?

T-BONE: It is possible to merchandise what you do and still maintain your integrity. The two aren't mutually exclusive at all. It doesn't matter much, though, in the long run, how music is merchandised—any more than it matters what the reviews say. Because the reviews and the marketing are both just firewood. Music will either mean something to people over a period of time or it won't. So, frankly, merchandising is not terribly important.

DOOR: So, back to our question. Can *you* merchandise your music and still maintain your integrity?

T-BONE: I am saying that I would not like to be in a position of having to deal with the proposition of merchandising the gospel. It's such a difficult and treacherous path, and I don't think very many people have navigated it well at all.

What I have to be concerned about is making beautiful music, making it better, and making music that touches people.

DOOR: How have you felt about the way the evangelical church has responded to Bob Dylan? First they embraced him, then they backed off.

T-BONE: The evangelical church is not the church, first of all. Whatever has gone on with Dylan is between him and God. I do know one thing, though. The church latched onto a tough customer when they latched onto Bob Dylan. If Christianity wants to manipulate Bob Dylan, they are going to have to be a lot smarter than they've been.

DOOR: What does the *real* church have to be concerned about today?

T-BONE: We are constantly being told what the real world is, and to face the facts. But the fact of the matter is that the facts don't matter. The real world is like a marriage between two people. It is completely unseen. It's a mystery. But we keep getting caught up in the facts. And that keeps us from knowing the real world.

DOOR: Uh, right, T-Bone. We've felt the same way ourselves . . . we think. But in this world, where the real is not real, and the facts don't matter, what does matter? What are the issues? Abortion? Nuclear armaments?

T-BONE: Abortion is a real shibboleth.

DOOR: Wait a minute, we have a policy against using ten-letter words in our magazine. Do you mean that abortion is a nonissue?

T-BONE: No.

DOOR: Uh, that's what we thought.

T-BONE: No. I don't think abortion is a nonissue. It is an issue that's distorted, and I think Christians need to rethink abortion. There has never been a person in history who has been *for* abortion. I don't think anyone has ever said, "You know what I'm going to do tonight? I'm going out to get laid so I can get pregnant and get an abortion." No one is *for* abortion. But the fact that people *think* people are for it is the problem.

What *we* need to do, as Christians, is to think. The Bible promises us a certain unity, and it also requires a certain unity among us. There is no Christian position on school prayer. There is no such thing. We have to sit down and talk these things out. We have to *think*. If Christianity requires us to toe the party line, if Christianity says we all have to agree or we are not Christians, then Christianity is no better than any other tyranny on earth.

RICHARD JOHN NEUHAUS

Name one of the most frightening realities of our time.

Nuclear war? Maybe.

Ronald Reagan? Possibly.

Punker Baptists? For sure.

But these are nothing compared to ... well ... you guessed it ... people with *three* names.

Sure, most of us *have* three names. But those of us who are normal never *use* all three of them. That's because we all know our parents worked very hard to give us at least one name that is horrible. Richard is a fine name. So is John. But Richard John?

Give us a break.

You probably think we interviewed Richard John Neuhaus because he's a scholar, or because he's a liberal—well, he's not really a liberal, he's actually very conservative on some issues, but on the other hand, lots of liberals don't like him, but, then, neither do a lot of conservatives—uh, where were we? Oh. We were discussing *why* we decided to interview Richard John Neuhaus. It's very simple. We have always interviewed by the quota system, and this issue was targeted for a New York, Lutheran male with three names. We knew there was some guy named Richard Milhous (see what we mean by horrible middle names?) who used to live in New York, but he wasn't a Lutheran, so we settled for Richard John.

Luckily, Richard John Neuhaus has never seen the *Door*. That's because he's always reading junk magazines like *Harper's* and *Atlantic Monthly*.

Richard John's most recent book is *The Naked Public Square*. His publisher must have told him that anything with the word *naked* in it would sell.

Neuhaus is director of the Center on Religion and Society (which is considering changing its name to the "Naked Center on Religion and Society"), and he was interviewed by Michael John Cromartie (who is considering changing his name to Naked Michael John Cromartie).

DOOR: In the sixties, you were very involved in the anti-Vietnam movement, yet recently, the *New York Times* called you a neoconservative who has moved to the right. Is that an accurate description of you?

NEUHAUS: I am a proponent of the once-and-future liberalism. I don't think I have moved to the right. It is enormously important to note, however, that what was considered a liberal, centrist position twenty years ago is today considered conservative or neoconservative.

DOOR: Then would it be fair to say that you still consider yourself a liberal, but that the definition of *left* has changed?

NEUHAUS: Yes, but even *left* and *right* are odd labels today.

DOOR: What do you mean?

NEUHAUS: Well, is the pro-life position on abortion considered a "left" or "right" position?

DOOR: Most would probably say it is a "right" position.

NEUHAUS: Exactly. At least that is what the *New York Times* and *Time* magazine would say. But they are making a great mistake. I am pro-life for the same reasons that I was engaged in the civil rights movement and the anti-Vietnam movement. It is the classic "liberal" position to *expand* the definition of the human community for which one provides protection and care. It is the classic "conservative" position to suggest that the way to deal with poverty is to get rid of poor people, and yet it is the Planned Parenthood organization who put out a booklet supporting abortion by showing how much money has been saved on welfare, education, etc., by virtue of aborting the children of the poor.

DOOR: In other words, on the issue of abortion, for example, it is the liberals who have abandoned their own classic positions?

NEUHAUS: Yes. In 1967, I wrote an article for *Commonweal* magazine called "Abortion: The Dangerous Assumptions.'" I said then what I say now to my friends on the left: We are making a very big mistake by buying into the pro-abortion position. It is not consistent with what has motored, impassioned, and sustained us in the past.

DOOR: It sounds like that might have made you a persona non grata at Planned Parenthood cocktail parties. Was that the beginning of your "breaking ranks" with the left?

NEUHAUS: Yes. Then, in 1976—a year after the fall of Saigon—Dan Berrigan, Jim Forest, and I drew up a petition protesting the fact that Hanoi was engaged in massive and systematic violations of human rights. The same so-called Third Force people among the Buddhists and others in Vietnam, with whom we had protested against the regime in Saigon, were now being jailed again or tortured or just disappearing under Hanoi. We drew up a list of 104 identifiable national leaders of the anti-war movement and asked them to join with us by going public with our protest. About fifty percent refused to sign the petition and were very candid in saying, "Hanoi is on the correct side of the global revolution and, therefore, even if Hanoi is doing some unseemly things like imprisoning hundreds of thousands of people or murdering many thousands, you are not to say anything about it." That was a very sobering experience.

DOOR: Uh . . . we can understand that.

NEUHAUS: I learned some very significant lessons from that experience. One lesson was that I will never again, in the public arena, enter into a common or united front with people whose presuppositions or beliefs are fundamentally opposed to mine. I also learned never to say that a situation is so bad that it can't be worse. There were many who suggested that if the U.S. were to withdraw from Vietnam, a bloodbath would follow. The standard retort from those of us in the anti-war movement was, "Look, nobody knows what will happen in the future. We do know what is happening now. We also know that whatever happens in the future cannot be worse than what is happening now." The dismal, sobering fact is that what happened after 1975 *was* worse, if you measure worse in terms of the totality of human suffering. Look at what happened—hundreds of thousands of boat people, hundreds of thousands who perished at sea, the genocide and veritable holocaust that took place in Kampuchea under Pol Pot—all of that was many times worse than the war in Vietnam. Believe me, I hope I will never again be cavalier about the possible horrible consequences of making the wrong political decision.

DOOR: You have written a book entitled *The Naked Public Square*. We assume that it is a book about the problem of nudity in downtown areas?

NEUHAUS: Not exactly. *The Naked Public Square* means that, in the last three or four decades, it has been increasingly assumed, and in some places explicitly articulated, that religion or religiously "tainted" values should be systematically and constitutionally excluded from American public life.

DOOR: Uh, you mean that we are now seeing a move toward freedom *from* religion instead of freedom *of* religion?

NEUHAUS: Well, let me give you an example. I have been very involved in conversations with every sector of the Jewish community and leadership. Years ago, the Jewish community decided that the more secular a society is, the safer it will be for Jews. They, of course, were attempting to keep themselves from becoming a religious minority in contrast to the Judeo-Christian mainstream. I urged them to reconsider.

It is my opinion that a totally secular society, where there are not transcendent or metaphysical inhibitions against evil—including the evil of anti-Semitism—is very dangerous. It is of critical importance that the Jewish community be creatively and prominently involved in the redefining of the American democratic experiment so that it is more responsive to the religiously based values of the American people.

DOOR: What do you think of the religious new right?

NEUHAUS: The religious new right, for all the problems it poses, has made an important contribution. They have "kicked the tripwire," alerting many in this society to how the elite culture in America has radically redefined the American experiment, and redefined it in a way that is alien and hostile to the religiously based values of the American people. The religious new right does have lots of problems. They are very simplistic to suggest, as Tim LaHaye says, that there are "x" number of secular humanists engaged in some kind of conspiracy. That is not helpful. But, as bizarre as the claims from the new right are sometimes, one has to acknowledge that even in bizarre claims there can be an element of truth. The new right did not recognize just how monumental and complex the issues they have taken on really are.

DOOR: Have you met Jerry Falwell?

NEUHAUS: Yes.

DOOR: And?

NEUHAUS: Well, he knows he is in way over his head. He is not hesitant in admitting that he doesn't know the points of reference by which American political theory and historical analyses have operated for decades. But he is learning. I don't want to sound condescending. I would be very unhappy if Jerry Falwell and his people fulfilled the hopes of those who say, "If we are very nice to the fundies, they will become like us; they will all eventually send their people to the University of Chicago Divinity School to get their Ph.D.s, and they will end up being indistinguishable from us." That would be disastrous. We are engaged in a *Kulturkampf*.

DOOR: God bless you.

NEUHAUS: ...

DOOR: Er ... we thought you sneezed, but you said "Kulturkampf." Uh ... we know, of course, what a *Kulturkampf* is, but for our readers' sake, just what is a *Kulturkampf*?

NEUHAUS: It is a German word which means war over the definition of the culture and over the controlling ideas by which we define life in public. You cannot fight for the democratic idea in a way that destroys the democratic reality. You have to contend for it in a way that enhances civility. But civility does not mean that we pretend we have no fundamental differences. It means that we do not exclude people

who we find religiously bothersome or excessively assertive about their moral convictions.

Many of those who advocate pluralism are really advocating a "monism of indifference," which means you hide, conceal, and do not permit those things that you care most about to become obtrusive. That is not like pluralism; that is monism. It is like having just one tone. Pluralism is the vibrant engagement of differences. I agree with the late Catholic social philosopher, John Courtney, when he says we can recognize that disagreement is an achievement; it is a rarity. Most of what is called disagreement is simply confusion.

The religious new right is here to stay. I hope they do not become co-opted or assimilated, because they provide the feistiness and sense of urgency we need. Frankly, we need the Jerry Falwells, because the churches need to find their nerve.

DOOR: The churches have had a failure of nerve?

NEUHAUS: An enormous failure of nerve. Some people think I am hostile toward the National Council of Churches and toward mainline Protestant denominations, but I am not. I am simply trying to make a pained appeal for these churches to resume their culture-forming task—a task which, at times in American history, they have performed with great distinction.

DOOR: In the past, but not now?

NEUHAUS: They have been persuaded or intimidated to believe that it is no longer plausible or respectable to engage intelligent people in reflecting on the place of America in influencing world history.

DOOR: And Jerry Falwell has not had a failure of nerve?

NEUHAUS: No. Of course he comes as an outsider, as someone who is breaking in on the discussion. He is not knocking gently, either. Instead, he is bashing the door down and saying, "Hello, everyone. We are here and you have to take us seriously. We are no longer dismissible as 'yahoos' and 'rednecks' and ignorant southern fundies. We are here to stay. And just in case you don't take us seriously, we happen to have these x-million number of votes."

DOOR: It occurs to us, in light of the bombings of the abortion clinics, that we are seeing a "radicalization" of the religious right. Do you agree? And does that concern you?

NEUHAUS: The religious right is becoming radicalized over a number of issues: school prayer, the aggressiveness of the IRS in controlling Christian education, and the increased involvement of the ACLU in these issues. There are an awful lot of Americans who do not understand—and I do not blame them for not understanding—why the Ten Commandments cannot be posted on a schoolroom wall (they have been taken down by court order). There are absurdities like this which eventually radicalize people. But I strongly hope that we will not see an increase in religious warfare. Rather, I hope we will see an increase in our efforts to construct a public policy which does not ignore the religious dimension but, instead, responds to the actual belief systems and commitments of the American people.

DOOR: You have commented on the new religious right. Do you have any comments on the evangelical left?

NEUHAUS: You mean people like *Sojourners*?

DOOR: Yes, as well as others like the *Other Side*.

NEUHAUS: Well, some question exists whether or not these folk should be called evangelicals. I think that question is legitimate because it is hard to see in what ways distinctively evangelical ideas control what they say. I have been profoundly disappointed by *Sojourners*. Ten years ago we desperately needed, as we need now, a distinctive, biblically directed, and biblically grounded vision of society to challenge us. *Sojourners* could have been that vision. Unfortunately, they are not a choice, but an echo. They are an echo of every predictable kind of far left, mainly pacifist far left, mishmash of conventional leftisms, presumptuously entertaining—and indeed, proclaiming—the conceit that they are prophetic, and I find that pathetic. But it is worse than pathetic because it contains an element of blasphemy.

DOOR: That is pretty strong language.

NEUHAUS: We need to understand, in biblical terms, what prophecy is. Prophets were taken by the scruffs of their necks, kicking and screaming all the way. They were compelled by the Lord to do their prophetic duty. Now, in the mainline denominations, we have commissions on prophecy, career patterns on prophecy, prophets with pension plans, and boards that specialize in prophetic utterances. This is blasphemy because, ironically and tragically, that kind of prophecy ends up becoming a destroyer of the prophetic possibility. And, of course, we have to remind ourselves that in scriptural times—and I'm sure it is the same today—most of the prophets were false prophets, especially the people who advertised themselves as prophets. They were most always false prophets.

DOOR: We have skirted all around the issue. Let's see if we can nail it down. It is obvious from your comments that you feel religion or faith cannot be kept out of the public world. So you do *not* believe in the separation of church and state?

NEUHAUS: No. The church and state are *both* public institutions, of which the state is one—a very important one, but it is not the only one. The media and education system in this country have reinforced the notion that if you say "public," you mean government or state.

DOOR: But doesn't the Constitution guarantee the separation of church and state?

NEUHAUS: First of all, we must underscore that the separation of church and state is not guaranteed in the Constitution. The Constitution *does* have, however, the "no establishment" clause and the "free exercise" clause. We have to understand that the "no establishment" clause is there to serve the "free exercise" clause.

DOOR: Huh?

NEUHAUS: In other words, we have a "no establishment" clause to insure that people will not be inhibited in the "free exercise" of their religion.

DOOR: But if we're honest, isn't the American society becoming more and more secularized? In reality, isn't religion slowly disappearing as a viable part of our lives?

NEUHAUS: I don't think as a society, we are secularized. The fact is that the overwhelming majority of Americans (the survey research says somewhere around ninety-five percent) believe in God, the Father of Abraham, Isaac, Jacob, and Jesus, and they believe the Bible is the authoritative reference for understanding that God.

DOOR: So you wouldn't agree with those who call this a "post-Christian age"?

NEUHAUS: No. When you have a society in which the overwhelming number of people claim to be Christian, and act like it in many ways; when you have a society where over forty percent of the people claim they were in church or synagogue the previous week; when you have a nation of people who spend billions and billions of dollars each year to transmit their faith to their children and the world; it seems ridiculous to say that this is a post-Christian society. It is like saying the week after the Super Bowl that this is a post-sports or post-football society.

DOOR: Then we take it that you are optimistic about the future integration of faith and public policy?

NEUHAUS: Not at all. No, I think it is quite likely that we will not pull it off. It may be that things have gone too far, and that there is no way of putting it back together. This is quite possible and would be very tragic. And, if I am right in believing that it is possible that God wills the democratic idea as part of his purpose in the unfolding of history, then it would be a tragedy of not only political but spiritual proportions. But we cannot be paralyzed by inhibitions and fears about the forces and ideas that are arrayed against us. We have to continue in faith knowing that, finally, it really isn't up to us— and not only this particular slice of history. The whole enterprise of history was God's idea to begin with and, if it's going to be pulled off, he is going to pull it off. Meanwhile, we just keep the faith and act in the courage of our uncertainties.

CALVIN MILLER

The swirling wind chased the dust into the hot unforgiving sun, blasting what little moisture there was into fearful submission. Heatmaker ruled the skies of Enid, Oklahoma.

Enid was the home of Calvin Miller . . . the Wordman. As darkness brought each day to a close, the Wordman would shout into the night, "Why Enid? Why not southern California?" His question would be met each night with the hot laughter of the Heatmaker who would taunt, "Born in East L.A." And then there would be silence. Suddenly, the silence would be broken with the thundering voice of the Earthmaker, "Because you're not cool, Calvin. And, besides, I want you to leave Enid and go to Kansas."

Calvin was stunned. Why did the Earthmaker want him to leave Enid? He couldn't understand. Actually, he could understand why he was asked to leave Enid. What he couldn't understand is why the Earthmaker thought Kansas was better. So one night, when Earthmaker was thundering in the silence, Calvin screamed, "Why should I leave Enid, if I'm just going to end up in Kansas?" The Earthmaker replied, "Because I want you to become a Southern Baptist." Calvin was shaken. "A Southern Baptist? But why?" The Earthmaker's answer shook the earth, "Because southern Baptists are much more needy than Southern Californians."

And so began the journey of Calvin Miller, the Wordmaker. He received his doctorate from Midwestern Baptist Seminary in Kansas City, then moved to Omaha, Nebraska. There he began meeting with ten people, and within twenty years those ten people grew into a church of over 2000 members. Until he published *The Singer*, *The Song*, and *The Finale*, no one but Southern Baptists had ever heard of him. Now, after hundreds of thousands of copies of the Singer trilogy have been sold (not to mention his more recent *A Requiem for Love*, the first of his Symphony trilogy), most everyone has heard of him . . . and most Southern Baptists are pretending that they never heard of him. After you read this interview, we think you'll understand why Calvin Miller is not one of your everyday, run-of-the-mill Southern Baptists. He did say to our interviewer, Michael Sanders (a closet Southern Baptist), that his first fear was that we would not publish his interview. His second fear was that we *would* publish it.

DOOR: *The Singer* has sold over 350,000 copies. Not bad for a beginner.

MILLER: I'm flattered, of course, that the book has sold as well as it has. But I try to be realistic. Sometimes the worst thing you can say about a book is that it is selling well. Most good books *don't* sell very well.

The Singer was my first work of fiction. There are things in it that I would change—places of inconsistency. I appreciate the acclaim I have received for the book, but I wonder sometimes if it is worth all the acclaim.

DOOR: Where did the idea for *The Singer* come from?

MILLER: I wrote *The Singer* when I was really down. I had a deacon in my church who wanted to fire me. He was doing everything he could to drive me from the church. I was spending a lot of time alone, crying out to God. I would wake up in the middle of the night desperately wanting God to make his presence known. One morning, I woke up at about two o'clock, and the first lines of *The Singer* were there. That's when I started working on the book. So *The Singer* came out of tremendous crisis in my life.

One Canadian reviewer panned the book, but he said something intriguing. He said, "The book isn't great, but Miller himself is the troubadour, singing a love song to his Lord." I think he was right. *The Singer is* my own love song to God. When I wrote it, I desperately needed God.

DOOR: We don't believe in the inerrancy of *The Singer,* of course, but when you write, do you sense the helping presence of God?

MILLER: We need to be real careful about that. Some of the most beautiful plays and poems have been written by atheists. I believe God is responsible for beauty, no matter who develops it. But I have always been a bit reluctant to give God the credit for anything, in case he doesn't want the credit. D. James Kennedy tells the story about a woman who came to him with a poem that "the Holy Spirit gave me." After he read the poem, he said that to accuse the Holy Spirit of a poem like that was not fair to God. In my arrogance, I would like to say that *The Singer* came from God. But in case God doesn't want the credit for it, I would rather not force him into that position. Fiction can move people to see the truth. I hope *The Singer* has at least done that.

DOOR: Do you think most writers write best when they are depressed?

MILLER: When an artist cries, he may not do his best work, but his work seems to come out better. The verbiage is better, the phraseology is better, and the words cohere better. When my two children left home, I wrote a little sonnet about their leaving called "A Soldier and a Maid." Both of them were married and gone within a couple of weeks, and I missed them. A friend of mine said, "When my kids left home, I just cried. But when your kids left home, you cried so beautifully." I think artists cry in a little bit different way. We "glory in our agony."

Dostoyevski said that "we groan loudest when we have a toothache"—

DOOR: Dostoyevski said that? Ed Dunlap, our dentist, was saying that yesterday.

MILLER: —I think the artist's groanings often come out in a more poetic way.

Sometimes I am embarrassed about what I create. I seem to feel so deeply when I write something, and three weeks later, when I look at it, I think, "Did I really feel that deeply?" Artists often overstate their emotions. It's typical of neurotic artistic types.

DOOR: Hmm. You are an artist *and* a Southern Baptist preacher. You certainly don't fit the mold of most Southern Baptist preachers we know . . . er . . . except when you took an offering when we arrived. Just who is Calvin Miller?

MILLER: We find out who we are by how we find ourselves acting. I have no idea what the content of my life really is. I know I have a hunger for excellence. I think artists (and I'm not sure I am one) have a dream of leaving something behind when they die. I have always loved the words of Robert Sherman in a song from the movie *Mary Poppins*—"A man has dreams of walking with giants to carve his niche in the edifice of time. Before the mortar of his zeal has a chance to congeal, the cup is dashed from his lips, the flame is snuffed aborning, and he's brought to rack and ruin in his prime." I think all of us have a fear of being brought to rack and ruin before we've really done anything or said anything. We all would like life to continue.

Ernie Becker, in his book *The Denial of Death*, says that we deny death in one of two ways: either by becoming a hero or by worshiping a hero. People dream of escaping anonymity. I'm not sure what that says about me, but I do know I want to do the best job that I can.

Ayn Rand defined art as "man defining himself." Art *is* an attempt at self-definition. I don't think any artist can be satisfied with the mediocre. I remember backpacking to a waterfall in New Mexico a few years ago. I painted a picture while I was there. I wanted it to be a great picture. But the more I painted, the worse the painting became. When I finished the painting, I didn't want my name on it. So I signed the name "Kris Kringle" to it, and I left it in the wilderness leaning up against a tree. I was unwilling for that picture to stand for something that I had done. That painting was not me, and I didn't want my name on it. I actually gave someone one of my paintings and then took it back a few years later because I didn't want that earlier painting to be a definition of who I am. I also bought the copyrights on my first five books. I am very embarrassed about some of the early things I wrote, and I don't want to have those books out there alongside *The Singer*—whatever value they might have. They will never be in print again. I am very excited about that because I don't want those books to represent me. They are not me.

DOOR: What good writers do you read?

MILLER: Secular writers, for the most part.

DOOR: What? No Tammy Faye Bakker?

MILLER: The trouble with most popular evangelical writers is that they are very predictable. You know what they are going to say and how they are going to say it. If you know how a person thinks and how they are going to answer every question—often without any artistry—then what's the point? I learn so much from people whose theology I don't agree with. I learn from people who don't have *any* theology. I even enjoy reading the work of secular humanists.

DOOR: You didn't say "secular humanists," did you?

MILLER: I don't happen to believe that humanism is a conspiracy. Most secular humanists I know are not conspirators. They work in various fields. It doesn't matter where they work. They don't get up every morning, put on black clothes, and slink down the street trying to kill Christians or figure out a way to destroy the church. Secular humanists go to work in laboratories, offices, and schools. Jonas Salk works in science and, I might add, we readily accept Dr. Salk's vaccine even though he would be considered a secular humanist. So while we're out there criticizing these great minds and great people, we continue to benefit from everything they have done. To enjoy the blessings given to us by such people and then lump them all together into one basket seems a bit hypocritical.

I find myself growing from people like Rene Dubois, the late J. Bronkowski, Lewis Mumford, Barbara Tuchmann, and even Carl Sagan.

DOOR: Please. Anyone but Carl Sagan.

MILLER: In terms of poetry, I am big on Dylan Thomas, Gerard Manley Hopkins, and Emily Dickinson.

DOOR: Surely there are some Christian writers. . . .

MILLER: There are two or three outstanding Christian writers: Frederick Buechner, Walter Wangerin, Virginia Stem Owens, and Madeleine L'Engle.

DOOR: That's four.

MILLER: That's four what?

DOOR: You said there were two or three outstanding Christian writers, but you named four.

MILLER: Is this interview over yet?

DOOR: If Christian writers are so bad, why do they sell so many books?

MILLER: Most of the popular books are popular because the writer has succeeded in some other area. Chuck Swindoll, Chuck Colson, James Dobson are all bouncing off something that has made them well-known. There just aren't many evangelical books that are popular because they are written well. There are some pastors—like Stephen Brown—who write well.

DOOR: That's encouraging—one pastor who can write. But then, evangelicals are not exactly known for their great writing, are they?

MILLER: Unfortunately, that's true, because the whole evangelical scene is a very "gross-national-product" kind of affair. Everything is evaluated in light of the product.

DOOR: What product?

MILLER: The product is what comes down the aisle after singing "Just As I Am." If the product is the only justification for art, then nothing can have value merely because it's beautiful. So if a person paints a picture or writes a poem that isn't about Jesus—even though it's beautiful—it doesn't count. I've always agreed with James that "every perfect gift comes down from the Father." I believe that great art of any kind comes from God, even if it's created by an atheist.

DOOR: What do you think about Christian music?

MILLER: Unfortunately, nowadays, music in the church is usually celebrated on a very shallow level. The music and the lyrics are very "ditty-like." So much of the music today is simply relational little songs that you clap or sing to. It is not the kind of music that is in the tradition of great composers.

DOOR: In one of your books you say, "Gospel music has been a mood-centered movement. This adoration has spawned a kind of giddy populism that speaks sweet of Jesus but does not always appear intelligent. There is no hunger to *know*, only to *feel* Christ."

MILLER: Absolutely. People come into church looking for love. Certainly, healing does come from touching each other and hugging each other. But church services must do more than just give us mood-centered experiences. A good sermon must not only inspire; it must also instruct. And the instruction must be solid enough that it is remembered for a lifetime. A good sermon is one from which people have learned something and have had their minds stimulated. Sermons should not be entirely emotive.

A good worship service motivates people to use their hearts *and* their minds in worship. Using stories laden with emotional impact to make people feel guilty or to get people down the aisle may make the minister feel good, but people need to encounter Christ. People's wills need to be changed. Sermons need to reach into people's minds and result in a change for the better over the long haul.

DOOR: Don't you think it's the function of the sermon to motivate people to make decisions about the things in their lives which need to be changed?

MILLER: People don't come down the aisle because of anybody's sermon. I have found that almost anytime a person makes an emotional decision in our church, it is not because they were motivated by my sermon. They didn't hear my sermon and start to cry. *They were crying when they came into the service.* We flatter ourselves, sometimes, by thinking that people make great emotional responses because of our sermons.

DOOR: You're not saying the sermon isn't important, are you?

MILLER: Of course not. Just overrated. To be honest, part of the problem in evangelical circles is that there is a tremendous lack of imagination in preaching. Most sermons preached in evangelical churches could have been preached a hundred years ago because there is no effort to relate to the modern world.

DOOR: You are primarily known as a writer, but you are also a pastor. What do you see as the greatest challenge of the modern pastor?

MILLER: The greatest challenge for any minister is modeling the Christ-life. I agree with what Lincoln said: "The world will little note nor long remember what we say here." The quality of person that we are stands over us—as Emerson said, it "thunders so loud people cannot hear what we say." When I live out the Christ-life, it makes real what I say.

DOOR: Someone has said that we often talk about the "priesthood of the believer" but say nothing about the "priesthood of the pastor."

MILLER: I knew you would try to get me in trouble with my fellow Southern Baptists. The truth is, a lot of people come to my office and tell me what's on their heart for the same reasons that a Catholic would go to a confessional and talk with a priest. Carlisle Barney said that Christians are priests to each other. That's true. We are priests to each other if we remember that the priest is a go-between. I define a priest as "common soil"—that square yard of dirt on which people meet God. Walt Whitman said, "If you want me, look for me beneath the soles of your feet." I guess, as a pastor, I would want to say, "If you want me, look for me under the soles of your feet, as you stand on a little plot of soil that is my life to make friends with God." Priests do that. Priests introduce people to God.

DOOR: Since we've already created some problems for you with your Southern Baptist brothers and sisters, let's keep going. We've all heard about the fighting and feuding going on among Southern Baptists. It all came to a head at the Southern Baptist Convention last summer. How do you feel about what's going on in the Southern Baptist church?

MILLER: I'm embarrassed by the current "theological crisis" that is going on in the Southern Baptist church—especially since I'm here in the North. There aren't many Southern Baptists in Omaha. In fact, in my city of 700,000 people there are less than 3000 Southern Baptists. Omaha is a mission field for Southern Baptists, and I have always believed that the Bible is not up for debate on the mission field. Most of the people in my church haven't heard that there is a crisis, and I'm not going to tell them about it. In the book of Nehemiah, Nehemiah is on the wall, the city is in rubble behind him, and the enemy is out in front of him. The people want to hear the Word of God at that moment. Not one person brings up the subject of inerrancy. The crisis of their lives, at that moment, was too severe. They didn't have time to debate the Bible. And that is what bothers me about this whole thing. Great debates over medicine do not erupt on the battlefield. The debates erupt in institutions where everything is settled and calm. Quarrels about inerrancy erupt in places like Texas where everyone says they are born again.

DOOR: But isn't the battle going on with the Southern Baptists more than just a battle about the inerrancy of Scripture? Isn't it a battle between conservative and liberal?

MILLER: Frankly, I don't think most Southern Baptists care what you believe. What they want to know is if you're on their side. Sadly, it has become an issue of power more than an issue of truth.

HENRI NOUWEN

Henri Nouwen is from Holland, a chaplain for the Holland-America cruise-ship line, an author, professor, and, most of all, a priest who understands and loves the common man. Henri has lived and worked with the prisoner, the handicapped, the laborer in the mines, and the poor in South America.

Although he has often rubbed shoulders with the rich and elite, you get the feeling that he is uncomfortable with such people. He seems much more at home with your basic, ordinary person. Maybe that is why he consented to be interviewed by your basic, ordinary magazine.

Father Nouwen has written a number of very helpful books including, *The Wounded Healer*, *Reaching Out*, *Love in a Fearful Land*, *Lifesigns*, *The Road to Daybreak*, and *Letters to Marc About Jesus*. This interview took place in 1985 at Harvard and was done by the *Door*'s token Harvard Divinity School correspondent, James D. Smith III.

DOOR: You are a priest, but you also have an extensive background in psychology. Many people in the church are leery of psychology. They think it's dangerous. Obviously, you don't. Why not?

NOUWEN: There is much in Scripture that actually enriches psychological concepts. In psychology, we talk a lot about "contracts." But, for those of us who are pastors, we have a much richer concept—the covenant. God didn't make contracts with his people. He made covenants. The concept of the covenant in the Old and New Testaments helps us to understand the nature of a helping relationship. Understanding a contract is helpful, but put into the biblical perspective of a covenant (where, even though there are limits to *our* faithfulness, God is always faithful), it broadens our view of what it means to minister to others.

DOOR: What *does* it mean to minister to others?

NOUWEN: First of all, your prayer life and your ministry are not two separate things. In order to understand what it means to minister, you have to ask what it means to lay down your life for your friends. Laying down your life doesn't mean to be killed or to be a physical martyr. It means that you make your own relationship with God the source of healing and new life for the people to whom you minister. Some people think that your spiritual life is your private life with God, and then your ministry is helping people and preaching to people. They see their spiritual life as a private relationship with God and their ministry as a place where they help others but keep themselves out of the relationship. No. It is *our* relationship with God that *is* the source of our ministry. So when you preach, you shouldn't be an exhibitionist, but you should use your own faith experiences. You want to heal people, but you want to be aware of your own woundedness. That's not a bad thing, because your own experiences of failure and sinfulness can indeed be a source of bringing the Good News. On the other hand, if your wounds haven't been taken care of and you're bleeding all over the place, then you'd better stay out of the pulpit for a while. To lay down our life for others means that we make our own faith experience a source of healing for others. That's what *The Wounded Healer* is about.

DOOR: You are Catholic, but you don't *seem* very Catholic.

NOUWEN: Well, my language is not very Roman Catholic, and I've never felt very attracted to the typical Roman Catholic ecclesiastical problems. In fact, many people do not even know that I am a Roman Catholic. But I *am* very Catholic. I personally like to worship God by using pictures or icons or candles. I need something to see,

something to smell, or something to touch. I still pray the rosary. I like to touch the beads because I feel very strongly that worship involves the whole body.

DOOR: *Now* you are sounding more Catholic. Some of our Protestant readers out there may be breaking out in a cold sweat.

NOUWEN: I speak in many Protestant churches, and I have been in many Protestant services. I like a lot of what they do, but on the whole their worship is very much directed to the mind. But we are getting off the subject. . . .

DOOR: But we are getting off the subject. We are pointing out that, other than your lapse a few minutes ago, you don't seem very Catholic.

NOUWEN: It is just that my psychological training made me aware that the real issues cut much deeper than whether someone is a Catholic or not.

DOOR: What *are* some of those deeper issues?

NOUWEN: The real spiritual issues are questions like, What does it mean to belong? What is faithfulness? What is commitment? How do you deal with loneliness? How do you move from loneliness to solitude?

DOOR: What, in your opinion, is the most important issue that people are struggling with today?

NOUWEN: Fear.

DOOR: Fear of what?

NOUWEN: There are many kinds of fear. First, there are the inner fears. (I am a terribly fearful person. For example, I am afraid of my own inner life, my own passions and struggles, the unknown within me, the demons within me.) Inner fears not only make us fearful of what we are like, but they keep us from saying what we feel to others.

Another kind of fear is fear of the other, the fear of the stranger. There is an enormous amount of fear today of the person who is not like us because of color, race, or sex. When I travel this country, I am overwhelmed by the fear people have for the stranger. We lock everything up. We are constantly afraid that someone will attack us or rob our house. We are afraid of the Latin Americans—that they might cross the border and take our jobs. We are afraid of the Russians.

There is also the fear of God. Even though many people might have a solid healthy theology about God, they still have the fear that one day God is going to get them. Even though many of us have learned a lot of good things about God, still there is this fear that when we get to heaven our computer print-out had better look good. There is this fear that God is a stranger even though the gospel keeps telling us that God is not a stranger. In fact, I see the Bible as an ongoing plea from God to us saying, "Come closer."

DOOR: How does one deal with these fears?

NOUWEN: You don't attack fear directly. Fear engenders fear. Obviously, there are times when you have to look at your fear, when you have to be aware of your fear. But letting go of fear is only possible when you are in love. It's fascinating that, in Scripture, the opposite of love is not hate but fear. Jesus kept saying, "Don't be afraid, it's me. You have to pay attention to me." In other words, we have to pay attention to the place where love is. We must go where love is. To the degree which people are in touch with love, to *that* degree, people can let go

of their fear. I know for myself, if I feel that I am really loved and someone attacks me or screams at me, it hurts me but it doesn't destroy me.

DOOR: Love casts out fear. Hmm. We think we've seen that written somewhere.

NOUWEN: Yes. In a strange way, when we know we are loved, life is no longer full of strangers. Somehow, alienation, separation, and the sense of not belonging or of being alone, disappear once we have the sense of being really loved. That is what happened with the apostles. They knew they were so fully loved that they were willing to leave father, mother, sister, and brother. They traveled the world and still felt at home. They never felt "not-at-home." There is a sense of belonging that love gives. Love does not keep you from having any fear at all—fear creeps up on us all the time—but it does cause fear to lose its manipulative power over us. Our decisions should increasingly be made on the basis of love, not on the basis of fear.

DOOR: What do you mean we should make decisions out of love, not out of fear?

NOUWEN: Well, frankly, my concern with the anti-nuclear movement and with *all* the issue movements is that sometimes people are acting out of fear more than they are acting out of love. It worries me when people try to scare others into things like, "If you don't do this, then you're going to lose your job," or "There is going to be nuclear war," or "You're going to get a terrible illness." That's what the world *wants* us to do—act out of fear. Getting us to buy into the agenda of fear is how people have power over us.

There is a story about two monks.

One of the monks said to the other, "We have never had a conflict. We don't even know how it feels to have a conflict. Let's have one, just for the fun of it, and see how it works." The other monk asked, "How do we have a conflict?" The first monk replied, "I'll put this brick between us. I will say that it is mine and you will reply by saying, 'No, no. That brick is mine.' And then we'll have a conflict." So the first monk placed the brick between them and said, "This brick is mine!" The other monk replied, "Well, if it's yours, take it!"

They could not have a conflict.

Fear is always connected to something we want to hold on to. It is true at a personal level and at a national level. The world tries to rule us by fear. The Christian is the person who says, "No. Love is stronger than fear."

DOOR: That's interesting, because it seems like there are many in the church who are opting for power nowadays.

NOUWEN: People who are afraid are always interested in power. Whereas people who are in love are always willing to give up power. That is what Jesus did, and that is what everyone who is in love says.

DOOR: So far, what you are saying sounds terrific. But *how* do we, as you said earlier, "go where the love is"?

NOUWEN: You nurture the places of love. That means prayer, because prayer is the central way of experiencing love. I wish we had more time to talk about prayer, because a lot of prayers are prayers of fear. And when that happens, it's not prayer anymore. Prayer is entering into communication with the unconditional love of God. That's what prayer is all about.

DOOR: What does it mean to be a spiritual person?

NOUWEN: The spiritual life is the life in which you try to fulfill the great commandment which says that we are to love God with all our heart, with all our soul, and with all our mind, and we are to love our neighbor as ourself. That's very important because there are many who think that means we give thirty-three percent to God, thirty-three percent to neighbor, and thirty-three percent to ourselves. The spiritual life means we love God with our *whole* heart, our *whole* soul, and our *whole* mind, and as a result we discover who our neighbor is and who we are. That's one way of looking at it.

DOOR: Keep going.

NOUWEN: The spiritual life is the life of God's Spirit within us. Jesus said, "It is good for you that I leave because unless I leave I cannot send the Spirit. And when I leave I will send the Spirit and he will lead you into full truth." Truth does not mean doctrines; it means betrothal. In other words, the Spirit will lead us into a full relationship (betrothal) with God. The spiritual life is God's breath in us. Paul said we can't even pray unless the Spirit prays in us. Jesus said that all he knew from God was for *us* to know as well. He didn't say that he knew a lot and we would get to know a few things. Jesus invites us to live the same life he lived.

DOOR: Now you're on a roll.

NOUWEN: Another way to speak of the spiritual life is to remember that the spiritual life *is* the Christian life. It's not something on top of the Christian life. It's not unique or special. The spiritual life is not a life that has something to *do* with prayer or monasteries. It is the core. *It is the Christian life.*

DOOR: Why does it seem that more and more people seem to be turned off by religion?

NOUWEN: Because most people don't see its connection with their life anymore. Churches, ministers, and sermons are not connecting with people's basic needs. People don't experience religion enhancing their lives. In fact, it appears to many of them that religion is the enemy.

Another problem is that, in this country, Christianity is a moral system. It's a behavioral system. Religion tells you what you are supposed to do and not supposed to do. It is perceived by many as a sort of policeman. To many, the church is becoming a "no-sayer." It tells people they can't do this and they can't do that. People don't realize that the spiritual life is a life in Christ where one can experience the joy and beauty of God. People will be willing to accept the discipline of the church if they are aware that there is a treasure to go after. And that treasure is that God wants to love us. When Jesus questions Peter, "Do you love me?" he then says to feed his lambs, his sheep, and to go to work. It's interesting, isn't it, that Jesus first asks, "Are you burning with love?" He knew that someone who is really in love doesn't even notice the suffering.

A lot of people have a hard time with Christianity because they look at the *last* thing Jesus said (about going the way of the cross), and they miss the *first* thing, which is that Jesus is a revelation of God's love. One of the reasons the charismatic movement is so successful is because it is bringing people back to that fact.

DOOR: Frankly, we don't see much of that "burning love" you are talking about.

NOUWEN: Christianity has to start dealing with this. We have to start dealing with this "mystical" quality to the faith.

DOOR: Mystical?

NOUWEN: For many people, mystical means unreal. They are wrong. Mystical means real. It is the intimate quality of the spiritual life. God is a jealous God. He wants lovers. He wants us to respond to him. Too many people still think of Jesus as someone who lived long ago. When you think of Jesus this way, you *remember* him. You tell stories about him. You are inspired by his example. But that is only *part* of the Christian life. Jesus is the risen Lord who is *now* among us. He is present here and now. He is not just someone who lived long ago. God is the God of the present—of this moment. We have to learn to live in the present. We have to learn to live in communion with God.

DOOR: You left teaching at Yale and went to Latin America. Why?

NOUWEN: From the very first moment I came to the United States, I wanted to know Spanish, because I felt that the future of the U.S. would depend very much on how we related to the Latin American world. I knew that from the very beginning. I knew that was going to be *the* question in the eighties and nineties. It's becoming more apparent every day. I felt that you couldn't be a real American if you didn't know Spanish.

DOOR: Si.

NOUWEN: So I went to language school in Bolivia. I feel North America and South America, from a spiritual perspective, are so intimately con-

nected to one another that if we are to understand the Word of God in North America 'we have to know how the Word of God works in Latin America.
DOOR: And what did you learn from Latin America?
NOUWEN: I originally went there to help. I felt that I had come from a wealthy, abundant culture—not only financially, but also educationally—and that, therefore, I needed to dedicate part of my life to the poor. However, what I found was that, in a spiritual sense, *they* are the wealthy ones. I found, amongst the poor and the oppressed, an enormous amount of spiritual gifts. I have never been in a place where I have seen so much joy or gratitude or care as I saw in Latin America. I also saw violence and poverty and injustice. But the closer I came to the people, the more I saw how God loved these people and how these people were richly blessed in the midst of their poverty and misery. I discovered that my task was not to bring them goodies but, instead, to allow them to give their gifts to me. I began to realize that it was more important for me to bring the Good News from the people of Latin America back to America. I began to see that it was more important for me to share the fruits of their sufferings for *our* conversion.
DOOR: So you came back to Harvard to share what you had learned about Latin America?
NOUWEN: I came here primarily to share what I learned about *Christ* in Latin America, not to talk about liberation theology or the Sandinistas. I feel the Latin American people can teach us a lot about peace, about joy, about the love of God, and about the Spirit of God. There is a lot of interest in Latin

America here. Americans want to know what Latin Americans do and how they do it. But I believe it is *more* important for us to learn about the faith of the Latin American people. They are oppressed and live under enormous pressure, but they have a very pure faith—an enormous faith and an enormous love. A deep spiritual life exists in the people there. We need to learn about the quality of spiritual life. But, to be honest, I have been overwhelmed by how terribly serious people are over here.
DOOR: What do you mean, "serious"?
NOUWEN: People in this country are always worrying about something. They worry about money. They worry about relationships. They worry about their image and about how well known they are. In my opinion, that kind of worrying is very unchristian. The people in Latin America are not that way. They are much more able to live in the present. We have so much to learn from the poor. They are much more joyful than the rich.
DOOR: So when you returned from Latin America, you found an abundance of spiritual poverty in America?
NOUWEN: Yes. Somehow Americans need to discover that their worth and identity are not connected with their importance, or with how much money they make, or how many cars they own. True self-identity and self-worth is rooted in God. The deepest sense of who we are is rooted in the fact that we are loved.

Americans need to learn about joy and gratitude. They need to learn about forgiveness. They need to become vulnerable and quit clinging so much to success so that they can discover the joy and peace of Christ. They need to go beyond the competitiveness of our society. The gospel is critical of a highly competitive way of life that drives us to excel and to win at any cost. The drive for "upward mobility" is causing people to lose touch with Christ, who has called us to "downward mobility." We cannot have community when everyone is competing. There is real suffering going on right here. There are so many Americans who are so lonely, so isolated, and so guilt-ridden, and they are choosing the adulation of the world as a means of coping. The people of Latin America are suffering, too, with poverty and oppression. But many of them have at least discovered real joy and real peace.

DOOR: What you have said has the ring of truth to it. So many of us in this country experience extreme spiritual poverty. We know we are impoverished, but we can't seem to do anything about it. Why?

NOUWEN: Being a Christian in America doesn't require a great cost. You can be a Christian and fully participate in the secular culture. I have a sense that, more and more, being a Christian in this country will require a choice. The Christian will have to be willing to make big sacrifices. (The Sanctuary Movement is a good example.)

Right now, in this culture, you can have your cake and eat it too. But that is an illusion. You cannot be a fat sprinter. If you want to sprint to the kingdom, you had better be lean.

WALTER WANGERIN

We met at the airport in Evansville, Indiana. That's right, Evansville. Interesting town. Oh . . . yeah. Walter Wangerin lives there. And, believe it or not, there is a school there . . . er . . . a university. The University of Evansville. We're not kidding.

Walter Wangerin met us at the airport. He was totally decked out for an Evansville summer—white shirt, white shorts, white socks, white shoes, and, of course, the coveted Evansville tan (beyond white). We thought we'd stumbled into an Assembly of God pastor's convention. But Walter Wangerin is a Lutheran . . . well . . . some Lutherans wonder about that . . . um . . . he went to Seminex.

Walter drove us around Evansville to see the points of interest. Five minutes later we were at his house.

Until 1985 Walter Wangerin was the pastor of a small, mostly black, inner-city congregation: Grace Lutheran Church. He is currently writing full-time (aided by his wife, an author's administrator for him) and working on his tan.

Walter Wangerin has written a number of best-selling books, including *The Book of the Dun Cow, The Book of Sorrows, Ragman and Other Cries of Faith, As for Me and My House: Crafting a Marriage To Last, Miz Lil and the Chronicles of Grace*, and *The Orphean Passages*.

Walter Wangerin is an eloquent preacher and a gifted writer. He is a deeply passionate and committed man who takes his faith *and* its implications seriously . . . even though he doesn't look too good in shorts. After you read this interview, we think you'll join us in the hope that we'll hear much more from Walter Wangerin in the future.

DOOR: If the Christian faith is true, then why doesn't it work better than it does? It seems like more and more people who call themselves Christians are bailing out of the faith or, at best, are not able to consistently stick with their faith. Why is that?

WANGERIN: It is because we no longer value covenants. We have raised the rights of the individual to such a celestial level that the value of the covenant has been lost. We give more credence to individual whims, desires, and rights, than we do to covenants. That is worth grieving over because there is something very valuable and trustworthy about covenants. If that value could be recognized, then our society could begin experiencing the blessing of covenants. So, for example, if you covenant with your subscribers to publish a magazine on time, then you—

DOOR: Hey, wait a minute. Let's don't get off the subject. What do you mean by "the blessing of covenants"?

WANGERIN: Covenants are difficult. Often you don't know what the covenant is in the beginning. All you know is that it exists. You discover *what* the covenant is in the painful, passionate business of living it out. And, if the covenant is real, if the commitment is real—even not knowing the future, even though we have no idea what the covenant is going to be—then a third being comes to exist between us (the parties who make the covenant). It has a life of its own, and it grows if it has the opportunity. *That* is a blessing. It is a blessing from the beginning because it holds us together while we discover what the covenant is and what the relationship is going to be. The covenant itself creates an arena for discovering and working out relationships. But covenants take time. In fact, they require time. You have to trust that the other person isn't going to cut and run. But when the members of society are too eager to cut and run, covenants cannot flourish.

DOOR: Are there any times when the breaking of a covenant is the lesser of two evils?

WANGERIN: I guess I would have to say yes, but I say it reluctantly. I have suffered with people through the obviously necessary decision of divorce.

DOOR: Why do you say "reluctantly"?

WANGERIN: Because I have seen the suffering that occurs when people get divorced, and so often it is a wasted suffering. It is a suffering that does not finally heal or bless or bring people to a new level of understanding. But suffering under the covenant and with the covenant, with the third being living between the parties, isn't a wasted suffering. It is often a generative suffering, a creative suffering. It is suffering, nonetheless; but if it arises out of covenant, then those who have made the covenant can grow wise and strong. They can grow into something different from what either one of them were, because the suffering forced them into new territory. Then the covenant becomes the blessing. It is a blessing from the beginning even though it feels like imprisonment at certain times.

DOOR: In response to what you have just said, what does the church do? Do we sound the alarm and prophetically call this society back to honoring their covenants?

WANGERIN: Historically, among the people of God, there have always been both prophets and priests. Priests consoled and comforted and tried to ease the relationship between God and the people. Priests said positive things and gave strokes to the people. But the prophets were different. They cried out against sinfulness. And, when the prophets cried out against sin, they generally cried out to the people of

God. (Even though prophets, like Amos, would speak to the nations around Israel, their strongest words were reserved for the people of Israel who knew the Law and knew the Lord.) Jeremiah spoke to Israel. Isaiah spoke to Israel. The prophets did not speak to the whole world. They spoke to the people of God.

DOOR: Hmm. What does that say about people like Jerry Falwell, Jimmy Swaggart, and others who are trying to call America back to God?

WANGERIN: I have a problem with any Christian who intends to be a prophet for the whole nation—especially when they are very harsh on secular society and very kind to the people of God and to the church. They have it reversed. They have forgotten a significant principle of prophecy: *Prophecy is to be spoken to those who have the Law, know the Law, and have messed up on the law.*

DOOR: In other words, these modern-day prophets should be speaking the prophetic word to their churches and not to the nation.

WANGERIN: Yes. Prophets are strange people. More often than not, the prophets are oddballs. They are often lonely outcasts who are never invited to anyone's parties. But what I see today are "prophets" who are unwilling to be outcasts. They are unwilling to experience the isolation and the loneliness that it takes to be a prophet. I am afraid it is not much of a witness if you are unwilling to die.

DOOR: It almost appears like these churches and organizations have decided to fight power with power.

WANGERIN: Well, the trouble is that these churches are generally using an Old Testament model instead of a New Testament model. The model for the church today should be Christ, not Jeremiah. Christ's action was diametrically different from the action of power. He suffered. He died. He evidenced the consequence of our sin right before our eyes in bloody dramatic fashion. When the church tries to arrogate power to enforce its righteous principles upon the whole world, it is in no way dying. This is in no way a sacrifice.

DOOR: Sacrifice. Interesting word. Seems like the church is always asking us to sacrifice. It usually means financially, of course.

WANGERIN: But sacrifice must always be self-sacrifice. We can never demand or command another one to make a sacrifice for us. I am the only one I can command into sacrifice. Jesus said, "Tell my disciples that I go before them." He was implying that his disciples can expect to go where he went and to have the same life he did. Jesus was, of course, whispering the comforting word to those who would face persecution. But I think he was also declaring the harder word. He was suggesting that if we follow him, he will go before us, but *both* of us will go to Jerusalem again. If we follow him, we will end up on a cross. A cross is giving up. A cross is sacrifice. That is very clear. A church that cares about power—the power of a large membership, power in the world, political power, television power, or persuasive opinion power—doesn't know the principle of sacrifice. Sacrifice is a word a power-hungry church just doesn't understand.

DOOR: So if someone says, "Sacrifice $1000 to our ministry and you will receive a blessing," what would you say?

WANGERIN: A sacrifice *does* hold a blessing. But sacrifice is always the blessing for another. When the bullock died on the altar, it got nothing for its death. When Jesus hung on the cross, the blessing was the world's and not his own. His resurrection was not the reward for having died; it was the declaration to the world that the dying worked.

DOOR: Uh . . . how about this? "If you sacrifice $1000 to this ministry, you will prosper"? What would you say to that?

WANGERIN: They are using the wrong word. The word they should use is not "sacrifice." The word is "invest." To suffer now for a later reward is not sacrifice.

DOOR: Let's go back to our original question—the question of what is causing the decline of faith in this country. You have given one cause— the deterioration of the value of the covenant. What else is contributing to the decline of faith in this society?

WANGERIN: The misunderstanding or the misuse of the word *faith*. The word *faith* can be used in many ways, of course. It can mean "a body of beliefs," but my fear is that we have made "a body of beliefs" the only definition of faith. As a result, real faith is being suffocated. *Faith is a relationship with the living God which is enacted in this world as well as in the world to come.* I have chosen every one of those words carefully. Faith is a relationship with the *living God*, not a stone god. By "living God" I mean a being who is alive and who is, where we are concerned, a changing God. The contradiction is that God is also the same yesterday, today, and forever. He is the God who never changes. That is a marvel. "Living God" does not mean God is like an eternal sun that just keeps burning whether

we are here or not. A living God lives in relationship to us like a ewe sheep lives in a relationship to its little lamb. It's a caring, watchful, directive, punishing, disciplining relationship. As a parent, one minute I am overwhelmed with love for my children, and just a few minutes later I can be so angry at them. My feelings change toward my children, but my love does not change.

DOOR: But what does faith look like?

WANGERIN: Faith looks different at different periods. Sometimes faith looks pious. Sometimes faith looks like dying. Sometimes faith looks like doubt. Faith can even look like despair. Each one of these faces are different peaks of the same mountain range. The problem is that the church often wants to latch onto one face of faith and give the impression that one characteristic is all that faith is. So they turn that one characteristic into a standard instead of recognizing that it is only an experience in the process of faith.

DOOR: All right, you've intrigued us. What do you mean faith can look like despair?

WANGERIN: For you and I to know forgiveness, we must first know our sin. I cannot know *my* forgiveness until I am first desolated by *my* sin. There must be a time when I lay my head down and say, "The Lord cannot love me," and mean it because I do not like what I see when I look at myself. When I finally become honest, when all the clothing falls away and I look at my spiritual nakedness and it is ugly, and when I can feel the Lord turn away from such ugliness—*then* "My God, my God, why have you forsaken me?" becomes more than just a question. It becomes a cry—a despairing acknowledgment of my forsaken state. At that very point, I am in the pigpen with the prodigal son. There is no hope, no healing possible. It is the end. Desolation and despair. That is necessary. It is an essential part of the drama.

DOOR: Now you have us depressed. Is this despair really necessary to faith?

WANGERIN: In order for grief to be true and valuable, in order for despair to be good and blessed, we have to come to the place where we can see no farther *than* the despair or the grief. It's terrible. Only when we deserve nothing and something comes anyway, can we know what grace is. Grace is undeserved. You can't just toss grace around like it is just another word. You can't teach people the doctrine of grace. Well, you can teach the doctrine of grace, but we cannot *know* grace until we are prepared to live the rest of our lives as a death apart from God . . . and then God comes and loves us nevertheless. We will never know the "nevertheless" of God until we have suffered.

DOOR: Somehow, it is hard to put despair and faith together.

WANGERIN: I understand. When we see someone in despair, we wonder if this person believes in anything. In fact, he or she is believing very much, and he or she is believing more than a lot of us whose faith is nothing more than feeling good when we sing "Amazing Grace."

DOOR: You make faith sound so difficult.

WANGERIN: Faith is work. It is a struggle. You must struggle with all your heart.

DOOR: What do you mean by struggle? Pray? Read the Bible?

WANGERIN: Yes. Do all that stuff. But just remember that those things are not the end; they are the means to God. They prepare you and, on the way, God will ambush you. All those things teach you the language so that when someone finally speaks the language, you understand it.

DOOR: If we're honest, we cannot help but feel a sense of panic as we watch what is happening in this society. We want desperately to *do* something. Not only are people running off after other gods, but these other gods are seducing all of us. There is something in us that wants to go smash down the false gods and force people into worshiping the one and only true God.

WANGERIN: That is a temptation, but we have to remember that false idols always fail. If you trust the wrong thing, the wrong thing will fail you. What you and I need to do for those who are trusting in false gods is to watch, wait, and be there, because the false gods *will* fall—but we do not precipitate that fall. Just look at Jeremiah. The whole time Jeremiah spoke to Israel, Israel did not listen. Jeremiah hoped from the beginning, silly fellow, that his words would change the people and wake them. But things did not go as Jeremiah planned. The people did not listen to Jeremiah. In fact, his words irritated the pants off of them, and then they were carried off into exile. Jeremiah died without seeing the people changed or awakened, but the false god had failed. And when the exile was in full force, the people remembered the words of Jeremiah. Those words, which were all empty and vacuous during Jeremiah's time, suddenly became substantive and real during the Exile. So Jeremiah says the words and they have no effect and he dies. But after he died, God put meaning into the words and the experience of people.

The same principle applies to us. As a pastor, I get upset when I see someone whose life is on a collision course with disaster. I am upset and torn because they won't listen to my advice. But, finally, I realize that the crisis is often what God uses to put meaning into the words that God spoke through me.

DOOR: What you are saying is that people have to experience the truth, not just hear it.

WANGERIN: Exactly. What we *don't* want to do in this culture is to reach out and snatch people's false gods away from them. That is not effectual because the people will hold onto their false gods all the more, and they will hate us besides. Instead, what we should do is to continue to speak the truth and continue to define the consequence. God is writing the script. God is directing the play. We are the reviewers who describe what the play means so that, when our society faces a crisis, it can remember the truth we spoke. But we must wait for God to put meaning to our words.

DOOR: Okay. We've talked about what faith looks like. Let's push that question a bit further. What difference does faith make? Shouldn't there be a distinguishable result of faith in our lives?

WANGERIN: Yes, there should be a difference. But the difference isn't in the surface things (drinking, smoking, dancing, or whatever). We should be different at our core, at our hearts. "A new commandment I give unto you, that you love one another," Jesus said. But he added five words to that statement because he knew us. He knew we would compromise the concept of love and try to take all the power and the pain out of it. So he added, "as I have loved you." How did Jesus love us? Through the Cross and his death. Sacrifice. We are different, all right. And that difference is a costly difference. But it is also a quiet difference. It is an invisible difference because the precise character of this love is that it doesn't look for, nor reap, reward. You don't get an Oscar for this kind of love. No one writes a magazine article about you because no one knows who you are. It is an unpublic love. Ultimately, the love will become visible. But the lover never does. The Christian is different—not in degree but in kind—from the rest of the world, and doesn't even know it.

DOOR: What about the overt differences like smoking, drinking, and the rest? Are you saying those differences don't matter?

WANGERIN: Pieties, such as you have just mentioned, *do* matter. But they are not between me and the world; they are between me and God. They are blessed in that they are the way I can concretely discover, *for myself*, the difference in my soul. They are *not* blessed for announcing my difference to the world. Yes, piety has its place. I want to underline and italicize that. Those pieties (not drinking, not smoking, or whatever) are good for meditation. They are good for working out the walk. But pieties are not good to hang like bangles on your being so that I can see what a good person you are. The only thing people ought to see is that we love them.

DOOR: That all sounds great, but all of us *do* expect faith to have observable consequences. All of us have people of faith whom we look up to because they prove to us that deep commitment is possible. And when these people fall—as a lot of them have done lately—our faith is shaken because we *do* equate true faith with observable differences.

WANGERIN: But what you are really saying is that sometimes the *object* of our faith is the wrong thing. Sometimes, instead of trusting in the Lord directly, we trust in intermediate things between God and us. So we end up trusting in a certain person, instead of in the God of that person. So when that person fails or falls, we are devastated. But that is good. Remember what I said earlier? Anytime we trust in a false god, that false god will fail us somewhere along the way. That is a devastating experience. But the blessing is that *when* the false god fails, the true God becomes apparent and you can put the false god in perspective. Let me give you an example. You have a godly, wonderful pastor whom you greatly admire. He fails you. He commits adultery, and your faith begins to collapse. But in the process, you begin to discover the true God in Jesus Christ, and you realize that you don't need your pastor for faith. You begin to trust in God and discover, in your relationship with him, the purity of forgiveness. So you return to your pastor and you pastor him. You evidence forgiveness to him. You wash his face, set him up once again to his position, and allow him to continue to serve as evidence of the Lord's forgiveness and presence.

DOOR: So where does hope come from? Obviously, it doesn't come from looking to other people. Certainly, it is ultimately in Jesus. But what does it look like?

WANGERIN: Hope and love are not far apart. The best example *I* can give you of how the two are intertwined is to look at the relationship between my wife and me. When we are apart, my love fires my hope that we will be together. When we are mad at each other, the love makes real the illogical, absurd hope that the fight we are having isn't all, and that we can survive beyond this moment. Love causes us to look to the future by trusting in the covenant of the past. In my marriage, there was a time when my wife and I stood in a church and made a promise to each other. We made that promise publicly and before God. I heard her promise. I have witnesses. Our hope is based on that covenant. And that covenant is held together by Jesus. Ultimately and finally, then, my hope is in Jesus.

BEN PATTERSON

He looks like a bouncer at the local pub or a man whose hemorrhoids are bothering him. Actually, he's the distinguished senior minister at Irvine Presbyterian Church (Irvine is a wealthy suburb in Orange County, located somewhere between Chuck Smith's Calvary Chapel and Bob Schuller's Crystal Cathedral).

Married, forty-seven years old, three children, graduate of the American Baptist Seminary of the West, editorial writer for the *Door*, contributor to *Leadership*, author of (most recently) *The Grand Essentials*, and avid runner, Ben Patterson is increasingly recognized as a significant spokesperson for the church. Ben has never been afraid to express his view regarding issues facing the church, including the Rapture mania of eight or so years ago that infected so many local congregations. From a 1981 conversation with Ben, here are some of his comments.

DOOR: Why are people so interested in the Second Coming?

PATTERSON: There's an apocalyptic mood in the whole culture. Most people have given up on any hope for a meaningful future. Because of that, they have retreated to purely personal pleasures. They want the feeling of security, the feeling of psychic health and well-being. White, middle-class Americans see the return of Christ as an escape from the horror of the future. They are despairing of losing what they have, so they are interested in the return of Christ because it's a rescue from judgment.

DOOR: Other reasons?

PATTERSON: Well, one would have to be a fool to not be worried about nuclear and economic instability. It's frightening.

DOOR: All right, let's get down to basics. There are a lot of folks out there who have Christ's second coming all figured out. They know the whole scenario based on the prophetic books in the Bible.

PATTERSON: That's true. Let's look at one of the books in the Bible that they use: the book of Daniel. Daniel's visions provide the framework for many of the prophetic schemes you are talking about. The problem, of course, is the dating of Daniel. Depending on how you date the book of Daniel, it has a different impact on the kind of scenario you come up with. Traditional, conservative scholarship has dated the book of Daniel at sometime during the Jewish captivity in Babylon, because that's the setting of the book. However, a minority of conservative scholars date the book of Daniel much later than the Babylonian captivity, suggesting that the book of Daniel was written during the early part of the second century B.C. There's almost a 400-year difference in the two datings. This is crucial, of course, because during that period there were two and maybe three major world empires. So if the book was written during the Babylonian period then you have one series of empires to account for, and if it was written during the Greek persecution of the Jews, you have another set of empires to account for.

DOOR: ...

PATTERSON: Did you get that?

DOOR: ...

PATTERSON: Hello?

DOOR: Hmm? Wha. . . . oh, uh, yeah, you have a son named Daniel? What is your point?

PATTERSON: Well, Hal Lindsey in his book deals with this issue by saying, in effect, "Godless liberals hold to a late date, but the rest of us Christians hold to an early date on the book of Daniel."

DOOR: And your point is. . . .

PATTERSON: That doesn't deal with the problem. It has nothing to do with liberal or conservative scholarship; it's a question of language and historical setting. The problem is that most of the people who write on this subject do not have a real understanding of the nature of apocalyptic literature.

This kind of literature came into full flower in the first century A.D., and the book of Revelation is probably the culmination of this kind of writing.

DOOR: Explain *your* understanding of apocalyptic literature then.

PATTERSON: It's a different kind of writing. It's always talking about strange kinds of beasts and cosmic upheavals. It is visionary and very emotional. The apocalyptic writers felt their way through a problem rather than thought their way through. Apocalyptic language is very Hebrew, and Hebrews are not of the Greek logical mentality. Their literature, therefore, does not lend itself to nice linear kinds of analysis, but all of the scenarists want to mold the book of Revelation into a nice logical sequence. Apocalyptic language doesn't lend itself to that. When was the last time you had a dream that was linear and logical? I'm not suggesting that dreams are not filled with a lot of truth, but the presentation of the truth into your own psyche or the world around you is anything but linear and analytic.

DOOR: So the Bible and its apocalyptic books are not there to tell us the particulars of Christ's second coming?

PATTERSON: I think Jesus is very clear that no one knows the day or the hour.

DOOR: People like Lindsey and Smith say they are not suggesting the day or the hour; they are just saying we're in the last generation.

PATTERSON: The moment you say the Second Coming can't be much more than forty years after the establishment of the state of Israel, it gets pretty academic as to whether or not you're predicting the day or the hour. To me, that's a clear violation of Jesus' injunction to be watchful and ready, always on the alert.

DOOR: Don't you ever wonder if maybe, just maybe, these people are right, and Jesus *is* going to return in 1983?

PATTERSON: I have a lot of confidence in my criticism of the modern-day scenarios. That in no way rules out the imminent return of Jesus Christ, but in all honesty, I get so upset at what these scenarios have done to the blessed hope, I have the feeling that if I were caught up in the clouds to meet Christ in 1983, and I saw Lindsey going up with me, I'd probably be mad about it.

DOOR: Interesting mix of feelings. You leave yourself wide open for the criticism that your attack of those who construct scenarios is an indication of a liberal theology which either doesn't take the Second Coming of Christ seriously, or doesn't believe in it period.

PATTERSON: Of course I believe he is coming back. I long for the consummation of the kingdom. I like Oscar Cullman's image. He said, "We Christians live in a situation similar to the Second World War, and the invasion of Normandy, D day." The decisive battle was won there, and we Christians live in the in-between-time between D day and V day, when the final victory was consummated. The battle has been won, and we Christians are just waiting for the consummation.

In my opinion, this obsession with calendarizing and timetables takes away from trusting in God. I describe what these people are doing as theological backseat driving. Instead of saying, "God, it's in your hands, and I'm going to let you unfold your history and your plan," they want to look over

his shoulder and make sure they understand just what his plan is. What happens is that people begin to place their faith in the plan, the scenario, the timetable, instead of God. I've actually had people come to our church who would not join when they found out I didn't necessarily believe that Christ was going to come back in this generation. (I don't necessarily *not* believe it either.) That's an example of someone getting the calendar thing way out of proportion.

DOOR: Matthew 24 says, "Therefore, be on the alert. . . ." Aren't we supposed to watch and be alert for the signs of Christ's imminent return?

PATTERSON: The King James Version uses the word *watch*. To be watchful is to be alert and to be faithful. People have defined being watchful as a command to decipher the code of history as it is secretly revealed in the book of Revelation or Daniel. However, when Jesus says "watch," he is not saying to be ready to decipher the code; he is admonishing us to be faithful, to realize the significance and the urgency of the moment we live in. Jesus' call, then, is a call to a discernment of the urgency of the times.

DOOR: Why is it that, if we're honest, we all would like to know the precise scenario of the last times?

PATTERSON: I can't speak for everyone else, but I can speak for myself. For me, it is the temptation to avoid the passion which is involved in trusting God. By passion, I mean that you really have to let go all your props and assurances. To radically trust God is to let go of all of our worldly, fleshly assurances and let God be the one who decides and determines for us. All of these plans and scenarios are acts of faithlessness, in my opinion. They urge people to make a decision about God, and that's good, but too often they cause people not to trust God, but to trust the plan.

DOOR: In twenty-five words or less, what is the book of Revelation all about?

PATTERSON: It's about Jesus. That's the first line of the book. It is about the glory of the resurrected Christ. It was written to beleaguered, persecuted Christians, and God chooses to give them comfort and encouragement by giving them a vision of the resurrected Christ. The controlling image of the resurrected Christ in the book of Revelation is that he is a lamb, the one slain for the sins of the world, the servant lamb whose strength is his vulnerability, whose power is his servanthood.

DOOR: Doesn't the book of Revelation have anything to say about the future?

PATTERSON: It tells us a lot about the future. It tells us that evil will compound itself as we approach the end. Some say it is about the first century only, others say it is about the end times only. I think it is both. We can learn a lot about the early church in the first century, and frankly, the things that happened in the first century are universals. Those things keep happening again and again.

DOOR: But what about the specifics in Revelation, like the number 666? Do you believe that the literal number 666 will somehow literally function as a part of the last days?

PATTERSON: Well, the number 666 is the number of man in Revelation 13. That number is needed to do business, buy and sell, get food. In other words, to play the world's game, you have to have the world's mark on you. Where is the mark put? On your forehead— biblically, that is where you think, and on your hand—biblically, that describes what you do. So both the center of your thinking and doing have to belong to the world. I think the question regarding whether there will be literal tattoos on your forehead misses the point. The point is that you have to have the mark of the beast if you're going to get along in this world.

DOOR: Some people believe that the number 666 will literally become the mark of the beast. For example, some form of 666 will appear on all our credit cards or even on our address label.

PATTERSON: I suppose that's possible.

DOOR: Not on *our* address labels.

PATTERSON: I couldn't imagine that happening to yours, but my point is that even John felt the mark of the beast was being given right then.

DOOR: Earl Palmer said once that the only thing we can say for sure about the future is this: "Jesus is coming back, and God is not done with Israel yet." Do you agree with that?

PATTERSON: Absolutely. But interestingly, Earl's argument that God is not done with Israel comes out of Romans 9 and 10, not out of the book of Revelation. It is very difficult to make a good case for the book of Revelation having anything to say about the state of Israel.

DOOR: Now you're talking heresy.

PATTERSON: That's a biggie, I know. Revelation 6 and the 144,000 Jews and all of that, but I am awestruck at the way people who claim to have a high view of the Bible twist Scripture and do things to the Bible to work up their prophetic schemes that would make the most thorough liberal blush. I think you have to make the text walk on all fours to suggest that the reference to the 144,000 has anything to do with the converted Jews after the Rapture.

DOOR: Don't any of the beasts described in Revelation and, for that matter, the ones described in Daniel and other places, have any reference to actual historical events?

PATTERSON: I'm sure they do. We just don't happen to have any clues as to which empires are being talked about. If you read the description of the beast in Revelation, it is an amalgamation of all the beasts in prophetic visions. This beast, this final manifestation of evil, will be an amalgam of all those which proceeded it. It will be the worst of everything that came before it. I don't think it will be a computer or world empire or leader, but it will be a worldly power that aligns itself against God, and it will be the quintessence of evil.

DOOR: Quintessence? We're impressed!

PATTERSON: You are? Do you know what it means?

DOOR: Sure.

PATTERSON: Then what does it mean?

DOOR: What?

PATTERSON: Quit stalling.

DOOR: It has something to do with five.

PATTERSON: It means the essence of . . . pure.

DOOR: Of course, Ben, we knew that. We were just tricking you.

PATTERSON: Um hmm. Okay guys, next question.

DOOR: For the Christian, what do you think is a healthy view of the future?

PATTERSON: A healthy view of the future begins with the calm assurance that God has the future in his hands. Someone has said, "He who holds the last moment need not fear the next minute." Therefore, I need not fear the next minute. A healthy view of the future sets you free to be in the present. When we know that the future is assured and believe that God is going to wind this whole thing up, then the result ought to be increased faithfulness and activity in the present. Jacques Ellul said that for the Christian the future is more real than the present. What that means is that the future has a way of invading the present for the Christian. We fight against injustice. We seek to be faithful to Christ, not because we're going to make the kingdom happen ourselves, but because God has already put it together for us. If I felt that the impulses growing out of all this interest in the return of Christ were ones toward greater activity in social justice or evangelism, I would trust the legitimacy of it more than I do.

DOOR: Are you suggesting that we could bring in or establish the kingdom of God here on earth?

PATTERSON: I don't think there is a thing we can do to bring the kingdom of God in. Not a thing. It is all the work of God, but that is not a call to irresponsibility. We are not to sit back, but I must never think that I will bring the kingdom in. The moment I do that, I forget that I am a sinner, that my every enterprise is tainted with sin. As John Carnell put it, "Even the cup of cold water that I hand to someone has my fingers sticking in it." I think what we do is work because we know the kingdom is coming. We involve ourselves in justice and works of righteousness that are signs of the coming kingdom. What we do is always provisional, always temporary, and always a sign of God's ultimate sign.

DOOR: What do you think of all the interest in pre-millennial, post-millenial, pre-trib, post-trib?

PATTERSON: The book of Revelation doesn't give us a very clear case for any of those positions. All of the talk about them centers around one tiny section of the book of Revelation (just part of the twentieth chapter). In my opinion, it's only the calendar-type minds who worry about things like that. I agree with Earl Palmer. I am a pro-millennialist.

DOOR: How literal is the Bible when it describes two people sleeping and one will be gone? Does the Bible mean that people really will be lifted up in the air with their cars left driverless, etc.?

PATTERSON: The examples you have given are very wooden, literalistic responses to the Hebraic, parabolic style of prophetic language. Those words are pictorial statements of the reality that the judgments of God will be sudden and unexpected, and that there will be a sifting of people.

DOOR: So you wouldn't make a movie of the Rapture?

PATTERSON: No, I wouldn't make a movie of it. When we get to the end of the book of Revelation, John lapses into pictures that are almost wild. He is transported by his vision, he's lost in rapture to try to express something that is beyond expression. So I think it is futile to try and literally show what it would be like to see Jerusalem descending from heaven like a bride adorned for her husband. How do you picture something like that? For example, in Revelation 7, it says that God

has sheltered us with his presence and the Lamb is our shepherd who leads us to streams of living water where we will never thirst, nor hunger, nor be scorched by the sun. That is so far beyond our experience. It really is a matter of "eye hath not seen, nor ear heard, nor entered into the heart of man, the things that God has prepared." It just eviscerates the blessed hope to make movies about it, or worse, paintings.

DOOR: Then what is the Christian hope? What should we be looking for?

PATTERSON: First of all, we know that history is going somewhere, and that God has it firmly in his grip. Therefore, we ought to be steadfast and immovable in always abounding in the work of the Lord because our labor isn't in vain. In the last lines of W. H. Auden's *For The Time Being,* there is a wonderful admonition to trust Christ and follow him. It says something like, "You should return to a city that has long awaited your return." I think of all the loneliness in my own life, at times, the hunger, the craving, and the restlessness I feel; this world is not my home. I'm just passing through. I've got a job to do here, but I'm made for something else and that place I'm made for is going to descend to earth one day.

DOOR: And so our hope is. . . .?

PATTERSON: That those who hunger and thirst after righteousness will be filled. That God will satisfy us in our deepest hungers, in the redemption of history, and in our bodies, during the final and complete reign of God over all of us. Our hope can be best summarized in the first line of the Lord's prayer: "Thy kingdom come. Thy will be done."

MADELEINE L'ENGLE

Madeleine L'Engle is very intimidating.

The Keepers of the *Door* were not intimidated by the fact that she graduated cum laude from Smith College. (After all, the editor of this magazine graduated cum boot from Bob Jones University.) We certainly were not intimidated by her writing achievements, which include *A Wrinkle in Time* (Newbery Medal Book, ALA Notable Book, Lewis Carroll Shelf Award), *A Swiftly Tilting Planet* (The American Book Award), and *A Ring of Endless Light* (Newbery Honor Book, ALA Notable Book, Children's Choices). The Keepers have a writing achievement of their own—*101 Things to Do During a Dull Sermon* (Noodlebery Award, CIA Award, Irangate Contra Award, Oral Roberts' Fund-raiser Award). And we were not intimidated by her wit, her charm, and her incredible energy at the age of sixty-eight when we spoke with her in 1986. (The Keepers are very well known for their lack of wit and charm.)

Nope. We were intimidated by Madeleine L'Engle's last name. (Is it Luh-ing-gul? Lah-ing-gul? Lllllll-ing-gul? Lih-nnng-ghil? Ling-glll?) We gave up and just called her Madeleine.

The Keepers of the *Door* traveled to San Diego while Ms. L'Engle was in the midst of a speaking tour. She graciously agreed to be interviewed even though she was recovering from reading one of our issues of the *Door*.

DOOR: Have you ever heard of the *Door*?

L'ENGLE: Scott Peck gave me a subscription and I read it, but—I'm embarrassed to say this—I haven't seen a current issue. The last one I read was a six-month-old issue.

DOOR: Uh . . . that *was* the current issue.

L'ENGLE: Oh. I'm sorry.

DOOR: It's Okay. You've been criticized by some evangelicals.

L'ENGLE: I never knew the evangelical church *existed* until I was invited to Wheaton.

DOOR: They exist all right, and some of them think your book *A Wrinkle in Time* is dangerous because it is about "witches, crystal balls, demons, and the power of the mind."

L'ENGLE: I had a reporter ask me about that, and I told her I didn't understand what these people meant by "the power of the mind." The reporter said that my critics were concerned because Meg (the central character in the story) thought "powerful, loving thoughts."

DOOR: Oh no.

L'ENGLE: I know. I said to the reporter, "So? Is something wrong with 'powerful, loving thoughts'"? The reporter said, "No, I don't think so, but I'm an Episcopalian."

DOOR: Well, that explains it for us.

L'ENGLE: For some reason, these people are very much afraid of the power of the mind. They are terrified of the imagination. Remember the parents in Tennessee who were afraid that certain books might "stimulate their children's imaginations"? They wanted their children's imaginations *bound*. I mean, really, how under the sun can you look at the Incarnation without an incredible leap of the imagination? Christianity demands *enormous* imagination.

DOOR: You have also been accused of being a universalist.

L'ENGLE: Frankly, when I was first accused of that, I had no idea what they were talking about. I thought they meant I was someone who thought that Jesus was good, Buddha was good, Muhammad was good, and all ways to God were equally good. That's not what they meant a'tall.

DOOR: A'tall? A'tall? Is that similar to the phrase "at all"?

L'ENGLE: I'm being asked this by a magazine known for its grammatical astuteness and proofreading genius?

DOOR: Uh. . . .

L'ENGLE: Now, where was I?

DOOR: Universalism.

L'ENGLE: Apparently, these people thought I believe that God, for no particular reason, is just going to wave a magic wand and say, "Okay, everybody out of hell. Home free." I am not a universalist. I do not believe in playing trivially with free will.

I was speaking at Evangel College, an Assembly of God school, and a young man stood up and said, "Your books *do* seem to indicate that you think God is forgiving." I said, "What an incredible statement." He quickly clarified his statement: "What I mean is, your books seem to indicate that you think ultimately God is going to forgive everybody." I told him that I don't believe God is going to fail with creation. I asked him if he believed in a failing God. He said, "There has to be absolute justice." Then I asked him, "If you die tonight, you would be nineteen or twenty; is that what you want? Absolute justice? Don't you want the teensiest, weensiest bit of mercy?" Personally, I want lots and *lots* and LOTS of mercy. Apparently, it never occurred to him that *he* might need some mercy.

DOOR: Do you think you convinced him that he might need some mercy?

L'ENGLE: No, I think he was convinced of his own moral superiority.

DOOR: Where did your faith begin?

L'ENGLE: My father was gassed in the First World War. It didn't kill him right away, but mustard gas just goes on eating lungs. It took my father until I was eighteen to finish coughing his lungs out. Because of his lungs, he worked best in the afternoon and evening. My parents slept late, so there was no one to take me to Sunday school. For that, I am very blessed.

DOOR: Because you didn't go to Sunday school?

L'ENGLE: Yes. I have met so many people who have spent most of their adult lives trying to unlearn the stuff they were given in Sunday school. I just read the Bible at home because it was a terrific storybook. It told stories about ordinary, unqualified people. I was alone a lot as a child.

DOOR: Did that bother you?

L'ENGLE: No. I came late in my parents' marriage. My mother was focused on my father. My parents ate dinner at 8:00, and I had a tray in my room . . . and, of course, a book on my chest. I was deliriously happy. I loved my solitude.

DOOR: Uh . . . where were we? Oh, yes. Your faith and stories.

L'ENGLE: I found that the only thing which answered the questions that I thought were important was story. Basically, what good stories do is not answer your questions, but give you more questions.

DOOR: Some people would disagree. They would say that the Bible has a lot of answers. They would point out that the Bible says a lot about morals, about ethics.

L'ENGLE: The Bible is not a moral book. It is not an ethical book. It is a magnificent storybook. It's no coincidence that Jesus taught almost entirely by telling stories. The Bible grapples with all of the age-old problems like why the innocent suffer and the wicked flourish. It doesn't give any answers; it just tells more stories.

DOOR: So you came to your own faith by reading the Bible?

L'ENGLE: And by asking questions that nobody could answer. My parents were wonderful in that regard. They did not answer questions they couldn't answer. And they did not lie. Sometimes I didn't like their answers, but I was grateful that their answers were truthful.

DOOR: Are you a Christian writer? A Christian who happens to write?

L'ENGLE: I am a writer who happens to be a Christian. I am a writer first.

DOOR: Is there a difference between "Christian fiction" and other kinds of fiction?

L'ENGLE: If it's good fiction, then it's Christian. If it's bad fiction, then it's not Christian, no matter what the subject matter.

DOOR: Respond to the statement, "If you can understand the writing, it's Christian; if you can't understand the writing, if it's too abstract, then it is not Christian."

L'ENGLE: I don't think writing should be abstract. Good writing is particular, which is probably why I'm a Christian because Christianity deals with the particular—God particularly in Jesus. That is why the Romans called Christ "The Scandal of the Particular." In fiction, you don't write about generalities. You write about particular people, in particular situations, making particular choices and decisions.

DOOR: Why have you chosen to write fiction as opposed to a nonfictional statement of what you believe?

L'ENGLE: If I wanted to write a statement of what I believe, I'd go off and get ordained. I'm a storyteller. I think my talent is for story. As a storyteller, my first job is to tell a story. The theology is underneath if you want to find it. You can say more in story than you can in a sermon. In fact, let me show you what I mean. There are three Hasidic stories which more or less express my theology:

Story number one: A young student goes to the wise old rabbi and says, "Rabbi, in the olden days, there were people who *saw* God. Why doesn't anybody see God nowadays?" The rabbi responded, "Nowadays, nobody can stoop so low."

Story number two: A student goes to the study of the wise old rabbi and says, "Oh, Rabbi, I love you so much." The rabbi says, "Do you know what hurts me?" Confused, the student replies, "Rabbi! I just wanted to tell you how much I love you, and you confuse me with irrelevant questions." The rabbi remains silent for a while and then says, "My question was neither confusing nor irrelevant. If you do not know what hurts me, how can you love me?"

Story number three: A very good man died and went to heaven. Peter kissed him on both cheeks, flung open the Pearly Gates, and invited him in. It was a day of bliss for the good man. Heaven was all milk and honey and alabaster—everything he had been taught to believe. But after awhile he realized he hadn't seen anyone. He walked and walked and saw no one. Finally, he went back to the Pearly Gates and asked Peter if he really was in heaven. Peter assured him it was heaven. "But where is everyone?" the man asked. "Where are the prophets? Where are the saints? Where is the Holy Family?" And Peter replied, "Oh, they're all down in hell ministering to the damned. If you'd like to join them, I'll show you the way."

DOOR: Somehow we have the feeling that if we had asked Jimmy Swaggart to tell us about his theology, he wouldn't have told us those stories.

L'ENGLE: Jimmy who?

DOOR: Never mind. What makes a good writer?

L'ENGLE: Technique and God. Writing technique is like any other technique. You have to work at it. You have to practice. In my case, I have to write every day.

DOOR: Oh, we know exactly what you mean. Magazine publishing is an exacting job requiring precise technique. You really have to work at it.

L'ENGLE: You're joking, right?

DOOR: It doesn't take a subscriber long before they feel free to attack. You said technique *and* God.

L'ENGLE: In a sense, the act of writing is an act of focused listening. I listen. Sooner or later I hear the story. I try to hear it and I try to serve it. I have to believe that God has something to do with that process of hearing.

DOOR: You and your husband, Hugh, were married for forty years. That's a long time.

L'ENGLE: In the Episcopal prayer book, marriage promises are big promises. And when Hugh and I made those mighty promises, we meant them. We live in a society that teaches us to act out all that we feel. The fact that you are married to one woman or one man doesn't mean you aren't going to be attracted by others. The fact that you've chosen this one doesn't mean very much if nobody else attracts you. But you don't act on it. You don't act out everything you feel. My husband was an actor. He worked with a lot of glamorous women and a lot of them were after him, but I trusted him completely. Pragmatically, however, I was ready and waiting for him when he came home from the theater. Why should he come home and find me asleep? I watched a lot of women who, while they were dating, were always beautifully dressed and always had their faces made up, but after they were married they walked around like slobs. I refused to do that. Every morning I was up and dressed. I put on my makeup. I think you owe your husband that much honor and he owes you that much honor in an equal way. You have to honor each other all through your marriage. We promised to honor each other, and that's what it means.

DOOR: You certainly didn't have the ideal situation. You both worked. Hugh came home late at night. You had children to raise in downtown New York.

L'ENGLE: First of all, I don't believe in a child-centered household. I don't believe in being a martyr for children. When I had a choice, it was better for the kids when I chose Hugh. When we moved to New York City, I wanted to be up for Hugh when he came home at 11:30. But I couldn't burn the candle at both ends. We had a family conference and I said, "Your father needs me more when he comes home from the theater than you need me in the morning. So you will have to get to school by yourselves if you want to have a living mother. When you get home from school, I'm yours, but I have to sleep in the morning." My theory about the kids is if their parents aren't happy, they're not going to be happy. Someone asked me once, "What do you and Hugh do that's best for your kids?" I answered off the top of my head, "We love each other."

DOOR: But love is work, isn't it?

L'ENGLE: Of course it is. I will be honest with you; there were times when simply the fact that I had these rings on kept me to my commitment and my honoring. I never had those moments for very long, but I had them. There are a lot of marriages today that break up just at the point where they could mature and deepen. We are taught to quit when it hurts. But often, it is the times of pain that produce the most growth in a relationship. I don't know what there was in our marriage that was basically right, but I do know it was worth all of the effort and struggle.

DOOR: It must have been very difficult when he died.

L'ENGLE: A couple of years ago, I received a phone call from a woman who was in the hospital. She wanted to know if I believed what I have written in my books. She was getting ready to have a mastectomy and she needed to know that. After my husband died, I discovered that I *do* believe what I have written.

When his wife died, someone said "I've been all the way down to the bottom and it's solid." I found that to be true. There *is* rock down there, and I believe it. I didn't want my husband to die. I loved him. We had a tumultuous marriage, but a very good marriage. It was terrific, and I didn't want it to end this soon.

DOOR: We sense that "tumultuous" for you meant "good," not "bad"; that it meant passion—real passion.

L'ENGLE: We need more passion. I understand passion—hot blood. In the French legal system, a murder committed in hot blood is treated very differently than one committed in cold blood. George MacDonald, whom I adore, said that it would be infinitely worse to refuse to forgive someone than to kill, because the latter may be a moment's madness, but the former is the cold-blooded reasoning of the heart. I understand that. I do react in hot blood, so Hugh and I had some good, rousing, passionate fights. I am passionate about everything. I'm passionate about my work. I'm passionate about what I believe in. I think sex is nice too. Life without passion would be half death.

DOOR: So you not only miss Hugh, you miss the passion as well.

L'ENGLE: Thank God we did not have any unfinished business. We didn't have any loose strings, no false guilt. I was with him till the end. I was holding him when he died. At least my grief is a clean grief.

DOOR: What can we do to help people in their grief?

L'ENGLE: Nothing. You hold them. You cry with them. You say, "I love you and I care." One of the most difficult things for me since Hugh died has been to break the ice with people. They don't know what to say. They are *embarrassed*. That is quite a burden to put on the person who is grieving. I end up having to minister to *them*. I don't want people to talk to me about pie in the sky. I've been sent dozens of books, and I asked a friend why I was so reluctant to read those books. He said, "Because they're no good." I guess I wouldn't mind reading about someone else's experience, but I don't want to be told how to grieve. I have to do it my own way.

DOOR: How do you feel about the church?

L'ENGLE: It's awful, but it's all we have. We have to have a commitment to the church as we do in marriage, except the church is a lot worse than marriage. The minute things become institutionalized, the church becomes awful. The larger a church, the more difficult it becomes. The closest I ever came to Christian community was during the early years of our marriage when we were having our kids and my husband left the theater "forever" (which, thank God, only lasted nine years). We were living in northwest Connecticut and attending a small, local Congregational church. It really was the center of our lives. We really did have community. We loved each other. If a mother was sick, everyone else came in and took the kids, did the cooking, cleaned the house. No big deal was made out of it. We did it without realizing what we were doing. It was spontaneous and it was good. You get too big and it becomes more and more difficult. I remember a woman telling me about the time a famous preacher came to her church and only a few people turned out. He berated the faithful few who came. She told me disgustedly, "Our Lord said to *feed* my sheep, not count them." The church too often counts instead of feeds.

DOOR: Any thoughts about preaching?

L'ENGLE: I do quite a bit of it myself. And when I preach, I try to talk about where I am now. And when I hear a sermon, I don't want to be preached at. I want to feel like we're all in this together. I want to hear the gospel, the Good News. I want it to be real. Preaching has to do with how much you're willing to reveal, how much you are willing to undress yourself.

DOOR: How about television evangelists?

L'ENGLE: I can't watch them. I don't have high blood pressure, but I think I would if I watched them. They have God in such a tiny little box. They have him tamed. So many of these TV evangelists make false promises. We were never promised that people were not going to die, or that people were not going to hurt. All we were promised was that God was going to be with us. If we love, we will be hurt. People we love will take sick and die. But the Good News is that God is in it with us. Think about it. To be born like any human baby—*that* was the sacrifice, not the Cross. The Good News is that God is here with us. We're writing the story together.

DOOR: You *do* have a gift. You have told your stories well. We have sensed that God has helped you write your stories.

L'ENGLE: One of the great things about the Bible is that the people God chooses to do his work are always unqualified.

We're all unqualified. Sometimes it seems as though God goes to great extremes to choose the *most* unqualified people possible. I guess if we think we're qualified, we might think we did it ourselves. It's wonderful, because I don't have to feel qualified to do what I'm doing. I just have to *believe* it is what God is calling me to do, not what *I* am calling me to do. And if I really believe that, the Holy Spirit will give me the grace that's needed to do it.

DOOR: We hope that the Holy Spirit will continue to give you the grace to do much, much more.

L'ENGLE: I wouldn't have missed this journey of life for anything in the world. I hope it's going to continue awhile longer. I've got books I want to write. And yet, I wrote in my journal when I was twenty-nine that I didn't expect to die soon, but that if I did, I knew I had lived.